W9-CDN-000

Methods in Behavioral Research

ELEVENTH EDITION

PAUL C. COZBY

California State University, Fullerton

SCOTT C. BATES

Utah State University

 McGraw Hill — Connect Learn Succeed™

The McGraw·Hill Companies

Connect
Learn
Succeed™

Published by McGraw-Hill, an imprint of The McGraw-Hill Companies, Inc., 1221 Avenue of the Americas, New York, NY 10020. Copyright © 2012, 2009, 2007, 2004. All rights reserved. Printed in the United States of America. Previous editions © 2001, 1997, 1993, 1989, 1985, 1981 by Mayfield Publishing Company, © 1977 by Paul C. Cozby. No part of this publication may be reproduced or distributed in any form or by any means, or stored in a database or retrieval system, without the prior written consent of The McGraw-Hill Companies, Inc., including, but not limited to, in any network or other electronic storage or transmission, or broadcast fordistance learning.

1 2 3 4 5 6 7 8 9 0 DOC/DOC 10 9 8 7 6 5 4 3 2 1

ISBN: 978-0-07-803515-9
MHID: 0-07-803515-5

Sponsoring Editor: *Krista Bettino*
Marketing Manager: *Julia Larkin Flohr*
Development Editor: *Kirk Bomont*
Managing Editor: *Anne Fuzellier*
Production Editor: *Margaret Young*
Interior and Cover Designer: *Preston Thomas, Cadence Design*
Buyer: *Louis Swaim*
Production Service: *Scratchgravel Publishing Services*
Composition: *MPS Limited, a Macmillan Company*
Printing: *45# New Era Matte Plus by R.R. Donnelley*
Vice President Editorial: *Michael Ryan*
Publisher: *Michael Sugarman*
Cover Images: © artpartner-images/Photographer's Choice/Getty Images
Credits: *The credits section for this book is on page 406 and is considered an extension of the copyright page.*

Library of Congress Cataloging-in-Publication Data

Cozby, Paul C.
    Methods in behavioral research/Paul Cozby, Scott Bates. — 11th ed.
        p. cm.
    Includes bibliographical references and index.
    ISBN-13: 978-0-07-803515-9 (alk. paper)
    ISBN-10: 0-07-803515-5 (alk. paper)
    1. Psychology—Research—Methodology. 2. Social sciences—Research—Methodology. I. Bates, Scott, 1969–
II. Title.
    BF76.5.C67 2011
    150.72—dc23

                                                                                    2011025421

The Internet addresses listed in the text were accurate at the time of publication. The inclusion of a website does not indicate an endorsement by the authors or McGraw-Hill, and McGraw-Hill does not guarantee the accuracy of the information presented at these sites.

www.mhhe.com

To Ingrid and Pierre

For your energy and smiles.
—PCC

To María Luisa and Ana Cecilia

My extraordinary girls, who helped me find my invincible summer.
—SCB

Contents

4 FUNDAMENTAL RESEARCH ISSUES   68

5 MEASUREMENT CONCEPTS   95

OBSERVATIONAL METHODS   113

ASKING PEOPLE ABOUT THEMSELVES: SURVEY RESEARCH   128

8 EXPERIMENTAL DESIGN 156

Confounding and Internal Validity 157
Basic Experiments 158
Assigning Participants to Experimental Conditions 163
Independent Groups Design 163
Repeated Measures Design 164
Matched Pairs Design 169
Illustrative Article: Experimental Design 170
Study Terms *171*
Review Questions *171*
Activity Questions *172*

9 CONDUCTING EXPERIMENTS 173

Selecting Research Participants 174
Manipulating the Independent Variable 175
Measuring the Dependent Variable 181
Additional Controls 184
Additional Considerations 188
Analyzing and Interpreting Results 191
Communicating Research to Others 191
Illustrative Article: Conducting Experiments 192
Study Terms *193*
Review Questions *193*
Activity Questions *194*
Answers *195*

10 COMPLEX EXPERIMENTAL DESIGNS 196

Increasing the Number of Levels of an Independent Variable 197
Increasing the Number of Independent Variables: Factorial Designs 199
Illustrative Article: Complex Experimental Designs 212
Study Terms *212*
Review Questions *213*
Activity Questions *213*
Answers *214*

11

SINGLE-CASE, QUASI-EXPERIMENTAL, AND DEVELOPMENTAL RESEARCH 215

12

UNDERSTANDING RESEARCH RESULTS: DESCRIPTION AND CORRELATION 239

13

UNDERSTANDING RESEARCH RESULTS: STATISTICAL INFERENCE 262

14 GENERALIZING RESULTS   287

APPENDIX A: WRITING RESEARCH REPORTS   304

Preface

The eleventh edition of *Methods in Behavioral Research* has benefited greatly from the addition of a new author, Scott C. Bates of Utah State University. The primary focus of the book remains constant: We continue to believe that teaching and learning about research methods is both challenging and great fun, and so we emphasize clear communication of concepts using interesting examples as our highest priority.

We have added to and updated our examples, clarified concepts throughout, and removed material that was distracting or confusing. We continue to enhance learning by describing important concepts in several contexts throughout the book; research shows that redundancy aids understanding. We also emphasize the need to study behavior using a variety of research approaches. An important change is the addition of Illustrative Articles in most chapters: Students are asked to find and read a specific recent journal article and answer questions that require use of concepts introduced in the chapter.

VALIDITY

The eleventh edition expands and emphasizes coverage of *validity* in behavioral research. By highlighting the key concepts of *internal, external,* and *construct validity* throughout the text, we hope to support students' understanding of these fundamental ideas. Furthermore, *validity* now provides a theme that runs throughout the text—just as validity is a theme that runs throughout behavioral research.

ORGANIZATION

The organization generally follows the sequence of planning and conducting a research investigation. Chapter 1 gives an overview of the scientific approach to knowledge and distinguishes between basic and applied research. Chapter 2 discusses sources of ideas for research and the importance of library research. Chapter 3 focuses on research ethics; ethical issues are covered in depth here and emphasized throughout the book. Chapter 4 introduces validity and examines psychological variables and the distinction between experimental and non-experimental approaches to studying relationships among variables. Chapter 5 focuses on measurement issues, including reliability and validity. Nonexperimental research approaches—including naturalistic observation, cases studies, and content analysis—are described in Chapter 6. Chapter 7 covers sampling as well as the design of questionnaires and interviews. Chapters 8 and 9 present the basics of designing and conducting experiments. Factorial designs are emphasized in Chapter 10. Chapter 11 discusses the designs for special applications: single-case experimental designs, developmental research designs, and quasi-experimental designs. Chapters 12 and 13 focus on the use of statistics to help students understand research results. These chapters include material on effect size and confidence intervals. Finally, Chapter 14 discusses generalization issues, meta-analyses, and the importance of replications.

Appendices on writing research reports and conducting statistical analyses are included as well. Appendix A presents a thorough treatment of current APA style plus an example of an actual published paper as illustration. Appendix B provides examples of formulas and calculations to help students conduct and present their own research. Appendix C presents useful values of chi-square, t, and F.

FLEXIBILITY

Chapters are relatively independent, providing instructors maximum flexibility in assigning the order of chapters. For example, chapters on research ethics and survey research methods are presented early in the book, but instructors who wish to present this material later in a course can easily do so. It is also relatively easy to eliminate sections of material within most chapters.

FEATURES

Clarity. The eleventh edition retains the strength of direct, clear writing. Concepts are described in different contexts to enhance understanding.

Compelling examples. Well-chosen research examples help students interpret challenging concepts and complex research designs.

Illustrative Articles. For most chapters, we selected an article from the professional literature that demonstrates and illustrates the content of the chapter in a meaningful way. Each article provides an interesting, engaging, and student-relevant example as a chapter-closing capstone exercise. In each case, an APA-style reference to a published empirical article is included, along with a brief introduction and summary. Three to five key discussion questions provide an applied, critical thinking–oriented, and summative learning experience for the chapter. (Note: We did not include Illustrative Articles for Chapters 2, 12, and 13, as reviewers suggested that most instructors would prefer to develop their own involvement activities for these chapters.)

Flexibility. Instructors are able to easily customize the chapter sequence to match their syllabi.

Decision-making emphasis. Distinguishing among a variety of research designs helps students understand when to use one type of design over another.

Strong pedagogy. Learning Objectives open each chapter. Review and activity questions provide practice for students to help them understand the material. Boldface key terms are listed at the end of each chapter, and many are also defined in a Glossary at the end of the book.

RESOURCES FOR STUDENTS AND INSTRUCTORS

The Online Learning Center is available for both students and instructors at www.mhhe.com/cozby11e.

For **students,** this online resource provides numerous study aids, authored by Kimberley Duff at Cerritos College, to enhance their learning experience. Students will be able to take a variety of practice quizzes, as well as explore the Internet through exercises and links that complement the text.

For **instructors,** the password-protected Instructor's Edition of the Online Learning Center contains an Instructor's Manual, edited by Martha Hubertz at Florida Atlantic University, and Test Bank, edited by Kimberley Duff at Cerritos College; a set of customizable PowerPoint slides, authored by James Neuse at California State University, Fullerton; and an image gallery and web links to help prepare course material. The Instructor's Manual includes numerous student activities and assignments.

In addition, Paul C. Cozby maintains a website devoted to learning about research methods at http://methods.fullerton.edu. This site provides easy access to more information about topics presented in the text through resources available on the Internet.

Ready, Set, Go! A Student Guide to IBM® SPSS® Statistics 19.0 and 20.0, by Thomas Pavkov and Kent Pierce, is a unique workbook/handbook that guides students through SPSS 19.0 and 20.0. The SPSS Student Version is ideal for students who are just beginning to learn statistics. It provides students with affordable, professional statistical analysis and modeling tools. The easy-to-use interface and comprehensive online help system enable students to learn statistics, not software.

ACKNOWLEDGMENTS

Many individuals helped to produce this and previous editions of this book. The executive editor at McGraw-Hill was Krista Bettino; we are also indebted to the editors of previous editions, Franklin Graham, Ken King, and Mike Sugarman, for their guidance. Thanks go to development editor Kirk Bomont, who was invaluable in developing the manuscript. Thanks also to individuals who have provided important input, particularly Diana Kyle, Jennifer Siciliani, and Kathy Brown. We are extremely grateful for the input from numerous students and instructors, including the following individuals, who provided detailed reviews for this edition:

Kimberley Duff, *Cerritos College*
Traci Giuliano, *Southwestern University*
Leona Johnson, *Hampton University*
Michael MacLean, *Buffalo State College*
Mark Stellmack, *University of Minnesota*

We are always interested in receiving comments and suggestions from students and instructors. Please e-mail us at scott.bates@usu.edu or cozby@fullerton.edu.

About the Authors

Paul C. Cozby is Emeritus Professor of Psychology at California State University, Fullerton. Dr. Cozby was an undergraduate at the University of California, Riverside, and received his Ph.D. in psychology from the University of Minnesota. He is a fellow of the American Psychological Association and a member of the Association for Psychological Science; he has served as officer of the Society for Computers in Psychology. He is Executive Officer of the Western Psychological Association. He is the author of *Using Computers in the Behavioral Sciences* and co-editor with Daniel Perlman of *Social Psychology*.

Scott C. Bates is Associate Professor of Psychology at Utah State University. He earned a B.S. in psychology from Whitman College, an M.S. in experimental psychology from Western Washington University, and a Ph.D. in social psychology from Colorado State University. His research interests and experiences are varied. He has conducted research in areas as wide-ranging as adolescent problem behavior and problem-behavior prevention, teaching and learning in higher education, and the psychological consequences of growing and tending plants in outer space.

1

Scientific Understanding of Behavior

LEARNING OBJECTIVES

- Explain the reasons for understanding research methods.
- Describe the scientific approach to learning about behavior and contrast it with pseudoscientific research.
- Define and give examples of the four goals of scientific research: description, prediction, determination of cause, and explanation of behavior.
- Discuss the three elements for inferring causation: temporal order, covariation of cause and effect, and elimination of alternative explanations.
- Define and describe basic and applied research.

What are the causes of aggression and violence? How do we remember things, what causes us to forget, and how can memory be improved? What are the effects of stressful environments on health? How do early childhood experiences affect later development? What are the best ways to treat depression? How can we reduce prejudice and intergroup conflict?

Curiosity about questions such as these is probably the most important reason that many students decide to take courses in the behavioral sciences. Scientific research provides us with the best means of addressing such questions and providing answers. In this book, we will examine the methods of scientific research in the behavioral sciences. In this introductory chapter, we will focus on ways in which knowledge of research methods can be useful in understanding the world around us. Further, we will review the characteristics of a scientific approach to the study of behavior and the general types of research questions that concern behavioral scientists.

USES OF RESEARCH METHODS

Informed citizens in our society increasingly need knowledge of research methods. Daily newspapers, general-interest magazines, and other media continually report research results: "Happiness Wards Off Heart Disease," "Recession Causes Increase in Teen Dating Violence," "Breast-Fed Children Found Smarter," "Facebook Users Get Worse Grades in College." Articles and books make claims about the beneficial or harmful effects of particular diets or vitamins on one's sex life, personality, or health. Survey results are frequently reported that draw conclusions about our beliefs concerning a variety of topics. The key question is, how do you evaluate such reports? Do you simply accept the findings because they are supposed to be scientific? A background in research methods will help you to read these reports critically, evaluate the methods employed, and decide whether the conclusions are reasonable.

Many occupations require the use of research findings. For example, mental health professionals must make decisions about treatment methods, assignment of clients to different types of facilities, medications, and testing procedures. Such decisions are made on the basis of research; to make good decisions, mental health professionals must be able to read the research literature in the field and apply it in their professional lives. Similarly, people who work in business environments frequently rely on research to make decisions about marketing strategies, ways of improving employee productivity and morale, and methods of selecting and training new employees. Educators must keep up with research on topics such as the effectiveness of different teaching strategies or programs to deal with special student problems. Knowledge of research methods and the ability to evaluate research reports are useful in many fields.

It is also important to recognize that scientific research has become increasingly prominent in public policy decisions. Legislators and political leaders at all levels of government frequently take political positions and propose legislation based on research findings. Research may also influence judicial decisions: A prime example of this is the *Social Science Brief* that was prepared by psychologists and accepted as evidence in the landmark 1954 case of *Brown v. Board of Education* in which the U.S. Supreme Court banned school segregation in the United States. One of the studies cited in the brief was conducted by Clark and Clark (1947), who found that when allowed to choose between light-skinned and dark-skinned dolls, both Black and White children preferred to play with the light-skinned dolls (see Stephan, 1983, for a further discussion of the implications of this study).

Behavioral research on human development has influenced U.S. Supreme Court decisions related to juvenile crime. In 2005, for instance, the Supreme Court decided that juveniles could not face the death penalty (*Roper v. Simmons*), and the decision was informed by neurological and behavioral research showing that the brain, social, and character differences between adults and juveniles make juveniles less culpable than adults for the same crimes. Similarly, in the 2010 Supreme Court decision *Graham v. Florida*, the Supreme Court decided that juvenile offenders could not be sentenced to life in prison without parole for non-homicide offenses. This decision was influenced by a friend of the court brief filed by the American Psychological Association that cited research in developmental psychology and neuroscience. The court majority pointed to this research in their conclusion that assessment of blame and standards for sentencing should be different for juveniles and adults because of juveniles' lack of maturity and poorly formed character development (Clay, 2010).

In addition, psychologists studying ways to improve the accuracy of eyewitness identification (e.g., Wells et al., 1998; Wells, 2001) greatly influenced recommended procedures for law enforcement agencies to follow in criminal investigations (U.S. Department of Justice, 1999) and provided science-based perspectives on the value of confessions.

Research is also important when developing and assessing the effectiveness of programs designed to achieve certain goals—for example, to increase retention of students in school, influence people to engage in behaviors that reduce their risk of contracting HIV, or teach employees how to reduce the effects of stress. We need to be able to determine whether these programs are successfully meeting their goals.

THE SCIENTIFIC APPROACH

We opened this chapter with several questions about human behavior and suggested that scientific research is a valuable means of answering them. How does the scientific approach differ from other ways of learning about behavior? People have always observed the world around them and sought explanations for what they see and experience. However, instead of using a scientific approach, many people rely on **intuition** and **authority** as ways of knowing.

The Limitations of Intuition and Authority

Intuition   Most of us either know or have heard about a married couple who, after years of trying to conceive, adopt a child. Then, within a very short period of time, they find that the woman is pregnant. This observation leads to a common belief that adoption increases the likelihood of pregnancy among couples who are having difficulties conceiving a child. Such a conclusion seems intuitively reasonable, and people usually have an explanation for this effect—for example, the adoption reduces a major source of marital stress, and the stress reduction in turn increases the chances of conception (see Gilovich, 1991).

This example illustrates the use of intuition and anecdotal evidence to draw general conclusions about the world around us. When you rely on intuition, you accept unquestioningly what your own personal judgment or a single story about one person's experience tells you. The intuitive approach takes many forms. Often, it involves finding an explanation for our own behaviors or the behaviors of others. For example, you might develop an explanation for why you keep having conflicts with your roommate, such as "he hates me" or "having to share a bathroom creates conflict." Other times, intuition is used to explain intriguing events that you observe, as in the case of concluding that adoption increases the chances of conception among couples having difficulty conceiving a child.

A problem with intuition is that numerous cognitive and motivational biases affect our perceptions, and so we may draw erroneous conclusions about cause and effect (cf. Fiske & Taylor, 1984; Gilovich, 1991; Nisbett & Ross, 1980; Nisbett & Wilson, 1977). Gilovich points out that there is in fact no relationship between adoption and subsequent pregnancy, according to scientific research investigations. So why do we hold this belief? Most likely it is because of a cognitive bias called *illusory correlation* that occurs when we focus on two events that stand out and occur together. When an adoption is closely followed by a pregnancy, our attention is drawn to the situation, and we are biased to conclude that there must be a causal connection. Such illusory correlations are also likely to occur when we are highly motivated to believe in the causal relationship. Although this is a natural thing for us to do, it is not scientific. A scientific approach requires much more evidence before conclusions can be drawn.

Authority   The philosopher Aristotle was concerned with the factors associated with persuasion or attitude change. In his *Rhetoric*, Aristotle describes the relationship between persuasion and credibility: "Persuasion is achieved by the speaker's personal character when the speech is so spoken as to make us think him credible. We believe good men more fully and readily than others." Thus, Aristotle would argue that we are more likely to be persuaded by a speaker who seems prestigious, trustworthy, and respectable than by one who appears to lack such qualities.

Many of us might accept Aristotle's arguments simply because he is considered a prestigious authority—a convincing and influential source—and his writings remain important. Similarly, many people are all too ready to accept anything they learn from the Internet, news media, books, government officials, or religious figures. They believe that the statements of such authorities must be true. The problem, of course, is that the statements may not be true. The scientific approach rejects the notion that one can accept *on faith* the statements of any authority; again, more evidence is needed before we can draw scientific conclusions.

Skepticism, Science, and the Empirical Approach

The scientific approach to acquiring knowledge recognizes that both intuition and authority can be sources of ideas about behavior. However, scientists do not unquestioningly accept anyone's intuitions—including their own. Scientists recognize that their ideas are just as likely to be wrong as anyone else's. Also, scientists do not accept on faith the pronouncements of anyone, regardless of that person's prestige or authority. Thus, scientists are very skeptical about what they see and hear. Scientific **skepticism** means that ideas must be evaluated on the basis of careful logic and results from scientific investigations.

If scientists reject intuition and blind acceptance of authority as ways of knowing about the world, how do they go about gaining knowledge? The fundamental characteristic of the scientific method is **empiricism**—the idea that knowledge is based on observations. Data are collected that form the basis of conclusions about the nature of the world. The scientific method embodies a number of rules for collecting and evaluating data; these rules will be explored throughout the book.

The power of the scientific approach can be seen all around us. Whether you look at biology, chemistry, medicine, physics, anthropology, or psychology, you will see amazing advances over the past 25, 50, or 100 years. We have a greater understanding of the world around us, and the applications of that understanding have kept pace. Goodstein (2000) describes an "evolved theory of science" that defines the characteristics of scientific inquiry. These characteristics are summarized below.

Data play a central role. For scientists, knowledge is primarily based on observations. Scientists enthusiastically search for observations that will verify their ideas about the world. They develop theories, argue that existing data support their theories, and conduct research that can increase our confidence that the theories are correct. Observations can be criticized, alternatives can be suggested, and data collection methods can be called into question. But in each of these cases, the role of data is central and fundamental. Scientists have a "show me, don't tell me" attitude.

Scientists are not alone. Scientists make observations that are accurately reported to other scientists and the public. You can be sure that many other scientists will follow up on the findings by conducting research that replicates and extends these observations.

Science is adversarial. Science is a way of thinking in which ideas do battle with other ideas in order to move ever closer to truth. Research can be conducted to test any idea; supporters of the idea and those who disagree with the idea can report their research findings, and these can be evaluated by others. Some ideas, even some very good ideas, may prove to be wrong if research fails to provide support for them. Good scientific ideas are testable. They can be supported or they can be falsified by data—the latter concept called **falsifiability** (Popper, 2002). If an idea is falsified when it is tested, science is thereby advanced because this result will spur the development of new and better ideas.

Scientific evidence is peer reviewed. Before a study is published in a top-quality scientific journal, other scientists who have the expertise to carefully evaluate the research review it. This process is called **peer review.** The role of these reviewers is to recommend whether the research should be published. This review process ensures that research with major flaws will not become part of the scientific literature. In essence, science exists in a free market of ideas in which the best ideas are supported by research and scientists can build upon the research of others to make further advances.

Integrating Intuition, Skepticism, and Authority

The advantage of the scientific approach over other ways of knowing about the world is that it provides an objective set of rules for gathering, evaluating, and reporting information. It is an open system that allows ideas to be refuted or supported by others. This does not mean that intuition and authority are unimportant, however. As noted previously, scientists often rely on intuition and assertions of authorities for ideas for research. Moreover, there is nothing wrong with accepting the assertions of authority as long as we do not accept them as scientific evidence. Often, scientific evidence is not obtainable, as, for example, when a religious figure or text asks us to accept certain beliefs on faith. Some beliefs cannot be tested and thus are beyond the realm of science. In science, however, ideas must be evaluated on the basis of available evidence that can be used to support or refute the ideas.

There is also nothing wrong with having opinions or beliefs as long as they are presented simply as opinions or beliefs. However, we should always ask whether the opinion can be tested scientifically or whether scientific evidence exists that relates to the opinion. For example, opinions on whether exposure to media violence increases aggression are only opinions until scientific evidence on the issue is gathered.

As you learn more about scientific methods, you will become increasingly skeptical of the research results reported in the media and the assertions of scientists as well. You should be aware that scientists often become authorities when they express their ideas. When someone claims to be a scientist, should we be more willing to accept what he or she has to say? First, ask about the credentials of the individual. It is usually wise to pay more attention to someone with an established reputation in the field and attend to the reputation of the institution represented by the person. It is also worthwhile to examine the researcher's funding source; you might be a bit suspicious when research funded by a drug company supports the effectiveness of a drug manufactured by that company, for example. Similarly, when an organization with a particular social-political agenda funds the research that supports that agenda, you should be skeptical of the findings and closely examine the methods of the study.

You should also be skeptical of pseudoscientific research. **Pseudoscience** is "fake" science in which seemingly scientific terms and demonstrations are used to substantiate claims that have no basis in scientific research. The claim may be that a product or procedure will enhance your memory, relieve depression, or treat autism or post-traumatic stress disorder. The fact that these are all worthy outcomes makes us very susceptible to believing pseudoscientific claims and forgetting to ask whether there is a valid scientific basis for the claims. In Chapter 2, we will discuss a procedure called *facilitated communication* that has been used by therapists working with children with autism. These children lack verbal skills for communication; to help them communicate, a facilitator holds the child's hand while the child presses keys to type messages on a keyboard. This technique produces impressive results, as the children are now able to express themselves. In Chapter 2, we will explore the scientific research that demonstrated that the facilitators, not the children, controlled the typing. The problem with all pseudoscience is that hopes are raised and promises will not be realized. Often the techniques can be dangerous as well. In the case of facilitated communication, a number of facilitators typed messages accusing a parent of physically or sexually abusing the child. Some parents were actually convicted of child abuse. In these legal cases, the scientific research on facilitated communication was used to help the defendant parent. Cases such as this have led to a movement to promote the exclusive use of evidence-based therapies—therapeutic interventions grounded in scientific research findings that demonstrate their effectiveness (cf. Lilienfied, Lynn, & Lohr, 2004). Figure 1.1 lists some of the characteristics of pseudoscientific claims you may hear about.

- Hypotheses generated are typically not testable.
- If scientific tests are reported, methodology is not scientific and validity of data is questionable.
- Supportive evidence tends to be anecdotal or to rely heavily on authorities that are so-called experts in the area of interest. Genuine scientific references are not cited.
- Claims ignore conflicting evidence.
- Claims are stated in scientific-sounding terminology and ideas.
- Claims tend to be vague, rationalize strongly held beliefs, and appeal to preconceived ideas.
- Claims are never revised.

FIGURE 1.1
Some characteristics of pseudoscience

Finally, we are all increasingly susceptible to false reports of scientific findings circulated via the Internet. Many of these claim to be associated with a reputable scientist or scientific organization, and then they take on a life of their own. A recent widely covered report, supposedly from the World Health Organization, claimed that the gene for blond hair was being selected out of the human gene pool. Blond hair would be a disappearing trait! General rules to follow are (1) be highly skeptical of scientific assertions that are supported by only vague or improbable evidence, and (2) take the time to do an Internet search for supportive evidence. You can check many of the claims that are on the Internet on www.snopes.com and www.truthorfiction.com.

GOALS OF BEHAVIORAL SCIENCE

Scientific research on behavior has four general goals: (1) to describe behavior, (2) to predict behavior, (3) to determine the causes of behavior, and (4) to understand or explain behavior.

Description of Behavior

The scientist begins with careful observation, because the first goal of science is to describe behavior—which can be something directly observable (such as running speed, eye gaze, or loudness of laughter) or something less observable (like perceptions of attractiveness). Cunningham and his colleagues examined judgments of physical attractiveness over time (Cunningham, Druen, & Barbee, 1997). Male college students in 1976 rated the attractiveness of a large number of females shown in photographs. The same photographs were rated in 1993 by another group of students. The judgments of attractiveness of the females were virtually identical; standards of attractiveness apparently changed very little over this time period. In another study, Cunningham compared the facial characteristics of females who were movie stars in the 1930s and 1940s with those of female stars of the 1990s. Such measures included eye height, eye width, nose length, cheekbone prominence, and smile width, among others. These facial characteristics were highly similar across the two time periods, again indicating that standards of attractiveness remain constant over time.

Researchers are often interested in describing the ways in which events are systematically related to one another. Do jurors judge attractive defendants more leniently than unattractive defendants? Are people more likely to be persuaded by a speaker who has high credibility? In what ways do cognitive abilities change as people grow older? Do students who study with a television set on score lower on exams than students who study in a quiet environment? Do taller people make more money than shorter people? Do men find women wearing red clothing more attractive than women wearing a dark blue color?

Prediction of Behavior

Another goal of science is to predict behavior. Once it has been observed with some regularity that two events are systematically related to one another (e.g., greater attractiveness is associated with more lenient sentencing), it becomes possible to make predictions. One implication of this process is that it allows us to anticipate events. If you read about an upcoming trial of a very attractive defendant, you can predict that the person will likely receive a lenient sentence. Further, the ability to predict often helps us make better decisions. For example, if you study the behavioral science research literature on attraction and relationships, you will learn about factors that predict long-term relationship satisfaction. You may be able to then use that information when predicting the likely success of your own relationships. You can even take a test that was designed to measure these predictors of relationship success. Tests such as RELATE, FOCCUS, and PREPARE can be completed online by yourself, with a partner, or with the help of a professional counselor (Larson, Newell, & Nichols, 2002).

Determining the Causes of Behavior

A third goal of science is to determine the causes of behavior. Although we might accurately predict the occurrence of a behavior, we might not correctly identify its cause. Research shows that a child's aggressive behavior may be predicted by knowing how much violence the child views on television. Unfortunately, unless we know that exposure to television violence is a *cause* of behavior, we cannot assert that aggressive behavior can be reduced by limiting scenes of violence on television. A child who is highly aggressive may prefer to watch violence when choosing television programs. Or consider this example: Research by Elliot and Niesta (2008) indicates that men find women wearing red are more attractive than women wearing a color such as blue. Does the red clothing cause the perception of greater attractiveness? Or is it possible that attractive women choose to wear brighter colors (including red) and less attractive women choose to wear darker colors? Should a woman wear red to help her be perceived as more attractive? We can only recommend this strategy if we know that the color red causes perception of greater attractiveness. We are now confronting questions of cause and effect: To know how to *change* behavior, we need to know the *causes* of behavior.

Cook and Campbell (1979) describe three types of evidence (drawn from the work of philosopher John Stuart Mill) used to identify the cause of a behavior. It is not enough to know that two events occur together, as in the case of knowing that watching television violence is a predictor of actual aggression. To conclude causation, three things must occur:

1. There is a temporal order of events in which the cause *precedes* the effect. This is called **temporal precedence.** Thus, we need to know that television viewing occurred first and aggression followed.

2. When the cause is present, the effect occurs; when the cause is not present, the effect does not occur. This is called **covariation of cause and effect.** We need to know that children who watch television violence behave aggressively and that children who do not watch television violence do not behave aggressively.

3. Nothing other than a causal variable could be responsible for the observed effect. This is called elimination of **alternative explanations.** There should be no other plausible alternative explanation for the relationship. This third point about alternative explanations is very important: Suppose that the children who watch a lot of television violence are left alone more than are children who don't view television violence. In this case, the increased aggression could have an alternative explanation: lack of parental supervision. Causation will be discussed again in Chapter 4.

Explanation of Behavior

A final goal of science is to explain the events that have been described. The scientist seeks to understand *why* the behavior occurs. Consider the relationship between television violence and aggression: Even if we know that TV violence is a cause of aggressiveness, we need to explain this relationship. Is it due to imitation or "modeling" of the violence seen on TV? Is it the result of psychological desensitization to violence and its effects? Or does watching TV violence lead to a belief that aggression is a normal response to frustration and conflict? Further research is necessary to shed light on possible explanations of what has been observed. Usually, additional research like this is carried out by testing theories that are developed to explain particular behaviors.

Description, prediction, determination of cause, and explanation are all closely intertwined. Determining cause and explaining behavior are particularly closely related because it is difficult ever to know the true cause or all the causes of any behavior. An explanation that appears satisfactory may turn out to be inadequate when other causes are identified in subsequent research. For example, when early research showed that speaker credibility is related to attitude change, the researchers explained the finding by stating that people are more willing to believe what is said by a person with high credibility than by one with low credibility. However, this explanation has given way to a more complex theory of attitude change that takes into account many other factors that are related to persuasion (Petty & Cacioppo, 1986). In short, there is a certain amount of ambiguity in the enterprise of scientific inquiry. New research findings almost always pose new questions that must be addressed by further research; explanations of behavior often must be discarded or revised as new evidence is gathered. Such ambiguity is part of the excitement and fun of science.

BASIC AND APPLIED RESEARCH

Basic Research

Basic research tries to answer fundamental questions about the nature of behavior. Studies are often designed to address theoretical issues concerning phenomena such as cognition, emotion, motivation, learning, neuropsychology, personality development, and social behavior. Here are descriptions of a few journal articles that pertain to some basic research questions:

> Kool, W., McGuire, J., Rosen, Z., & Botvinick, M. (2010). Decision making and the avoidance of cognitive demand. *Journal of Experimental Psychology: General, 139,* 665–682. doi:10.1037/a0020198
>
> Past research documented that people choose the least physically demanding option when choosing among different behaviors. This study investigated choices that differed in the amount of required cognitive effort. As expected, the participants chose to pursue options with the fewest cognitive demands.

> Rydell, R. J., Rydell, M. T., & Boucher, K. L. (2010). The effect of negative performance stereotypes on learning. *Journal of Personality and Social Psychology, 99,* 883–896. doi:10.1037/a0021139
>
> Female participants studied a tutorial on a particular approach to solving math problems. After completing the first half of the tutorial, they were given math problems to solve. At this point, a stereotype was invoked. Some participants were told that the purpose of the experiment was to examine reasons why females perform poorly in math. The other participants were not given this information. The second half of the tutorial was then presented and a second math performance measure was administered. The participants receiving the negative stereotype information did perform poorly on the second math test; the other participants performed the same on both math tests.

> Jacovina, M. E., & Gerreg, R. J. (2010). How readers experience characters' decisions. *Memory & Cognition, 38,* 753–761. doi:10.3758/MC.38.6.753
>
> This study focused on the way that readers process information about decisions that a story's characters make along with the consequences of the decisions. Participants read a story in which there was a match of the reader's decision preference and outcome (e.g., the preferred decision was made and there were positive consequences) or there was a mismatch (e.g., the preferred choice was made but there were negative outcomes). Readers took longer to read the information about decision outcomes when there was a mismatch of decision preference and outcome.

Applied Research

The research articles listed above were concerned with basic processes of behavior and cognition rather than any immediate practical implications. In contrast, **applied research** is conducted to address issues in which there are practical problems and potential solutions. To illustrate, here are a few summaries of journal articles about applied research:

Ramesh, A., & Gelfand, M. (2010). Will they stay or will they go? The role of job embeddedness in predicting turnover in individualistic and collectivistic cultures. *Journal of Applied Psychology, 95,* 807–823. doi:10.1037/a0019464

In the individualistic United States, employee turnover was predicted by the fit between the person's skills and the requirements of the job. In the more collectivist society of India, turnover was more strongly related to the fit between the person's values and the values of the organization.

Young, C., Fang, D., & Zisook, S. (2010). Depression in Asian-American and Caucasian undergraduate students. *Journal of Affective Disorders, 125,* 379–382. doi:10.1016/j.jad.2010.02.124

Asian-American college students reported higher levels of depression than Caucasian students. The results have implications for campus mental health programs.

Braver, S. L., Ellman, I. M., & Fabricus, W. V. (2003). Relocation of children after divorce and children's best interests: New evidence and legal considerations. *Journal of Family Psychology, 17,* 206–219. doi:10.1037/0893-3200.17.2.206

College students whose parents had divorced were categorized into groups based on whether the parent had moved more than an hour's drive away. The students whose parents had not moved had more positive scores on a number of adjustment measures.

Killen, J. D., Robinson, T. N., Ammerman, S., Hayward, C., Rogers, J., Stone, C., . . . Schatzberg, A. F. (2004). Randomized clinical trial of the efficacy of Bupropion combined with nicotine patch in the treatment of adolescent smokers. *Journal of Clinical and Consulting Psychology, 72,* 722–729. doi:10.1037/0022-006X.72.4.729

A randomized clinical trial is an experiment testing the effects of a medical procedure. In this study, adolescent smokers who received the antidepressant Bupropion along with a nicotine patch had the same success rate in stopping smoking as a group who received the nicotine patch alone.

Hyman, I., Boss, S., Wise, B., McKenzie, K., & Caggiano, J. (2010). Did you see the unicycling clown? Inattentional blindness while walking and talking on a cell phone. *Applied Cognitive Psychology, 24,* 597–607. doi:10.1002/acp.1638

Does talking on a cell phone while walking produce an inattentional blindness—a failure to notice events in the environment? In one study, pedestrians walking across a campus square while using a cell phone walked more slowly and changed directions more frequently than others walking in the same location. In a second study, a clown rode a unicycle on the square. Pedestrians were asked if they noticed a clown on a unicycle after they had crossed the square. The cell phone users were much less likely to notice than pedestrians walking alone, with a friend, or while listening to music.

TABLE 1.1   Test yourself

Examples of research questions	Basic	Applied
1. Is extraversion related to sensation-seeking?		
2. Do video games such as *Grand Theft Auto* increase aggression among children and young adults?		
3. How do neurons generate neurotransmitters?		
4. Does memory process visual images and sound simultaneously?		
5. How can a city increase recycling by residents?		
6. Which strategies are best for coping with natural disasters?		

At this point, you may be wondering if there is a definitive way to know whether a study should be considered basic or applied. The distinction between basic and applied research is a convenient typology but is probably more accurately viewed as a continuum. Notice in the listing of applied research studies that some are more applied than others. The study on adolescent smoking is very much applied—the data will be valuable for people who are planning smoking cessation programs for adolescents. The study on depression among college students would be valuable on campuses that have mental health awareness and intervention programs for students. The study on child custody could be used as part of an argument in actual court cases. It could even be used by counselors working with couples in the process of divorce. The study on cell phone use is applied because of the widespread use of cell phones and the documentation of the problems they may cause. However, the study would not necessarily lead to a solution to the problem. All of these studies are grounded in applied issues and solutions to problems, but they differ in how quickly and easily the results of the study can actually be used. Table 1.1 gives you a chance to test your understanding of this distinction.

A major area of applied research is called **program evaluation,** which assesses the social reforms and innovations that occur in government, education, the criminal justice system, industry, health care, and mental health institutions. In an influential paper on "reforms as experiments," Campbell (1969) noted that social programs are really experiments designed to achieve certain outcomes. He argued persuasively that social scientists should evaluate each program to determine whether it is having its intended effect. If it is not, alternative programs should be tried. This is an important point that people in all organizations too often fail to remember when new ideas are implemented; the scientific approach dictates that new programs should be evaluated. Here are three sample journal articles about program evaluation:

Reid, R., Mullen, K., D'Angelo, M., Aitken, D., Papadakis, S., Haley, P., . . . Pipe, A. L. (2010). Smoking cessation for hospitalized smokers: An evaluation of the "Ottawa Model." *Nicotine & Tobacco Research, 12*, 11–18. doi:10.1093/ntr/ntp165

A smoking cessation program for patients was implemented in nine Canadian hospitals. Smoking rates were measured for a year following the treatment. The program was successful in reducing smoking.

Grossman, J. B., & Tierney, J. P. (1998). Does mentoring work? An impact study of the Big Brothers Big Sisters program. *Evaluation Review, 22*, 403–426. doi:10.1177/0193841X9802200304

An experiment was conducted to evaluate the impact of participation in the Big Brothers Big Sisters program. The 10- to 16-year-old youths participating in the program were less likely to skip school, begin using drugs or alcohol, or get into fights than the youths in the control group.

Kumpfer, K., Whiteside, H., Greene, J., & Allen, K. (2010). Effectiveness outcomes of four age versions of the Strengthening Families Program in statewide field sites. *Group Dynamics: Theory, Research, and Practice, 14*(3), 211–229. doi:10.1037/a0020602

A large-scale Strengthening Families Program was implemented over a 5-year period with over 1,600 high-risk families in Utah. For most measures of improvement in family functioning, the program was effective across all child age groups.

Much applied research is conducted in settings such as large business firms, marketing research companies, government agencies, and public polling organizations and is not published but rather is used within the company or by clients of the company. Whether or not such results are published, however, they are used to help people make better decisions concerning problems that require immediate action.

Comparing Basic and Applied Research

Both basic and applied research are important, and neither can be considered superior to the other. In fact, progress in science is dependent on a synergy between basic and applied research. Much applied research is guided by the theories and findings of basic research investigations. For example, one of the most effective treatment strategies for specific phobia—an anxiety disorder characterized by extreme fear reactions to specific objects or situations—is called *exposure therapy* (Chambless et al., 1996). In exposure therapy, people who suffer from a phobia are exposed to the object of their fears in a safe setting while a therapist trains them in relaxation techniques in order to counter-program their fear reaction. This behavioral treatment emerged from the work of Pavlov and Watson, who studied the processes by which animals acquire, maintain, and critically lose reflexive reactions to stimuli (Wolpe, 1982).

In recent years, many in our society, including legislators who control the budgets of research-granting agencies of the government, have demanded that research be directly relevant to specific social issues. The problem with this attitude toward research is that we can never predict the ultimate applications of basic research. Psychologist B. F. Skinner, for example, conducted basic research in the 1930s on operant conditioning, which carefully described the effects of reinforcement on such behaviors as bar pressing by rats. Years later, this research led to many practical applications in therapy, education, and industrial psychology. Research with no apparent practical value ultimately can be very useful. The fact that no one can predict the eventual impact of basic research leads to the conclusion that support of basic research is necessary both to advance science and to benefit society.

Behavioral research is important in many fields and has significant applications to public policy. This chapter has introduced you to the major goals and general types of research. All researchers use scientific methods, whether they are interested in basic, applied, or program evaluation questions. The themes and concepts in this chapter will be expanded in the remainder of the book. They will be the basis on which you evaluate the research of others and plan your own research projects as well.

This chapter emphasized that scientists are skeptical about what is true in the world; they insist that propositions be tested empirically. In the next two chapters, we will focus on two other characteristics of scientists. First, scientists have an intense curiosity about the world and find inspiration for ideas in many places. Second, scientists have strong ethical principles; they are committed to treating those who participate in research investigations with respect and dignity.

ILLUSTRATIVE ARTICLE: INTRODUCTION

Most chapters in this book include a chapter closing feature called *Illustrative Article,* which is designed to relate some of the key points in the chapter to information in a published journal article. In each case you will be asked to obtain a copy of the article using some of the skills that will be presented in Chapter 2, read the article, and answer some questions that are closely aligned with the material in the chapter.

For this chapter, instead of reading articles from scientific journals, we invite you to read two columns in which *New York Times* columnist David Brooks describes the value and excitement he has discovered by reading social science research literature. His enthusiasm for research is summed up by his comment that "a day without social science is like a day without sunshine." The two articles can be found via the *New York Times* website or using a newspaper database in your library that includes the *New York Times*:

Brooks, D. (2010, December 7). Social science palooza. *New York Times,* p. A33. Retrieved from www.nytimes.com/2010/12/07/opinion/07brooks.html

Brooks, D. (2011, March 18). Social science palooza II. *New York Times,* p. A29. Retrieved from www.nytimes.com/2011/03/18/opinion/18brooks.html

After reading the newspaper columns, consider the following:

1. Which of the articles that Brooks describes did you find most interesting (i.e., you would like to conduct research on the topic, you would be motivated to read the original journal article). Why do you find this interesting?

2. Of all the articles described, which one would you describe as being the most applied and which one most reflects basic research? Why?

Study Terms

Alternative explanations (p. 10)

Applied research (p. 11)

Authority (p. 3)

Basic research (p. 11)

Covariation of cause and effect (p. 10)

Empiricism (p. 5)

Falsifiability (p. 6)

Goals of behavioral science (p. 8)

Intuition (p. 3)

Peer review (p. 6)

Program evaluation (p. 13)

Pseudoscience (p. 7)

Skepticism (p. 5)

Temporal precedence (p. 9)

Review Questions

1. Why is it important for anyone in our society to have knowledge of research methods?

2. Why is scientific skepticism useful in furthering our knowledge of behavior? How does the scientific approach differ from other ways of gaining knowledge about behavior?

3. Provide definitions and examples of description, prediction, determination of cause, and explanation as goals of scientific research.

4. Describe the three elements for inferring causation.

5. Describe the characteristics of the way that science works, according to Goodstein (2000).

6. How does basic research differ from applied research?

Activity Questions

1. Read several editorials in your daily newspaper and identify the sources used to support the assertions and conclusions. Did the writer use intuition, appeals to authority, scientific evidence, or a combination of these? Give specific examples.

2. Imagine a debate on the following assertion: Behavioral scientists should only conduct research that has immediate practical applications. Develop arguments that support (pro) and oppose (con) the assertion.

3. Imagine a debate on the following assertion: Knowledge of research methods is unnecessary for students who intend to pursue careers in clinical and counseling psychology. Develop arguments that support (pro) and oppose (con) the assertion.

4. A newspaper headline says, "Eating Disorders May Be More Common in Warm Places." You read the article to discover that a researcher found that the incidence of eating disorders among female students at a university in Florida was higher than at a university in Pennsylvania. Assume that this study accurately describes a difference between students at the two universities. Discuss the finding in terms of the issues of identification of cause and effect and explanation. Come back to this question after you have read the next few chapters. For more information, see Sloan, D. M. (2002). Does warm weather climate affect eating disorder pathology? *International Journal of Eating Disorders, 32,* 240–244.

5. Identify ways that you might have allowed yourself to accept beliefs or engage in practices that you might have rejected if you had engaged in scientific skepticism. For example, we continually have to remind some of our friends that a claim made in an e-mail may be a hoax or a rumor. Provide specific details of the experience(s). How might you go about investigating whether the claim is valid?

Answers

TABLE 1.1:

basic = 1, 3, 4   applied = 2, 5, 6

2

Where to Start

LEARNING OBJECTIVES

- Discuss how a hypothesis differs from a prediction.
- Describe the different sources of ideas for research, including common sense, observation, theories, past research, and practical problems.
- Identify the two functions of a theory.
- Summarize the fundamentals of conducting library research in psychology, including the use of *PsycINFO*.
- Summarize the information included in the abstract, introduction, method, results, and discussion sections of research articles.

The motivation to conduct scientific research derives from a natural curiosity about the world. Most people have their first experience with research when their curiosity leads them to ask, "I wonder what would happen if..." or "I wonder why...," followed by an attempt to answer the question. What are the sources of inspiration for such questions? How do you find out about other people's ideas and past research? In this chapter, we will explore some sources of scientific ideas. We will also consider the nature of research reports published in professional journals.

HYPOTHESES AND PREDICTIONS

Most research studies are attempts to test a hypothesis formulated by the researcher. A hypothesis is a type of idea or question; it makes a statement about something that may be true. Thus, a **hypothesis** is a tentative idea or question that is waiting for evidence to support or refute it. Once the hypothesis is proposed, data must be gathered and evaluated in terms of whether the evidence is consistent or inconsistent with the hypothesis. Sometimes, hypotheses are stated as informal research questions. For example, Cramer, Mayer, and Ryan (2007) had general questions about college students' use of cell phones while driving: "Do males and females differ in their use of cell phones while driving?" or "Does having a passenger in the car make a difference in cell phone use?" or "How will college student cell phone use compare with a recent national sample of young adults?" With such questions in mind, the researchers developed a procedure for collecting data to answer the questions.

Such research questions can be stated in more formal terms. The first research question can be phrased as a hypothesis that "there is a gender difference in use of cell phones while driving." In either case, we are putting forth an idea that two variables, gender and cell phone use while driving, may be related. Similarly, other researchers might formulate hypotheses such as "crowding results in lowered performance on mental tasks" or "attending to more features of something to be learned will result in greater memory." After formulating the hypothesis, the researcher will design a study to test the hypothesis. In the example on crowding, the researcher might conduct an experiment in which research participants in either a crowded or an uncrowded room work on a series of tasks; performance on these tasks is then measured.

At this point, the researcher would make a specific **prediction** concerning the outcome of this experiment. Here the prediction might be that "participants in the uncrowded condition will perform better on the tasks than will participants in the crowded condition." If this prediction is confirmed by the results of the study, the hypothesis is supported. If the prediction is not confirmed, the researcher will either reject the hypothesis (and believe that crowding does not lead to poor performance) or conduct further research using different methods to study the hypothesis. It is important to note that when the results of a study confirm a prediction, the hypothesis is only *supported*, not *proven*. Researchers study the same hypothesis using a variety of methods, and each time this hypothesis is supported by a research study, we become more confident that the hypothesis is correct.

WHO WE STUDY: A NOTE ON TERMINOLOGY

We have been using the term *participants* to refer to the individuals who participate in research projects. An equivalent term in psychological research is *subjects*. The *Publication Manual of the American Psychological Association* (APA, 2010) now allows the use of either *participants* or *subjects* when describing humans who take part in psychological research. You will see both terms when you read about research; both terms will be used in this book. Other terms that you may encounter include *respondents* and *informants*. The individuals who take part in survey research are usually called *respondents*. *Informants* are the people who help researchers understand the dynamics of particular cultural and organizational settings—this term originated in anthropological and sociological research, and is now being used by psychologists as well. In many research reports more specific descriptions of the participants will be used, for example: *employees* in an organization, *students* in a classroom, or *residents* of an assisted living facility.

SOURCES OF IDEAS

It is not easy to say where good ideas come from. Many people are capable of coming up with worthwhile ideas but find it difficult to verbalize the process by which they are generated. Cartoonists know this—they show a brilliant idea as a lightbulb flashing on over the person's head. But where does the electricity come from? Let's consider five sources of ideas: common sense, observation of the world around us, theories, past research, and practical problems.

Common Sense

One source of ideas that can be tested is the body of knowledge called common sense—the things we all believe to be true. Do "opposites attract" or do "birds of a feather flock together"? If you "spare the rod," do you "spoil the child"? Is a "picture worth a thousand words"? Asking questions such as these can lead to research programs studying attraction, the effects of punishment, and the role of visual images in learning and memory.

Testing a commonsense idea can be valuable because such notions don't always turn out to be correct, or research may show that the real world is much more complicated than our commonsense ideas would have it. For example, pictures can aid memory under certain circumstances, but sometimes pictures detract from learning (see Levin, 1983). Conducting research to test commonsense ideas often forces us to go beyond a commonsense theory of behavior.

Observation of the World Around Us

Observations of personal and social events can provide many ideas for research. The curiosity sparked by your observations and experiences can lead you to ask questions about all sorts of phenomena. In fact, this type of curiosity is what drives many students to engage in their first research project.

Have you ever had the experience of storing something away in a "special place" where you were sure you could find it later (and where no one else would possibly look for it), only to later discover that you couldn't recall where you had stored it? Such an experience could lead to systematic research on whether it is a good idea to put things in special places. In fact, Winograd and Soloway (1986) conducted a series of experiments on this very topic. Their research demonstrated that people are likely to forget where something is placed when two conditions are present: (1) The location where the object is placed is judged to be highly memorable *and* (2) the location is considered a very unlikely place for the object. Thus, although it may seem to be a good idea at the time, storing something in an unusual place is generally not a good idea.

A more recent example demonstrates the diversity of ideas that can be generated by curiosity about things that happen around you. During the past few years, there has been a great deal of controversy about the effects of music lyrics, with fears that certain types of rock and hip hop music lead to sexual promiscuity, drug use, and violence. Martino et al. (2006), as an example, interviewed adolescents over a 3-year period to explore the impact that music with degrading sexual lyrics had on sexual behavior. They found that over time, listening to music with degrading sexual lyrics predicted a wide range of early sexual behaviors.

The world around us is a rich source of material for scientific investigation. When he was a college student, psychologist Michael Lynn worked as a waiter dependent upon tips from customers. The experience sparked an interest that fueled an academic career (Crawford, 2000). For many years, Lynn has studied tipping behavior in restaurants and hotels in the United States and in other countries. He has looked at factors that increase tips, such as posture, touching, and phrases written on a check, and his research has had an impact on the hotel and restaurant industry. If you have ever worked in restaurants, you have undoubtedly formed many of your own hypotheses about tipping behavior. Lynn went one step further and took a scientific approach to testing his ideas. His research illustrates that taking a scientific approach to a problem can lead to new discoveries and important applications.

Finally, we should mention the role of serendipity—sometimes the most interesting discoveries are the result of accident or sheer luck. Ivan Pavlov is best known for discovering what is called *classical conditioning*, wherein a neutral stimulus (such as a tone), if paired repeatedly with an unconditioned stimulus (food) that produces a reflex response (salivation), will eventually produce the response when presented alone. Pavlov did not set out to discover classical conditioning. Instead, he was studying the digestive system in dogs by measuring their salivation when given food. He accidentally discovered that the dogs were salivating prior to the actual feeding and then studied the ways that the stimuli preceding the feeding could produce a salivation response. Of course, such accidental discoveries are made only when viewing the world with an inquisitive eye.

Theories

Much research in the behavioral sciences tests theories of behavior. A **theory** consists of a systematic body of ideas about a particular topic or phenomenon. Psychologists have theories relating to human behavior including learning, memory, and personality, for example. These ideas form a coherent and logically consistent structure that serves two important functions. First, theories *organize and explain* a variety of specific facts or descriptions of behavior. Such facts and descriptions are not very meaningful by themselves, and so theories are needed to impose a framework on them. This framework makes the world more comprehensible by providing a few abstract concepts around which we can organize and explain a variety of behaviors. As an example, consider how Charles Darwin's theory of evolution organized and explained a variety of facts concerning the characteristics of animal species. Similarly, in psychology one theory of memory asserts that there are separate systems of short-term memory and long-term memory. This theory accounts for a number of specific observations about learning and memory, including such phenomena as the different types of memory deficits that result from a blow to the head versus damage to the hippocampus area of the brain and the rate at which a person forgets material he or she has just read.

Second, theories *generate new knowledge* by focusing our thinking so that we notice new aspects of behavior—theories guide our observations of the world. The theory generates hypotheses about behavior, and the researcher conducts studies to test the hypotheses. If the studies confirm the hypotheses, the theory is supported. As more and more evidence accumulates that is consistent with the theory, we become more confident that the theory is correct.

Sometimes people describe a theory as "just an idea" that may or may not be true. We need to separate this use of the term—which implies that a theory is essentially the same as a hypothesis—from the scientific meaning of *theory*. In fact, a scientific theory consists of much more than a simple "idea." A scientific theory is grounded in actual data from prior research as well as numerous hypotheses that are consistent with the theory. These hypotheses can be tested through further research. Such testable hypotheses are falsifiable—the data can either support or refute the hypotheses (see Chapter 1). As a theory develops with more and more evidence that supports the theory, it is wrong to say that it is "just an idea." Instead, the theory becomes well established as it enables us to explain a great many observable facts. It is true that research may reveal a weakness in a theory when a hypothesis generated by the theory is not supported. When this happens, the theory can be modified to account for the new data. Sometimes a new theory will emerge that accounts for both new data and the existing body of knowledge. This process defines the way that science continually develops with new data that expand our knowledge of the world around us.

Evolutionary theory has influenced our understanding of sexual attraction and mating patterns (Buss, 2007). For example, Buss describes a well-established finding that males experience more intense feelings of jealousy when a partner has a sexual relationship with someone else (sexual infidelity) than when the partner has developed an emotional bond only (emotional infidelity); females in contrast are more jealous when the partner has engaged in emotional infidelity than sexual infidelity. This finding is consistent with evolutionary theory, which asserts that males and females have evolved different strategies for mate selection. All individuals have an evolutionary interest in passing their genes on to future generations. However, females have relatively few opportunities to reproduce, have a limited age range during which to reproduce, and must exert a tremendous amount of time and energy caring for their children. Males, in contrast, can reproduce at any time and have a reproductive advantage by their ability to produce more offspring than a given female can. Because of these differences, the theory predicts that females and males will have different perspectives of infidelity. Females will be more threatened if the partner might no longer provide support and resources for childrearing by developing an emotional bond with another partner. Males are more distressed if it is possible that they will be caring for a child who does not share their genes. Although research supports evolutionary theory, alternative theories can be developed that may better explain the same findings, because theories are living and dynamic. Levy and Kelly (2010) suggest that attachment theory may provide a better explanation. They point out that both males and females differ in their level of attachment in relationships. Also, females in general show greater attachment than do males. From the perspective of attachment theory, the amount of attachment will be related to the distress experienced by an instance of emotional infidelity. Research by Levy and Kelly found that high attachment individuals were most upset by emotional infidelity; individuals with low attachment to the relationship were more distressed by sexual infidelity. These findings will lead to more research to test the two theoretical perspectives.

Theories are usually modified as new research defines the scope of the theory. The necessity of modifying theories is illustrated by the theory of short-term versus long-term memory mentioned previously. The original conception of the long-term memory system described long-term memory as a storehouse of permanent, fixed memories. However, now-classic research by cognitive psychologists, including Loftus (1979), has shown that memories are easily reconstructed and reinterpreted. In one study, participants watched a film of an automobile accident and later were asked to tell what they saw in the film. Loftus found that participants' memories were influenced by the way they were questioned. For example, participants who were asked whether they saw "the" broken headlight were more likely to answer yes than were participants who were asked whether they saw "a" broken headlight. Results such as these have required a more complex theory of how long-term memory operates.

Past Research

A fourth source of ideas is past research. Becoming familiar with a body of research on a topic is perhaps the best way to generate ideas for new research. Because the results of research are published, researchers can use the body of past literature on a topic to continually refine and expand our knowledge. Virtually every study raises questions that can be addressed in subsequent research. The research may lead to an attempt to apply the findings in a different setting, to study the topic with a different age group, or to use a different methodology to replicate the results. In the Cramer et al. (2007) study on cell phone use while driving, trained observers noted cell phone use of 3,650 students leaving campus parking structures during a 3-hour period on 2 different days. They reported that 11% of all drivers were using cell phones. Females were more likely than males to be using a cell phone, and drivers with passengers were less likely to be talking than solitary drivers. Knowledge of this study might lead to research on ways to reduce students' cell phone use while driving.

In addition, as you become familiar with the research literature on a topic, you may see inconsistencies in research results that need to be investigated, or you may want to study alternative explanations for the results. Also, what you know about one research area often can be successfully applied to another research area.

Let's look at a concrete example of a study that was designed to address methodological flaws in previous research. In Chapter 1, we discussed research on a method—called *facilitated communication*—intended to help children who are diagnosed with autism. Childhood autism is characterized by a number of symptoms including severe impairments in language and communication ability. Parents and care providers were greatly encouraged by facilitated communication, which allowed an autistic child to communicate with others by pressing keys on a keyboard showing letters and other symbols. A facilitator held the child's hand to facilitate the child's ability to determine which key to press. With this technique, many autistic children began communicating their thoughts and feelings and answered questions posed to them. Most people who saw facilitated communication in action regarded the technique as a miraculous breakthrough.

The conclusion that facilitated communication was effective was based on a comparison of the autistic child's ability to communicate with and without the facilitator. The difference is impressive to most observers. Recall, however, that scientists are by nature skeptical. They examine all evidence carefully and ask whether claims are justified. In the case of facilitated communication, Montee, Miltenberger, and Wittrock (1995) noted that the facilitator might have been unintentionally guiding the child's fingers to type meaningful sentences. In other words, the facilitator, and not the autistic individual, might be controlling the communication. Montee et al. conducted a study to test this idea. In one condition, both the facilitator and the autistic child were shown a picture, and the child was asked to indicate what was shown in the picture by typing a response with the facilitator. This was done on a number of trials. In another condition, only the child saw the pictures. In a third condition, the child and facilitator were shown different pictures (but the facilitator was unaware of this fact). Consistent with the hypothesis that the facilitator is controlling the child's responses, the pictures were correctly identified only in the condition in which both saw the same pictures. Moreover, when the child and facilitator viewed different pictures, the child never made the correct response, and usually the picture the facilitator had seen was the one identified.

Practical Problems

Research is also stimulated by practical problems that can have immediate applications. Groups of city planners and citizens might survey bicycle riders to determine the most desirable route for a city bike path, for example. On a larger scale, researchers have guided public policy by conducting research on obesity and eating disorders, as well as other social and health issues. Much of the applied and evaluation research described in Chapter 1 addresses issues such as these.

LIBRARY RESEARCH

Before conducting any research project, an investigator must have a thorough knowledge of previous research findings. Even if the researcher formulates the basic idea, a review of past studies will help the researcher clarify the idea and design the study. Thus, it is important to know how to search the literature on a topic and how to read research reports in professional journals. In this section, we will discuss only the fundamentals of conducting library research; for further information, you should go to your college library and talk with a librarian (large libraries may have a librarian devoted to providing assistance in psychology and other behavioral sciences). Librarians have specialized training and a lot of practical experience in conducting library research. You may also refer to a more detailed guide to library research in psychology, such as Reed and Baxter (2003), or to the numerous library guides available on the Internet. You may also find guides to help you prepare a paper that reviews research; Rosnow and Rosnow (2009) is an example.

The Nature of Journals

If you've wandered through the periodicals section of your library, you've noticed the enormous number of professional journals. In these journals, researchers publish the results of their investigations. After a research project has been completed, the study is written as a report, which then may be submitted to the editor of an appropriate journal. The editor solicits reviews from other scientists in the same field and then decides whether the report is to be accepted for publication. (This is the process of peer review described in Chapter 1.) Because each journal has a limited amount of space and receives many more papers than it has room to publish, most papers are rejected. Those that are accepted are published about a year later, although sometimes online editions are published more quickly.

Most psychology journals specialize in one or two areas of human or animal behavior. Even so, the number of journals in many areas is so large that it is almost impossible for anyone to read them all. Table 2.1 lists some of the major

TABLE 2.1 Some major journals in psychology

General

American Psychologist * (general articles on a variety of topics)	*Psychological Methods* *
	Current Directions in Psychological Science
Contemporary Psychology * (book reviews)	*Psychological Science in the Public Interest*
Psychological Bulletin * (literature reviews)	*History of Psychology* *
Psychological Review * (theoretical articles)	*Review of General Psychology* *
Psychological Science	

Clinical and counseling psychology

Journal of Abnormal Psychology *	*Behavior Therapy*
Journal of Consulting and Clinical Psychology *	*Journal of Abnormal Child Psychology*
Journal of Counseling Psychology *	*Journal of Social and Clinical Psychology*
Behavior Research and Therapy	*Professional Psychology: Research and Practice* *
Journal of Clinical Psychology	

Experimental areas of psychology

Journal of Experimental Psychology:	*Memory & Cognition*
General *	*Cognitive Psychology*
Applied *	*Cognition*
Learning, Memory, and Cognition *	*Cognitive Science*
Human Perception and Performance *	*Discourse Processes*
Animal Behavior Processes *	*Journal of the Experimental Analysis of Behavior*
Journal of Comparative Psychology *	*Animal Learning and Behavior*
Behavioral Neuroscience *	*Neuropsychology* *
Bulletin of the Psychonomic Society	*Emotion* *
Learning and Motivation	*Experimental and Clinical Psychopharmacology* *

Developmental psychology

Developmental Psychology *	*Developmental Review*
Psychology and Aging *	*Infant Behavior and Development*
Child Development	*Experimental Aging Research*
Journal of Experimental Child Psychology	*Merrill–Palmer Quarterly*
Journal of Applied Developmental Psychology	

TABLE 2.1 (continued)

Personality and social psychology

*Journal of Personality and Social Psychology**	*Social Psychology Quarterly*
Personality and Social Psychology Bulletin	*Journal of Applied Social Psychology*
Journal of Experimental Social Psychology	*Basic and Applied Social Psychology*
Journal of Research in Personality	*Journal of Social and Personal Relationships*
Journal of Social Issues	

Applied areas of psychology

*Journal of Applied Psychology**	*Evaluation Review*
*Journal of Educational Psychology**	*Evaluation and Program Planning*
Journal of Applied Behavior Analysis	*Environment and Behavior*
*Health Psychology**	*Journal of Environmental Psychology*
*Psychological Assessment**	*Journal of Consumer Research*
*Psychology, Public Policy, and Law**	*Journal of Marketing Research*
Law and Human Behavior	*Rehabilitation Psychology*
Educational and Psychological Measurement	*Journal of Business and Psychology*
American Educational Research Journal	

Family studies and sexual behavior

*Journal of Family Psychology**	*Journal of Sex Research*
Families, Systems and Health	*Journal of Sexual Behavior*
Journal of Marriage and the Family	*Journal of Homosexuality*
Journal of Marital and Family Therapy	

Ethnic, gender, and cross-cultural issues

Hispanic Journal of Behavioral Sciences	*Journal of Cross-Cultural Psychology*
Journal of Black Psychology	*Cultural Diversity and Ethnic Minority Psychology**
Sex Roles	*Psychology of Men and Masculinity*
Psychology of Women Quarterly	

Some Canadian and British journals

Canadian Journal of Experimental Psychology	*British Journal of Psychology*
Canadian Journal of Behavioral Science	*British Journal of Social and Clinical Psychology*

*Published by the American Psychological Association.

journals in several areas of psychology; the table does not list any journals that are published only on the Internet, and it does not include many journals that publish in areas closely related to psychology as well as highly specialized areas within psychology. Clearly, it would be difficult to read all of the journals listed, even if you restricted your reading to a single research area in psychology such as learning and memory. If you were seeking research on a single specific topic, it would be impractical to look at every issue of every journal in which relevant research might be published. Fortunately, you don't have to.

Online Scholarly Research Databases: PsycINFO

The American Psychological Association began the monthly publication of *Psychological Abstracts,* or *Psych Abstracts,* in 1927. The abstracts are brief summaries of articles in psychology and related disciplines indexed by topic area. Today, the abstracts are maintained in a computer database called **PsycINFO,** which is accessed via the Internet and is updated weekly. The exact procedures you will use to search *PsycINFO* will depend on how your library has arranged to obtain access to the database. In all cases, you will obtain a list of abstracts that are related to your particular topic of interest. You can then find and read the articles in your library or, in many cases, link to full text that your library subscribes to. If an important article is not available in your library, ask a librarian about services to obtain articles from other libraries.

Conducting a PsycINFO Search

The exact look and feel of the system you will use to search *PsycINFO* will depend on your library website. Your most important task is to specify the search terms that you want the database to use. These are typed into a search box. How do you know what words to type in the search box? Most commonly, you will want to use standard psychological terms. The "Thesaurus of Psychological Index Terms" lists all the standard terms that are used to index the abstracts, and it can be accessed directly with most *PsycINFO* systems. Suppose you are interested in the topic of test anxiety. It turns out that both *test* and *anxiety* are major descriptors in the thesaurus. If you look under *anxiety* you will see all of the related terms, including *separation anxiety, social anxiety,* and *test anxiety.* While using the thesaurus, you can check any term and then request a search of that term. Of course, you can search using any term or phrase that is relevant to your topic. When you give the command to start the search, the results of the search will be displayed.

Below is the output of one of the articles found with a search on test anxiety. The exact appearance of the output that you receive will depend on the your library's search system. The default output includes citation information that you will need along with the abstract itself. Notice that the output is organized into "fields" of information. The full name of each field is included here; many systems allow abbreviations. You will almost always want to see the *title, author, source/publication title,* and *abstract.* Note that you also have fields such as publication type, keywords to briefly describe the article, and age group. When you do the search, some fields will appear as hyperlinks to lead you to other information in your library database or to other websites. Systems are continually being upgraded to enable users to more easily obtain full-text access to the articles and find other articles on similar topics. The *Digital Object Identifier* (DOI) is particularly helpful in finding full-text sources of the article and is now provided with other publication information when journal articles are referenced.

The reference for the article is

Nelson, D., & Knight, A. (2010). The power of positive recollections: Reducing test anxiety and enhancing college student efficacy and performance. *Journal of Applied Social Psychology, 40*(3), 732–745. doi:10.1111/j.1559-1816.2010.00595.x

PsycINFO output for Nelson and Knight (2010) appears as follows:

Title:	The Power of Positive Recollections: Reducing Test Anxiety and Enhancing College Student Efficacy and Performance.
Authors:	Nelson, Donna Webster, Winthrop University, Rock Hill, SC, US, nelsond@winthrop.edu Knight, Ashley E., Winthrop University, Rock Hill, SC, US
Address:	Nelson, Donna Webster, Department of Psychology, Winthrop University, Rock Hill, SC, US, 29733, nelsond@winthrop.edu
Source:	Journal of Applied Social Psychology, Vol 40(3), Mar, 2010. pp. 732-745.
Page Count:	14
Publisher:	United Kingdom: Wiley-Blackwell Publishing Ltd.
ISSN:	0021-9029 (Print)
Language:	English
Keywords:	positive recollections; test anxiety; college student efficacy & performance
Abstract:	This research sought to develop an intervention (targeting positive emotions and thoughts) as a mechanism for reducing test anxiety and raising confidence and performance in a sample of college students. Participants were randomly assigned to a positive thought task or a control task. Those in the positive-thought condition, who were assigned to write about successful personal experiences, derived several benefits, when compared with control participants who wrote

about their morning routines. Specifically, they experienced more positive affect and less negative affect, exhibited a more optimistic outlook, and reported less test anxiety. They were more likely to appraise the quiz confidently, perceiving it as a challenge rather than a threat. Perhaps most importantly, they exhibited superior performance on the quiz. (PsycINFO Database Record (c) 2010 APA, all rights reserved)

Subjects:	*College Students; *Performance; *Positivism; *Self Efficacy; *Test Anxiety
Classification:	Academic Learning & Achievement (3550)
Age Group:	Adulthood (18 yrs & older) (300)
Tests & Measures:	Positive and Negative Affect Scale
Methodology:	Empirical Study; Quantitative Study
Publication Type:	Journal; Peer Reviewed Journal
Document Type:	Journal Article
Release Date:	20100503
Copyright:	the Authors & Wiley Periodicals, Inc. 2010.
Digital Object Identifier:	10.1111/j.1559-1816.2010.00595.x
Accession Number:	2010-06157-011
Database:	PsycINFO

When you do a simple search with a single word or a phrase such as *test anxiety,* the default search yields articles that have that word or phrase anywhere in any of the fields listed. Often you will find that this produces too many articles, including articles that are not directly relevant to your interests. One way to narrow the search is to limit it to certain fields. Your *PsycINFO* search screen will allow you to limit the search to one field, such as the title of the article. You can also learn how to type a search that includes the field you want. For example, you could specify *test anxiety in TITLE* to limit your search to articles that have the term in the title of the article. Your search screen will also allow you to set limits on your search to specify, for instance, that the search should find only journal articles (not books or dissertations) or include participants from certain age groups.

Most *PsycINFO* systems have advanced search screens that enable you to use the Boolean operators AND and OR and NOT. These can be typed as discussed below, but the advanced search screen uses prompts to help you design the search. Suppose you want to restrict the *test anxiety in TITLE* search to studies of college students only. You can do this by asking for *(test anxiety in TITLE) AND (college students in SUBJECTS).* The AND forces both conditions to be true for an article to be included. The parentheses are used to separate different parts of your search specification and are useful when your searches become increasingly complicated.

The OR operation is used to expand a search that is too narrow. Suppose you want to find articles that discuss romantic relationships on the Internet. A *PsycINFO* search for *Internet AND romance* in any field produces 59 articles; changing the specification to *Internet AND (romance OR dating OR love)* yields 330 articles. Articles that have the term *Internet* and any of the other three terms specified were included in the second search.

The NOT operation will exclude sources based on a criterion you specify. The NOT operation is used when you anticipate that the search criteria will be met by some irrelevant abstracts. In the Internet example, it is possible that the search will include articles on *child predators*. To exclude the term *child* from the results of the search, the following adjustment can be made: *Internet AND (romance OR dating OR love) NOT child.* When this search was conducted, 303 abstracts were found instead of the 330 obtained previously.

Another helpful search tool is the "wildcard" asterisk (*). The asterisk stands for any set of letters in a word and so it can expand your search. Consider the word *romance* in the search above—by using *roman**, the search will expand to include both *romance* and *romantic*. The wildcard can be very useful with the term *child** to find *child, children, childhood,* and so on. You have to be careful when doing this, however; the *roman** search would also find *Romania* and *romanticism.* In this case, it might be more efficient to simply add *OR romantic* to the search. These and other search strategies are summarized in Figure 2.1.

It is a good idea to give careful thought to your search terms. Consider the case of a student who decided to do a paper on the topic of road rage. She wanted to know what might cause drivers to become so angry at other drivers that they become physically aggressive. A search on the term *road rage* led to a number of interesting articles. However, when looking at the output from the search, she noticed that the major keywords included *driving behavior* and *anger* but not *road rage.* When she asked about this, we realized that she had only found articles that included the term *road rage* in the title or abstract. This term has become popular, but it may not be used in many academic studies of the topic. She then expanded the search to include *driving AND anger.* The new search yielded many articles not found in the original search.

As you review the results of your search, you can print, save, or send information to your e-mail address. Other options such as printing a citation in APA style may also be available.

Science Citation Index and Social Sciences Citation Index

Two related search resources are the **Science Citation Index** (SCI) and the **Social Sciences Citation Index** (SSCI). These are usually accessed together using the **Web of Science** computer database. Both allow you to search through citation information such as the name of the author or article title. The SCI includes disciplines such as biology, chemistry, biomedicine, and pharmacology, whereas the SSCI includes social and behavioral sciences such as sociology and criminal justice. The most important feature of both resources is the ability to use the "key

General Strategies

- Use several databases—for example, both *PsycINFO* and Google Scholar. Become familiar with the databases available in your library to expand the range of information available to you.

- Record your search terms and repeat your searches to find updates.

- Do not restrict yourself to full-text articles, as this introduces a bias in your results.

- Try a variety of key words: *angry driving* and *road rage* generate two sets of results that do not completely overlap.

- Consider using the words *review* and *meta-analysis* in the title of an article to find literature reviews.

- Look for the perfect key article and then use that one to identify additional articles. Use the results that you do find to generate new results.

- Use the "times cited in this database" information from PsycINFO or the "related articles" information in Google Scholar.

- Use the "cited references" information provided by PsycINFO and Google Scholar.

PsycINFO Search Strategies

- Use fields such as the TITLE and AUTHOR. Example: Typing *divorce* in TITLE requires that the term appear in the title.

- Use AND, OR, and NOT. AND limits the search. Example: Typing *divorce AND child* requires both terms to be included.

- Use OR to expand search. Example: Typing *divorce OR breakup* includes either terms.

- Use NOT to exclude search terms. Example: Typing *shyness NOT therapy* excludes any shyness articles that have the term *therapy*.

- Use the wildcard asterisk (*). Example: Typing *child** finds any word that begins with *child* (childhood, child's, etc.).

- Find the procedure for restricting the search to peer-reviewed articles.

- Review and use keywords that were selected by article authors (in PsycINFO, these are found in the more detailed result output).

Google Search Strategies

- Follow the link to Advanced Search. The advanced search screen allows you to

  ○ Search for a specific phrase

  ○ Specify a set of "AND" words or phrases so the each of the results of your search will include all the words or phrases

  ○ Specify a set of "OR" words or phrases to expand your search

  ○ Specify a set of "NOT" words or phrases to limit your search

FIGURE 2.1
Some strategies for searching research databases

article" method. Here you need to first identify a key article on your topic that is particularly relevant to your interests. Choose an article that was published sufficiently long ago to allow time for subsequent related research to be conducted and reported. You can then search for the subsequent articles that cited the key article. This search will give you a bibliography of articles relevant to your topic. To provide an example of this process, we chose the following article:

> Fleming, M., & Rickwood, D. (2001). Effects of violent versus nonviolent video games on children's arousal, aggressive mood, and positive mood. *Journal of Applied Social Psychology, 31*(10), 2047–2071. doi:10.1111/j.1559-1816.2001. tb00163.x

When we did an article search using the SSCI, we found 17 articles that had cited the Fleming and Rickwood paper since it was published in 2001. Here is one of them:

> Lim, S., & Reeves, B. (2009). Being in the game: Effects of avatar choice and point of view on psychophysiological responses during play. *Media Psychology, 12*(4), 348–370. doi:10.1080/15213260903287242

This article as well as the others on the list might then be retrieved. It may then turn out that one or more of the articles might become new key articles for further searches. It is also possible to specify a "key person" in order to find all articles written by or citing a particular person after a given date.

Literature Reviews

Articles that summarize the research in a particular area are also useful; these are known as **literature reviews.** The journal *Psychological Bulletin* publishes reviews of the literature in various topic areas in psychology. Each year, the *Annual Review of Psychology* publishes articles that summarize recent developments in various areas of psychology. Other disciplines have similar annual reviews.

The following article is an example of a literature review:

> Gatchel, R. J., Peng, Y. B., Peters, M. L., Fuchs, P. N., & Turk, D. C. (2007). The biopsychosocial approach to chronic pain: Scientific advances and future directions. *Psychological Bulletin, 133,* 581–624. doi:10.1037/0033-2909.133.4.581

The authors of this article reviewed the past literature relating the biopsychosocial approach to understanding chronic pain. They described a very large number of studies on the biological aspects of pain along with research on psychological and social influences. They also point to new methods and directions for the field.

When conducting a search, you might want to focus on finding review articles. Adding *review* as a search term in the title of the article will generate review articles in your results.

Other Electronic Search Resources

The American Psychological Association maintains several databases in addition to *PsycINFO*. These include *PsycARTICLES,* consisting of full-text scholarly articles, and *PsycBOOKS,* a database of full-text books and book chapters. Other major databases include *Sociological Abstracts*, *PubMed*, and *ERIC (Educational Resources Information Center)*. In addition, services such as LexisNexis Academic and Factiva allow you to search general media resources such as newspapers. A reference librarian can help you use these and other resources available to you.

Internet Searches

The most widely available information resource is the wealth of material that is available on the Internet and located using search services such as Google. The Internet is a wonderful source of information; any given search may help you find websites devoted to your topic, articles that people have made available to others, book reviews, and even online discussions. Although it is incredibly easy to search (just type something in a dialog box and press the Enter key), you can improve the quality of your searches by learning (1) the differences in the way each service finds and stores information; (2) advanced search rules, including how to make searches more narrow and how to find exact phrases; and (3) ways to critically evaluate the quality of the information that you find. You also need to make sure that you carefully record the search service and search terms you used, the dates of your search, and the exact location of any websites that you will be using in your research; this information will be useful as you provide documentation in the papers that you prepare.

Google Scholar

Google Scholar is a specialized scholarly search engine that can be accessed via any web browser at http://scholar.google.com. When you do a search using Google Scholar, you find articles, theses, books, abstracts, and court opinions from a wide range of sources, including academic publishers, professional societies, online repositories, universities, and other websites. Just like Google ranks the output of a standard search, Google Scholar ranks the output of a Google Scholar search. In the case of Google Scholar, search output is ranked by the contents of the article (i.e., did the article contain the keywords that were used in the search?) along with an article's overall prominence based on author, journal, and how often it is cited in other articles.

Google Scholar operates like any other Google search. Access Google Scholar at http://scholar.google.com and type in a keyword as you would in a basic *PsycINFO* search. The key difference is that whereas the universe of content for *PsycINFO* comes from the published works in the psychology and related sciences, the universe for Google Scholar includes the entire Internet. This can be both a strength and a weakness. If your topic is broad—for example, if you were interested in doing a search for *depression* or *ADHD* or *color perception*—Google Scholar would generate many more hits than would *PsycINFO*. Indeed, many of those hits would not be from the scientific literature. On the other hand, if you have a narrow search (e.g., *adult ADHD treatment* or *color perception and reading speed*), then Google Scholar would generate a set of results more closely aligned with your intentions.

Evaluating web information   Your own library and a variety of websites have information on evaluating the quality of information found on the Internet. Some of the most important things to look for are listed here.

- Is the site associated with a major educational institution or research organization? A site sponsored by a single individual or an organization with a clear bias should be viewed with skepticism.
- Is information provided on the people who are responsible for the site? Can you check on the credentials of these individuals?
- Is the information current?
- Do links from the site lead to legitimate organizations?

ANATOMY OF A RESEARCH ARTICLE

Your literature search has helped you to find research articles to read. What can you expect to find in these articles? Research articles usually have five sections: (1) an *abstract,* such as the ones found in *PsycINFO;* (2) an *Introduction* that explains the problem under investigation and the specific hypotheses being tested; (3) a *Method* section that describes in detail the exact procedures used in the study; (4) a *Results* section in which the findings are presented; and (5) a *Discussion* section in which the researcher may speculate on the broader implications of the results, propose alternative explanations for the results, discuss reasons that a particular hypothesis may not have been supported by the data, and/or make suggestions for further research on the problem. In addition to the five major sections, you will find a list of all the references that were cited.

Abstract

The **abstract** is a summary of the research report and typically runs no more than 120 words in length. It includes information about the hypothesis, the procedure, and the broad pattern of results. Generally, little information is abstracted from the discussion section of the paper.

Introduction

In the **Introduction section,** the researcher outlines the problem that has been investigated. Past research and theories relevant to the problem are described in detail. The specific expectations of the researcher are noted, often as formal hypotheses. In other words, the investigator introduces the research in a logical format that shows how past research and theory are connected to the current research problem and the expected results.

Method

The **Method section** is divided into subsections, with the number of subsections determined by the author and dependent on the complexity of the research design. Sometimes, the first subsection presents an overview of the design to prepare the reader for the material that follows. The next subsection describes the characteristics of the participants. Were they male or female, or were both sexes used? What was the average age? How many participants were included? If the study used human participants, some mention of how participants were recruited for the study would be needed. The next subsection details the procedure used in the study. In describing any stimulus materials presented to the participants, the way the behavior of the participants was recorded, and so on, it is important that no potentially crucial detail be omitted. Such detail allows the reader to know exactly how the study was conducted, and it provides other researchers with the information necessary to replicate the study. Other subsections may be necessary to describe in detail any equipment or testing materials that were used.

Results

In the **Results section,** the researcher presents the findings, usually in three ways. First, there is a description in narrative form—for example, "The location of items was most likely to be forgotten when the location was both highly memorable and an unusual place for the item to be stored." Second, the results are described in statistical language. Third, the material is often depicted in tables and graphs.

The statistical terminology of the results section may appear formidable. However, lack of knowledge about the calculations isn't really a deterrent to understanding the article or the logic behind the statistics. Statistics are only a tool the researcher uses in evaluating the outcomes of the study.

Discussion

In the **Discussion section,** the researcher reviews the research from various perspectives. Do the results support the hypothesis? If they do, the author should give all possible explanations for the results and discuss why one explanation is superior to another. If the hypothesis has not been supported, the author should suggest potential reasons. What might have been wrong with the methodology, the hypothesis, or both? The researcher may also discuss how the results compare with past research results on the topic. This section may also include suggestions for possible practical applications of the research and for future research on the topic.

You should familiarize yourself with some actual research articles. Appendix A includes an entire article in manuscript form. An easy way to find more articles in areas that interest you is to visit the website of the American Psychological Association (APA) at www.apa.org. All the APA journals listed in Table 2.1 have links that you can find by going to www.apa.org/journals. When you select a journal that interests you, you will go to a page that allows you to read recent articles published in the journal. Read articles to become familiar with the way information is presented in reports. As you read, you will develop ways of efficiently processing the information in the articles. It is usually best to read the abstract first, then skim the article to decide whether you can use the information provided. If you can, go back and read the article carefully. Note the hypotheses and theories presented in the introduction, write down anything that seems unclear or problematic in the method, and read the results in view of the material in the introduction. Be critical when you read the article; students often generate the best criticism. Most important, as you read more research on a topic, you will become more familiar with the variables being studied, the methods used to study the variables, the important theoretical issues being considered, and the problems that need to be addressed by future research. In short, you will find yourself generating your own research ideas and planning your own studies.

Study Terms

Abstract (p. 35)

Discussion section (p. 36)

Hypothesis (p. 19)

Introduction section (p. 35)

Literature review (p. 33)

Method section (p. 36)

Prediction (p. 19)

PsycINFO (p. 28)

Results section (p. 36)

Science Citation Index (SCI) (p. 31)

Social Sciences Citation Index (SSCI) (p. 31)

Theory (p. 22)

Web of Science (p. 31)

Review Questions

1. What is a hypothesis? What is the distinction between a hypothesis and a prediction?
2. What are the two functions of a theory?
3. Describe the difference in the way that past research is found when you use *PsycINFO* versus the "key article" method of the *Science Citation Index/Social Sciences Citation Index (Web of Science)*.
4. What information does the researcher communicate in each of the sections of a research article?

Activity Questions _____

1. Think of at least five "commonsense" sayings about behavior (e.g., "Spare the rod, spoil the child"; "Like father, like son"; "Absence makes the heart grow fonder"). For each, develop a hypothesis that is suggested by the saying and a prediction that follows from the hypothesis. (Based on Gardner, 1988.)

2. Choose one of the hypotheses formulated in Activity Question 1 and develop a strategy for finding research on the topic using the computer database in your library.

3. Theories serve two purposes: (1) to organize and explain observable events and (2) to generate new knowledge by guiding our way of looking at these events. Identify a consistent behavior pattern in yourself or somebody close to you (e.g., you consistently get into an argument with your sister on Friday nights). Generate two possible theories (explanations) for this occurrence (e.g., because you work long hours on Friday, you're usually stressed and exhausted when you get home; because your sister has a chemistry quiz every Friday afternoon and she's not doing well in the course, she is very irritable on Fridays). How would you gather evidence to determine which explanation might be correct? How might each explanation lead to different approaches to changing the behavior pattern, either to decrease or increase its occurrence?

3

Ethical Research

LEARNING OBJECTIVES

- Summarize Milgram's obedience experiment.
- Discuss the three ethical principles outlined in the *Belmont Report:* beneficence, autonomy, and justice.
- Define deception and discuss the ethical issues surrounding its use in research.
- List the information contained in an informed consent form.
- Discuss potential problems in obtaining informed consent.
- Describe the purpose of debriefing research participants.
- Describe the function of an Institutional Review Board.
- Contrast the categories of risk involved in research activities: exempt, minimal risk, and greater than minimal risk.
- Summarize the ethical principles in the APA ethics code concerning research with human participants.
- Summarize the ethical principles in the APA ethics code concerning research with animals.
- Discuss how potential risks and benefits of research are evaluated.
- Discuss the ethical issue surrounding misrepresentation of research findings.

E thical concerns are paramount when planning, conducting, and evaluating research. In this chapter, we will explore ethical issues in detail, and we will examine some guidelines for dealing with these problems.

MILGRAM'S OBEDIENCE EXPERIMENT

Stanley Milgram conducted a series of experiments (1963, 1964, 1965) to study the phenomenon of obedience to an authority figure. He placed an ad in the local newspaper in New Haven, Connecticut, offering a small stipend to men to participate in a "scientific study of memory and learning" being conducted at Yale University. The participants reported to Milgram's laboratory at Yale, where they met a scientist dressed in a lab coat and another participant in the study, a middle-aged man named "Mr. Wallace." Mr. Wallace was actually a confederate (i.e., accomplice) of the experimenter, but the participants didn't know this. The scientist explained that the study would examine the effects of punishment on learning. One person would be a "teacher" who would administer the punishment, and the other would be the "learner." Mr. Wallace and the volunteer participant then drew slips of paper to determine who would be the teacher and who would be the learner. The drawing was rigged, however—Mr. Wallace was always the learner and the volunteer was always the teacher.

The scientist attached electrodes to Mr. Wallace and placed the teacher in front of an impressive-looking shock machine. The shock machine had a series of levers that, the individual was told, when pressed would deliver shocks to Mr. Wallace. The first lever was labeled 15 volts, the second 30 volts, the third 45 volts, and so on up to 450 volts. The levers were also labeled "Slight Shock," "Moderate Shock," and so on up to "Danger: Severe Shock," followed by red X's above 400 volts.

Mr. Wallace was instructed to learn a series of word pairs. Then he was given a test to see if he could identify which words went together. Every time Mr. Wallace made a mistake, the teacher was to deliver a shock as punishment. The first mistake was supposed to be answered by a 15-volt shock, the second by a 30-volt shock, and so on. Each time a mistake was made, the learner received a greater shock. The learner, Mr. Wallace, never actually received any shocks, but the participants in the study didn't know that. In the experiment, Mr. Wallace made mistake after mistake. When the teacher "shocked" him with about 120 volts, Mr. Wallace began screaming in pain and eventually yelled that he wanted out. What if the teacher wanted to quit? This happened—the volunteer participants became visibly upset by the pain that Mr. Wallace seemed to be experiencing. The scientist told the teacher that he could quit but urged him to continue, using a series of verbal prods that stressed the importance of continuing the experiment.

The study purportedly was to be an experiment on memory and learning, but Milgram really was interested in learning whether participants would continue to obey the experimenter by administering ever higher levels of shock to the learner. What happened? Approximately 65% of the participants continued to deliver shocks all the way to 450 volts. Milgram's study received a great deal of publicity, and the results challenged many of our beliefs about our ability to resist authority. Milgram's study is important, and the results have implications for understanding obedience in real-life situations, such as the Holocaust in Nazi Germany and the Jonestown mass suicide (see Miller, 1986). What about the ethics of the Milgram study? How should we make decisions about whether the Milgram study or any other study is ethical?

THE *BELMONT REPORT*

Current ethical guidelines for both behavioral and medical researchers have their origins in ***The Belmont Report:*** *Ethical Principles and Guidelines for the Protection of Human Subjects of Research* (National Commission for the Protection of Human Subjects of Biomedical and Behavioral Research, 1979). This report defined the principles and applications that have guided more detailed regulations and the American Psychological Association Ethics Code. The three basic ethical principles are beneficence, respect for persons (autonomy), and justice. The associated applications of these principles are assessment of risks and benefits, informed consent, and selection of subjects. These topics will guide our discussion of ethical issues in research.

ASSESSMENT OF RISKS AND BENEFITS

The principle of **beneficence** in the *Belmont Report* refers to the need for research to maximize benefits and minimize any possible harmful effects of participation. In most decisions we make in life, we consider the relative risks (or costs) and benefits of the decision. In decisions about the ethics of research, we must calculate potential risks and benefits that are likely to result; this is called a ***risk-benefit analysis.*** Ethical principles require asking whether the research procedures have minimized risk to participants.

The potential **risks** to the participants include such factors as psychological or physical harm and loss of confidentiality; we will discuss these in detail. In addition, the cost of *not* conducting the study if in fact the proposed procedure is the only way to collect potentially valuable data can be considered (cf. Christensen, 1988). The benefits include direct benefits to the participants, such as an educational benefit, acquisition of a new skill, or treatment for a psychological or medical problem. There may also be material benefits such as a monetary payment, some sort of gift, or even the possibility of winning a prize in a raffle. Other less tangible benefits include the satisfaction gained through being part of a scientific investigation and the potential beneficial applications of the research findings (e.g., the knowledge gained through the research might improve future educational practices, psychotherapy, or social policy). As we will see, current regulations concerning the conduct of research with human participants require a risk-benefit analysis before research can be approved.

Risks in Psychological Research

Let's return to a consideration of Milgram's research. The risk of experiencing stress and psychological harm is obvious. It is not difficult to imagine the effect of delivering intense shocks to an obviously unwilling learner. A film that Milgram made shows participants protesting, sweating, and even laughing nervously while delivering the shocks. You might ask whether subjecting people to such a stressful experiment is justified, and you might wonder whether the experience had any long-range consequences for the volunteers. For example, did participants who obeyed the experimenter feel continuing remorse or begin to see themselves as cruel, inhumane people? A defense of Milgram's study follows, but first let's consider some potentially stressful research procedures.

Physical harm   Procedures that could conceivably cause some physical harm to participants are rare but possible. Many medical procedures fall in this category—for example, administering a drug such as alcohol or caffeine, or depriving people of sleep for an extended period of time. The risks in such procedures require that great care be taken to make them ethically acceptable. Moreover, there would need to be clear benefits of the research that would outweigh the potential risks.

Stress   More common than physical stress is psychological stress. For example, participants might be told that they will receive some extremely intense electric shocks. They never actually receive the shocks; it is the fear or anxiety during the waiting period that is the variable of interest. Research by Schachter (1959) employing a procedure like this showed that the anxiety produced a desire to affiliate with others during the waiting period.

In another procedure that produces psychological stress, participants are given unfavorable feedback about their personalities or abilities. Researchers interested in self-esteem have typically given a subject a bogus test of personality or ability. The test is followed by an evaluation that lowers self-esteem by indicating that the participant has an unfavorable personality trait or a low ability score.

Asking people about traumatic or unpleasant events in their lives might also cause stress for some participants. Thus, research that asks people to think about the deaths of a parent, spouse, or friend or their memories of living through a disaster could trigger a stressful reaction.

When stress is possible, the researcher must ask whether all safeguards have been taken to help participants deal with the stress. Usually a debriefing session following the study is designed in part to address any potential problems that may arise during the research.

Loss of privacy and confidentiality   Another risk is the loss of expected privacy and confidentiality. Researchers must take care to protect the privacy of individuals. At a minimum, researchers should protect privacy by keeping all data locked in a secure place. **Confidentiality** becomes particularly important when studying topics such as sexual behavior, divorce, family violence, or drug abuse; in these cases, researchers may need to ask people very sensitive questions about their private lives. It is extremely important that responses to such questions be confidential. In most cases, the responses are completely anonymous—there is no way to connect any person's identity with the data. This happens, for example, when questionnaires are administered to groups of people and no information is asked that could be used to identify an individual (such as name, Social Security number, or phone number). In other cases, such as a personal interview in which the identity of the person might be known, the researcher must carefully plan ways of coding data, storing data, and explaining the procedures to participants so that there is no question concerning the confidentiality of responses.

In some research, there is a real need to be able to identify individual participants. This occurs when individuals are studied on multiple occasions over time or when personal feedback, such as a test score, must be given. In such cases, the researcher should develop a way to identify the individuals but to separate the information about their identity from the actual data. Thus, if questionnaires or the computerized data files were seen by anyone, the data could not be linked to specific individuals.

In some cases, the risks entailed with loss of confidentiality are so great that researchers may wish to apply for a Certificate of Confidentiality from the U.S. Department of Health and Human Services. Obtaining this certificate is appropriate when the data could conceivably be the target of a legal subpoena.

Another privacy issue concerns concealed observation of behavior. In some studies, researchers make observations of behavior in public places. Observing people in shopping malls or in their cars does not seem to present any major ethical problems. However, what if a researcher wishes to observe behavior in more private settings or in ways that may violate individuals' privacy (see Wilson & Donnerstein, 1976)? For example, would it be ethical to rummage through people's trash or watch people in public restrooms? The Internet has posed other issues of privacy. Every day, thousands of people post messages on websites. The messages can potentially be used as data to understand attitudes, disclosure of personal information, and expressions of emotion. Many messages are public postings, much like a letter sent to a newspaper or magazine. But consider websites devoted to psychological and physical problems that people seek out for information and support. Many of these sites require registration to post messages. Consider a researcher interested in using one of these sites for data. What ethical issues arise in this case? Buchanan and Williams (2010) address these and other ethical issues that arise when doing research using the Internet.

INFORMED CONSENT

The *Belmont Report*'s principle of *respect for persons* or **autonomy** states that participants are treated as autonomous; they are capable of making deliberate decisions about whether to participate in research. The application here is **informed consent**—potential participants in a research project should be provided with all information that might influence their decision of whether to participate. Thus, research participants should be informed about the purposes of the study, the risks and benefits of participation, and their rights to refuse or terminate participation in the study. They can then freely consent or refuse to participate in the research.

Informed Consent Form

Participants are usually provided with some type of informed consent form that contains the information that participants need to make their decision. Most commonly, the form is printed for the participant to read and sign. There are numerous examples of informed consent forms available on the Internet. Your college may have developed examples through the research office. A checklist for an informed consent form is provided in Figure 3.1. Note that the checklist addresses both content and format. The content will typically cover (1) the purpose of the research, (2) procedures that will be used including time involved (remember that you do not need to tell participants exactly what is being studied), (3) risks and benefits, (4) any compensation, (5) confidentiality, (6) assurance of voluntary participation and permission to withdraw, and (7) contact information for questions.

The form must be written so that participants understand the information in the form. In some cases, the form was so technical or loaded with legal terminology that it is very unlikely that the participants fully realized what they were signing. In general, consent forms should be written in simple and straightforward language that avoids jargon and technical terminology (generally at a sixth- to eighth-grade reading level; most word processors provide grade-level information with the Grammar Check feature). To make the form easier to understand, it should not be written in the first person. Instead, information should be provided as if the researcher were simply having a conversation with the participant. Thus, the form might say:

> *Participation in this study is voluntary. You may decline to participate without penalty.*

instead of

> *I understand that participation in this study is voluntary. I may decline to participate without penalty.*

The first statement is providing information to the participant in a straightforward way using the second person ("you"), whereas the second statement has a legalistic tone that may be more difficult to understand. Finally, if participants are non-English speakers, they should receive a translated version of the form.

Check to make sure the informed consent form includes the following:

☐ Statement that participants are being asked to participate in a research study

☐ Explanation of the purposes of the research in clear language

☐ Expected duration of the subject's participation

☐ Description of the procedures

☐ Description of any reasonably foreseeable risks or discomforts and safeguards to minimize the risks

☐ Description of any benefits to the individual or to others that may reasonably be expected from the research

☐ If applicable, a disclosure of appropriate alternative procedures or courses of treatment, if any, that might be advantageous to the individual

☐ Description of the extent, if any, to which confidentiality of records identifying the individual will be maintained

☐ If an incentive is offered, a description of the incentive and requirement to obtain it; also, a description of the impact of a decision to discontinue participation

☐ Contact information for questions about the study (usually phone contacts for the researcher, faculty advisor, and the Institutional Review Board office)

☐ Statement that participation is voluntary, refusal to participate will involve no penalty or loss of benefits to which the subject is otherwise entitled, and the subject may discontinue participation at any time without penalty or loss of benefits to which the individual is otherwise entitled

☐ Form is printed in no smaller than 11-point type (no "fine print")

☐ Form is free of technical jargon and written at sixth- to eighth-grade level

☐ Form is not written in the first person (statements such as "I understand . . ." are discouraged)

Other information may be needed for research with high-risk or medical procedures. Much more information on developing an informed consent form is readily available on university and federal government websites, for example, *Tips on Informed Consent* from the Department of Health and Human Services: http://www.hhs.gov/ohrp/policy/ictips.html

FIGURE 3.1
Checklist for informed consent form

Autonomy Issues

Informed consent seems simple enough; however, there are important issues to consider. The first concerns lack of autonomy. What happens when the participants may lack the ability to make a free and informed decision to voluntarily participate? Special populations such as minors, patients in psychiatric hospitals, or adults with cognitive impairments require special precautions. When minors are asked to participate, for example, a written consent form signed by a parent or guardian is generally required in addition to agreement by the minor; this agreement by a minor is formally called *assent*. The Division of Developmental Psychology of the American Psychological Association and the Society for Research on Child Development have established their own guidelines for ethical research with children.

Coercion is another threat to autonomy. Any procedure that limits an individual's freedom to consent is potentially coercive. For example, a supervisor who asks employees to fill out a survey during a staff meeting or a professor requiring students to participate in a study in order to pass the course is applying considerable pressure on potential participants. The employees may believe that the supervisor will somehow punish them if they do not participate; they also risk embarrassment if they refuse in front of co-workers. Sometimes benefits are so great that they become coercive. For example, a prisoner may believe that increased privileges or even a favorable parole decision may result from participation. Researchers must consider these issues and make sure that autonomy is preserved.

Information Issues: Withholding Information and Deception

It may have occurred to you that providing all information about the study to participants might be unwise. Providing too much information could potentially invalidate the results of the study; for example, researchers usually will withhold information about the hypothesis of the study or the particular condition an individual is participating in (see Sieber, 1992). It is generally acceptable to withhold information when the information would not affect the decision to participate and when the information will later be provided, usually in a debriefing session when the study is completed. Most people who volunteer for psychology research do not expect full disclosure about the study prior to participation. However, they do expect a thorough debriefing after they have completed the study. Debriefing will be described after we consider the more problematic issue of deception.

It may also have occurred to you that there are research procedures in which informed consent is not necessary or even possible. If you choose to observe the number of same-sex and mixed-sex study groups in your library, you probably don't need to announce your presence and obtain anyone's permission. If you study the content of the self-descriptions that people write for an online dating service, do you need to contact each person to include their information in your study? When planning research, it is important to make sure that you do have good reasons not to obtain informed consent.

Deception occurs when there is active misrepresentation of information. The Milgram experiment illustrates two types of deception. First, participants were deceived about the purpose of the study. Participants in the Milgram experiment agreed to take part in a study of memory and learning, but they actually took part in a study on obedience. Who could imagine that a memory and learning experiment (that title does sound tame, after all) would involve delivering high-intensity, painful electric shocks to another person? Participants in the Milgram experiment didn't know what they were letting themselves in for.

Milgram's study was conducted before informed consent was routine; however, you can imagine that Milgram's consent form would inaccurately have participants agree to be in a memory study. They would also be told that they are free to withdraw from the study at any time. Is it possible that the informed consent procedure would affect the outcome of the study? Knowledge that the research is designed to study obedience would likely alter the behavior of the participants. Few of us like to think of ourselves as obedient, and we would probably go out of our way to prove that we are not. Research indicates that providing informed consent may in fact bias participants' responses, at least in some research areas. For example, research on stressors such as noise or crowding has shown that a feeling of "control" over a stressor reduces its negative impact. If you know that you can terminate a loud, obnoxious noise, the noise produces less stress than when the noise is uncontrollable. Studies by Gardner (1978) and Dill, Gilden, Hill, and Hanslka (1982) have demonstrated that informed consent procedures do increase perceptions of control in stress experiments and therefore can affect the conclusions drawn from the research.

It is also possible that the informed consent procedure may bias the sample. In Milgram's experiment, if participants had prior knowledge that they would be asked to give severe shocks to the other person, some might have declined to be in the experiment. Therefore, we might limit our ability to generalize the results only to those "types" who agreed to participate. If this were true, anyone could say that the obedient behavior seen in the Milgram experiment occurred simply because the people who agreed to participate were sadists in the first place!

Second, the Milgram study also illustrates a type of deception in which participants become part of a series of events staged for the purposes of the study. A confederate of the experimenter played the part of another participant in the study; Milgram created a reality for the participant in which obedience to authority could be observed. Such deception has been most common in social psychology research; it is much less frequent in areas of experimental psychology such as human perception, learning, memory, and motor performance. Even in these areas, researchers may use a cover story to make the experiment seem plausible and involving (e.g., telling participants that they are reading actual newspaper stories for a study on readability when the true purpose is to examine memory errors or organizational schemes).

The problem of deception is not limited to laboratory research. Procedures in which observers conceal their purposes, presence, or identity are also deceptive. For example, Humphreys (1970) studied the sexual behavior of men who frequented public restrooms (called *tearooms*). Humphreys did not directly participate in sexual activities, but he served as a lookout who would warn the others of possible intruders. In addition to observing the activities in the tearoom, Humphreys wrote down license plate numbers of tearoom visitors. Later, he obtained the addresses of the men, disguised himself, and visited their homes to interview them. Humphreys' procedure is certainly one way of finding out about anonymous sex in public places, but it employs considerable deception.

Is Deception a Major Ethical Problem in Psychological Research?

Many psychologists believe that the problem of deception has been exaggerated (Bröder, 1998; Kimmel, 1998; Korn, 1998; Smith & Richardson, 1985). Bröder argues that the extreme examples of elaborate deception cited by these critics are rare. Moreover, there is evidence that the college students who participate in research do not mind deception and may in fact enjoy experiments with deception (Christensen, 1988).

In the decades since the Milgram experiments in the 1960s, some researchers have attempted to assess the use of deception to see if elaborate deception has indeed become less common. Because most of the concern over this type of deception arises in social psychological research, attempts to address this issue have focused on social psychology. Gross and Fleming (1982) reviewed 691 social psychological studies published in the 1960s and 1970s. Although most research in the 1970s still used deception, the deception primarily involved false cover stories.

Has the trend away from deception continued? Sieber, Iannuzzo, and Rodriguez (1995) examined the studies published in the *Journal of Personality and Social Psychology* in 1969, 1978, 1986, and 1992. The number of studies that used some form of deception decreased from 66% in 1969 to 47% in 1978 and to 32% in 1986 but increased again to 47% in 1992. The large drop in 1986 may be due to an increase that year in the number of studies on such topics as personality that require no deception to carry out. Also, informed consent was more likely to be explicitly described in 1992 than in previous years, and debriefing was more likely to be mentioned in the years after 1969. However, false cover stories are still frequently used. Korn (1997) has also concluded that use of deception is decreasing in social psychology.

There are three primary reasons for a decrease in the type of elaborate deception seen in the Milgram study. First, more researchers have become interested in cognitive variables rather than emotions and so use methods that are similar to those used by researchers in memory and cognitive psychology. Second, the general level of awareness of ethical issues as described in this chapter has led researchers to conduct studies in other ways (some alternatives to deception are described below). Third, ethics committees at universities and colleges now review proposed research more carefully, so elaborate deception is likely to be approved only when the research is important and there are no alternative procedures available (ethics review boards are described later in this chapter).

THE IMPORTANCE OF DEBRIEFING

Debriefing occurs after the completion of the study. It is an opportunity for the researcher to deal with issues of withholding information, deception, and potential harmful effects of participation.

If participants were deceived in any way, the researcher needs to explain why the deception was necessary. If the research altered a participant's physical or psychological state in some way—as in a study that produces stress—the researcher must make sure that the participant has calmed down and is comfortable about having participated. If a participant needs to receive additional information or to speak with someone else about the study, the researcher should provide access to these resources. The participants should leave the experiment without any ill feelings toward the field of psychology, and they may even leave with some new insight into their own behavior or personality.

Debriefing also provides an opportunity for the researcher to explain the purpose of the study and tell participants what kinds of results are expected and perhaps discuss the practical implications of the results. In some cases, researchers may contact participants later to inform them of the actual results of the study. Thus, debriefing has both an educational and an ethical purpose.

Is debriefing sufficient to remove any negative effects when stress and elaborate deception are involved? Let's turn again to Milgram's research. Milgram went to great lengths to provide a thorough debriefing session. Participants who were obedient were told that their behavior was normal in that they had acted no differently from most other participants. They were made aware of the strong situational pressure that was exerted on them, and efforts were made to reduce any tension they felt. Participants were assured that no shock was actually delivered, and there was a friendly reconciliation with the confederate, Mr. Wallace. Milgram also mailed a report of his research findings to the participants and at the same time asked about their reactions to the experiment. The responses showed that 84% were glad that they had participated, and 74% said they had benefited from the experience. Only 1% said they were sorry they had participated. When a psychiatrist interviewed participants a year later, no ill effects of participation could be detected. We can only conclude that debriefing did have its intended effect. Other researchers who have conducted further work on the ethics of Milgram's study reached the same conclusion (Ring, Wallston, & Corey, 1970). Other research on debriefing has also concluded that debriefing is effective as a way of dealing with deception and other ethical issues that arise in research investigations (Oczak, 2007; Smith, 1983; Smith & Richardson, 1983).

ALTERNATIVES TO DECEPTION

After criticizing the use of deception in research, Kelman (1967) called for the development of alternative procedures. Such procedures include role-playing, simulations, and "honest" experiments.

Role-Playing and Simulations

In one **role-playing** procedure, the experimenter describes a situation to participants and then asks them how they would respond to the situation. Sometimes, participants are asked to say how they themselves would behave in the situation; other times, they are asked to predict how real participants in such a situation would behave. It isn't clear whether these two instructions produce any difference in results.

The most serious defect of role-playing is that, no matter what results are obtained, critics can always claim that the results would have been different if the participants had been in a real situation. This criticism is based on the assumption that people aren't always able to accurately predict their own behavior or the behavior of others. This would be particularly true when undesirable behavior—such as conformity, obedience, or aggression—is involved. For example, if Milgram had used a role-playing procedure, how many people do you think would have predicted that they would be completely obedient? In fact, Milgram asked a group of psychiatrists to predict the results of his study and found that even these experts could not accurately anticipate what would happen. A similar problem would arise if people were asked to predict whether they would help someone in need. Most of us would probably overestimate our altruistic tendencies.

A different type of role-playing uses **simulation** of a real-world situation. Simulations can be used to examine conflict between competing individuals, driving behavior using driving simulators, or jury deliberations, for example. Such simulations can create high degrees of involvement among participants.

Even simulations may present ethical problems. A dramatic example is the Stanford Prison Experiment conducted by Zimbardo (1973; Haney & Zimbardo, 1998). Zimbardo set up a simulated prison in the basement of the psychology building at Stanford University. He then recruited college students who were paid to play the role of either prisoner or guard for a period of 2 weeks. Guards were outfitted in uniforms and given sunglasses and clubs. Prisoners were assigned numbers and wore nylon stocking caps to simulate prison haircuts and reduce feelings of individuality. The participants became so deeply involved in their roles that Zimbardo had to stop the simulation after 6 days because of the cruel behavior of the "guards" and the stressful reactions of the "prisoners." This was only a simulation—participants knew that they were not really prisoners or guards. Yet they became so involved in their roles that the experiment produced higher levels of stress than in almost any other experiment one can imagine. An interesting follow-up to the Stanford Prison Experiment was conducted in 2001 in a collaborative effort between research psychologists and the BBC (http://www.bbcprisonstudy.org). The BBC Prison Experiment was very similar to the Stanford version but the researchers did concentrate on ethical issues. A five-person review panel monitored the progress of the experiment continuously, an emergency medical team and security personnel were present, and two clinical psychologists were on call. The study was scheduled for 8 days, and film crews recorded all events for a 4-hour series broadcast in 2002. The differences in the outcomes of the two studies are the subject of continuing discussion among psychologists; for example, the guards' relationship to the inmates was quite different in the BBC study.

Honest Experiments

Rubin (1973) encouraged researchers to take advantage of situations in which behavior could be studied without elaborate deception, in **honest experiments.** In the first such strategy, participants agree to have their behavior studied and know exactly what the researchers hope to accomplish. For example, speed dating studies have become a very useful way to study romantic attraction (Finkel, Eastwick, & Matthews, 2007; Fisman, Iyengar, Kamenica, & Simonson, 2006). Student participants can be recruited to engage in an actual speed-dating event held on campus or at a local restaurant; they complete numerous questionnaires and make choices that can lead to possible dates. Because everyone meets with everyone else, the situation allows for a systematic examination of many factors that might be related to date selection.

A related strategy presents itself when people seek out information or services that they need. Students who volunteer for a study skills improvement program at their college may be assigned to either an in-class or an online version of the course, and the researcher can administer measures to examine whether one version is superior to the other.

Another strategy involves situations in which a naturally occurring event presents an opportunity for research. For example, researchers were able to study the effects of crowding when a shortage of student housing forced Rutgers University to assign entering students randomly to crowded and un-crowded dormitory rooms (Aiello, Baum, & Gormley, 1981). Baum, Gachtel, and Schaeffer (1983) studied the stressful effects associated with nuclear power plant disasters by comparing people who lived near the Three Mile Island nuclear plant with others who lived near an undamaged nuclear plant or a conventional coal-fired power plant. Science depends on replicability of results, so it is notable that the same pattern of results as shown in the Three Mile Island study was obtained following the September 11 terrorist attacks (Schlenger et al., 2002). More than 2,000 adult residents of New York City, Washington, DC, and other metropolitan areas throughout the United States completed a Posttraumatic Stress Disorder (PTSD) checklist to determine incidence of the disorder. PTSD was indicated in 11.2% of the New York residents in contrast with 2.7% of the residents of Washington, DC, and 3.6% of those living in other metropolitan areas. Such natural experiments are valuable sources of data.

JUSTICE AND THE SELECTION OF PARTICIPANTS

The third ethical principle defined in the *Belmont Report* is termed **justice.** The principle of justice addresses issues of fairness in receiving the benefits of research as well as bearing the burdens of accepting risks. The history of medical research includes too many examples of high-risk research that was conducted with individuals selected because they were powerless and marginalized within the society. One of the most horrific is the Tuskegee Syphilis Study, in which 399 poor African Americans in Alabama were not treated for syphilis in order to track the long-term effects of this disease (Reverby, 2000). This study took place from 1932 to 1972, when the details of the study were made public. The outrage over the fact that this study was done at all and that the subjects were unsuspecting African Americans spurred scientists to overhaul ethical regulations in both medical and behavioral research. The fact that the Tuskegee study was not an isolated incident was brought to light in 2010 when documentation of another syphilis study done from 1946 to 1948 in Guatemala was discovered (Reverby, 2011). Men in this study were infected with syphilis and then treated with penicillin. Reverby describes the study in detail and focuses on one doctor who was involved in both the Guatemala and Tuskegee studies.

The justice principle requires researchers to address issues of equity. Any decisions to include or exclude certain people from a research study must be justified on scientific grounds. Thus, if age, ethnicity, gender, or other criteria are used to select participants, the researcher must provide a scientific rationale.

RESEARCHER COMMITMENTS

Researchers make several implicit contracts with participants during the course of a study. For example, if participants agree to be present for a study at a specific time, the researcher should also be there. The issue of punctuality is never mentioned by researchers, yet research participants note it when asked about the obligations of the researcher (Epstein, Suedfeld, & Silverstein, 1973). If researchers promise to send a summary of the results to participants, they should do so. If participants are to receive course credit for participation, the researcher must immediately let the instructor know that the person took part in the study. These may seem to be little details, but they are very important in maintaining trust between participants and researchers.

FEDERAL REGULATIONS AND THE INSTITUTIONAL REVIEW BOARD

The *Belmont Report* provided an outline for issues of research ethics. The actual rules and regulations for the protection of human research participants were issued by the U.S. Department of Health and Human Services (HHS). Under these regulations (U.S. Department of Health and Human Services, 2001), every institution that receives federal funds must have an **Institutional Review Board (IRB)** that is responsible for the review of research conducted within the institution. The IRB is a local review agency composed of at least five individuals; at least one member of the IRB must be from outside the institution. Every college and university in the United States that receives federal funding has an IRB; in addition, most psychology departments have their own research review committee (Chastain & Landrum, 1999). All research conducted by faculty, students, and staff associated with the institution is reviewed in some way by the IRB. This includes research that may be conducted at another location such as a school, community agency, hospital, or via the Internet.

The federal regulations for IRB oversight of research continue to evolve. For example, all researchers must now complete specified educational requirements. Most colleges and universities require students and faculty to complete one or more online tutorials on research ethics to meet these requirements.

The HHS regulations also categorized research according to the amount of risk involved in the research. This concept of risk was later incorporated into the Ethics Code of the American Psychological Association.

Exempt Research

Research in which there is *no risk* is exempt from review. Thus, anonymous questionnaires, surveys, and educational tests are all considered **exempt research,** as is naturalistic observation in public places when there is no threat to anonymity. Archival research in which the data being studied are publicly available or the participants cannot be identified is exempt as well. This type of research requires no informed consent. However, researchers cannot decide by themselves that research is exempt; instead, the IRB at the institution formulates a procedure to allow a researcher to apply for exempt status.

Minimal Risk Research

A second type of research activity is called **minimal risk,** which means that the risks of harm to participants are no greater than risks encountered in daily life or in routine physical or psychological tests. When minimal risk research is being conducted, elaborate safeguards are less of a concern, and approval by the IRB is routine. Some of the research activities considered minimal risk are (1) recording routine physiological data from adult participants (e.g., weighing, tests of sensory acuity, electrocardiography, electroencephalography, diagnostic echography, and voice recordings)—note that this would not include recordings that might involve invasion of privacy; (2) moderate exercise by healthy volunteers; and (3) research on individual or group behavior or characteristics of individuals—such as studies of perception, cognition, game theory, or test development—in which the researcher does not manipulate participants' behavior and the research will not involve stress to participants.

Greater Than Minimal Risk Research

Any research procedure that places participants at greater than minimal risk is subject to thorough review by the IRB. Complete informed consent and other safeguards may be required before approval is granted.

Researchers planning to conduct an investigation are required to submit an application to the IRB. The application requires description of risks and benefits, procedures for minimizing risk, the exact wording of the informed consent form, how participants will be debriefed, and procedures for maintaining confidentiality. Even after a project is approved, there is continuing review. If it is a long-term project, it will be reviewed at least once each year. If there are any changes in procedures, researchers are required to obtain approval from the IRB. The three risk categories are summarized in Table 3.1.

TABLE 3.1   Assessment of risk

Risk assessment	Examples	Special actions
No risk	Studying normal educational practices Cognitive aptitude/achievement measures Anonymous surveys Observation of nonsensitive public behaviors where participants cannot be identified	No informed consent needed, but protocol must be judged as no risk by IRB
Minimal risk	Standard psychological measures Voice recordings not involving danger to participants Studies of cognition/perception not involving stress	Fully informed consent generally not required, but debriefing/ethical concerns are important
Greater than minimal risk	Research involving physical stress, psychological stress, invasion of privacy, measures of sensitive information where participants may be identified	Full IRB review required, and special ethical procedures may be imposed

IRB Impact on Research

Some researchers have voiced their frustration about the procedures necessary to obtain IRB approval for research. The review process can take a long time, and the IRB may ask for revisions and clarifications. Moreover, the policies and procedures that govern IRB operations apply to all areas of research, so the extreme caution necessary for medical research is applied to psychology research (see Collins, 2002). Unfortunately, little can be done to change the basic IRB structure. Researchers must plan carefully, allow time for the approval process, and submit all materials requested in the application (Collins, 2002).

With the HHS regulations and review of research by the IRB, the rights and safety of human participants are well protected. Both researchers and review board members tend to be very cautious in terms of what is considered ethical. In fact, several studies have shown that students who have participated in research studies are more lenient in their judgments of the ethics of experiments than are researchers or IRB members (Epstein et al., 1973; Smith, 1983; Sullivan & Deiker, 1973). Moreover, individuals who have taken part in research that used deception report that they did not mind the deception and evaluated the experience positively (Christensen, 1988).

APA ETHICS CODE

Psychologists recognize the ethical issues we have discussed, and the American Psychological Association (APA) has provided leadership in formulating ethical principles and standards. The *Ethical Principles of Psychologists and Code of Conduct*—known as the **APA Ethics Code**—was revised in 2002, and updates and amendments are issued periodically. The most recent version of the *Ethics Code* is available at http://apa.org/ethics/code/index.aspx. The preamble to the Ethics Code states the following:

> Psychologists are committed to increasing scientific and professional knowledge of behavior and people's understanding of themselves and others and to the use of such knowledge to improve the condition of individuals, organizations, and society. Psychologists respect and protect civil and human rights and the central importance of freedom of inquiry and expression in research, teaching, and publication. They strive to help the public in developing informed judgments and choices concerning human behavior. In doing so, they perform many roles, such as researcher, educator, diagnostician, therapist, supervisor, consultant, administrator, social interventionist, and expert witness. This Ethics Code provides a common set of principles and standards upon which psychologists build their professional and scientific work.

The five general principles relate to beneficence, responsibility, integrity, justice, and respect for the rights and dignity of others. Ten ethical standards address specific issues concerning the conduct of psychologists in teaching, research, therapy, counseling, testing, and other professional roles and responsibilities. We will be most concerned with Ethical Standard 8: Research and Publication.

RESEARCH WITH HUMAN PARTICIPANTS

The sections of Ethical Standard 8 that most directly deal with research using human participants are included below.

8.01 Institutional approval

When institutional approval is required, psychologists provide accurate information about their research proposals and obtain approval prior to conducting the research. They conduct the research in accordance with the approved research protocol.

8.02 Informed consent to research

a. When obtaining informed consent as required in Standard 3.10, Informed Consent, psychologists inform participants about (1) the purpose of the research, expected duration, and procedures; (2) their right to decline to participate and to withdraw from the research once participation has begun; (3) the foreseeable consequences of declining or withdrawing; (4) reasonably foreseeable factors that may be expected to influence their willingness to participate such as potential risks, discomfort, or adverse effects; (5) any prospective research benefits; (6) limits of confidentiality; (7) incentives for participation; and (8) whom to contact for questions about the research and research participants' rights. They provide opportunity for the prospective participants to ask questions and receive answers. (See also Standards 8.03, Informed consent for recording voices and images in research; 8.05, Dispensing with informed consent for research; and 8.07, Deception in research.)

b. Psychologists conducting intervention research involving the use of experimental treatments clarify to participants at the outset of the research (1) the experimental nature of the treatment; (2) the services that will or will not be available to the control group(s) if appropriate; (3) the means by which assignment to treatment and control groups will be made; (4) available treatment alternatives if an individual does not wish to participate in the research or wishes to withdraw once a study has begun; and (5) compensation for or monetary costs of participating including, if appropriate, whether reimbursement from the participant or a third-party payor will be sought. (See also Standard 8.02a, Informed Consent to Research.)

8.03 Informed consent for recording voices and images in research

Psychologists obtain informed consent from research participants prior to recording their voices or images for data collection unless (1) the research consists solely of naturalistic observations in public places, and it is not anticipated that the recording will be used in a manner that could cause personal identification or harm, or (2) the research design includes deception, and consent for the use of the recording is obtained during debriefing. (See also Standard 8.07, Deception in Research.)

8.04 Client/patient, student, and subordinate research participants

a. When psychologists conduct research with clients/patients, students, or subordinates as participants, psychologists take steps to protect the prospective participants from adverse consequences of declining or withdrawing from participation.

b. When research participation is a course requirement or an opportunity for extra credit, the prospective participant is given the choice of equitable alternative activities.

8.05 Dispensing with informed consent for research

Psychologists may dispense with informed consent only (1) where research would not reasonably be assumed to create distress or harm and involves (a) the study of normal educational practices, curricula, or classroom management methods conducted in educational settings; (b) only anonymous questionnaires, naturalistic observations, or archival research for which disclosure of responses would not place participants at risk of criminal or civil liability or damage their financial standing, employability, or reputation, and confidentiality is protected; or (c) the study of factors related to job or organization effectiveness conducted in organizational settings for which there is no risk to participants' employability, and confidentiality is protected or (2) where otherwise permitted by law or federal or institutional regulations.

8.06 Offering inducements for research participation

a. Psychologists make reasonable efforts to avoid offering excessive or inappropriate financial or other inducements for research participation when such inducements are likely to coerce participation.

b. When offering professional services as an inducement for research participation, psychologists clarify the nature of the services, as well as the risks, obligations, and limitations. (See also Standard 6.05, Barter With Clients/Patients.)

8.07 Deception in research

a. Psychologists do not conduct a study involving deception unless they have determined that the use of deceptive techniques is justified by the study's significant prospective scientific, educational, or applied value and that effective nondeceptive alternative procedures are not feasible.

b. Psychologists do not deceive prospective participants about research that is reasonably expected to cause physical pain or severe emotional distress.

c. Psychologists explain any deception that is an integral feature of the design and conduct of an experiment to participants as early as is feasible, preferably at the conclusion of their participation, but no later than at the conclusion of the data collection, and permit participants to withdraw their data. (See also Standard 8.08, Debriefing.)

8.08 Debriefing

a. Psychologists provide a prompt opportunity for participants to obtain appropriate information about the nature, results, and conclusions of the research, and they take reasonable steps to correct any misconceptions that participants may have of which the psychologists are aware.

b. If scientific or humane values justify delaying or withholding this information, psychologists take reasonable measures to reduce the risk of harm.

c. When psychologists become aware that research procedures have harmed a participant, they take reasonable steps to minimize the harm.

These standards complement the HSS regulations and the *Belmont Report.* They stress the importance of informed consent as a fundamental part of ethical practice. However, fully informed consent may not always be possible, and deception may sometimes be necessary. In such cases, the researcher's responsibilities to participants are increased. Obviously, decisions as to what should be considered ethical or unethical are not simple; there are no ironclad rules.

ETHICS AND ANIMAL RESEARCH

Although this chapter has been concerned with the ethics of research with humans, you are no doubt well aware that psychologists sometimes conduct research with animals (Akins, Panicker, & Cunningham, 2004). Animals are used for a variety of reasons. The researcher can carefully control the environmental conditions of the animals, study the same animals over a long period, and monitor their behavior 24 hours a day if necessary. Animals are also used to test the effects of drugs and to study physiological and genetic mechanisms underlying behavior. About 7% of the articles in *Psychological Abstracts* (now *PsycINFO*) in 1979 described studies involving animals (Gallup & Suarez, 1985), and data indicate that the amount of research done with animals has been steadily declining (Thomas & Blackman, 1992). Most commonly, psychologists work with rats and mice, and to a lesser extent, birds; according to one survey of animal research in psychology, over 95% of the animals used in research were rats, mice, and birds (see Gallup & Suarez, 1985).

In recent years, groups opposed to animal research in medicine, psychology, biology, and other sciences have become more vocal and militant. Animal rights groups have staged protests at conventions of the American Psychological Association, animal research laboratories in numerous cities have been vandalized, and researchers have received threats of physical harm.

Scientists argue that animal research benefits humans and point to many discoveries that would not have been possible without animal research (Carroll & Overmier, 2001; Miller, 1985). Also, animal rights groups often exaggerate the amount of research that involves any pain or suffering whatsoever (Coile & Miller, 1984).

Plous (1996a, 1996b) conducted a national survey of attitudes toward the use of animals in research and education among psychologists and psychology majors. The attitudes of both psychologists and students were quite similar. In general, there is support for animal research: 72% of the students support such research, 18% oppose it, and 10% are unsure (the psychologists "strongly" support animal research more than the students, however). In addition, 68% believe that animal research is necessary for progress in psychology. Still, there is some ambivalence and uncertainty about the use of animals: When asked whether animals in psychological research are treated humanely, 12% of the students said "no" and 44% were "unsure." In addition, research involving rats or pigeons was viewed more positively than research with dogs or primates unless the research is strictly observational. Finally, females have less positive views toward animal research than males. Plous concluded that animal research in psychology will continue to be important for the field but will likely continue to decline as a proportion of the total amount of research conducted.

Animal research is indeed very important and will continue to be necessary to study many types of research questions (see http://www.apa.org/science/anguide.html). It is crucial to recognize that strict laws and ethical guidelines govern both research with animals and teaching procedures in which animals are used. Such regulations deal with the need for proper housing, feeding, cleanliness, and health care. They specify that the research must avoid any cruelty in the form of unnecessary pain to the animal. In addition, institutions in which animal research is carried out must have an *Institutional Animal Care and Use Committee (IACUC)* composed of at least one scientist, one veterinarian, and a community member. The **IACUC** is charged with reviewing animal research procedures and ensuring that all regulations are adhered to (see Holden, 1987). This section of the Ethics Code is of particular importance here:

8.09 Humane care and use of animals in research

a. Psychologists acquire, care for, use, and dispose of animals in compliance with current federal, state, and local laws and regulations, and with professional standards.

b. Psychologists trained in research methods and experienced in the care of laboratory animals supervise all procedures involving animals and are responsible for ensuring appropriate consideration of their comfort, health, and humane treatment.

c. Psychologists ensure that all individuals under their supervision who are using animals have received instruction in research methods and in the care, maintenance, and handling of the species being used, to the extent appropriate to their role. (See also Standard 2.05, Delegation of Work to Others.)

d. Psychologists make reasonable efforts to minimize the discomfort, infection, illness, and pain of animal subjects.

e. Psychologists use a procedure subjecting animals to pain, stress, or privation only when an alternative procedure is unavailable and the goal is justified by its prospective scientific, educational, or applied value.

f. Psychologists perform surgical procedures under appropriate anesthesia and follow techniques to avoid infection and minimize pain during and after surgery.

g. When it is appropriate that an animal's life be terminated, psychologists proceed rapidly, with an effort to minimize pain and in accordance with accepted procedures.

APA has also developed a more detailed *Guidelines for Ethical Conduct in the Care and Use of Animals* (http://www.apa.org/science/leadership/care/guidelines .aspx). Clearly, psychologists are concerned about the welfare of animals used in research. Nonetheless, this issue likely will continue to be controversial.

RISKS AND BENEFITS REVISITED

You are now familiar with the ethical issues that confront researchers who study human and animal behavior. When you make decisions about research ethics, you need to consider the many factors associated with risk to the participants. Are there risks of psychological harm or loss of confidentiality? Who are the research participants? What types of deception, if any, are used in the procedure? How will informed consent be obtained? What debriefing procedures are being used? You also need to weigh the direct benefits of the research to the participants, as well as the scientific importance of the research and the educational benefits to the students who may be conducting the research for a class or degree requirement (see Figure 3.2).

These are not easy decisions. Consider a study in which a male confederate insults the male participant. This study, conducted by Cohen, Nisbett, Bowdle, and Schwarz (1996), compared the reactions of college students living in the northern United States with those of students living in the southern United States. The purpose was to investigate whether males in the South had developed a "culture of honor" that expects them to respond aggressively when insulted. Indeed, the students in the North had little response to the insult, whereas the Southerners responded with heightened physiological and cognitive indicators of anger. The fact that so much violence in the world is committed by males who are often avenging some perceived insult to their honor makes this topic particularly relevant to society. Do you believe that the potential benefits of the study to society and science outweigh the risks involved in the procedure?

Obviously, an IRB reviewing this study concluded that the researchers had sufficiently minimized risks to the participants such that the benefits outweighed

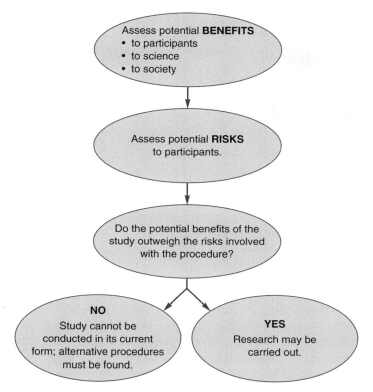

FIGURE 3.2
Analysis of risks and benefits

the costs. If you ultimately decide that the costs outweigh the benefits, you must conclude that the study cannot be conducted in its current form. You may suggest alternative procedures that could make it acceptable. If the benefits outweigh the costs, you will likely decide that the research should be carried out. Your calculation might differ from another person's calculation, which is precisely why having ethics review boards is such a good idea. An appropriate review of research proposals makes it highly unlikely that unethical research will be approved.

MISREPRESENTATION: FRAUD AND PLAGIARISM

Two other elements of the Ethics Code should be noted:

8.10 Reporting research results

a. Psychologists do not fabricate data. (See also Standard 5.01a, Avoidance of False or Deceptive Statements.)

b. If psychologists discover significant errors in their published data, they take reasonable steps to correct such errors in a correction, retraction, erratum, or other appropriate publication means.

8.11 Plagiarism

Psychologists do not present portions of another's work or data as their own, even if the other work or data source is cited occasionally.

Fraud

The fabrication of data is **fraud.** We must be able to believe the reported results of research; otherwise, the entire foundation of the scientific method as a means of knowledge is threatened. In fact, although fraud may occur in many fields, it probably is most serious in two areas: science and journalism. This is because science and journalism are both fields in which written reports are assumed to be accurate descriptions of actual events. There are no independent accounting agencies to check on the activities of scientists and journalists.

Instances of fraud in the field of psychology are considered to be very serious (cf. Hostetler, 1987; Riordan & Marlin, 1987), but fortunately, they are very rare (Murray, 2002). Perhaps the most famous case is that of Sir Cyril Burt, who reported that the IQ scores of identical twins reared apart were highly similar. The data were used to support the argument that genetic influences on IQ are extremely important. However, Kamin (1974) noted some irregularities in Burt's data. A number of correlations for different sets of twins were exactly the same to the third decimal place, virtually a mathematical impossibility. This observation led to the discovery that some of Burt's presumed co-workers had not in fact worked with him or had simply been fabricated. Ironically, though, Burt's "data" were close to what has been reported by other investigators who have studied the IQ scores of twins.

In most cases, fraud is detected when other scientists cannot replicate the results of a study. Suspicions of fabrication of research data by social psychologist Karen Ruggiero arose when other researchers had difficulty replicating her published findings. The researcher subsequently resigned from her academic position and retracted her research findings (Murray, 2002). Sometimes fraud is detected by a colleague who has worked with the researcher. For example, Stephen Breuning was guilty of faking data showing that stimulants could be used to reduce hyperactive and aggressive behavior in severely retarded children (Byrne, 1988). In this case, another researcher who had worked closely with Breuning had suspicions about the data; he then informed the federal agency that had funded the research.

Fraud is not a major problem in science in part because researchers know that others will read their reports and conduct further studies, including replications. They know that their reputations and careers will be seriously damaged if other scientists conclude that the results are fraudulent. In addition, the likelihood of detection of fraud has increased in recent years as data accessibility has become more open: Regulations of most funding agencies require researchers to make their data accessible to other scientists.

Why, then, do researchers sometimes commit fraud? For one thing, scientists occasionally find themselves in jobs with extreme pressure to produce impressive results. This is not a sufficient explanation, of course, because many researchers maintain high ethical standards under such pressure. Another reason is that researchers who feel a need to produce fraudulent data have an exaggerated fear of failure, as well as a great need for success and the admiration that comes with it. If you wish to explore further the dynamics of fraud, you might wish to begin with Hearnshaw's (1979) book on Sir Cyril Burt. Controversy has continued to surround the case: One edited volume is titled *Cyril Burt: Fraud or Framed?* (Macintosh, 1995). Most analyses conclude, however, that the research was fraudulent (Tucker, 1997).

One final point: Allegations of fraud should not be made lightly. If you disagree with someone's results on philosophical, political, religious, or other grounds, it does not mean that they are fraudulent. Even if you cannot replicate the results, the reason may lie in aspects of the methodology of the study rather than deliberate fraud. However, the fact that fraud could be a possible explanation of results stresses the importance of careful record keeping and documentation of the procedures and results.

Plagiarism

Plagiarism refers to misrepresenting another's work as your own. You must give proper citation of your sources. Plagiarism can take the form of submitting an entire paper written by someone else. It can also mean including a paragraph or even a sentence that is copied without using quotation marks and a reference to the source of the quotation. Plagiarism also occurs when you present another person's ideas as your own rather than properly acknowledging the source of the ideas. Thus, even if you paraphrase the actual words used by a source, it is plagiarism if the source is not cited.

Although plagiarism is certainly not a new problem, access to Internet resources and the ease of copying material from the Internet may be increasing its prevalence. In fact, Szabo and Underwood (2004) report that more than 50% of a sample of British university students believe that using Internet resources for academically dishonest activities is acceptable. It is little wonder that many schools are turning to computer-based mechanisms of detecting plagiarism (e.g., http://www.turnitin.com).

Plagiarism is ethically wrong and can lead to many strong consequences, including academic sanctions such as a failing grade or expulsion from the school. Because plagiarism is often a violation of copyright law, it can be prosecuted as a criminal offense as well. Finally, it is interesting to note that some students believe that citing sources weakens their paper—that they are not being sufficiently original. In fact, Harris (2002) notes that student papers are actually strengthened when sources are used and properly cited.

Ethical guidelines and regulations evolve over time. The APA Ethics Code and federal, state, and local regulations may be revised periodically. Researchers need to always be aware of the most current policies and procedures. In the following chapters, we will discuss many specific procedures for studying behavior. As you read about these procedures and apply them to research you may be interested in, remember that ethical considerations are always paramount.

ILLUSTRATIVE ARTICLE: ETHICAL ISSUES

Middlemist, Knowles, and Matter (1976) measured the time to onset of urination and the duration of urination of males in restrooms at a college. The purpose of the research was to study the effect of personal space on a measure of physiological arousal (urination times). The students were observed while alone or with a confederate of the experimenter, who stood at the next stall or a more distant stall in the restroom. The presence and closeness of the confederate did have the effect of delaying urination and shortening the duration of urination.

First, acquire and read the article:

Middlemist, R.D., Knowles, E.S., & Matter, C.F. (1976). Personal space invasions in the lavatory: Suggestive evidence for arousal. *Journal of Personality and Social Psychology, 33*, 541–546. doi:10.1037/0022-3514.33.5.541

Then, after reading the article, consider the following:

1. Conduct an informal risk-benefit analysis. What are the risks and benefits inherent in this study as described? Do you think that the study is ethically justifiable given your analysis? Why or why not?

2. Redesign the study such that participants were given an opportunity to provide their informed consent. Do you think the results of the study would be affected by the changes that you suggest? Why or why not?

3. Describe some alternatives to the deception used in this study.

4. To what extent did the study adhere to the Ethics Code of the American Psychological Association?

5. If you were a member of your institution's IRB, would you vote to allow this study—as described—to be conducted? Why or why not?

Study Terms _____

APA Ethics Code (p. 55)
Autonomy (*Belmont Report*) (p. 44)
Belmont Report (p. 41)
Beneficence (*Belmont Report*) (p. 41)
Confidentiality (p. 43)
Debriefing (p. 48)
Deception (p. 46)
Exempt research (p. 53)
Fraud (p. 62)
Honest experiments (p. 51)

IACUC (p. 59)
Informed consent (p. 44)
Institutional Review Board (IRB; p. 52)
Justice (*Belmont Report*) (p. 51)
Minimal risk research (p. 53)
Plagiarism (p. 63)
Risk (p. 41)
Risk-benefit analysis (p. 41)
Role-playing (p. 49)
Simulation (p. 50)

Review Questions _____

1. Discuss the major ethical issues in behavioral research including risks, benefits, deception, debriefing, informed consent, and justice. How can researchers weigh the need to conduct research against the need for ethical procedures?

2. Why is informed consent an ethical principle? What are the potential problems with obtaining fully informed consent?

3. What alternatives to deception are described in the text?

4. Summarize the principles concerning research with human participants in the APA Ethics Code.

5. What is the difference between "no risk" and "minimal risk" research activities?

6. What is an Institutional Review Board?

7. Summarize the ethical procedures for research with animals.

8. What constitutes fraud, what are some reasons for its occurrence, and why doesn't it occur more frequently?

Activity Questions _____

1. Consider the following experiment, similar to one that was conducted by Smith, Lingle, and Brock (1978). Each participant interacted for an hour with another person who was actually an accomplice. After this interaction, both persons agreed to return one week later for another session with

each other. When the real participants returned, they were informed that the person they had met the week before had died. The researchers then measured reactions to the death of the person.

   a. Discuss the ethical issues raised by the experiment.

   b. Would the experiment violate the guidelines articulated in APA Ethical Standard 8 dealing with research with human participants? In what ways?

   c. What alternative methods for studying this problem (reactions to death) might you suggest?

   d. Would your reactions to this study be different if the participants had played with an infant and then later been told that the infant had died?

2. In a procedure described in this chapter, participants are given false feedback about an unfavorable personality trait or a low ability level. What are the ethical issues raised by this procedure? Compare your reactions to that procedure with your reactions to an analogous one in which people are given false feedback that they possess a very favorable personality trait or a very high ability level.

3. A social psychologist conducts a field experiment at a local bar that is popular with college students. Interested in observing flirting techniques, the investigator instructs male and female confederates to smile and make eye contact with others at the pub for varying amounts of time (e.g., 2 seconds, 5 seconds, etc.) and varying numbers of times (e.g., once, twice, etc.). The investigator observes the responses of those receiving the gaze. What ethical considerations, if any, do you perceive in this field experiment? Is there any deception involved?

4. Should people who are observed in field experiments be debriefed? Write a paragraph supporting the pro position and another paragraph supporting the con position.

5. Dr. Alucard conducted a study to examine various aspects of the sexual behaviors of college students. The students filled out a questionnaire in a classroom on the campus; about 50 students were tested at a time. The questionnaire asked about prior experience with various sexual practices. If a student had experience, a number of other detailed questions were asked. However, if the student did not have any prior experience, he or she skipped the detailed questions and simply went on to answer another general question about a sexual experience. What ethical issues arise when conducting research such as this? Do you detect any specific problems that might arise because of the "skip" procedure used in this study?

6. Read the following research scenarios and assess the risk to participants by placing a check mark in the appropriate box (answers below). Can you explain the basis for your answers?

Experiment Scenario	No Risk	Minimal Risk	Greater Than Minimal Risk
a. Researchers conducted a study on a college campus examining the physical attractiveness level among peer groups by taking pictures of students on campus and then asking students at another college to rate the attractiveness levels of each student in the photos.			
b. A group of researchers plan to measure differences in depth perception accuracy with and without perceptual cues. In one condition participants could use both eyes and in another condition one eye was covered with an eye patch.			
c. Researchers conducted an anonymous survey on attitudes toward gun control among shoppers at a local mall.			
d. College students watched a 10-minute video recording of either a male or female newscaster presenting the same news content. While the video played, an eye movement recording device tracked the amount of time the students were viewing the video.			

Answers

a. Greater than minimal risk

b. Minimal risk

c. No risk

d. Minimal risk

4

Fundamental Research Issues

LEARNING OBJECTIVES

- Define *variable* and describe the *operational definition* of a variable.
- Describe the different relationships between variables: positive, negative, curvilinear, and no relationship.
- Compare and contrast nonexperimental and experimental research methods.
- Distinguish between an independent variable and a dependent variable.
- Discuss the limitations of laboratory experiments and the advantage of using multiple methods of research.
- Distinguish between construct validity, internal validity, and external validity.

I n this chapter, we explore some of the basic issues and concepts that are necessary for understanding the scientific study of behavior. We begin by looking at the nature of variables and the relationships between variables. We also
examine general methods for studying these relationships. Most important, we
introduce the concept of validity in research.

VALIDITY: AN INTRODUCTION

You are likely aware of the concept of validity. You use the term when asking
whether the information that you found on a website is valid. A juror must decide whether the testimony given in a trial is valid. Someone on a diet may wonder if the weight shown on the bathroom scale is valid. After a first date, your
friend may try to decide whether her positive impressions of the date are valid.
Validity refers to truth or accuracy. Is the information on the website true? Does
the testimony reflect what actually happened? Is the scale really showing my actual weight? Should my friend believe that her positive impression is accurate?
In all these cases, someone is confronted with information and must make a
decision about the extent to which the information is valid.

Scientists are also concerned about the validity of their research findings. In
this chapter, we introduce three key types of validity:

- Construct validity concerns whether our methods of studying variables are
  accurate.
- Internal validity refers to the accuracy of conclusions about cause and effect.
- External validity concerns whether we can generalize the findings of a study
  to other settings.

These issues will be described in greater depth in this and subsequent chapters.
Before exploring issues of validity, we need to have a fundamental understanding of variables and the operational definition of variables.

VARIABLES

A **variable** is any event, situation, behavior, or individual characteristic that varies. Any variable must have two or more levels or values. Consider the following
examples of variables that you might encounter in research and your own life. As
you read a book, you encounter the variable of *word length*, with values defined
by the number of letters of each word. You can take this one step further and
think of the *average word length* used in paragraphs in the book. One book you
read may use a longer average word length than another. When you think about
yourself and your friends, you might categorize the people on a variable such as

extraversion. Some people can be considered relatively low on the extraversion variable (or introverted); others are high on extraversion. You might volunteer at an assisted living facility and notice that the residents differ in their *subjective well-being:* Some of the people seem much more satisfied with their lives than others. When you are driving and the car in front of you brakes to slow down or stop, the period of time before you apply the brakes in your own car is called *response time.* You might wonder if response time varies depending on the driver's age or whether the driver is talking to someone using a cell phone. In your biology class, you are studying for a final exam that is very important and you notice that you are experiencing the variable of *test anxiety.* Because the test is important, everyone in your study group says that they are very anxious about it. You might remember that you never felt anxious when studying for quizzes earlier in the course. As you can see, we all encounter variables continuously in our lives even though we don't formally use the term. Researchers, however, systematically study variables.

Examples of variables a psychologist might study include cognitive task performance, depression, intelligence, reaction time, rate of forgetting, aggression, speaker credibility, attitude change, anger, stress, age, and self-esteem. For some variables, the values will have true numeric, or quantitative, properties. Values for the number of free throws made, number of words correctly recalled, and the number of symptoms of major depression would all range from 0 to an actual value. The values of other variables are not numeric, but instead simply identify different categories. An example is gender; the values for gender are male and female. These are different, but they do not differ in amount or quantity.

OPERATIONAL DEFINITIONS OF VARIABLES

A variable such as *aggression, cognitive task performance, pain, self-esteem,* or even *word length* must be defined in terms of the specific method used to measure or manipulate it. The **operational definition** of a variable is the set of procedures used to measure or manipulate it.

A variable must have an operational definition to be studied empirically. The variable *bowling skill* could be operationalized as a person's average bowling score, or it could be operationalized as the number of pins knocked down in a single roll. Such a variable is concrete and easily operationalized in terms of score or number of pins. But things become more complicated when studying behavior. For example, a variable such as *pain* is very general and more abstract. Pain is a subjective state that cannot be directly observed, but that does not mean that we cannot create measures to infer how much pain someone is experiencing. A common pain measurement instrument in both clinical and research settings is the McGill Pain Questionnaire, which has both a long form and a short form (Melzack, 2005). The short form includes a 0 to 5 scale with descriptors *no pain, mild, discomforting, distressing, horrible, excruciating.* There is also a line with end points of *no pain* and *worst possible pain*; the person responds by making a mark at the appropriate place on the line. In addition, the questionnaire offers sensory descriptors such as *throbbing, shooting,* and *stabbing;* each of these descriptors has a rating of *none, mild, moderate,* or *severe.* This is a relatively complex set of questions and is targeted for use with adults. When working with children over 3, a better measurement instrument would be the Wong-Baker FACES™ Pain Rating Scale:

Using the FACES scale, a researcher could ask a child, "How much pain do you feel? Point to how much it hurts." These examples illustrate that the same variable of pain can be studied using different operational definitions.

There are two important benefits in operationally defining a variable. First, the task of developing an operational definition of a variable forces scientists to discuss abstract concepts in concrete terms. The process can result in the realization that the variable is too vague to study. This realization does not necessarily indicate that the concept is meaningless, but rather that systematic research is not possible until the concept can be operationally defined.

In addition, operational definitions also help researchers to communicate their ideas with others. If someone wishes to tell me about aggression, I need to know exactly what is meant by this term because there are many ways of operationally defining it. For example, aggression could be defined as (1) the number and duration of shocks delivered to another person, (2) the number of times a child punches an inflated toy clown, (3) the number of times a child fights with other children during recess, (4) homicide statistics gathered from police records, (5) a score on a personality measure of aggressiveness, or even (6) the number of times a batter is hit with a pitch during baseball games. Communication with another person will be easier if we agree on exactly what we mean when we use the term *aggression* in the context of our research.

Of course, a very important question arises once a variable is operationally defined: How good is the operational definition? How well does it match up with reality? How well does my average bowling score really represent my skill?

Construct validity refers to the adequacy of the operational definition of variables: Does the operational definition of a variable actually reflect the true theoretical meaning of the variable? If you wish to scientifically study the variable of extraversion, you need some way to measure that variable. Psychologists have developed measures that ask people whether they like to socialize with strangers or whether they prefer to avoid such situations. Do the answers on such a measure provide a good indication of the underlying variable of extraversion? If you are studying anger, will telling female college students that males had rated them unattractive create feelings of anger? Researchers are able to address these questions when they design their studies and examine the results.

RELATIONSHIPS BETWEEN VARIABLES

Many research studies investigate the relationship between two variables: Do the levels of the two variables vary systematically together? For example, does playing violent video games result in greater aggressiveness? Is physical attractiveness related to a speaker's credibility? As age increases, does the amount of cooperative play increase as well?

Recall that some variables have true numeric values whereas the levels of other variables are simply different categories (e.g., female versus male; being a student-athlete versus not being a student-athlete). This distinction will be expanded upon in Chapter 5. For the purposes of describing relationships among variables, we will begin by discussing relationships in which both variables have true numeric properties.

When both variables have values along a numeric scale, many different "shapes" can describe their relationship. We begin by focusing on the four most common relationships found in research: the **positive linear relationship,** the **negative linear relationship,** the **curvilinear relationship,** and, of course, the situation in which there is *no relationship* between the variables. These relationships are best illustrated by line graphs that show the way changes in one variable are accompanied by changes in a second variable. The four graphs in Figure 4.1 show these four types of relationships.

Positive Linear Relationship

In a positive linear relationship, increases in the values of one variable are accompanied by increases in the values of the second variable. In Chapter 1, we described a positive relationship between communicator credibility and persuasion; higher levels of credibility are associated with greater attitude change. Consider another communicator variable, rate of speech. Are "fast talkers" more persuasive? In a study conducted by Smith and Shaffer (1991), students listened to a speech delivered at a slow (144 words per minute), intermediate (162 wpm), or fast (214 wpm) speech rate. The speaker advocated a position favoring legislation to raise the legal drinking age; the students initially disagreed with this position. Graph A in Figure 4.1 shows the positive linear relationship between speech rate and attitude change that was found in this study. That is, as rate of speech increased, so did the amount of attitude change. In a graph like this, we see a horizontal and a vertical axis, termed the *x* axis and *y* axis, respectively. Values of the first variable are placed on the horizontal axis, labeled from low to high. Values of the second variable are placed on the vertical axis. Graph A shows that higher speech rates are associated with greater amounts of attitude change.

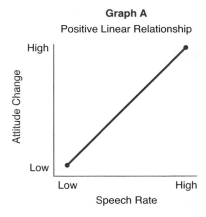

Graph A
Positive Linear Relationship

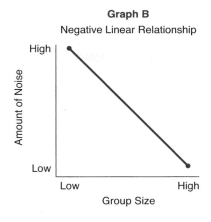

Graph B
Negative Linear Relationship

FIGURE 4.1
Four types
of relation-
ships
between
variables

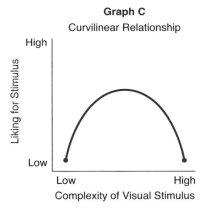

Graph C
Curvilinear Relationship

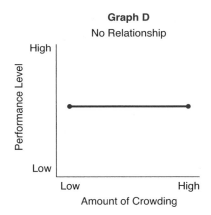

Graph D
No Relationship

Negative Linear Relationship

Variables can also be negatively related. In a negative linear relationship, *increases* in the values of one variable are accompanied by *decreases* in the values of the other variable. Latané, Williams, and Harkins (1979) were intrigued with reports that increasing the number of people working on a task may actually reduce group effort and productivity. The researchers designed an experiment to study this phenomenon, which they termed "social loafing" (which you may have ob- served in group projects!). The researchers asked participants to clap and shout to make as much noise as possible. They did this alone or in groups of two, four, or six people. Graph B in Figure 4.1 illustrates the negative relationship between number of people in the group and the amount of noise made by each person. As the size of the group *increased,* the amount of noise made by each individual *decreased.* The two variables are systematically related, just as in a positive rela- tionship; only the direction of the relationship is reversed.

Curvilinear Relationship

In a curvilinear relationship, increases in the values of one variable are accompanied by systematic increases and decreases in the values of the other variable. In other words, the direction of the relationship changes at least once. This type of relationship is sometimes referred to as a *nonmonotonic function*.

Graph C in Figure 4.1 shows a curvilinear relationship between complexity of visual stimuli and ratings of preferences for the stimuli. This particular relationship is called an *inverted-U relationship*. Increases in visual complexity are accompanied by increases in liking for the stimulus, but only up to a point. The relationship then becomes negative, as further increases in complexity are accompanied by *decreases* in liking for the stimulus (Vitz, 1966). Of course, it is also possible to have a U-shaped relationship. Research on the relationship between age and happiness indicates that adults in their 40s are less happy than younger and older adults (Blanchflower & Oswald, 2008). A U-shaped curve results when this relationship is graphed.

No Relationship

When there is no relationship between the two variables, the graph is simply a flat line. Graph D in Figure 4.1 illustrates the relationship between crowding and task performance found in a study by Freedman, Klevansky, and Ehrlich (1971). Unrelated variables vary independently of one another. Increases in crowding are not associated with any particular changes in performance; thus, a flat line describes the lack of relationship between the two variables.

These graphs illustrate several common shapes that describe the relationship between two variables. The positive and negative linear relationships just described are examples of a more general category of relationships described as monotonic, because the relationship between the variables is always positive or always negative. The curvilinear relationship shown in Graph C is a nonmonotonic relationship, because the direction of the relationship changes. Other monotonic or nonmonotonic relationships may be described by more complicated shapes. An example of a positive monotonic function that is not strictly linear is shown in Figure 4.2.

FIGURE 4.2
Positive
monotonic
function

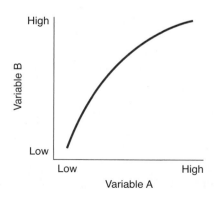

TABLE 4.1 Identify the type of relationship

Read the following examples and identify the relationship by placing a check mark in the appropriate box. (Answers are provided on the last page of the chapter.)	Positive	Negative	Curvilinear
Increased caloric intake is associated with increased body weight.			
As people gain experience speaking in public, their anxiety level decreases.			
Performance of basketball players increases as arousal increases from low to moderate levels, then decreases as arousal becomes extremely high.			
Increased partying behavior is associated with decreased grades.			
A decrease in the number of headaches is associated with a decrease in the amount of sugar consumed per day.			
Amount of education is associated with higher income.			
Liking for a song increases the more you hear it, but then after a while you like it less and less.			
The more you exercise your puppy, the less your puppy chews on things in your house.			

Remember that these are general patterns. Even if, in general, a positive linear relationship exists, it does not necessarily mean that everyone who scores high on one variable will also score high on the second variable. Individual deviations from the general pattern are likely. In addition to knowing the general type of relationship between two variables, it is also necessary to know the strength of the relationship. That is, we need to know the size of the correlation between the variables. Sometimes two variables are strongly related to each other and show little deviation from the general pattern. Other times the two variables are not highly correlated because many individuals deviate from the general pattern. A numerical index of the strength of relationship between variables is called a **correlation coefficient.** Correlation coefficients are very important because we need to know how strongly variables are related to one another. Correlation coefficients are discussed in detail in Chapter 12. Table 4.1 provides an opportunity to review types of relationships—for each example, identify the shape of the relationship as positive, negative, or curvilinear.

Relationships and Reduction of Uncertainty

When we detect a relationship between variables, we reduce uncertainty about the world by increasing our understanding of the variables we are examining.

The term *uncertainty* implies that there is randomness in events; scientists refer to this as *random variability* in events that occur. Research is aimed at reducing random variability by identifying systematic relationships between variables.

Identifying relationships between variables seems complex but is much easier to see in a simple example. For this example, the variables will have no quantitative properties—we will not describe *increases* in the values of variables but only differences in values—in this case whether a person likes to shop. Suppose you ask 200 students at your school to tell you whether they like to shop. Now suppose that 100 students said *Yes* and the remaining 100 said *No*. What do you do with this information? You know only that there is variability in people's shopping preferences—some people like to shop and others do not.

This variability is called *random variability*. If you walked up to anyone at your school and tried to guess whether the person liked shopping, you would have to make a random guess—you would be right about half the time and wrong half the time (because we know that 50% of the people like to shop and 50% do not, any guess you make will be right about half the time). However, if we could explain the variability, it would no longer be random. How can the random variability be reduced? The answer is to see if we can identify variables that are related to attitudes toward shopping.

Suppose you also asked people to indicate their gender—whether they are male or female. Now let's look at what happens when you examine whether gender is related to shopping preference. Table 4.2 shows one possible outcome. Note that there are 100 males and 100 females in the study. The important thing, though, is that 30 of the males say they like shopping and 70 of the females say they like shopping. Have we reduced the random variability? We clearly have. Before you had this information, there would be no way of predicting whether a given person would like to shop. Now that you have the research finding, you can predict the likelihood that any female would like to shop and any male would not like to shop. Now you will be right about 70% of the time; this is a big increase from the 50% when everything was random.

TABLE 4.2   Gender and shopping preference (hypothetical data)

		Participant Gender	
		Males	Females
Like to shop?	Yes	30	70
	No	70	30
	Number of participants	100	100

Is there still random variability? The answer is clearly yes. You will be wrong about 30% of the time, and you don't know when you will be wrong. For unknown reasons, some males will say they like to shop and some females will not. Can you reduce this remaining uncertainty? The quest to do so motivates additional research. With further studies, you may be able to identify other variables that are also related to liking to shop. For example, variables such as income and age may also be related to shopping preference.

This discussion underscores once again that relationships between variables are rarely perfect: There are males and females who do not fit the general pattern. The relationship between the variables is stronger when there is less random variability—for example, if 90% of females and 10% of males liked shopping, the relationship would be much stronger (with less uncertainty or randomness).

NONEXPERIMENTAL VERSUS EXPERIMENTAL METHODS

How can we determine whether variables are related? There are two general approaches to the study of relationships among variables, the nonexperimental method and the experimental method. With the **nonexperimental method,** relationships are studied by making observations or measures of the variables of interest. This may be done by asking people to describe their behavior, directly observing behavior, recording physiological responses, or even examining various public records such as census data. In all these cases, variables are observed as they occur naturally. A relationship between variables is established when the two variables vary together. For example, Steinberg and Dornbusch (1991) measured how many hours high school students worked at paying jobs and related this variable to grade point average. The two variables did vary together: Students who worked more hours tended to have lower grades.

The second approach to the study of relationships, the **experimental method,** involves direct manipulation and control of variables. The researcher manipulates the first variable of interest and then observes the response. For example, Ramirez and Beilock (2011) were interested in the anxiety produced by important "high-stakes" examinations. Because such anxiety may impair performance, it is important to find ways to reduce the anxiety. In their research, Ramirez and Beilock tested the hypothesis that writing about testing worries would improve performance on the exam. In their study, they used the experimental method. All students took a math test and were then given an opportunity to take the test again. To make this a high-stakes test, students were led to believe that the monetary payout to themselves and their partner was dependent on their performance. The writing variable was then manipulated. Some students spent 10 minutes before taking the test writing about what they were thinking and feeling about the test. The other students constituted a control group; these students simply sat quietly for 10 minutes prior to taking the test. Next, the new, important test was then administered. The researchers found that students in the writing condition improved their scores; the control group's scores actually decreased. With the experimental method, the two variables do not merely vary together; one variable is introduced first to determine whether it affects the second variable.

Nonexperimental Method

Suppose a researcher is interested in the relationship between exercise and anxiety. How could this topic be studied? Using the nonexperimental method, the researcher would devise operational definitions to measure both the amount of exercise that people engage in and their level of anxiety. There could be a variety of ways of operationally defining either of these variables; for example, the researcher might simply ask people to provide self-reports of their exercise patterns and current anxiety level. The important point to remember here is that *both* variables are measured when using the nonexperimental method, in contrast to the experimental variable in which only the *first* variable is manipulated. Now suppose that the researcher collects data on exercise and anxiety from a number of people and finds that exercise is negatively related to anxiety—that is, the people who exercise more also have lower levels of anxiety. The two variables covary, or correlate, with each other: Observed differences in exercise are associated with amount of anxiety. Because the nonexperimental method allows us to observe covariation between variables, another term that is frequently used to describe this procedure is the *correlational method.* With this method, we examine whether the variables correlate or vary together.

The nonexperimental method seems to be a reasonable approach to studying relationships between variables such as exercise and anxiety. A relationship is established by finding that the two variables vary together—the variables covary or correlate with each other. However, this method is not ideal when we ask questions about cause and effect. We know the two variables are related, but what can we say about the causal impact of one variable on the other? There are two problems with making causal statements when the nonexperimental method is used: (1) it can be difficult to determine the direction of cause and effect and (2) researchers face the third-variable problem—that is, extraneous variables may be causing an observed relationship (see Figure 4.3, in which arrows are used to depict causal links among variables).

Direction of cause and effect   The first problem involves *direction of cause and effect*. With the nonexperimental method, it is difficult to determine

Directionality Problem

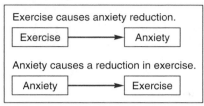

Third-Variable Problem

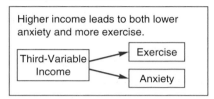

FIGURE 4.3
Causal possibilities in a nonexperimental study

which variable causes the other. In other words, it can't really be said that exercise causes a reduction in anxiety. Although there are plausible reasons for this particular pattern of cause and effect, there are also reasons why the opposite pattern might occur. Perhaps high anxiety causes people to reduce exercise. The issue here is one of temporal precedence; it is very important in making causal inferences (see Chapter 1). Knowledge of the correct direction of cause and effect in turn has implications for applications of research findings: If exercise reduces anxiety, then undertaking an exercise program would be a reasonable way to lower one's anxiety. However, if anxiety causes people to stop exercising, simply forcing someone to exercise is not likely to reduce the person's anxiety level.

The problem of direction of cause and effect is not the most serious drawback to the nonexperimental method, however. Scientists have pointed out, for example, that astronomers can make accurate predictions even though they cannot manipulate variables in an experiment. In addition, the direction of cause and effect is often not crucial because, for some pairs of variables, the causal pattern may operate in both directions. For instance, there seem to be two causal patterns in the relationship between the variables of similarity and liking: (1) Similarity causes people to like each other, and (2) liking causes people to become more similar. In general, the third-variable problem is a much more serious fault of the nonexperimental method.

The third-variable problem   When the nonexperimental method is used, there is the danger that no direct causal relationship exists between the two variables. Exercise may not influence anxiety, and anxiety may have no causal effect on exercise; this is known as a spurious relationship. Instead, there may be a relationship between the two variables because some other variable causes both exercise *and* anxiety. This is known as the **third-variable problem.** A third variable is any variable that is extraneous to the two variables being studied. Any number of other third variables may be responsible for an observed relationship between two variables. In the exercise and anxiety example, one such third variable could be income level. Perhaps high income allows people more free time to exercise (and the ability to afford a health club membership!) and also lowers anxiety. If income is the determining variable, there is no direct cause-and-effect relationship between exercise and anxiety; the relationship was caused by the third variable, income level. The third variable is an alternative explanation for the observed relationship between the variables. Recall from Chapter 1 that the ability to rule out alternative explanations for the observed relationship between two variables is another important factor when we try to infer that one variable causes another.

The fact that third variables could be operating is a serious problem, because third variables introduce alternative explanations that reduce the overall validity of a study. The fact that income could be related to exercise means that income level is an alternative explanation for an observed relationship between exercise and anxiety. The alternative explanation is that high income reduces anxiety level, so exercise has nothing to do with it. When we actually know that an uncontrolled third variable is operating, we can call the third variable a **confounding variable.** If two variables are confounded, they are intertwined so you cannot determine which of the variables is operating in a given situation. If income is confounded with exercise, income level will be an alternative explanation whenever you study exercise. Fortunately, there is a solution to this problem: the experimental method provides us with a way of controlling for the effects of third variables.

As you can see, direction of cause and effect and potential third variables represent serious limitations of the nonexperimental method. Often, they are not considered in media reports of research results. For instance, a newspaper may report the results of a nonexperimental study that found a positive relationship between amount of coffee consumed and likelihood of a heart attack. Obviously, there is not necessarily a cause-and-effect relationship between the two variables. Numerous third variables (e.g., occupation, personality, or genetic predisposition) could cause both a person's coffee-drinking behavior and the likelihood of a heart attack. In sum, the results of such studies are ambiguous and should be viewed with skepticism.

Experimental Method

The experimental method reduces ambiguity in the interpretation of results. With the experimental method, one variable is manipulated and the other is then measured (recall that both variables are measured when using the non-experimental method). If a researcher used the experimental method to study whether exercise reduces anxiety, exercise would be manipulated—perhaps by having one group of people exercise each day for a week and another group refrain from exercise. Anxiety would then be measured. Suppose that people in the exercise group have less anxiety than the people in the no-exercise group. The researcher could now say something about the direction of cause and effect: In the experiment, exercise came first in the sequence of events. Thus, anxiety level could not influence the amount of exercise that the people engaged in.

Another characteristic of the experimental method is that it attempts to eliminate the influence of all potential confounding third variables on the dependent variable. This is generally referred to as control of extraneous variables. Such control is usually achieved by making sure that every feature of the environment except the manipulated variable is held constant. Any variable that cannot be held constant is controlled by making sure that the effects of the variable are random. Through randomization, the influence of any extraneous variables is equal in the experimental conditions. Both procedures are used to ensure that any differences between the groups are due to the manipulated variable.

Experimental control
With **experimental control,** all extraneous variables are kept constant. If a variable is held constant, it cannot be responsible for the results of the experiment. In other words, any variable that is held constant cannot be a confounding variable. In the experiment on the effect of exercise, the researcher would want to make sure that the only difference between the exercise and no-exercise groups is the exercise. For example, because people in the exercise group are removed from their daily routine to engage in exercise, the people in the no-exercise group should be removed from their daily routine as well. Otherwise, the lower anxiety in the exercise condition could have resulted from the "rest" from the daily routine rather than from the exercise.

Experimental control is accomplished by treating participants in all groups in the experiment identically; the only difference between groups is the manipulated variable. In the Loftus experiment on memory (discussed in Chapter 2), both groups witnessed the same accident, the same experimenter asked the questions in both groups, the lighting and all other conditions were the same, and so on. When a difference occurred between the groups in reporting memory, researchers could be sure that the difference was the result of the method of questioning rather than of some other variable that was not held constant.

Randomization
The number of potential confounding variables is infinite, and sometimes it is difficult to keep a variable constant. The most obvious

such variable is any characteristic of the participants. Consider an experiment in which half the research participants are in the exercise condition and the other half are in the no-exercise condition; the participants in the two conditions might be different on some extraneous, third variable such as income. This difference could cause an apparent relationship between exercise and anxiety. How can the researcher eliminate the influence of such extraneous variables in an experiment?

The experimental method eliminates the influence of such variables by **randomization.** Randomization ensures that the extraneous variable is just as likely to affect one experimental group as it is to affect the other group. To eliminate the influence of individual characteristics, the researcher assigns participants to the two groups in a random fashion. In actual practice, this means that assignment to groups is determined using a list of random numbers. To understand this, think of the participants in the experiment as forming a line. As each person comes to the front of the line, a random number is assigned, much like random numbers are drawn for a lottery. If the number is even, the individual is assigned to one group (e.g., exercise); if the number is odd, the subject is assigned to the other group (e.g., no exercise). By using a random assignment procedure, the researcher is confident that the characteristics of the participants in the two groups will be virtually identical. In this "lottery," for instance, people with low, medium, and high incomes will be distributed equally in the two groups. In fact, randomization ensures that the individual characteristic composition of the two groups will be virtually identical in every way. This ability to randomly assign research participants to the conditions in the experiment is an important difference between the experimental and non-experimental methods.

To make the concept of random assignment more concrete, you might try an exercise such as the one we did with a box full of old baseball cards. The box contained cards of 50 American League players and 50 National League players. The cards were thoroughly mixed up; we then proceeded to select 32 of the cards and assign them to "groups" using a sequence of random numbers obtained from a website that generates random numbers (www.randomizer.org). As each card was drawn, we used the following decision rule: If the random number is even, the player is assigned to Group 1, and if the number is odd, the player is assigned to Group 2. We then checked to see whether the two groups differed in terms of league representation. Group 1 had nine American League players and seven National League players, whereas Group 2 had an equal number of players from the two leagues. The two groups were virtually identical!

Any other variable that cannot be held constant is also controlled by randomization. For instance, many experiments are conducted over a period of several days or weeks, with participants arriving for the experiment at various times during each day. In such cases, the researcher uses a random order for scheduling the sequence of the various experimental conditions. This procedure prevents a situation in which one condition is scheduled during the first days of the experiment whereas the other is studied during later days. Similarly, participants in one group will not be studied only during the morning and the others only in the afternoon.

Direct experimental control and randomization eliminate the influence of any extraneous variables (keeping variables constant across conditions). Thus, the experimental method allows a relatively unambiguous interpretation of the results. Any difference between groups on the observed variable can be attributed to the influence of the manipulated variable.

INDEPENDENT AND DEPENDENT VARIABLES

When researchers study the relationship between variables, the variables are usually conceptualized as having a cause-and-effect connection. That is, one variable is considered to be the cause and the other variable the effect. Thus, speaker credibility is viewed as a cause of attitude change, and exercise is viewed as having an effect on anxiety. Researchers using both experimental and nonexperimental methods view the variables in this fashion, even though, as we have seen, there is less ambiguity about the direction of cause and effect when the experimental method is used. Researchers use the terms **independent variable** and **dependent variable** when referring to the variables being studied. The variable that is considered to be the cause is called the independent variable, and the variable that is the effect is called the dependent variable. It is often helpful to actually draw a relationship between the independent and dependent variables using an arrow as we did in Figure 4.3. The arrow always indicates your hypothesized causal sequence:

In an experiment, the manipulated variable is the independent variable. After manipulating the independent variable, the researchers measure a second variable, called the dependent variable. The basic idea is that the researchers make changes in the independent variable and then see if the dependent variable changes in response.

One way to remember the distinction between the independent and dependent variables is to relate the terms to what happens to participants in an experiment. First, the participants are exposed to a situation, such as watching a violent versus a nonviolent program or exercising versus not exercising. This is the manipulated variable. It is called the independent variable because the participant has nothing to do with its occurrence; the researchers vary it independently of any characteristics of the participant or situation.

In the next step of the experiment, the researchers want to see what effect the independent variable had on the participant; to find this out, they measure the dependent variable. In this step, the participant is responding to what happened to him or her; whatever the participant does or says, the researcher assumes must be caused by—or be dependent on—the effect of the independent (manipulated) variable. The independent variable, then, is the variable manipulated by the experimenter, and the dependent variable is the participant's measured behavior, which is assumed to be caused by the independent variable.

When the relationship between an independent and a dependent variable is plotted in a graph, the independent variable is always placed on the horizontal axis and the dependent variable is always placed on the vertical axis. If you look back to Figure 4.1, you will see that this graphing method was used to present the four relationships. In Graph B, for example, the independent variable, "Group Size," is placed on the horizontal axis; the dependent variable, "Amount of Noise," is placed on the vertical axis.

Note that some research focuses primarily on the independent variable, with the researcher studying the effect of a single independent variable on numerous behaviors. Other researchers may focus on a specific dependent variable and study how various independent variables affect that one behavior. To make this distinction more concrete, consider a study of the effect of jury size, the independent variable, on the outcome of a trial, the dependent variable. One researcher studying this issue might be interested in the effect of group size on a variety of behaviors, including jury decisions and risk taking among business managers. Another researcher, interested solely in jury decisions, might study the effects of many aspects of trials, such as jury size and the judge's instructions, on juror behavior. Both emphases lead to important research. Figure 4.4 presents an opportunity to test your knowledge of the types of variables we have described.

Read the following and answer the questions below (answers are provided on the last page of the chapter). Researchers conducted a study to examine the effect of music on exam scores. They hypothesized that scores would be higher when students listened to soft music compared to no music during the exam because the soft music would reduce students' test anxiety. One hundred (50 male, 50 female) students were randomly assigned to either the soft music or no music conditions. Students in the music condition listened to music using headphones during the exam. Fifteen minutes after the exam began, researchers asked students to complete a questionnaire that measured test anxiety. Later, when the exams were completed and graded, the scores were recorded. As hypothesized, test anxiety was significantly lower and exam scores were significantly higher in the soft music condition compared to the no music condition.

The independent variable is: _____

The dependent variable is: _____

The potential confounding variable is: _____

FIGURE 4.4
Identify the relevant variables

INTERNAL VALIDITY: INFERRING CAUSALITY

Internal validity is the ability to draw conclusions about causal relationships from the results of a study. A study has high internal validity when strong inferences can be made that one variable caused changes in the other variable. We have seen that strong causal inferences can be made more easily when the experimental method is used.

Recall from Chapter 1 that inferences of cause and effect require three elements. So, strong internal validity requires an analysis of these three elements. First, there must be temporal precedence: The causal variable should come first in the temporal order of events and be followed by the effect. The experimental method addresses temporal order by first manipulating the independent variable and then observing whether it has an effect on the dependent variable. In other situations, you may observe the temporal order or you may logically conclude that one order is more plausible than another. Second, there must be covariation between the two variables. Covariation is demonstrated with the experimental method when participants in an experimental condition (e.g., an exercise condition) show the effect (e.g., a reduction in anxiety), whereas participants in a control condition (e.g., no exercise) do not show the effect. Third, there is a need to eliminate plausible alternative explanations for the observed relationship. An alternative explanation is based on the possibility that some confounding third variable is responsible for the observed relationship. When designing research, a great deal of attention is paid to eliminating alternative explanations, because doing so brings us closer to truth. Indeed, eliminating alternative explanations improves internal validity. The experimental method begins by attempting to keep such variables constant through random assignment and experimental control.

Other issues of control will be discussed in later chapters. The main point here is that inferences about causal relationships are stronger when there are fewer alternative explanations for the observed relationships.

EXTERNAL VALIDITY

Another important type of validity concerns the extent to which the results can be generalized to other populations and settings. This is known as the **external validity** of a study. In thinking about external validity, several questions arise: Can the results of a study be replicated with other operational definitions of the variables? Can the results be replicated with different participants? Can the results be replicated in other settings?

For example, Schumann and Ross (2010) examined whether there were gender differences in apology behavior (i.e., saying "sorry"). In this case, undergraduate students from the University of Waterloo in Canada were asked to complete an online questionnaire every evening for 12 days. The participants reported instances during the day when they "apologized to someone or did something to someone else that might have deserved an apology." They found that both males and females apologized at about the same rate (81% of the time) when they committed an offense; however, males reported fewer offenses deserving of an apology than did females. Now, in terms of external validity, this presents several things to think about. First, are Canadian undergraduates like other undergraduates? Indeed, are they like other Canadians? Next, what if Schumann and Ross decided to operationalize "apology behavior" differently than described above? What if the definition was changed to "admitted an error or discourtesy and accompanied it by an expression of regret"? Would the results be the same? If so, then we would have evidence for external validity, because the *results* generalized regardless of the specific operational definition. Likewise, if the study were replicated in China, Chile, Congo, and the Czech Republic with the same result, then we would have further evidence for external validity.

When examining a single study, we find internal validity to be generally in conflict with external validity. A researcher interested in establishing that there is a causal relationship between variables is most interested in internal validity. An experiment would be designed in which the independent variable is manipulated and other variables are kept constant (experimental control). This is most easily done in a laboratory setting, often with a highly restricted sample such as college students drawn from introductory psychology classes. A researcher more interested in the external validity of the research might conduct nonexperimental research with a sample drawn from a more diverse population. The issue of external validity is a complex one that will be discussed more fully in Chapter 14. We will now address some of the reasons that a researcher might choose a nonexperimental approach, including external validity.

CHOOSING A METHOD

The advantages of the experimental method for studying relationships between variables have been emphasized. However, there *are* disadvantages to experiments and many good reasons for using methods other than experiments. Let's examine some of the issues that arise when choosing a method.

Artificiality of Experiments

In a laboratory experiment, the independent variable is manipulated within the carefully controlled confines of a laboratory. This procedure permits relatively unambiguous inferences concerning cause and effect and reduces the possibility that extraneous variables could influence the results. These unambiguous inferences are another way of saying "strong internal validity." Laboratory experimentation is an extremely valuable way to study many problems. However, the high degree of control and the laboratory setting may sometimes create an artificial atmosphere that may limit either the questions that can be addressed or the generality of the results. So, although laboratory experiments often have strong internal validity, they may often have limited external validity. For this reason, researchers may decide to use some of the nonexperimental methods described above.

Another alternative is to try to conduct an experiment in a field setting. In a **field experiment,** the independent variable is manipulated in a natural setting. As in any experiment, the researcher attempts to control extraneous variables via either randomization or experimental control. As an example of a field experiment, consider Lee, Schwarz, Taubman, and Hou's (2010) study on the impact that public sneezing had on perceptions of risk resulting from flu. On a day that swine flu received broad media attention, students on a university campus were exposed to a confederate who either sneezed and coughed, or did not, as participants passed. Afterwards, participants were asked to complete a measure of perceived risks in order to help on a "class project." The researchers conducted a similar study at shopping malls and local businesses. In all three cases, they found that participants who were exposed to sneezing and coughing perceived higher risk of contracting a serious disease, having a heart attack prior to age 50, and dying from a crime or accident.

Many other field experiments take place in public spaces such as street corners, shopping malls, and parking lots. Ruback and Juieng (1997) measured the amount of time drivers in a parking lot took to leave their space under two conditions: (1) when another car (driven by the experimenter) waited a few spaces away or (2) when no other car was present. As you might expect, drivers took longer to leave when a car was waiting for the space. Apparently, the motive to protect a temporary territory is stronger than the motive to leave as quickly as possible! The advantage of the field experiment is that the independent variable is investigated in a natural context. The disadvantage is that the researcher loses the ability to directly control many aspects of the situation. For instance, in the parking lot, there are other shoppers in the area and security guards that might drive by. The laboratory experiment permits researchers to more easily keep extraneous variables constant, thereby eliminating their influence on the outcome of the experiment. Of course, it is precisely this control that leads to the artificiality of the laboratory investigation. Fortunately, when researchers have conducted experiments in both lab and field settings, the results of the experiments have been very similar (Anderson, Lindsay, & Bushman, 1999).

Ethical and Practical Considerations

Sometimes the experimental method is not a feasible alternative because experimentation would be either unethical or impractical. Child-rearing practices would be impractical to manipulate with the experimental method, for example. Further, even if it were possible to randomly assign parents to two child-rearing conditions, such as using withdrawal of love versus physical types of punishment, the manipulation would be unethical. Instead of manipulating variables such as child-rearing techniques, researchers usually study them as they occur in natural settings. Many important research areas present similar problems—for example, studies of the effects of alcoholism, divorce and its consequences, or the impact of corporal punishment on children's aggressiveness. Such problems need to be studied, and generally the only techniques possible are nonexperimental.

When such variables are studied, people are often categorized into groups based on their experiences. When studying corporal punishment, for example, one group would consist of individuals who were spanked as children and another group would consist of people who were not. This is sometimes called an *ex post facto* design. Ex post facto means "after the fact"—the term was coined to describe research in which groups are formed on the basis of some actual difference rather than through random assignment as in an experiment. It is extremely important to study these differences. However, it is important to recognize that this is nonexperimental research because there is no random assignment to the groups and no manipulation of an independent variable.

Participant Variables

Participant variables (also called *subject variables* and *personal attributes*) are characteristics of individuals, such as age, gender, ethnic group, nationality, birth order, personality, or marital status. These variables are by definition nonexperimental and so must be measured. For example, to study a personality characteristic such as extraversion, you might have people complete a personality test that is designed to measure this variable. Such variables may be studied in experiments along with manipulated independent variables (see Chapter 10).

Description of Behavior

A major goal of science is to provide an accurate description of events. Thus, the goal of much research is to describe behavior; in those cases, causal inferences are not relevant to the primary goals of the research. A classic example of descriptive research in psychology comes from the work of Jean Piaget, who carefully observed the behavior of his own children as they matured. He described in detail the changes in their ways of thinking about and responding to their environment (Piaget, 1952). Piaget's descriptions and his interpretations of his observations resulted in an important theory of cognitive development that greatly increased our understanding of this topic. Piaget's theory had a major impact on psychology that continues today (Flavell, 1996).

A more recent example of descriptive research in psychology is Meston and Buss's (2007) study on the motives for having sex. The purpose of the study was to describe the "multitude of reasons that people engage in sexual intercourse" (p. 496). In the study, 444 male and female college students were asked to list the reasons why they had engaged in sexual intercourse in the past. The researchers combed through the answers and identified 237 reasons including "I was attracted to the person," "I wanted to feel loved," "I wanted to make up after a fight," and "I wanted to defy my parents." The next step for the researchers was to categorize the reasons that their participants reported for having sex, including physical reasons (such as attraction) and goal attainment reasons (such as revenge). In this case, as with some of Piaget's work, the primary goal was to describe behavior rather than to understand its causes.

Successful Predictions of Future Behavior

In many real-life situations, a major concern is to make a successful prediction about a person's future behavior—for example, success in school, ability to learn a new job, or probable interest in various major fields in college. In such circumstances, there may be no need to be concerned about issues of cause and effect. It is possible to design measures that increase the accuracy of predicting future behavior. School counselors can give tests to decide whether students should be in "enriched" classroom programs, employers can test applicants to help determine whether they should be hired, and college students can take tests that help them decide on a major. These types of measures can lead to better decisions for many people. When researchers develop measures designed to predict future behavior, they must conduct research to demonstrate that the measure does, in fact, relate to the behavior in question. This research will be discussed in Chapter 5.

Advantages of Multiple Methods

Perhaps most important, complete understanding of any phenomenon requires study using multiple methods, both experimental and nonexperimental. No method is perfect, and no single study is definitive. To illustrate, consider a hypothesis developed by Frank and Gilovich (1988). They were intrigued by the observation that the color black represents evil and death across many cultures over time, and they wondered whether this has an influence on our behavior. They noted that several professional sports teams in the National Football League and National Hockey League wear black uniforms and hypothesized that these teams might be more aggressive than other teams in the leagues.

They first needed an operational definition of "black" and "nonblack" uniforms; they decided that a black uniform is one in which 50% or more of the uniform is black. Using this definition, five NFL and five NHL teams had black uniforms. They first asked people who had no knowledge of the NFL or NHL to view each team's uniform and then rate the teams on "malevolent" adjectives such as "mean" and "aggressive." Overall, the ratings of the black uniform teams were perceived to be more malevolent. They then compared the penalty yards of NFL black and nonblack teams and the penalty minutes of NHL teams. In both cases, black teams were assessed more penalties. But is there a causal pattern? Frank and Gilovich discovered that two NHL teams had switched uniforms from nonblack to black, so they compared penalty minutes before and after the switch; consistent with the hypothesis, penalties did increase for both teams. They also looked at the penalty minutes of a third team that had changed from a nonblack color to another nonblack color and found no change in penalty minutes. Note that none of these studies used the experimental method. In an experiment to test the hypothesis that people perceive black uniform teams as more aggressive, students watched videos of two plays from a staged football game in which the defense was wearing either black or white. Both plays included an aggressive act by the defense. On these plays, the students penalized the black uniform team more than the nonblack team. In a final experiment to see whether being on a black uniform team would increase aggressiveness, people were brought into the lab in groups of three. The groups were told they were a "team" that would be competing with another team. All members of the team were given either white or black clothing to wear for the competition; they were then asked to choose the games they would like to have for the competition. Some of the games were aggressive ("dart gun duel") and some were not ("putting contest"). As you might expect by now, the black uniform teams chose more aggressive games.

The important point here is that no study is a perfect test of a hypothesis. However, when multiple studies using multiple methods all lead to the same conclusion, our confidence in the findings and our understanding of the phenomenon are greatly increased.

EVALUATING RESEARCH: SUMMARY OF THE THREE VALIDITIES

The key concept of validity was introduced at the outset of this chapter. *Validity* refers to "truth" and the accurate representation of information. Research can be described and evaluated in terms of three types of validity:

- **Construct validity** refers to the adequacy of the operational definitions of variables.
- **Internal validity** refers to our ability to accurately draw conclusions about causal relationships.
- **External validity** is the extent to which results of a study can be generalized to other populations and settings.

Each gives us a different perspective on any particular research investigation, and every research study should be evaluated on these aspects of validity.

At this point, you may be wondering how researchers select a methodology to study a problem. A variety of methods are available, each with advantages and disadvantages. Researchers select the method that best enables them to address the questions they wish to answer. No method is inherently superior to another. Rather, the choice of method is made after considering the problem under investigation, ethics, cost and time constraints, and issues associated with the three types of validity. In the remainder of this book, many specific methods will be discussed, all of which are useful under different circumstances. In fact, all are necessary to understand the wide variety of behaviors that are of interest to behavioral scientists. Complete understanding of any problem or issue requires research using a variety of methodological approaches.

ILLUSTRATIVE ARTICLE: STUDYING BEHAVIOR

Many people have had the experience of anticipating something bad happening to them: "I'm not going to get that job" or "I'm going to fail this test" or "She'll laugh in my face if I ask her out!" Do you think that anticipating a negative outcome means that a person is less distressed when a negative outcome occurs? That is, is it better to think "I'm going to fail" if, indeed, you may fail?

In a study published by Golub, Gilbert, and Wilson (2009), two experiments and a field study were conducted in an effort to determine whether this negative expectation is a good thing or a bad thing.

In the two laboratory studies, participants were asked to complete a personality assessment and were then led to have either positive, negative, or no expectations about the results. Participants' affective (emotional) state was assessed prior to—and directly after—hearing a negative (in the case of study 1a) or positive (in the case of study 1b) outcome. In the field study, participants were undergraduate introductory psychology students who were asked about their expectations of their performance in an upcoming exam. Then, a day after the exam, positive and negative emotion was assessed. Taken together, the results of these three studies suggest that anticipating bad outcomes may be an ineffective path to positive emotion.

First, acquire and read the article:

Golub, S. A., Gilbert, D. T., & Wilson, T. D. (2009). Anticipating one's troubles: The costs and benefits of negative expectations. *Emotion, 9*, 227–281. doi:10.1037/a0014716

Then, after reading the article, consider the following:

1. For each of the studies, how did Golub, Gilbert, and Wilson (2009) operationally define the *positive expectations*? How did they operationally define *affect*?
2. In experiments 1a and 1b, what were the independent variable(s)? What where the dependent variable(s)?
3. This article includes three different studies. In this case, what are the advantages to answering the research question using multiple methods?
4. On what basis did the authors conclude, "our studies suggest that the affective benefits of negative expectations may be more elusive than their costs" (p. 280)?
5. Evaluate the external validity of the two experiments and one field study that Golub, Gilbert, and Wilson (2009) conducted.
6. How good was the internal validity?

Study Terms

Confounding variable (p. 80)

Construct validity (p. 71)

Correlation coefficient (p. 75)

Curvilinear relationship (p. 72)

Dependent variable (p. 83)

Experimental control (p. 81)

Experimental method (p. 77)

External validity (p. 85)

Field experiment (p. 87)

Independent variable (p. 83)

Internal validity (p. 85)

Negative linear relationship (p. 72)

Nonexperimental method (correlational method) (p. 77)

Operational definition (p. 70)

Participant (subject) variable (p. 88)

Positive linear relationship (p. 72)

Randomization (p. 82)

Third-variable problem (p. 80)

Variable (p. 69)

Review Questions

1. What is a variable? List at least five different variables and then describe at least two levels of each variable. For example, age is a variable. For adults, age has values that can be expressed in years starting at 18 and ranging upward. In an actual study, the age variable might be measured by asking for actual age in years, the year of birth, or providing a choice of age ranges such as 18–34, 35–54, and 55+. Sentence length is a variable. The values might be defined by the number of words in sentences that participants write in an essay.

2. Define "operational definition" of a variable. Give at least two operational definitions of the variables you thought of in the previous review question.

3. Distinguish among positive linear, negative linear, and curvilinear relationships.

4. What is the difference between the nonexperimental method and the experimental method?

5. What is the difference between an independent variable and a dependent variable?

6. Distinguish between laboratory and field experiments.

7. What is meant by the problem of direction of cause and effect and the third-variable problem?

8. How do direct experimental control and randomization influence the possible effects of extraneous variables?

9. What are some reasons for using the nonexperimental method to study relationships between variables?

Activity Questions _____

1. Males and females may differ in their approaches to helping others. For example, males may be more likely to help a person having car trouble, and females may be more likely to bring dinner to a sick friend. Develop two operational definitions for the concept of helping behavior, one that emphasizes the "male style" and the other the "female style." How might the use of one or the other lead to different conclusions from experimental results regarding who helps more, males or females? What does this tell you about the importance of operational definitions?

2. You observe that classmates who get good grades tend to sit toward the front of the classroom, and those who receive poorer grades tend to sit toward the back. What are three possible cause-and-effect relationships for this nonexperimental observation?

3. Consider the hypothesis that stress at work causes family conflict at home.
   a. What type of relationship is proposed (e.g., positive linear, negative linear)?
   b. Graph the proposed relationship.
   c. Identify the independent variable and the dependent variable in the statement of the hypothesis.
   d. How might you investigate the hypothesis using the experimental method?
   e. How might you investigate the hypothesis using the nonexperimental method (recognizing the problems of determining cause and effect)?
   f. What factors might you consider in deciding whether to use the experimental or nonexperimental method to study the relationship between work stress and family conflict?

4. Identify the independent and dependent variables in the following descriptions of experiments:
   a. Students watched a cartoon either alone or with others and then rated how funny they found the cartoon to be.
   b. A comprehension test was given to students after they had studied textbook material either in silence or with the television turned on.
   c. Some elementary school teachers were told that a child's parents were college graduates, and other teachers were told that the child's parents had not finished high school; they then rated the child's academic potential.
   d. Workers at a company were assigned to one of two conditions: One group completed a stress management training program; another group of workers did not participate in the training. The number of sick days taken by these workers was examined for the two subsequent months.

5. A few years ago, newspapers reported a finding that Americans who have a glass of wine a day are healthier than those who have no wine (or who have a lot of wine or other alcohol). What are some plausible alternative explanations for this finding; that is, what variables other than wine could explain the finding? (Hint: What sorts of people in the United States are most likely to have a glass of wine with dinner?)

6. The limitations of nonexperimental research were dramatically brought to the attention of the public by the results of an experiment on the effects of postmenopausal hormone replacement therapy (part of a larger study known as the Women's Health Initiative). An experiment is called a *clinical trial* in medical research. In the clinical trial, participants were randomly assigned to receive either the hormone replacement therapy or a placebo (no hormones). The hormone replacement therapy consisted of estrogen plus progestin. In 2002, the investigators concluded that women taking the hormone replacement therapy had a higher incidence of heart disease than did women in the placebo (no hormone) condition. At that point, they stopped the experiment and informed both the participants and the public that they should talk with their physicians about the advisability of this therapy. The finding dramatically contrasted with the results of nonexperimental research in which women taking hormones had a lower incidence of heart disease; in these studies, researchers compared women who were already taking the hormones with women not taking hormones. Why do you think the results were different with the experimental research and the nonexperimental research?

Answers

TABLE 4.1:

positive, negative, curvilinear, negative, positive, positive, curvilinear, negative

FIGURE 4.4:

Independent variable = music condition

Dependent variable = exam scores

Potential confounding variables = use of headphones, music preferences, music volume, music familiarity

5

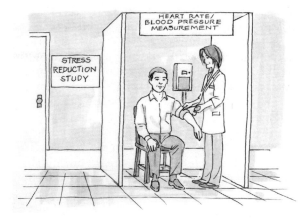

Measurement Concepts

LEARNING OBJECTIVES

- Define *reliability* of a measure of behavior and describe the difference between test-retest, internal consistency, and interrater reliability.
- Discuss ways to establish construct validity, including face validity, content validity, predictive validity, concurrent validity, convergent validity, and discriminant validity.
- Describe the problem of reactivity of a measure of behavior and discuss ways to minimize reactivity.
- Describe the properties of the four scales of measurement: nominal, ordinal, interval, and ratio.

We learn about behavior through careful measurement. As we discussed in Chapter 4, behavior can be measured in many ways. The most common measurement strategy is to ask people to tell you about themselves: How many times have you argued with your spouse in the past week? How would you rate your overall happiness? How much did you like your partner in this experiment? Of course, you can also directly observe behaviors. How many errors did someone make on a task? Will people that you approach in a shopping mall give you change for a dollar? How many times did a person smile during an interview? Physiological and neurological responses can be measured as well. How much did heart rate change while working on the problems? Did muscle tension increase during the interview? There is an endless supply of fascinating behaviors that can be studied. We will describe various methods of measuring variables at several points in subsequent chapters. In this chapter, however, we explore the technical aspects of measurement. We need to consider reliability, validity, and reactivity of measures. We will also consider scales of measurement.

RELIABILITY OF MEASURES

Reliability refers to the consistency or stability of a measure of behavior. Your everyday definition of reliability is quite close to the scientific definition. For example, you might say that Professor Fuentes is "reliable" because she begins class exactly at 10 a.m. each day; in contrast, Professor Fine might be called "unreliable" because, although she sometimes begins class exactly on the hour, on any given day she may appear anytime between 10 and 10:20 a.m.

Similarly, a reliable measure of a psychological variable such as intelligence will yield the same result each time you administer the intelligence test to the same person. The test would be unreliable if it measured the same person as average one week, low the next, and bright the next. Put simply, a reliable measure does not fluctuate from one reading to the next. If the measure does fluctuate, there is error in the measurement device.

A more formal way of understanding reliability is to use the concepts of true score and measurement error. Any measure that you make can be thought of as comprising two components: (1) a **true score,** which is the real score on the variable, and (2) **measurement error.** An unreliable measure of intelligence contains considerable measurement error and so does not provide an accurate indication of an individual's true intelligence. In contrast, a reliable measure of intelligence—one that contains little measurement error—will yield an identical (or nearly identical) intelligence score each time the same individual is measured.

To illustrate the concept of reliability further, imagine that you know someone whose "true" intelligence score is 100. Now suppose that you administer an unreliable intelligence test to this person each week for a year. After the year, you calculate the person's average score on the test based on the 52 scores you obtained. Now suppose that you test another friend who also has a true intelligence

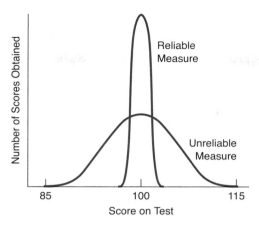

FIGURE 5.1
Comparing data of a reliable and unreliable measure

score of 100; however, this time you administer a highly reliable test. Again, you calculate the average score. What might your data look like? Typical data are shown in Figure 5.1. In each case, the average score is 100. However, scores on the unreliable test range from 85 to 115, whereas scores on the reliable test range from 97 to 103. The *measurement error* in the unreliable test is revealed in the greater variability shown by the person who took the unreliable test.

When conducting research, you can measure each person only once; you can't give the measure 50 or 100 times to discover a true score. Thus, it is very important that you use a reliable measure. Your single administration of the measure should closely reflect the person's true score.

The importance of reliability is obvious. An unreliable measure of length would be useless in building a table; an unreliable measure of a variable such as intelligence is equally useless in studying that variable. Researchers cannot use unreliable measures to systematically study variables or the relationships among variables. Trying to study behavior using unreliable measures is a waste of time because the results will be unstable and unable to be replicated.

Reliability is most likely to be achieved when researchers use careful measurement procedures. In some research areas, this might involve carefully training observers to record behavior; in other areas, it might mean paying close attention to the way questions are phrased or the way recording electrodes are placed on the body to measure physiological reactions. In many areas, reliability can be increased by making multiple measures. This is most commonly seen when assessing personality traits and cognitive abilities. A personality measure, for example, will typically have 10 or more questions (called *items*) designed to assess a trait. Reliability is increased when the number of items increases.

How can we assess reliability? We cannot directly observe the true score and error components of an actual score on the measure. However, we can assess the stability of measures using correlation coefficients. Recall from Chapter 4 that a correlation coefficient is a number that tells us how strongly two variables are related to each other. There are several ways of calculating correlation coefficients; the most common correlation coefficient when discussing reliability is the **Pearson product-moment correlation coefficient.** The Pearson correlation coefficient (symbolized as r) can range from 0.00 to $+1.00$ and 0.00 to -1.00. A correlation of 0.00 tells us that the two variables are not related at all. The closer a correlation is to 1.00, either $+1.00$ or -1.00, the stronger is the relationship. The positive and negative signs provide information about the direction of the relationship. When the correlation coefficient is positive (a plus sign), there is a positive linear relationship—high scores on one variable are associated with high scores on the second variable. A negative linear relationship is indicated by a minus sign—high scores on one variable are associated with low scores on the second variable. The Pearson correlation coefficient will be discussed further in Chapter 12.

To assess the reliability of a measure, we will need to obtain at least two scores on the measure from many individuals. If the measure is reliable, the two scores should be very similar; a Pearson correlation coefficient that relates the two scores should be a high positive correlation. When you read about reliability, the correlation will usually be called a *reliability coefficient.* Let's examine specific methods of assessing reliability.

Test-Retest Reliability

Test-retest reliability is assessed by measuring the same individuals at two points in time. For example, the reliability of a test of intelligence could be assessed by giving the measure to a group of people on one day and again a week later. We would then have two scores for each person, and a correlation coefficient could be calculated to determine the relationship between the first test score and the retest score. Recall that high reliability is indicated by a high correlation coefficient showing that the two scores are very similar. If many people have very similar scores, we conclude that the measure reflects true scores rather than measurement error. It is difficult to say how high the correlation should be before we accept the measure as reliable, but for most measures the reliability coefficient should probably be at least .80.

Given that test-retest reliability requires administering the same test twice, the correlation might be artificially high because the individuals remember how they responded the first time. Alternate forms reliability is sometimes used to avoid this problem; it requires administering two different forms of the same test to the same individuals at two points in time.

Intelligence is a variable that can be expected to stay relatively constant over time; thus, we expect the test-retest reliability for intelligence to be very high. However, some variables may be expected to change from one test period to the next. For example, a mood scale designed to measure a person's current mood state is a measure that might easily change from one test period to another, and so test-retest reliability might not be appropriate. On a more practical level, obtaining two measures from the same people at two points in time may sometimes be difficult. To address these issues, researchers have devised methods to assess reliability without two separate assessments.

Internal Consistency Reliability

It is possible to assess reliability by measuring individuals at only one point in time. We can do this because most psychological measures are made up of a number of different questions, called *items*. An intelligence test might have 100 items, a measure of extraversion might have 15 items, or a multiple-choice examination in a class might have 50 items. A person's test score would be based on the total of his or her responses on all items. In the class, an exam consists of a number of questions about the material, and the total score is the number of correct answers. An extraversion measure might ask people to agree or disagree with items such as "I enjoy the stimulation of a lively party." An individual's extraversion score is obtained by finding the total number of such items that are endorsed. Recall that reliability increases with increasing numbers of items.

Internal consistency reliability is the assessment of reliability using responses at only one point in time. Because all items measure the same variable, they should yield similar or consistent results. One indicator of internal consistency is **split-half reliability;** this is the correlation of the total score on one half of the test with the total score on the other half. The two halves are created by randomly dividing the items into two parts. The actual calculation of a split-half reliability coefficient is a bit more complicated because the final measure will include items from both halves. Thus, the combined measure will have more items and will be more reliable than either half by itself. This fact must be taken into account when calculating the reliability coefficient; the corrected reliability is termed the *Spearman-Brown split-half reliability coefficient.*

Split-half reliability is relatively straightforward and easy to calculate, even without a computer. One drawback is that it is based on only one of many possible ways of dividing the measure into halves. Another commonly used indicator of reliability based on internal consistency, called **Cronbach's alpha,** provides us with the average of all possible split-half reliability coefficients. To actually perform the calculation, scores on each item are correlated with scores on every other item. A large number of correlation coefficients are produced; you would only want to do this with a computer! The value of Cronbach's alpha is based on the average of all the inter-item correlation coefficients and the number of items in the measure. Again, you should note that more items will be associated with higher reliability.

It is also possible to examine the correlation of each item score with the total score based on all items. Such **item-total correlations** are very informative because they provide information about each individual item. Items that do not correlate with the total score on the measure are actually measuring a different variable; they can be eliminated to increase internal consistency reliability. This information is also useful when it is necessary to construct a brief version of a measure. Even though reliability increases with longer measures, a shorter version can be more convenient to administer and still retain acceptable reliability.

Interrater Reliability

In some research, raters observe behaviors and make ratings or judgments. To do this, a rater uses instructions for making judgments about the behaviors—for example, by rating whether a child's behavior on a playground is aggressive and how aggressive is the behavior. You could have one rater make judgments about aggression, but the single observations of one rater might be unreliable. The solution to this problem is to use at least two raters who observe the same behavior. **Interrater reliability** is the extent to which raters agree in their observations. Thus, if two raters are judging whether behaviors are aggressive, high interrater reliability is obtained when most of the observations result in the same judgment. A commonly used indicator of interrater reliability is called *Cohen's Kappa*.

The methods of assessing reliability are summarized in Figure 5.2.

Reliability and Accuracy of Measures

Reliability is clearly important when researchers develop measures of behavior. Reliability is not the only characteristic of a measure or the only thing that researchers worry about. Reliability tells us about measurement error but it does not tell us about whether we have a good measure of the variable of interest. To

---

Test-Retest Reliability

- A measure is taken two times. The correlation of a score at time 1 with the score at time 2 represents *test-retest reliability*.

Internal Consistency Reliability

- *Cronbach's Alpha*: Correlation of each item on the measure with every other item on the measure is the Cronbach's Alpha reliability coefficient.
- *Split-Half Reliability*: The correlation of total score on half of a measure with the score on the other half of the measure represents split-half reliability.

Interrater Reliability

- Evidence for reliablity is present when multiple raters agree in their observations of the same thing. *Cohen's Kappa* is a commonly used indicator of *interrater reliability*.

FIGURE 5.2
Three strategies for assessing reliability

use a silly example, suppose you want to measure intelligence. The measure you develop looks remarkably like the device that is used to measure shoe size at your local shoe store. You ask your best friend to place one foot in the device, and you use the gauge to measure their intelligence. Numbers on the device provide a scale of intelligence so you can immediately assess a person's intelligence level. Will these numbers result in a reliable measure of intelligence? The answer is that they will! Consider what a test-retest reliability coefficient would be. If you administer the "foot intelligence scale" on Monday, it will be almost the same the following Monday; the test-retest reliability is high. But is this an accurate measure of intelligence? Obviously, the scores have nothing to do with intelligence; just because the device is labeled an intelligence test does not mean that it is a *good* measure of intelligence.

Let's consider a less silly example. Suppose your neighborhood gas station pump puts the same amount of gas in your car every time you purchase a gallon (or liter) of fuel; the gas pump gauge is reliable. However, the issue of accuracy is still open. The only way you can know about accuracy of the pump is to compare the gallon (or liter) you receive with some standard measure. In fact, states have inspectors responsible for comparing the amount that the pump says is a gallon with an exact gallon measure. A pump with a gauge that does not deliver what it says must be repaired or replaced. This difference between the reliability and accuracy of measures leads us to a consideration of the validity of measures.

CONSTRUCT VALIDITY OF MEASURES

If something is valid, it is "true" in the sense that it is supported by available evidence. The amount of gasoline that the gauge indicates should match some standard measure of liquid volume; a measure of a personality characteristic such as shyness should be an accurate indicator of that trait. Recall from Chapter 4 that **construct validity** concerns whether our methods of studying variables are accurate. That is, it refers to the adequacy of the operational definition of variables. To what extent does the operational definition of a variable actually reflect the true theoretical meaning of the variable? In terms of measurement, construct validity is a question of whether the measure that is employed actually measures the construct it is intended to measure. Applicants for some jobs are required to take a Clerical Ability Test; this measure is supposed to predict an individual's clerical ability. The validity of such a test is determined by whether it actually does measure this ability. A measure of shyness is an operational definition of the shyness variable; the validity of this measure is determined by whether it does measure this construct.

Indicators of Construct Validity

Face validity   How do we know that a measure is valid? Ways that we can assess validity are summarized in Table 5.1. Construct validity information is gathered through a variety of methods. The simplest way to argue that a measure

TABLE 5.1   Indicators of construct validity of a measure

Validity	Definition	Example
Face Validity	The content of the measure appears to reflect the construct being measured.	If the new measure of depression includes items like "I feel sad" or "I feel down" or "I cry a lot," then it would have evidence for being face-valid.
Content Validity	The content of the measure is linked to the universe of content that defines the construct.	Depression is defined by a mood and by cognitive and physiological symptoms. If the new measure of depression was content-valid, it would include items from each of these domains.
Predictive Validity	Scores on the measure predict behavior on a criterion measured at a future time.	If the measure of depression predicts future diagnosis of depression, then it would have evidence of predictive validity.
Concurrent Validity	Scores on the measure are related to a criterion measured at the same time (concurrently).	If two groups of participants were given the measures, and they differed in predictable ways (e. g, if those in therapy for depression scored higher than those in therapy for an anxiety disorder), then this would be evidence for concurrent validity.
Convergent Validity	Scores on the measure are related to other measures of the same construct.	If scores from the new measure, collected at the same time as other measures of depression (e.g., Beck Depression Inventory or Duke Anxiety-Depression Scale), were related to scores from those other measures, then it could be said to have evidence for convergent validity.
Discriminant Validity	Scores on the measure are not related to other measures that are theoretically different.	If the new measure, collected at the same time as other measures of anxiety (e.g., state/trait anxiety), was unrelated to those measures, then it could be said to have evidence for discriminant validity because it would indicate that what was being measured was *not* anxiety.

is valid is to suggest that the measure appears to accurately assess the intended variable. This is called **face validity**—the evidence for validity is that the measure appears "on the face of it" to measure what it is supposed to measure. Face validity is not very sophisticated; it involves only a judgment of whether, given the theoretical definition of the variable, the content of the measure appears to actually measure the variable. That is, do the procedures used to measure the variable appear to be an accurate operational definition of the theoretical variable? Thus, a measure of a variable such as shyness will usually appear to measure that variable. A measure of shyness called the Shy Q (Bortnik, Henderson, & Zimbardo, 2002) includes items such as "I often feel insecure in social situations" but does not include an item such as "I learned to ride a bicycle at an early age"—the first item appears to be more closely related to shyness than does the second one. Note that the assessment of validity here is a very subjective, intuitive process. A way to improve the process somewhat is to systematically seek out experts in the field to make the face validity determination.

In either case, face validity is not sufficient to conclude that a measure is in fact valid. Appearance is not a very good indicator of accuracy. Some very poor measures may have face validity; for example, most personality measures that appear in popular magazines typically have several questions that look reasonable but often don't tell you anything meaningful. The interpretations of the scores may make fun reading, but there is no empirical evidence to support the conclusions that are drawn in the article. In addition, many good measures of variables do not have obvious face validity. For example, is it obvious that rapid eye movement during sleep is a measure of dreaming?

Content validity

Content validity is based on comparing the content of the measure with the universe of content that defines the construct. For example, a measure of depression would have content that links to each of the symptoms that define the depression construct. Or consider a measure of "knowledge of psychology" that could be administered to graduating seniors at your college. In this case, the faculty would need to define a universe of content that constitutes this knowledge. The measure would then have to reflect that universe. Thus, if classical conditioning is one of the content areas that defines knowledge of psychology, questions relating to this topic will be included in the measure.

Both face validity and content validity focus on assessing whether the content of a measure reflects the meaning of the construct being measured. Other indicators of validity rely on research that examines how scores on a measure relate to other measures of behavior. In validity research, the behavior is termed a *criterion*. These validity indicators are predictive validity, concurrent validity, convergent validity, and discriminant validity.

Predictive validity

Research that uses a measure to predict some future behavior is using **predictive validity.** Thus, with predictive validity, the criterion measure is based on future behavior or outcomes. Predictive validity is clearly important when studying measures that are designed to improve our ability to make predictions. A Clerical Ability Test is intended to provide a fast way to predict future performance in a clerical position. Similarly, many college students take the Graduate Record Exam (GRE), which was developed to predict success in graduate programs, or the Law School Admissions Test (LSAT), developed to predict success in law school. The construct validity of such measures is demonstrated when scores on the measure predict the future behaviors. For example, predictive validity of the LSAT is demonstrated when research shows that people who score high on the test do better in law school than people who score low on the test (i.e., there is a positive relationship between the test score and grades in law school). The measure can be used to advise people on whether they are likely to succeed in law school or to select applicants for law school admission.

Concurrent validity   **Concurrent validity** is demonstrated by research that examines the relationship between the measure and a criterion behavior at the same time (concurrently). Research using the concurrent validity approach can take many forms. A common method is to study whether two or more groups of people differ on the measure in expected ways. Suppose you have a measure of shyness. Your theory of shyness might lead you to expect that salespeople whose job requires making cold calls to potential customers would score lower on the shyness measure than salespeople in positions in which potential customers must make the effort to contact the company themselves.

Another approach to concurrent validity is to study how people who score either low or high on the measure behave in different situations. For example, you could ask people who score high versus low on the shyness scale to describe themselves to a stranger while you measure their level of anxiety. Here you would expect that the people who score high on the shyness scale would exhibit higher amounts of anxiety.

Convergent validity   Any given measure is a particular operational definition of the variable being measured. Often there will be other operational definitions—other measures—of the same or similar constructs. **Convergent validity** is the extent to which scores on the measure in question are related to scores on other measures of the same construct or similar constructs. Measures of similar constructs should converge—for example, one measure of shyness should correlate highly with another shyness measure or a measure of a similar construct such as social anxiety. In actual research on a shyness scale, the convergent validity of the Shy Q was demonstrated by showing that Shy Q scores were highly correlated (.77) with a scale called the Fear of Negative Evaluation (Bortnik et al., 2002). Because the constructs of shyness and fear of negative evaluation have many similarities (such fear is thought to be a component of shyness), the high correlation is expected and increases our confidence in the construct validity of the Shy Q measure.

Discriminant validity   When the measure is *not* related to variables with which it should not be related, **discriminant validity** is demonstrated. The

measure should discriminate between the construct being measured and other unrelated constructs. In research on the discriminant validity of their shyness measure, Bortnik et al. (2002) found no relationship between Shy Q scores and several conceptually unrelated interpersonal values such as valuing forcefulness with others.

REACTIVITY OF MEASURES

A potential problem when measuring behavior is **reactivity.** A measure is said to be reactive if awareness of being measured changes an individual's behavior. A reactive measure tells what the person is like when he or she is aware of being observed, but it doesn't tell how the person would behave under natural circumstances. Simply having various devices such as electrodes and blood pressure cuffs attached to your body may change the physiological responses being recorded. Knowing that a researcher is observing you or recording your behavior on tape might change the way you behave. Measures of behavior vary in terms of their potential reactivity. There are also ways to minimize reactivity, such as allowing time for individuals to become used to the presence of the observer or the recording equipment.

A book by Webb, Campbell, Schwartz, Sechrest, and Grove (1981) has drawn attention to a number of measures that are called *nonreactive* or *unobtrusive*. Many such measures involve clever ways of indirectly recording a variable. For example, an unobtrusive measure of preferences for paintings in an art museum is the frequency with which tiles around each painting must be replaced—the most popular paintings are the ones with the most tile wear. Levine (1990) studied the pace of life in cities, using indirect measures such as the accuracy of bank clocks and the speed of processing standard requests at post offices to measure pace of life. Some of the measures described by Webb et al. (1981) are simply humorous. For instance, in 1872, Sir Francis Galton studied the efficacy of prayer in producing long life. Galton wondered whether British royalty, who were frequently the recipients of prayers by the populace, lived longer than other people. He checked death records and found that members of royal families actually led shorter lives than other people, such as men of literature and science. The book by Webb and his colleagues is a rich source of such nonreactive measures. More important, it draws attention to the problem of reactivity and sensitizes researchers to the need to reduce reactivity whenever possible. We will return to this issue at several points in this book.

VARIABLES AND MEASUREMENT SCALES

Every variable that is studied must be operationally defined. The operational definition is the specific method used to manipulate or measure the variable (see Chapter 4). There must be at least two values or levels of the variable. In

Chapter 4, we mentioned that the values may be quantitatively different or they may reflect categorical differences. In actuality, the world is a bit more complex. The levels can be conceptualized as a scale that uses one of four kinds of measurement scales: nominal, ordinal, interval, and ratio (summarized in Table 5.2).

Nominal Scales

Nominal scales have no numerical or quantitative properties. Instead, categories or groups simply differ from one another (sometimes nominal variables are called "categorical" variables). An obvious example is the variable of gender. A person is classified as either male or female. Being male does not imply a greater amount of "sexness" than being female; the two levels are merely different. This is called a nominal scale because we simply assign names to different categories. Another example is the classification of undergraduates according to major. A psychology major would not be entitled to a higher number than a history major, for instance. Even if you were to assign numbers to the different categories, the numbers would be meaningless, except for identification.

In an experiment, the independent variable is often a nominal or categorical variable. For example, Hölzel et al. (2011) studied the effect of meditation

TABLE 5.2   Scales of measurement

Scale	Description	Examples	Distinction
Nominal	Categories with no numeric scales	Males/females Introverts/extroverts	Impossible to define any quantitative values and/or differences between/across categories
Ordinal	Rank ordering Numeric values limited	2-, 3-, and 4-star restaurants Ranking TV programs by popularity	Intervals between items not known
Interval	Numeric properties are literal Assume equal interval between values	Intelligence Aptitude test score Temperature (Fahrenheit or Celsius)	No true zero
Ratio	Zero indicates absence of variable measured	Reaction time Weight Age Frequencies of behaviors	Can form ratios (someone weighs twice as much as another person)

on brain structures using magnetic resonant imaging (MRI). They found that, after participants underwent an 8-week mindfulness meditation-based stress reduction program, their specific brain areas increased gray-matter density as compared with other participants who did not take part in the program. The independent variable in this case (participating in the program or not) was clearly nominal because the two levels are merely different; participants either did, or did not, participate in the stress reduction program.

Ordinal Scales

Ordinal scales allow us to rank order the levels of the variable being studied. Instead of having categories that are simply different, as in a nominal scale, the categories can be ordered from first to last. Letter grades are a good example of an ordinal scale. Another example of an ordinal scale is provided by the movie rating system used on a movie review website. Movies on TV are given one, two, three, or four checks, based on these descriptions:

✓ ✓ ✓ ✓	Great! New or old, a classic
✓ ✓ ✓	Good! First rate
✓ ✓	Flawed, but may have some good moments
✓	Poor! Desperation time

The rating system is not a nominal scale because the number of checks is meaningful in terms of a continuum of quality. However, the checks allow us only to rank order the movies. A four-check movie is better than a three-check movie; a three-check movie is better than a two-check movie; and so on. Although we have this quantitative information about the movies, we cannot say that the difference between a one-check and a two-check movie is always the same or that it is equal to the difference between a two-check and a three-check movie. No particular value is attached to the intervals between the numbers used in the rating scale.

Interval and Ratio Scales

In an **interval scale,** the difference between the numbers on the scale is meaningful. Specifically, the intervals between the numbers are equal in size. The difference between 1 and 2 on the scale, for example, is the same as the difference between 2 and 3. Interval scales generally have five or more quantitative levels.

A household thermometer (Fahrenheit or Celsius) measures temperature on an interval scale. The difference in temperature between 40° and 50° is equal to the difference between 70° and 80°. However, there is no absolute zero on the scale that would indicate the *absence* of temperature. The zero on any interval scale is only an arbitrary reference point. (Note that the zero point on the Celsius scale was chosen to reflect the temperature at which water freezes; this is the same as 32 degrees on the Fahrenheit scale. The zero on both scales is arbitrary, and there are even negative numbers on the scale.) Without an absolute zero point on interval scales, we cannot form ratios of the numbers. That is, we cannot say that one number on the scale represents twice as much (or three times as much, and so forth) temperature as another number. You cannot say, for example, that 60° is twice as warm as 30°.

An example of an interval scale in the behavioral sciences might be a personality measure of a trait such as extraversion. If the measurement is an interval scale, we cannot make a statement such as "the person who scored 20 is twice as extraverted as the person who scored 10" because there is no absolute zero point that indicates an absence of the trait being measured.

Ratio scales do have an absolute zero point that indicates the absence of the variable being measured. Examples include many physical measures, such as length, weight, or time. With a ratio scale, such statements as "a person who weighs 220 pounds weighs twice as much as a person who weighs 110 pounds" or "participants in the experimental group responded twice as fast as participants in the control group" are possible.

Ratio scales are used in the behavioral sciences when variables that involve physical measures are being studied—particularly time measures such as reaction time, rate of responding, and duration of response. However, many variables in the behavioral sciences are less precise and so use nominal, ordinal, or interval scale measures. It should also be noted that the statistical tests for interval and ratio scales are the same.

The Importance of the Measurement Scales

When you read about the operational definitions of variables, you'll recognize the levels of the variable in terms of these types of scales. The conclusions one draws about the meaning of a particular score on a variable depend on which type of scale was used. With interval and ratio scales, you can make quantitative distinctions that allow you to talk about amounts of the variable. With nominal scales, there is no quantitative information. To illustrate, suppose you are studying perceptions of physical attractiveness. In an experiment, you might show participants pictures of people with different characteristics such as their waist-to-hip ratio (waist size divided by hip size); this variable has been studied extensively by Singh and his colleagues (see Singh, Dixon, Jessop, Morgan, & Dixon, 2010). How should you measure the participants' physical attractiveness judgments? You could use a nominal scale such as:

_____ Not Attractive _____ Attractive

These scale values allow participants to state whether they find the person attractive or not, but do not allow you to know about the amount of attractiveness. As an alternative, you could use a scale that asks participants to rate amount of attractiveness:

Very Unattractive ____ ____ ____ ____ ____ ____ ____ Very Attractive

This rating scale provides you with quantitative information about amount of attractiveness because you can assign numeric values to each of the response options on the scale; in this case, the values would range from 1 to 7. A major finding of Singh's research is that males rate females with a .70 waist-to-hip ratio as most attractive. Singh interprets this finding in terms of evolutionary theory—this ratio presumably is a signal of reproductive capacity.

The scale that is used also determines the types of statistics that are appropriate when the results of a study are analyzed. For now, we do not need to worry about statistical analysis. However, we will return to this point in Chapter 12.

RESEARCH ON PERSONALITY AND INDIVIDUAL DIFFERENCES

Although reliability and validity are important characteristics of all measures, systematic and detailed research on validity is most often carried out on measures of personality and individual differences. Psychologists study psychological attributes such as intelligence, self-esteem, extraversion, and depression; they also measure abilities, attributes, and potential. They study compatibility of couples and cognitive abilities of children. Some research is aimed at informing us about basic personality processes. For example, Costa and McCrae (1985) developed the NEO Personality Inventory (NEO-PI) to measure five major dimensions of personality: neuroticism, extraversion, openness to experience, agreeableness, and conscientiousness. Other measures are important in applied settings. Clinical, counseling, and personnel psychologists use measures to help make better clinical diagnoses (e.g., MMPI-II), career choice decisions (e.g., Vocational Interest Inventory), and hiring decisions.

When you are interested in doing research in these areas, it is usually wise to use existing measures of psychological characteristics rather than develop your own. Existing measures have reliability and validity data to help you decide which measure to use. You will also be able to compare your findings with prior research that uses the measure. Many existing measures are owned and distributed by commercial test publishers and are primarily used by professional psychologists in applied settings such as schools and clinical practices. Many other measures are freely available for researchers to use in basic research investigations. Sources of information about psychological tests include the *Mental Measurements Yearbook,* which you can search online in many libraries, and this FAQ: www.apa.org/science/programs/testing/find-tests.aspx.

We are now ready to consider methods for measuring behavior. A variety of observational methods are described in Chapter 6. We will then focus on questionnaires and interviews in Chapter 7.

ILLUSTRATIVE ARTICLE: MEASUREMENT CONCEPTS

Every term, millions of students complete course evaluations in an effort to assess the quality and performance of their instructors. This specific measurement instrument can vary from campus to campus, but the overall goal is the same. Course evaluations are used to inform hiring decisions, promotion decisions, and classroom instruction decisions, and they are also used by individual instructors to improve the courses that they teach.

Brown (2008) was interested in student perceptions of course evaluations. He collected data from 80 undergraduates enrolled in an undergraduate research methods course and examined their perceptions of student evaluations of teaching, of mid-semester evaluations, and of the effectiveness of completing mid-semester evaluations.

He found, among other things, that although participants believed that students are honest in their evaluations and that the evaluations are important in hiring decisions, they were less sure that instructors took the evaluations seriously and also tended to believe that students evaluate courses based on the grade that they get, or to "get back" at instructors.

For this exercise, acquire, and read, the following article:

Brown, M. (2008). Student perceptions of teaching evaluations. *Journal of Instructional Psychology, 35*(2), 177–181.

After reading the article, consider the following:

1. Brown (2008) did not report any reliability data for his measures. How would you suggest that he go about assessing the reliability of his measures?

2. In the context of evaluating college teaching, how would you describe the construct validity of course evaluation measures generally (or the specific tool that is used on your campus)? That is, how well do student evaluations truly assess the construct of course quality? Specifically, how would you assess the content, predictive, concurrent, convergent, and discriminant validity of student course evaluation measures?

3. Brown did not report any validity information for his measures of participant perceptions. Assess the face validity of his measures.

4. Do you think that Brown's measures are reactive? How so? Likewise, do you think that course evaluations are reactive? How so?

5. Describe the level of measurement used in Brown's study. Generate two alternative strategies for measurement that would occur at different levels.

Study Terms

Concurrent validity (p. 104)
Construct validity (p. 101)
Content validity (p. 103)
Convergent validity (p. 104)
Cronbach's alpha (p. 99)
Discriminant validity (p. 104)
Face validity (p. 103)
Internal consistency reliability (p. 99)
Interrater reliability (p. 100)
Interval scale (p. 107)
Item-total correlation (p. 99)
Measurement error (p. 96)

Nominal scale (p. 106)
Ordinal scale (p. 107)
Pearson product-moment correlation coefficient (p. 98)
Predictive validity (p. 103)
Ratio scale (p. 108)
Reactivity (p. 105)
Reliability (p. 96)
Split-half reliability (p. 99)
Test-retest reliability (p. 98)
True score (p. 96)

Review Questions

1. What is meant by the reliability of a measure? Distinguish between true score and measurement error.
2. Describe the methods of determining the reliability of a measure.
3. Discuss the concept of construct validity. Distinguish among the indicators of construct validity.
4. Why isn't face validity sufficient to establish the validity of a measure?
5. What is a reactive measure?
6. Distinguish between nominal, ordinal, interval, and ratio scales.

Activity Questions

1. Conduct a PsycINFO search to find information on the construct validity of a psychological measure. Specify *construct validity* as a search term along with terms such as *aptitude test, personality test, intelligence test,* and so on. You can also specify particular psychological constructs such as *depression, self-esteem,* or *extraversion.* Read about a measure that interests you and describe the reliability and validity research reported.
2. Here are a number of references to variables. For each, identify whether a nominal, ordinal, interval, or ratio scale is being used:
    a. The temperatures in cities throughout the country that are listed in most newspapers.

    b. The birth weights of babies who were born at Wilshire General Hospital last week.

    c. The number of hours you spent studying each day during the past week.

    d. The amount of the tips left after each meal at a restaurant during a 3-hour period.

    e. The number of votes received by the Republican and Democratic candidates for Congress in your district in the last election.

    f. The brand listed third in a consumer magazine's ranking of DVD players.

    g. Connecticut's listing as the number one team in a poll of sportswriters, with Kansas listed number two.

    h. Your friend's score on an intelligence test.

    i. Yellow walls in your office and white walls in your boss's office.

    j. The type of programming on each radio station in your city (e.g., KPSY plays jazz, KSOC is talk radio).

    k. Ethnic group categories of people in a neighborhood.

3. Take a personality test on the Internet (you can find such tests using Internet search engines). Based on the information provided, what can you conclude about the test's reliability, construct validity, and reactivity?

4. Think of an important characteristic that you would look for in a potential romantic partner, such as humorous, intelligent, attractive, hardworking, religious, and so on. How might you measure that characteristic? Describe two methods that you might use to assess construct validity.

Observational Methods

LEARNING OBJECTIVES

■ Compare quantitative and qualitative methods of describing behavior.

■ Describe naturalistic observation and discuss methodological issues such as participation and concealment.

■ Describe systematic observation and discuss methodological issues such as the use of equipment, reactivity, reliability, and sampling.

■ Describe the features of a case study.

■ Describe archival research and the sources of archival data: statistical records, survey archives, and written records.

A ll scientific research requires careful observation. In this chapter, we will explore a variety of observational methods including observing behavior in natural settings, asking people to describe their behavior (self-report), and examining existing records of behavior, such as census data or hospital records. Because so much research involves surveys using questionnaires or interviews, we cover the topic of survey research separately in Chapter 7. Before we describe these methods in detail, it will be helpful to understand the distinction between quantitative and qualitative methods of describing behavior.

QUANTITATIVE AND QUALITATIVE APPROACHES

Observational methods can be broadly classified as primarily quantitative or qualitative. Qualitative research focuses on people behaving in natural settings and describing their world in their own words; quantitative research tends to focus on specific behaviors that can be easily quantified (i.e., counted). Qualitative researchers emphasize collecting in-depth information on a relatively few individuals or within a very limited setting; quantitative investigations generally include larger samples. The conclusions of qualitative research are based on interpretations drawn by the investigator; conclusions in quantitative research are based upon statistical analysis of data.

To more concretely understand the distinction, imagine that you are interested in describing the ways in which the lives of teenagers are affected by working. You might take a quantitative approach by developing a questionnaire that you would ask a sample of teenagers to complete. You could ask about the number of hours they work, the type of work they do, their levels of stress, their school grades, and their use of drugs. After assigning numerical values to the responses, you could subject the data to a quantitative, statistical analysis. A quantitative description of the results would focus on such things as the percentage of teenagers who work and the way this percentage varies by age. Some of the results of this type of survey are described in Chapter 7.

Suppose, instead, that you take a qualitative approach to describing behavior. You might conduct a series of focus groups in which you gather together groups of 8 to 10 teenagers and engage them in a discussion about their perceptions and experiences with the world of work. You would ask them to tell you about the topic using their own words and their own ways of thinking about the world. To record the focus group discussions, you might use a video- or audiotape recorder and have a transcript prepared later, or you might have observers take detailed notes during the discussions. A qualitative description of the findings would focus on the themes that emerge from the discussions and the manner in which the teenagers conceptualized the issues. Such description is qualitative because it is expressed in nonnumerical terms using language and images.

Other methods, both qualitative and quantitative, could also be used to study teenage employment. For example, a quantitative study could examine data collected from the state Department of Economic Development; a qualitative researcher might work in a fast-food restaurant as a management trainee. Keep in mind the distinction between quantitative and qualitative approaches to describing behavior as you read about other specific observational methods discussed in this chapter. Both approaches are valuable and provide us with different ways of understanding behavior.

NATURALISTIC OBSERVATION

Naturalistic observation is sometimes called *field work* or simply *field observation* (see Lofland, Snow, Anderson, & Lofland, 2006). In a **naturalistic observation** study, the researcher makes observations of individuals in their natural environments (the field). This research approach has roots in anthropology and the study of animal behavior and is currently widely used in the social sciences to study many phenomena in all types of social and organizational settings. Thus, you may encounter naturalistic observation studies that focus on employees in a business organization, members of a sports team, patrons of a bar, students and teachers in a school, or prairie dogs in a colony in Arizona.

Sylvia Scribner's (1997) research on "practical thinking" is a good example of naturalistic observation research in psychology. Scribner studied ways that people in a variety of occupations make decisions and solve problems. She describes the process of this research: ". . . my colleagues and I have driven around on a 3 a.m. milk route, helped cashiers total their receipts and watched machine operators logging in their production for the day . . . we made detailed records of how people were going about performing their jobs. We collected copies of all written materials they read or produced—everything from notes scribbled on brown paper bags to computer print-outs. We photographed devices in their working environment that required them to process other types of symbolic information—thermometers, gauges, scales, measurement instruments of all kinds" (Scribner, 1997, p. 223). One aspect of thinking that Scribner studied was the way that workers make mathematical calculations. She found that milk truck drivers and other workers make complex calculations that depend on their acquired knowledge. For example, a delivery invoice might require the driver to multiply 32 quarts of milk by $.68 per quart. To arrive at the answer, drivers use knowledge acquired on the job about how many quarts are in a case and the cost of a case; thus, they multiply 2 cases of milk by $10.88 per case. In general, the workers that Scribner observed employed complex but very efficient strategies to solve problems at work. More important, the strategies used could often not be predicted from formal models of problem solving. The Scribner research had a particular emphasis on people making decisions in their everyday environment. Scribner has since expanded her research to several different occupations and many types of decisions.

Other naturalistic research may examine a narrower range of behaviors. For example, Graham and her colleagues observed instances of aggression that occurred in bars in a large city late on weekend nights (Graham, Tremblay, Wells, Pernanen, Purcell, & Jelley, 2006). Both the Scribner and the Graham studies are instances of naturalistic research because the observations were made in natural settings and the researchers did not attempt to influence what occurred in the settings.

Description and Interpretation of Data

The goal of naturalistic observation is to provide a complete and accurate picture of what occurred in the setting, rather than to test hypotheses formed prior to the study. To achieve this goal, the researcher must keep detailed field notes—that is, write or dictate on a regular basis (at least once each day) everything that has happened. Field researchers rely on a variety of techniques to gather information, depending on the particular setting. In the Graham et al. (2006) study in bars, the observers were alert to any behaviors that might lead to an incident of aggression. They carefully watched and listened to what happened. They immediately made notes on what they observed; these were later given to a research coordinator. In other studies, the observers might interview key "informants" to provide inside information about the setting, talk to people about their lives, and examine documents produced in the setting, such as newspapers, newsletters, or memos. In addition to taking detailed field notes, researchers conducting naturalistic observation usually use audio or video recordings.

The researcher's first goal is to describe the setting, events, and persons observed. The second, equally important goal is to analyze what was observed. The researcher must interpret what occurred, essentially generating hypotheses that help explain the data and make them understandable. Such an analysis is done by building a coherent structure to describe the observations. The final report, although sensitive to the chronological order of events, is usually organized around the structure developed by the researcher. Specific examples of events that occurred during observation are used to support the researcher's interpretations.

A good naturalistic observation report will support the analysis by using multiple confirmations. For example, similar events may occur several times, similar information may be reported by two or more people, and several different events may occur that all support the same conclusion.

The data in naturalistic observation studies are primarily *qualitative* in nature; that is, they are the descriptions of the observations themselves rather than *quantitative* statistical summaries. Such qualitative descriptions are often richer and closer to the phenomenon being studied than are statistical representations. However, it is often useful to also gather quantitative data. Depending on the setting, data might be gathered on income, family size, education levels, age, or gender of individuals in the setting. Such data can be reported and interpreted along with qualitative data gathered from interviews and direct observations.

Issues in Naturalistic Observation

Participation and concealment   Two related issues facing the researcher are whether to be a participant or nonparticipant in the social setting and whether to conceal his or her purposes from the other people in the setting. Do you become an active participant in the group or do you observe from the outside? Do you conceal your purposes or even your presence, or do you openly let people know what you are doing?

A nonparticipant observer is an outsider who does not become an active part of the setting. In contrast, a participant observer assumes an active, insider role. Because **participant observation** allows the researcher to observe the setting from the inside, he or she may be able to experience events in the same way as natural participants. Friendships and other experiences of the participant observer may yield valuable data. A potential problem with participant observation, however, is that the observer may lose the objectivity necessary to conduct scientific observation. Remaining objective may be especially difficult when the researcher already belongs to the group being studied or is a dissatisfied former member of the group. Remember that naturalistic observation requires accurate description and objective interpretation with no prior hypotheses. If a researcher has some prior reason to either criticize people in the setting or give a glowing report of a particular group, the observations will likely be biased and the conclusions will lack objectivity.

Should the researcher remain concealed or be open about the research purposes? Concealed observation may be preferable because the presence of the observer may influence and alter the behavior of those being observed. Imagine how a nonconcealed observer might alter the behavior of high school students in many situations at a school. Thus, concealed observation is less reactive than nonconcealed observation because people are not aware that their behaviors are being observed and recorded. Still, nonconcealed observation may be preferable from an ethical viewpoint: Consider the invasion of privacy when researchers hid under beds in dormitory rooms to discover what college students talk about (Henle & Hubbell, 1938)! Also, people often quickly become used to the observer and behave naturally in the observer's presence. This fact allows documentary filmmakers to record very private aspects of people's lives, as was done in the 2009 British documentary *Love, Life, and Death in a Day*. The filmmaker, Sue Bourne, contacted funeral homes to find families willing to be filmed throughout their grieving over the death of a loved one.

The decision of whether to conceal one's purpose or presence depends on both ethical concerns and the nature of the particular group and setting being studied. Sometimes a participant observer is nonconcealed to certain members of the group, who give the researcher permission to be part of the group as a concealed observer. Often a concealed observer decides to say nothing directly about his or her purposes but will completely disclose the goals of the research if asked by anyone. Nonparticipant observers are also not concealed when they gain permission to "hang out" in a setting or use interview techniques to gather information. In actuality, then, there are degrees of participation and concealment: A nonparticipant observer may not become a member of the group, for example, but may over time become accepted as a friend or simply part of the ongoing activities of the group. In sum, researchers who use naturalistic observation to study behavior must carefully determine what their role in the setting will be.

You may be wondering about informed consent in naturalistic observation. Recall from Chapter 3 that observation in public places when anonymity is not threatened is considered exempt research. In these cases, informed consent may not be necessary. Moreover, in nonconcealed observation, informed consent may be given verbally or in written form. Nevertheless, researchers must be sensitive to ethical issues when conducting naturalistic observation. Of particular interest is whether the observations are made in a public place with no clear expectations that behaviors are private. For example, should a neighborhood bar be considered public or private?

Limits of naturalistic observation   Naturalistic observation obviously cannot be used to study all issues or phenomena. The approach is most useful when investigating complex social settings both to understand the settings and to develop theories based on the observations. It is less useful for studying well-defined hypotheses under precisely specified conditions.

Field research is also very difficult to do. Unlike a typical laboratory experiment, field research data collection cannot always be scheduled at a convenient time and place. In fact, field research can be extremely time-consuming, often placing the researcher in an unfamiliar setting for extended periods. In the Graham et al. (2006) investigation of aggression in bars, observers spent over 1,300 nights in 118 different bars (74 male–female pairs of observers were required to accomplish this feat).

Also, in more carefully controlled settings such as laboratory research, the procedures are well defined and the same for each participant, and the data analysis is planned in advance. In naturalistic observation research, however, there is an ever-changing pattern of events, some important and some unimportant; the researcher must record them all and remain flexible in order to adjust to them as research progresses. Finally, the process of analysis that follows the completion of the research is not simple (imagine the task of sorting through the field notes of every incident of aggression that occurred on over 1,300 nights). The researcher must repeatedly sort through the data to develop hypotheses to explain the data and then make sure all data are consistent with the hypotheses. Although naturalistic observation research is a difficult and challenging scientific procedure, it yields invaluable knowledge when done well.

SYSTEMATIC OBSERVATION

Systematic observation refers to the careful observation of one or more specific behaviors in a particular setting. This research approach is much less global than naturalistic observation research. The researcher is interested in only a few very specific behaviors, the observations are quantifiable, and the researcher frequently has developed prior hypotheses about the behaviors.

For example, Bakeman and Brownlee (1980; also see Bakeman, 2000) were interested in the social behavior of young children. Three-year-olds were video-taped in a room in a "free play" situation. Each child was taped for 100 minutes; observers viewed the videotapes and coded each child's behavior every 15 seconds, using the following coding system:

Unoccupied: Child is not doing anything in particular or is simply watching other children.

Solitary play: Child plays alone with toys but is not interested in or affected by the activities of other children.

Together: Child is with other children but is not occupied with any particular activity.

Parallel play: Child plays beside other children with similar toys but does not play with the others.

Group play: Child plays with other children, including sharing toys or participating in organized play activities as part of a group of children.

Bakeman and Brownlee were particularly interested in the sequence or order in which the different behaviors were engaged in by the children. They found, for example, that the children rarely went from being unoccupied to engaging in parallel play. However, they frequently went from parallel to group play, indicating that parallel play is a transition state in which children decide whether to interact in a group situation.

Coding Systems

Numerous behaviors can be studied using systematic observation. The researcher must decide which behaviors are of interest, choose a setting in which the behaviors can be observed, and most important, develop a **coding system,** such as the one described, to measure the behaviors. Rhoades and Stocker (2006) describe the use of the Marital Interaction Video Coding System. Couples are recorded for 10 minutes as they discuss an area of conflict; they then discuss a positive aspect of their relationship for 5 minutes. The video is later coded for hostility and affection displayed during each 5 minutes of the interaction. To code hostility, the observers rated the frequency of behaviors such as "blames other" and "provokes partner." Affection behaviors that were coded included "expresses concern" and "agrees with partner."

Methodological Issues

Equipment   We should briefly mention several methodological issues in systematic observation. The first concerns equipment. You can directly observe behavior and code it at the same time; for example, you could directly observe and record the behavior of children in a classroom or couples interacting on campus using paper-and-pencil measures. However, it is becoming more common to use video recording equipment to make such observations. Video recorders have the advantage of providing a permanent record of the behavior observed that can be coded later. Your observations can be coded on a clipboard; a stopwatch is sometimes useful for recording the duration of events. Alternatively, computer-based recording devices can be used to code the observed behaviors, as well as to keep track of their duration.

Reactivity
A second issue is **reactivity**—the possibility that the presence of the observer will affect people's behaviors (see Chapter 5). Reactivity can be reduced by concealed observation. Using small cameras and microphones can make the observation unobtrusive, even in situations in which the participant has been informed of the recording. Also, reactivity can be reduced by allowing time for people to become used to the observer and equipment.

Reliability
Recall from Chapter 5 that reliability refers to the degree to which a measurement reflects a true score rather than measurement error. Reliable measures are stable, consistent, and precise. When conducting systematic observation, two or more raters are usually used to code behavior. Reliability is indicated by a high agreement among the raters. Very high levels of agreement are reported in virtually all published research using systematic observation (generally 80% agreement or higher). For some large-scale research programs in which many observers will be employed over a period of years, observers are first trained using videotapes, and their observations during training are checked for agreement with results from previous observers.

Sampling
For many research questions, samples of behavior taken over an extended period provide more accurate and useful data than single, short observations. Consider a study on the behaviors of nursing home residents and staff during meals (Stabell, Eide, Solheim, Solberg, and Rustoen, 2004). The researchers were interested in the frequency of different resident behaviors such as independent eating, socially engaged eating, and dependent eating in which help is needed. The staff behaviors included supporting the behaviors of the residents (e.g., assisting, socializing). The researchers could have made observations during a single meal or two meals during a single day. However, such data might be distorted by short-term trends—the particular meal being served, an illness, a recent event such as a death among the residents. The researchers instead sampled behaviors during breakfast and lunch over a period of 6 weeks. Each person was randomly chosen to be observed for a 3-minute period during both meals on 10 of the days of the study. A major finding was that the staff members were most frequently engaged in supporting dependent behavior with little time spent supporting independent behaviors such as socializing. Interestingly, part-time nursing student staff were more likely to support independence.

CASE STUDIES

A **case study** is an observational method that provides a description of an individual. This individual is usually a person, but it may also be a setting such as a business, school, or neighborhood. A naturalistic observation study is sometimes called a case study, and in fact the naturalistic observation and case study approaches sometimes overlap. We have included case studies as a separate category in this chapter because case studies do not necessarily involve naturalistic observation. Instead, the case study may be a description of a patient by a clinical psychologist or a historical account of an event such as a model school that failed. A **psychobiography** is a type of case study in which a researcher applies psychological theory to explain the life of an individual, usually an important historical figure (Schultz, 2005). Thus, case studies may use such techniques as library research and telephone interviews with persons familiar with the case but no direct observation at all (Yin, 2009).

Depending on the purpose of the investigation, the case study may present the individual's history, symptoms, characteristic behaviors, reactions to situations, or responses to treatment. Typically, a case study is done when an individual possesses a particularly rare, unusual, or noteworthy condition. One famous case study involved a man with an amazing ability to recall information (Luria, 1968). The man, called "S.," could remember long lists and passages with ease, apparently using mental imagery for his memory abilities. Luria also described some of the drawbacks of S.'s ability. For example, he frequently had difficulty concentrating because mental images would spontaneously appear and interfere with his thinking. Another case study example concerns language development; it was provided by "Genie," a child who was kept isolated in her room, tied to a chair, and never spoken to until she was discovered at the age of 13½ (Curtiss, 1977). Genie, of course, lacked any language skills. Her case provided psychologists and linguists with the opportunity to attempt to teach her language skills and discover which skills could be learned. Apparently, Genie was able to acquire some rudimentary language skills, such as forming childlike sentences, but she never developed full language abilities.

Individuals with particular types of brain damage can allow researchers to test hypotheses (Stone, Cosmides, Tooby, Kroll, & Knight, 2002). The individual in their study, R.M., had extensive limbic system damage. The researchers were interested in studying the ability to detect cheaters in social exchange relationships. Social exchange is at the core of our relationships: One person provides goods or services for another person in exchange for some other resource. Stone et al. were seeking evidence that social exchange can evolve in a species only when there is a biological mechanism for detecting cheaters; that is, those who do not reciprocate by fulfilling their end of the bargain. R.M. completed two types of reasoning problems. One type involved detecting violations of social exchange rules (e.g., you must fulfill a requirement if you receive a particular benefit); the other type focused on nonsocial precautionary action rules (e.g., you must take this precaution if you engage in a particular hazardous behavior). Individuals with no brain injury do equally well on both types of measures. However, R.M. performed very poorly on the social exchange problems but did well on the precautionary problems, as well as other general measures of cognitive ability. This finding supports the hypothesis that our ability to engage in social exchange relationships is grounded in the development of a biological mechanism that differs from general cognitive abilities.

Case studies are valuable in informing us of conditions that are rare or unusual and thus providing unique data about some psychological phenomenon, such as memory, language, or social exchange. Insights gained through a case study may also lead to the development of hypotheses that can be tested using other methods.

ARCHIVAL RESEARCH

Archival research involves using previously compiled information to answer research questions. The researcher does not actually collect the original data. Instead, he or she analyzes existing data such as statistics that are part of public records (e.g., number of divorce petitions filed), reports of anthropologists, the content of letters to the editor, or information contained in databases. Judd, Smith, and Kidder (1991) distinguish among three types of archival research data: statistical records, survey archives, and written records.

Statistical Records

Statistical records are collected by many public and private organizations. The U.S. Census Bureau maintains the most extensive set of statistical records available, but state and local agencies also maintain such records. In a study using public records, Bushman, Wang, and Anderson (2005) examined the relationship between temperature and aggression. They used temperature data in Minneapolis that was recorded in 3-hour periods in 1987 and 1988; data on assaults were available through police records. They found that higher temperature is related to more aggression; however, this effect was limited to data recorded between 9:00 p.m. and 3:00 a.m.

There are also numerous less obvious sources of statistical records, including public health statistics, test score records kept by testing organizations such as the Educational Testing Service, and even sports organizations. Major League Baseball is known for the extensive records that are kept on virtually every aspect of every game and every player. Abel and Kruger (2010) took advantage of this fact to investigate the relationship between positive emotions and longevity. They began with photographs of 230 major league players published in 1952. The photographs were then rated for smile intensity to provide a measure of emotional positivity. The longevity of players who had died by the end of 2009 was then examined in relation to smile intensity. The results indicated that these two variables are indeed related. Further, ratings of attractiveness were unrelated to longevity.

Survey Archives

Survey archives consist of data from surveys that are stored on computers and available to researchers who wish to analyze them. Major polling organizations make many of their surveys available. Also, many universities are part of the Inter-university Consortium for Political and Social Research (ICPSR; http://www.icpsr.umich.edu/), which makes survey archive data available. One very useful data set is the General Social Survey (GSS; see their website at http://www.norc.uchicago.edu/GSS+Website/), a series of surveys funded by the National Science Foundation. Each survey includes over 200 questions covering a range of topics such as attitudes, life satisfaction, health, religion, education, age, gender, and race. Survey archives are now becoming available via the Internet at sites that enable researchers to analyze the data online. Survey archives are extremely important because most researchers do not have the financial resources to conduct surveys of randomly selected national samples; the archives allow them to access such samples to test their ideas. A study by Robinson and Martin (2009) illustrates how the GSS can be used to test hypotheses. The study examined whether Internet users differed from non-users in their social attitudes. Clearly, the findings would have implications for interpreting the results of surveys conducted via the Internet. The results showed that although Internet users were somewhat more optimistic, there were no systematic differences between those who use and do not use the Internet.

Written and Mass Communication Records

Written records are documents such as diaries and letters that have been preserved by historical societies, ethnographies of other cultures written by anthropologists, and public documents as diverse as speeches by politicians or discussion board messages left by Internet users. Mass communication records include books, magazine articles, movies, television programs, and newspapers.

An example of archival research using such records is a study of 487 anti-smoking ads that was conducted by Rhodes, Roskos-Ewoldsen, Eno, and Monahan (2009). They found that there were an increasing number of ads attacking the tobacco industry over time and that many of the ads emphasized the negative health impact of smoking. However, few ads attacked claims for the benefits of smoking such as stress reduction or preventing weight gain.

Content Analysis of Documents

Content analysis is the systematic analysis of existing documents. Like systematic observation, content analysis requires researchers to devise coding systems that raters can use to quantify the information in the documents. Sometimes the coding is quite simple and straightforward; for example, it is easy to code whether the addresses of the applicants on marriage license applications are the same or different. More often, the researcher must define categories in order to code the information. In the study of smoking ads, researchers had to define categories to describe the ads, for example, *attacks tobacco companies* or *causes cancer*. Similar procedures would be used in studies examining archival documents such as speeches, magazine articles, television shows, and reader comments on articles published on the Internet.

The use of archival data allows researchers to study interesting questions, some of which could not be studied in any other way. Archival data are a valuable supplement to more traditional data collection methods. There are at least two major problems with the use of archival data, however. First, the desired records may be difficult to obtain: They may be placed in long-forgotten storage places, or they may have been destroyed. Second, we can never be completely sure of the accuracy of information collected by someone else.

This chapter has provided a great deal of information about important qualitative and quantitative observational methods that can be used to study a variety of questions about behavior. In the next chapter, we will explore a very common way of finding out about human behavior—simply asking people to use self-reports to tell us about themselves.

ILLUSTRATIVE ARTICLE: OBSERVATIONAL METHODS

Happiness, according to Aristotle, is the most desirable of all things. In the past few decades, many researchers have been studying predictors of happiness in an attempt to understand the construct.

Mehl, Vazire, Holleran, and Clark (2010) conducted a naturalistic observation on the topic of happiness using electronically activated recorders (a device that unobtrusively records snippets of sound at regular intervals, for a fixed amount of time). In this study, 79 undergraduate students wore the device for four days; 30-second recordings were made every 12.5 minutes. Each snippet was coded as having been taken while the participant was alone or with people. If the participant was with somebody, the recordings were also coded for "small talk" and "substantial talk." Other measures administered were well-being and happiness.

First, acquire and read the article:

Mehl, M. R., Vazire, S., Holleran, S. E., & Clark, C. S. (2010). Eavesdropping on happiness: Well-being is related to having less small talk and more substantive conversations. *Psychological Science, 21*, 539–541.

Then, after reading the article, consider the following:

1. What is the research question for this study?
2. Is the basic approach in this study qualitative or quantitative?

3. Is this study an example of concealed or nonconcealed observation? What are the ethical issues present in this study?

4. Do you think that participants would be reactive to this data collection method?

5. How reliable were the coders? How did the authors assess their reliability?

6. How did the researchers operationally define *small talk, substantive talk, well-being,* and *happiness*? What do you think about the quality of these operational definitions?

7. Does this study suffer from the problem involving the direction of causation (p. 79)? How so?

8. Does this study suffer from the third-variable problem (p. 80)? How so?

9. Do you think that this study included any confounding variables? Provide examples.

10. Given the topic of this study, what other ways can you think of to conduct this study using an observational method?

Study Terms

Archival research (p. 122)

Case study (p. 121)

Coding system (p. 119)

Content analysis (p. 123)

Naturalistic observation (p. 115)

Participant observation (p. 117)

Psychobiography (p. 121)

Reactivity (p. 120)

Systematic observation (p. 118)

Review Questions

1. What is naturalistic observation? How does a researcher collect data when conducting naturalistic observation research?

2. Why are the data in naturalistic observation research primarily qualitative?

3. Distinguish between participant and nonparticipant observation; between concealed and nonconcealed observation.

4. What is systematic observation? Why are the data from systematic observation primarily quantitative?

5. What is a coding system? What are some important considerations when developing a coding system?

6. What is a case study? When are case studies used? What is a psychobiography?

7. What is archival research? What are the major sources of archival data?
8. What is content analysis?

Activity Questions

1. Some questions are more readily answered using quantitative techniques, and others are best addressed through qualitative techniques or a combination of both approaches. Suppose you are interested in how a parent's alcoholism affects the life of an adolescent. Develop a research question best answered using quantitative techniques and another research question better suited to qualitative techniques. A quantitative question is, "Are adolescents with alcoholic parents more likely to have criminal records?" and a qualitative question is, "What issues do alcoholic parents introduce in their adolescent's peer relationships?"

2. Devise a simple coding system to do a content analysis of print advertisements in popular magazines. Begin by examining the ads to choose the content dimensions you wish to use (e.g., gender). Apply the system to an issue of a magazine and describe your findings.

3. Read each scenario below and determine whether a case study, naturalistic observation, systematic observation, or archival research was used.

Scenario	Case study	Naturalistic observation	Systematic observation	Archival research
Researchers conducted an in-depth study with certain 9/11 victims to understand the psychological impact of the attack on the World Trade Center in 2001.				
Researchers recorded the time it took drivers in parking lots to back out of a parking stall. They also measured the age and gender of the drivers, and whether another car was waiting for the space.				
Contents of Craigslist personal ads in three major cities were coded to determine whether men and women differ in terms of their self-descriptions.				

(Continued)

Scenario	Case study	Naturalistic observation	Systematic observation	Archival research
The researcher spent over a year meeting with and interviewing Aileen Wuornos, the infamous female serial killer who was the subject of the film *Monster*, to construct a psychobiography.				
Researchers examined unemployment rates and the incidence of domestic violence police calls in six cities.				
A group of researchers studied recycling behavior at three local parks over a 6-month period. They concealed their presence and kept detailed field notes.				

Answers

case study, systematic observation, archival research, case study, archival research, naturalistic observation

7

Asking People About Themselves: Survey Research

LEARNING OBJECTIVES

- Discuss reasons for conducting survey research.
- Identify factors to consider when writing questions for interviews and questionnaires, including defining research objectives and question wording.
- Describe different ways to construct questionnaire responses, including closed-ended questions, open-ended questions, and rating scales.
- Compare the two ways to administer surveys: written questionnaires and oral interviews.
- Define interviewer bias.
- Describe a panel study.
- Distinguish between probability and nonprobability sampling techniques.
- Describe simple random sampling, stratified random sampling, and cluster sampling.
- Describe haphazard sampling, purposive sampling, and quota sampling.
- Describe the ways that samples are evaluated for potential bias, including sampling frame and response rate.

S urvey research employs questionnaires and interviews to ask people to provide information about themselves—their attitudes and beliefs, demographics (age, gender, income, marital status, and so on) and other facts, and past or intended future behaviors. In this chapter we will explore methods of designing and conducting surveys, including sampling techniques.

WHY CONDUCT SURVEYS?

Surveys are a research tool that is used to ask people to tell us about themselves. They have become extremely important as society demands data about issues rather than only intuition and anecdotes.

Surveys are being conducted all the time. Just look at your daily newspaper, local TV news broadcast, or the Internet. The Centers for Disease Control and Prevention is reporting results of a survey of new mothers asking about breastfeeding. A college survey center is reporting the results of a telephone survey asking about political attitudes. If you look around your campus, you will find academic departments conducting surveys of seniors or recent graduates. If you make a major purchase, you will likely receive a request to complete a survey that asks about your satisfaction. If you visit the American Psychological Association website, you can read a report called *Stress in America* that presents the results of an Internet survey of over 1,300 adults that was conducted in 2010.

Surveys are clearly a common and important method of studying behavior. Every university needs data from graduates to help determine changes that should be made to the curriculum and student services. Auto companies want data from buyers to assess and improve product quality and customer satisfaction. Without collecting such data, we are totally dependent upon stories we might hear or letters that a graduate or customer might write. Other surveys can be important for making public policy decisions by lawmakers and public agencies. In basic research, many important variables—including attitudes, current emotional states, and self-reports of behaviors—are most easily studied using questionnaires or interviews.

We often think of survey data providing a snapshot of how people think and behave at a given point in time. However, the survey method is also an important way for researchers to study relationships among variables and ways that attitudes and behaviors change over time. For example, the *Monitoring the Future* project (http://monitoringthefuture.org) has been conducted every year since 1975—its purpose is to monitor the behaviors, attitudes, and values of American high school and college students. Each year, 50,000 8th, 10th, and 12th grade students participate in the survey. Figure 7.1 shows a typical finding: Each line on the graph represents the percentage of survey respondents who reported using marijuana in the past 12 months. Note the trend that shows the peak of marijuana popularity occurring in the late 1970s and the least reported use in the early 1990s.

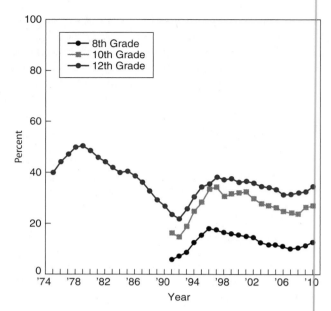

FIGURE 7.1
Percentage of survey respondents who reported using marijuana in the past 12 months, over time.
Adapted from *Monitoring the Future*, http://monitoringthefuture.org/data/10data/fig10_3.pdf

Survey research is also important as a complement to experimental research findings. Recall from Chapter 2 that Winograd and Soloway (1986) conducted experiments on the conditions that lead to forgetting where we place something. To study this topic using survey methods, Brown and Rahhal (1994) asked both younger and older adults about their actual experiences when they hid something and later forgot its location. They reported that older adults take longer than younger adults to find the object and that older adults hide objects from potential thieves, whereas younger people hide things from friends and relatives. Interestingly, most lost objects are eventually found, usually by accident in a location that had been searched previously. This research illustrates a point made in previous chapters that multiple methods are needed to understand any behavior.

An assumption that underlies the use of questionnaires and interviews is that people are willing and able to provide truthful and accurate answers. Researchers have addressed this issue by studying possible biases in the way people respond. A **response set** is a tendency to respond to all questions from a particular perspective rather than to provide answers that are directly related to the questions. Thus, response sets can affect the usefulness of data obtained from self-reports. The most common response set is called social desirability, or "faking good." The social desirability response set leads the individual to answer in the most socially acceptable way—the way that "most people" are perceived to respond or the way that would reflect most favorably on the person. Social desirability can be a problem in many research areas, but it is probably most acute when the question concerns a sensitive topic such as violent or aggressive behavior, substance abuse, or sexual practices. However, it should not be assumed that people consistently misrepresent themselves. If the researcher openly and honestly communicates the purposes and uses of the research, promises to provide feedback about the results, and assures confidentiality, then the participants can reasonably be expected to give honest responses.

We turn now to the major considerations in survey research: constructing the questions that are asked, choosing the methods for presenting the questions, and sampling the individuals taking part in the research.

CONSTRUCTING QUESTIONS TO ASK

A great deal of thought must be given to writing questions for questionnaires and interviews. This section describes some of the most important factors to consider when constructing questions.

Defining the Research Objectives

When constructing questions for a survey, the first thing the researcher must do is explicitly determine the research objectives: What is it that he or she wishes to know? The survey questions must be tied to the research questions that are being addressed. Too often, surveys get out of hand when researchers begin to ask any question that comes to mind about a topic without considering exactly what useful information will be gained by doing so. This process will usually require the researcher to decide on the type of questions to ask. There are three general types of survey questions (Judd, Smith, & Kidder, 1991).

Attitudes and beliefs Questions about attitudes and beliefs focus on the ways that people evaluate and think about issues. Should more money be spent on mental health services? Are you satisfied with the way that police responded to your call? How do you evaluate this instructor?

Facts and demographics Factual questions ask people to indicate things they know about themselves and their situation. In most studies, asking some demographic information is necessary to adequately describe your sample. Age, gender, and ethnicity are typically asked. Depending on the topic of the study, questions on such information as income, marital status, employment status, and number of children might be included. Obviously, if you are interested in making comparisons among groups, such as males and females, you must ask the relevant information about group membership. You may also need such information to adequately describe the sample. It is unwise to ask such questions if you have no real reason to use the information, however.

Other factual information you might ask will depend on the topic of your survey. Each year, *Consumer Reports* magazine asks readers to tell them about the repairs that have been necessary on many of the products that the readers owned, such as cars and dishwashers. Factual questions about illnesses and other medical information would be asked in a survey of health and quality of life.

Behaviors   Other survey questions can focus on past behaviors or intended future behaviors. How many days last week did you exercise for 20 minutes or longer? How many children do you plan to have? Have you ever been so depressed that you called in sick to work?

Question Wording

A great deal of care is necessary to write the very best questions for a survey. Cognitive psychologists have identified a number of potential problems with question wording (see Graesser, Kennedy, Wiemer-Hastings, & Ottati, 1999). Many of the problems stem from a difficulty with understanding the question, including (a) unfamiliar technical terms, (b) vague or imprecise terms, (c) ungrammatical sentence structure, (d) phrasing that overloads working memory, and (e) embedding the question with misleading information. Here is a question that illustrates some of the problems identified by Graesser et al.:

> Did your mother, father, full-blooded sisters, full-blooded brothers, daughters, or sons ever have a heart attack or myocardial infarction?

This is an example of memory overload because of the length of the question and the need to keep track of all those relatives while reading the question. The respondent must also worry about two different diagnoses with regard to each relative. Further, the term *myocardial infarction* may be unfamiliar to most people. How do you write questions to avoid such problems? The following items are important to consider when you are writing questions.

Simplicity   The questions asked in a survey should be relatively simple. People should be able to easily understand and respond to the questions. Avoid jargon and technical terms that people won't understand. Sometimes, however, you have to make the question a bit more complex—or longer—to make it easier to understand. Usually this occurs when you need to define a term or describe an issue prior to asking the question. Thus, before asking whether someone approves of Proposition J, you will probably want to provide a brief description of the content of this ballot measure. Likewise, if you want to know about the frequency of alcohol use in a population, asking, "Have you had a drink of alcohol in the past 30 days?" may generate a slightly different answer than "Have you had a drink of alcohol (meaning one full can of beer, shot of liquor, or glass of wine) in the past 30 days?" The latter case is probably closer to what you would be interested in knowing.

Double-barreled questions   Avoid double-barreled questions that ask two things at once. A question such as "Should senior citizens be given more money for recreation centers and food assistance programs?" is difficult to answer because it taps two potentially very different attitudes. If you are interested in both issues, ask two questions.

Loaded questions   A loaded question is written to lead people to respond in one way. For example, the questions "Do you favor eliminating the wasteful excesses in the public school budget?" and "Do you favor reducing the public school budget?" will likely elicit different answers. Or consider that men are less likely to say they have "raped" someone than that they have "forced sex"; similarly, women are less likely to say they have been raped than forced to have unwanted sex (Koss, 1992). Questions that include emotionally charged words such as *rape, waste, immoral, ungodly,* or *dangerous* may influence the way that people respond and thus lead to biased conclusions.

Negative wording   Avoid phrasing questions with negatives. This question is phrased negatively: "Do you feel that the city should not approve the proposed women's shelter?" Agreement with this question means disagreement with the proposal. This phrasing can confuse people and result in inaccurate answers. A better format would be: "Do you believe that the city should approve the proposed women's shelter?"

"Yea-saying" and "nay-saying"   When you ask several questions about a topic, a respondent may employ a response set to agree or disagree with all the questions. Such a tendency is referred to as **"yea-saying"** or **"nay-saying."** The problem here is that the respondent may in fact be expressing true agreement, but alternatively may simply be agreeing with anything you say. One way to detect this response set is to word the questions so that consistent agreement is unlikely. For example, a study of family communication patterns might ask people how much they agree with the following statements: "The members of my family spend a lot of time together" and "I spend most of my weekends with friends." Similarly, a measure of loneliness could phrase some questions so that agreement means the respondent is lonely ("I feel isolated from others") and others with the meaning reversed so that disagreement indicates loneliness (e.g., "I feel part of a group of friends"). Although it is possible that someone could legitimately agree with both items, consistently agreeing or disagreeing with a set of related questions phrased in both standard and reversed formats is an indicator that the individual is "yea-saying" or "nay-saying."

Graesser and his colleagues have developed a computer program called *QUAID* (Question Understanding Aid) that analyzes question wording. Researchers can try out their questions online at the QUAID website (http://mnemosyne.csl.psyc.memphis.edu/quaid/quaidindex.html). You should also review the question wording examples in Table 7.1.

TABLE 7.1   Question wording: What is the problem?

Read each of the following questions and identify the problems for each.	Negative wording	Simplicity	Double-barreled	Loaded
Professors should not be required to take daily attendance. 1 = (Strongly Disagree) and 5 = (Strongly Agree)				
I enjoy studying and spending time with friends on weekends.				
Do you support the legislation that would unfairly tax hard-working farmers?				
I would describe myself as attractive and intelligent.				
Do you believe the relationship between cell phone behavior and consumption of fast food is orthogonal?				
Restaurants should not have to be inspected each month.				
Are you in favor of the boss's whim to cut lunchtime to 30 minutes?				

Answers are provided at the end of the chapter.

RESPONSES TO QUESTIONS

Closed- Versus Open-Ended Questions

Questions may be either closed- or open-ended. With **closed-ended questions,** a limited number of response alternatives are given; with **open-ended questions,** respondents are free to answer in any way they like. Thus, you could ask a person, "What is the most important thing children should learn to prepare them for life?" followed by a list of answers from which to choose (a closed-ended question), or you could leave this question open-ended for the person to provide the answer.

Using closed-ended questions is a more structured approach; they are easier to code and the response alternatives are the same for everyone. Open-ended questions require time to categorize and code the responses and are therefore more costly. Sometimes a respondent's response cannot be categorized at all because the response doesn't make sense or the person couldn't think of an answer.

Still, an open-ended question can yield valuable insights into what people are thinking. Open-ended questions are most useful when the researcher needs to know what people are thinking and how they naturally view their world; closed-ended questions are more likely to be used when the dimensions of the variables are well defined.

Schwarz (1999) points out that the two approaches can sometimes lead to different conclusions. He cites the results of a survey question about preparing children for life. When "To think for themselves" was one alternative in a closed-ended list, 62% chose this option; however, only 5% gave this answer when the open-ended format was used. This finding points to the need to have a good understanding of the topic when asking closed-ended questions.

Number of Response Alternatives

With closed-ended questions, there are a fixed number of response alternatives. In public opinion surveys, a simple "yes or no" or "agree or disagree" dichotomy is often sufficient. In more basic research, it is often preferable to have a sufficient number of alternatives to allow people to express themselves—for example, a 5- or 7-point scale ranging from "*strongly agree* to *strongly disagree*" or "*very positive* to *very negative*." Such a scale might appear as follows:

Strongly agree ____ ____ ____ ____ ____ ____ ____ Strongly disagree

Rating Scales

Rating scales such as the one shown above are very common in many areas of research. Rating scales ask people to provide "how much" judgments on any number of dimensions—amount of agreement, liking, or confidence, for example. Rating scales can have many different formats. The format that is used depends on factors such as the topic being investigated. Perhaps the best way to gain an understanding of the variety of formats is simply to look at a few examples. The simplest and most direct scale presents people with five or seven response alternatives with the endpoints on the scale labeled to define the extremes. For example,

Students at the university should be required to pass a comprehensive examination to graduate.

Strongly agree ____ ____ ____ ____ ____ ____ ____ Strongly disagree

How confident are you that the defendant is guilty of attempted murder?

Not at all confident ____ ____ ____ ____ ____ Very confident

Graphic rating scale

A **graphic rating scale** requires a mark along a continuous 100-millimeter line that is anchored with descriptions at each end.

How would you rate the movie you just saw?

Not very enjoyable _____ Very enjoyable

A ruler is then placed on the line to obtain the score on a scale that ranges from 0 to 100.

Semantic differential scale

The **semantic differential scale** is a measure of the meaning of concepts that was developed by Osgood and his associates (Osgood, Suci, & Tannenbaum, 1957). Respondents rate any concept—persons, objects, behaviors, ideas—on a series of bipolar adjectives using 7-point scales, as follows:

Smoking cigarettes

Good	___	___	___	___	___	___	___	Bad
Strong	___	___	___	___	___	___	___	Weak
Active	___	___	___	___	___	___	___	Passive

Research on the semantic differential shows that virtually anything can be measured using this technique. Ratings of specific things (marijuana), places (the student center), people (the governor, accountants), ideas (abortion, tax reduction), and behaviors (attending church, using public transit) can be obtained. A large body of research shows that the concepts are rated along three basic dimensions: the first and most important is *evaluation* (e.g., adjectives such as good–bad, wise–foolish, kind–cruel); the second is *activity* (active–passive, slow–fast, excitable–calm); and the third is *potency* (weak–strong, hard–soft, large–small).

Nonverbal scales for children

Young children may not understand the types of scales we've just described, but they are able to give ratings. Think back to the example in Chapter 4 (page 71) that uses drawings of faces to aid in the assessment of the level of pain that a child is experiencing. Similar face scales can be used to ask children to make ratings of other things such as a toy.

Labeling Response Alternatives

The examples thus far have labeled only the endpoints on the rating scale. Respondents decide the meaning of the response alternatives that are not labeled. This is a reasonable approach, and people are usually able to use such scales without difficulty. Sometimes researchers need to provide labels to more clearly define the meaning of each alternative. Here is a fairly standard alternative to the *agree-disagree* scale shown above:

_____	_____	_____	_____	_____
Strongly agree	Agree	Undecided	Disagree	Strongly disagree

This type of scale assumes that the middle alternative is a "neutral" point halfway between the endpoints. Sometimes, however, a perfectly balanced scale may not be possible or desirable. Consider a scale asking a college professor to rate a student for a job or graduate program. This particular scale asks for comparative ratings of students:

> In comparison with other graduates, how would you rate this student's potential for success?

_____	_____	_____	_____	_____
Lower 50%	Upper 50%	Upper 25%	Upper 10%	Upper 5%

Notice that most of the alternatives ask people to make a rating within the top 25% of students. This is done because students who apply for such programs tend to be very bright and motivated, and so professors rate them favorably. The wording of the alternatives attempts to force the raters to make finer distinctions among generally very good students.

Labeling alternatives is particularly interesting when asking about the frequency of a behavior. For example, you might ask, "How often do you exercise for at least 20 minutes?" What kind of scale should you use to let people answer this question? You could list (1) never, (2) rarely, (3) sometimes, (4) frequently. These terms convey your meaning but they are vague. Here is another set of alternatives, similar to ones described by Schwarz (1999):

_____ less than twice a week

_____ about twice a week

_____ about four times a week

_____ about six times a week

_____ at least once each day

A different scale might be:

_____ less than once per month

_____ about once a month

_____ about once every two weeks

_____ about once a week

_____ more than once per week

Schwarz (1999) calls the first scale a *high-frequency scale* because most alternatives indicate a high frequency of exercise. The other scale is referred to as low frequency. Schwarz points out that the labels should be chosen carefully because people may interpret the meaning of the scale differently, depending on the labels used. If you were actually asking the exercise question, you might decide on alternatives different from the ones described here. Moreover, your choice should be influenced by factors such as the population you are studying. If you are studying people who generally exercise a lot, you will be more likely to use a higher-frequency scale than you would if you were studying people who generally don't exercise a great deal.

FINALIZING THE QUESTIONNAIRE

Formatting the Questionnaire

The printed questionnaire should appear attractive and professional. It should be neatly typed and free of spelling errors. Respondents should find it easy to identify the questions and the response alternatives to the questions. Leave enough space between questions so people don't become confused when reading the questionnaire. If you have a particular scale format, such as a 5-point rating scale, use it consistently. Don't change from 5- to 4- to 7-point scales, for example.

It is also a good idea to carefully consider the sequence in which you will ask your questions. In general, it is best to ask the most interesting and important questions first to capture the attention of your respondents and motivate them to complete the survey. Roberson and Sundstrom (1990) obtained the highest return rates in an employee attitude survey when important questions were presented first and demographic questions were asked last. In addition, it is a good idea to group questions together when they address a similar theme or topic. Doing so will make your survey appear more professional, and your respondents will be more likely to take it seriously.

Refining Questions

Before actually administering the survey, it is a good idea to give the questions to a small group of people and have them think aloud while answering them. The participants might be chosen from the population being studied, or they could be friends or colleagues who can give reasonable responses to the questions. For the think-aloud procedure, you will need to ask the individuals to tell you how they interpret each question and how they respond to the response alternatives. This procedure can provide valuable information that you can use to improve the questions. (The importance of pilot studies such as this is discussed further in Chapter 9.)

ADMINISTERING SURVEYS

There are two ways to administer surveys. One is to use a written questionnaire, wherein respondents read the questions and indicate their responses on a form. The other way is to use an interview format. An interviewer asks the questions and records the responses in a personal verbal interaction. Both questionnaires and interviews can be presented to respondents in several ways. Let's examine the various methods of administering surveys.

Questionnaires

With questionnaires, the questions are presented in written format and the respondents write their answers. There are several positive features of using questionnaires. First, they are generally less costly than interviews. They also allow the respondent to be completely anonymous as long as no identifying information (e.g., name, Social Security number, or driver's license number) is asked. However, questionnaires require that the respondents be able to read and understand the questions. In addition, many people find it boring to sit by themselves reading questions and then providing answers; thus, a problem of motivation may arise. Questionnaires can be administered in person to groups or individuals, through the mail, on the Internet, and with other technologies.

Personal administration to groups or individuals   Often researchers are able to distribute questionnaires to groups of individuals. This might be a college class, parents attending a school meeting, people attending a new employee orientation, or students waiting for an appointment with an advisor. An advantage of this approach is that you have a captive audience that is likely to complete the questionnaire once they start it. Also, the researcher is present so people can ask questions if necessary.

Mail surveys   Surveys can be mailed to individuals at a home or business address. This is a very inexpensive way of contacting the people who were selected for the sample. However, the mail format is a drawback because of potentially low response rates: The questionnaire can easily be placed aside and forgotten among all the other tasks that people must attend to at home and work. Even if people start to fill out the questionnaire, something may happen to distract them, or they may become bored and simply throw the form in the trash. Some of the methods for increasing response rates are described later in this chapter. Another drawback is that no one is present to help if the person becomes confused or has a question about something.

Internet surveys   It is very easy to design a questionnaire for administration on the Internet. Both open- and closed-ended questions can be written and presented as **Internet surveys** to respondents. After the questionnaire is

completed, the responses are immediately sent to the researcher. One of the first problems to consider is how to sample people. Most commonly, surveys are listed on search engines so people who are interested in a topic can discover that someone is interested in collecting data. Some of the major polling organizations are building a database of people interested in participating in surveys. Every time they conduct a survey, they select a sample from the database and send an e-mail invitation to participate. The Internet is also making it easier to obtain samples of people with particular characteristics. There are all sorts of Internet special interest groups for people with a particular illness or of a particular age, marital status, or occupational group. Members of these groups use social networking sites, e-mail discussions, bulletin boards, and chat rooms to exchange ideas and information. Researchers can ask people who use these resources to volunteer for surveys. One concern about Internet data collection is whether the results will be at all similar to what might be found using traditional methods.

Another problem with Internet data is the inherent ambiguity about the characteristics of the individuals providing information for the study. To meet ethical guidelines, the researcher will usually state that only persons 18 years of age or older are eligible; yet how is that controlled? People may also misrepresent their age, gender, or ethnicity. We simply do not know if this is a major problem. However, for most research topics it is unlikely that people will go to the trouble of misrepresenting themselves on the Internet to a greater extent than they would with any other method of collecting data. Kraut et al. (2004) and Buchanan and Williams (2010) describe the ethical issues of Internet research in detail.

Other technologies   Researchers are taking advantage of new technologies to assist with the collection of data. An interesting application is seen in studies aimed at sampling people's behaviors and emotions over an extended period of time. The usual approach would be to ask people to provide retrospective accounts of their behaviors or emotions (e.g., how often have you felt angry during the last week?). With cell phones and other wireless communication devices, it is possible to contact people at various times and ask them to provide an immediate report of their current activities and emotions. Barrett and Barrett (2001) refer to this as "computerized experience-sampling."

Interviews

The fact that an interview requires an interaction between people has important implications. First, people are often more likely to agree to answer questions for a real person than to answer a mailed questionnaire. Good interviewers become quite skilled in convincing people to participate. Thus, response rates tend to be higher when interviews are used. The interviewer and respondent often establish a rapport that helps motivate the person to answer all the questions and complete the survey. People are more likely to leave questions unanswered on a written questionnaire than in an interview. An important advantage of an interview is that the interviewer can clarify any problems the person might have in understanding questions. Further, an interviewer can ask follow-up questions if needed to help clarify answers.

One potential problem in interviews is called **interviewer bias.** This term describes all of the biases that can arise from the fact that the interviewer is a unique human being interacting with another human. Thus, one potential problem is that the interviewer could subtly bias the respondent's answers by inadvertently showing approval or disapproval of certain answers. Or, if there are several interviewers, each could possess different characteristics (e.g., level of physical attractiveness, age, or race) that might influence the way respondents answer. Another problem is that interviewers may have expectations that could lead them to "see what they are looking for" in the respondents' answers. Such expectations could bias their interpretations of responses or lead them to probe further for an answer from certain respondents but not from others—for example, when questioning Whites but not people from other groups or when testing boys but not girls. Careful screening and training of interviewers help to limit such biases.

We can now examine three methods of conducting interviews: face-to-face, telephone, and focus groups.

Face-to-face interviews

Face-to-face interviews require that the interviewer and respondent meet to conduct the interview. Usually the interviewer travels to the person's home or office, although sometimes the respondent goes to the interviewer's office. Such interviews tend to be quite expensive and time-consuming. Therefore, they are most likely to be used when the sample size is fairly small and there are clear benefits to a face-to-face interaction.

Telephone interviews

Almost all interviews for large-scale surveys are done via telephone. **Telephone interviews** are less expensive than face-to-face interviews, and they allow data to be collected relatively quickly because many interviewers can work on the same survey at once. Also, computerized telephone survey techniques lower the cost of telephone surveys by reducing labor and data analysis costs. With a **computer-assisted telephone interview (CATI)** system, the interviewer's questions are prompted on the computer screen, and the data are entered directly into the computer for analysis.

Focus group interviews

An interview strategy that is often used in industry is the focus group interview. A **focus group** is an interview with a group of about 6 to 10 individuals brought together for a period of usually 2–3 hours. Virtually any topic can be explored in a focus group. Often the group members are selected because they have a particular knowledge or interest in the topic. Because the focus group requires people to both spend time and incur some costs traveling to the focus group location, participants usually receive some sort of monetary or gift incentive.

The questions tend to be open-ended, and they are asked of the whole group. An advantage here is that group interaction is possible: People can respond to one another, and one comment can trigger a variety of responses. The interviewer must be skilled in working with groups both to facilitate communication and to deal with problems that may arise, such as one or two persons trying to dominate the discussion or hostility between group members. The group discussion is usually recorded and may be transcribed. The tapes and transcripts are then analyzed to find themes and areas of group consensus and disagreement. Sometimes the transcripts are analyzed with a computer program to search for certain words and phrases. Researchers usually prefer to conduct at least two or three discussion groups on a given topic to make sure that the information gathered is not unique to one group of people. However, because each focus group is time-consuming and costly and provides a great deal of information, researchers don't do very many such groups on any one topic.

SURVEY DESIGNS TO STUDY CHANGES OVER TIME

Surveys most frequently study people at one point in time. On many occasions, however, researchers wish to make comparisons over time. For example, local newspapers often hire firms to conduct an annual random survey of county residents. Because the questions are the same each year, it is possible to track changes over time in such variables as satisfaction with the area, attitudes toward the school system, and perceived major problems facing the county. Similarly, a large number of first-year students are surveyed each year at colleges throughout the United States to study changes in the composition, attitudes, and aspirations of this group (Pryor, Hurtado, DeAngelo, Palucki Blake, & Tran, 2011). First-year college students today, for instance, come from more ethnically diverse backgrounds than those in the 1970s (90.9% of respondents in 1971 were White whereas in 2006, 76.5% were). Political attitudes have also shifted over time among this group: Trends in opinions about paying taxes and abortion rights can be seen. Finally, the percentage of new students who think that their "emotional health" is above average or in the "top 10%" hit a 25-year low in 2010: In 1985, 64% of respondents reported good emotional health; in 2010, 52% of students did.

Another way to study changes over time is to conduct a **panel study** in which the same people are surveyed at two or more points in time. In a two-wave panel study, people are surveyed at two points in time; in a three-wave panel study, three surveys are conducted; and so on. Panel studies are particularly important when the research question addresses the relationship between one variable at "time 1" and another variable at some later "time 2." For example, Chandra et al. (2008) examined the relationship between exposure to sexual content on television and teen pregnancy over time. Data were collected from over 2,000 teens over a 3-year period. Exposure to sexual content on television was assessed using a survey that asked the participants to report on their television viewing habits, along with their sexual knowledge, attitudes, and behavior. Participants were surveyed three times over the course of 3 years. Chandra and her colleagues found that higher levels of exposure to sexual content on television were, indeed,

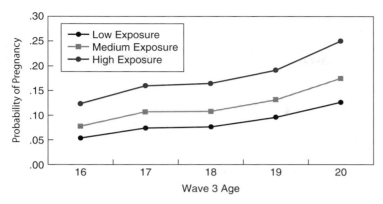

FIGURE 7.2
Probability of pregnancy at "time 3" related to exposure to low, medium, or high levels of sexual content on television at "time 1."

Adapted from "Does watching sex on television predict teen pregnancy? Findings from a national longitudinal survey of youth," by A. Chandra, S. C. Martino, R. L. Collins, M. N. Elliott, S. H. Berry, D. E. Kanouse, and A. Miu, 2008, *Pediatrics, 122*, pp. 1047–1054.

predictive of higher rates of teen pregnancy—as shown in Figure 7.2. Indeed, they reported that "high rates of exposure corresponded to twice the rate of observed pregnancies seen with low rates of exposure" (p. 1052).

SAMPLING FROM A POPULATION

Most research projects involve **sampling** participants from a population of interest. The **population** is composed of all individuals of interest to the researcher. One population of interest in a large public opinion poll, for instance, might be all eligible voters in the United States. This implies that the population of interest does not include people under the age of 18, convicted prisoners, visitors from other countries, and anyone else not eligible to vote. You might conduct a survey in which your population consists of all students at your college or university. With enough time and money, a survey researcher could conceivably contact everyone in the population. The United States attempts to do this every 10 years with an official census of the entire population. With a relatively small population, you might find it easy to study the entire population.

In most cases, however, studying the entire population would be a massive undertaking. Fortunately, it can be avoided by selecting a sample from the population of interest. With proper sampling, we can use information obtained from the participants (or "respondents") who were sampled to precisely estimate characteristics of the population as a whole. Statistical theory allows us to infer what the population is like, based on data obtained from a sample (the logic underlying what is called *statistical significance* will be addressed in Chapter 13).

Confidence Intervals

When researchers make inferences about populations, they do so with a certain degree of confidence. Here is a statement that you might see when you read the results of a survey: "The results from the survey are accurate within 3 percentage points, using a 95% level of confidence." What does this tell you? Suppose you asked students to tell you whether they prefer to study at home or at school, and the survey results indicate that 61% prefer to study at home. Using the same degree of confidence, you would now know that the actual population value is probably between 58% and 64%. This is called a **confidence interval**—you can have 95% confidence that the true population value lies within this interval around the obtained sample result. Your best estimate of the population value is the sample value. However, because you have only a sample and not the entire population, your result may be in error. The confidence interval gives you information about the likely amount of the error. The formal term for this error is **sampling error,** although you are probably more familiar with the term *margin of error*. Recall the concept of measurement error discussed in Chapter 5: When you measure a single individual on a variable, the obtained score may deviate from the true score because of measurement error. Similarly, when you study one sample, the obtained result may deviate from the true population value because of sampling error.

The surveys you often read about in newspapers and the previous example deal with percentages. What about questions that ask for more quantitative information? The logic in this instance is very much the same. For example, if you also ask students to report how many hours and minutes they studied during the previous day, you might find that the average amount of time was 76 minutes. A confidence interval could then be calculated based on the size of the sample; for example, the 95% confidence interval is 76 minutes plus or minus 10 minutes. It is highly likely that the true population value lies within the interval of 66 to 86 minutes. The topic of confidence intervals is discussed again in Chapter 13.

Sample Size

It is important to note that a larger sample size will reduce the size of the confidence interval. Although the size of the interval is determined by several factors, the most important is sample size. Larger samples are more likely to yield data that accurately reflect the true population value. This statement should make intuitive sense to you; a sample of 200 people from your school should yield more accurate data about your school than a sample of 25 people.

How large should the sample be? The sample size can be determined using a mathematical formula that takes into account the size of the confidence interval and the size of the population you are studying. Table 7.2 shows the sample size needed for a sample percentage to be accurate within plus or minus 3%, 5%, and 10%, given a 95% level of confidence. Note first that you need a larger sample size for increased accuracy. With a population size of 10,000, you need a sample of 370 for accuracy within ±5%; the needed sample size increases to 964 for accuracy within ±3%. Note that sample size is *not* a constant percentage of the population

TABLE 7.2   Sample size and precision of population estimates (95% confidence level)

Size of population	Precision of estimate		
	±3%	±5%	±10%
2,000	696	322	92
5,000	879	357	94
10,000	964	370	95
50,000	1,045	381	96
100,000	1,055	383	96
Over 100,000	1,067	384	96

Note: The sample sizes were calculated using conservative assumptions about the nature of the true population values.

size. Many people believe that proper sampling requires a certain percentage of the population; these people often complain about survey results when they discover that a survey of an entire state was done with "only" 700 or 1,000 people. However, you can see in the table that the needed sample size does not change much, even as the population size increases from 5,000 to 100,000 or more. As Fowler (2009) notes, "a sample of 150 people will describe a population of 1,500 or 15 million with virtually the same degree of accuracy . . ." (p. 45).

SAMPLING TECHNIQUES

There are two basic techniques for sampling individuals from a population: probability sampling and nonprobability sampling. In **probability sampling,** each member of the population has a specifiable probability of being chosen. Probability sampling is required when you want to make precise statements about a specific population on the basis of the results of your survey. In **nonprobability sampling,** we don't know the probability of any particular member of the population being chosen. Although this approach is not as sophisticated as probability sampling, we shall see that nonprobability sampling is quite common and useful in many circumstances.

Probability Sampling

Simple random sampling   With **simple random sampling,** every member of the population has an equal probability of being selected for the sample. If the population has 1,000 members, each has one chance out of a thousand of being selected. Suppose you want to sample students who attend your school.

A list of all students would be needed; from that list, students would be chosen at random to form the sample.

When conducting telephone interviews, researchers commonly have a computer randomly generate a list of telephone numbers with the dialing prefixes used for residences in the city or area being studied. This will produce a **random sample** of the population because most residences have telephones (if many people do not have phones, the sample would be biased). Some companies will even provide researchers with a list of telephone numbers for a survey in which the phone numbers of businesses and numbers that phone companies do not use have been removed. You might note that this procedure results in a random sample of households rather than individuals. Survey researchers use other procedures when it is important to select one person at random from the household.

Stratified random sampling   A somewhat more complicated procedure is **stratified random sampling.** The population is divided into subgroups (also known as *strata*), and random sampling techniques are then used to select sample members from each stratum. Any number of dimensions could be used to divide the population, but the dimension (or dimensions) chosen should be relevant to the problem under study. For instance, a survey of sexual attitudes might stratify on the basis of age, gender, and amount of education because these factors are related to sexual attitudes. Stratification on the basis of height or hair color would be ridiculous for this survey.

Stratified random sampling has the advantage of a built-in assurance that the sample will accurately reflect the numerical composition of the various subgroups. This kind of accuracy is particularly important when some subgroups represent very small percentages of the population. For instance, if African Americans make up 5% of a city of 100,000, a simple random sample of 100 people might not include any African Americans; a stratified random sample would include 5 African Americans chosen randomly from the population. In practice, when it is important to represent a small group within a population, researchers will "oversample" that group to ensure that a representative sample of the group is surveyed; a large enough sample must be obtained to be able to make inferences about the population. Thus, if your campus has a distribution of students similar to the city described here and you need to compare attitudes of African Americans and Whites, you will need to sample a large percentage of the African American students and only a small percentage of the White students to obtain a reasonable number of respondents from each group.

Cluster sampling   It might have occurred to you that obtaining a list of all members of a population might be difficult. What if officials at your school decide that you cannot have access to a list of all students? What if you want to study a population that has no list of members, such as people who work in county health care agencies? In such situations, a technique called **cluster sampling** can be used. Rather than randomly sampling from a list of individuals, the researcher can identify "clusters" of individuals and then sample from these clusters. After the clusters are chosen, all individuals in each cluster are included in the sample. For example, you might conduct the survey of students using cluster sampling by identifying all classes being taught—the classes are the clusters of students. You could then randomly sample from this list of classes and have all members of the chosen classes complete your survey (making sure, of course, that no one completes the survey twice).

Most often, use of cluster sampling requires a series of samples from larger to smaller clusters—a multistage approach. For example, a researcher interested in studying county health care agencies might first randomly determine a number of states to sample and then randomly sample counties from each state chosen. The researcher would then go to the health care agencies in each of these counties and study the people who work in them. Note that the main advantage of cluster sampling is that the researcher does not have to sample from lists of individuals to obtain a truly random sample of individuals.

Nonprobability Sampling

In contrast to probability sampling, where the probability of every member is knowable, in nonprobability sampling, the probability of being selected is not known. Nonprobability sampling techniques are quite arbitrary. A population may be defined, but little effort is expended to ensure that the sample accurately represents the population. However, among other things, nonprobability samples are cheap and convenient. Three types of nonprobability sampling are haphazard sampling, purposive sampling, and quota sampling.

Haphazard sampling
One form of nonprobability sampling is **haphazard sampling** or "convenience" sampling. Haphazard sampling could be called a "take-them-where-you-find-them" method of obtaining participants. Thus, you would select a sample of students from your school in any way that is convenient. You might stand in front of the student union at 9 a.m., ask people who sit around you in your classes to participate, or visit a couple of fraternity and sorority houses. Unfortunately, such procedures are likely to introduce biases into the sample so that the sample may not be an accurate representation of the population of all students. Thus, if you selected your sample from students walking by the student union at 11 a.m., your sample excludes students who don't frequent this location, and it may also eliminate afternoon and evening students. On my own campus, this sample would differ from the population of all students by being younger, working fewer hours, and being more likely to belong to a fraternity or sorority. Sample biases such as these limit your ability to use your sample data to estimate the actual population values. Your results may not generalize to your intended population but instead may describe only the biased sample that you obtained.

Purposive sampling
A second form of nonprobability sampling is **purposive sampling.** The *purpose* is to obtain a sample of people who meet some predetermined criterion. Sometimes at a large movie complex, you may see researchers asking customers to fill out a questionnaire about one or more

movies. They are always doing purposive sampling. Instead of sampling anyone walking toward the theater, they take a look at each person to make sure that they fit some criterion—under the age of 30 or an adult with one or more children, for example. This is a good way to limit the sample to a certain group of people. However, it is not a probability sample.

Quota sampling   A third form of nonprobability sampling is **quota sampling.** A researcher who uses this technique chooses a sample that reflects the numerical composition of various subgroups in the population. Thus, quota sampling is similar to the stratified sampling procedure previously described; however, random sampling does not occur when you use quota sampling. To illustrate, suppose you want to ensure that your sample of students includes 19% first-year students, 23% sophomores, 26% juniors, 22% seniors, and 10% graduate students because these are the percentages of the classes in the total population. A quota sampling technique would make sure you have these percentages, but you would still collect your data using haphazard techniques. If you didn't get enough graduate students in front of the student union, perhaps you could go to a graduate class to complete the sample. Although quota sampling is a bit more sophisticated than haphazard sampling, the problem remains that no restrictions are placed on how individuals in the various subgroups are chosen. The sample does reflect the numerical composition of the whole population of interest, but respondents within each subgroup are selected in a haphazard manner. These techniques are summarized in Table 7.3.

EVALUATING SAMPLES

Samples should be representative of the population from which they are drawn. A completely unbiased sample is one that is highly representative of the population. How do you create a completely unbiased sample? First, you would randomly sample from a population that contains *all* individuals in the population. Second, you would contact and obtain completed responses from *all* individuals selected to be in the sample. Such standards are rarely achieved. Even if random sampling is used, bias can be introduced from two sources: the sampling frame used and poor response rates. Moreover, even though nonprobability samples have more potential sources of bias than probability samples, there are many reasons (summarized in Table 7.3) why they are used and should be evaluated positively.

Sampling Frame

The **sampling frame** is the *actual* population of individuals (or clusters) from which a random sample will be drawn. Rarely will this perfectly coincide with the population of interest—some biases will be introduced. If you define your population as "residents of my city," the sampling frame may be a list of telephone numbers that you will use to contact residents between 5 p.m. and 9 p.m. This sampling frame excludes persons who do not have telephones or whose schedule

TABLE 7.3   Advantages and disadvantages of sampling techniques

Sample technique	Example	Advantages	Disadvantages
Probability sampling techniques			
Simple random sampling	A computer program randomly chooses 100 students from a list of all 10,000 students at College X.	Representative of population.	May cost more. May be difficult to get full list of all members of any population of interest.
Stratified random sampling	The names of all 10,000 College X students are sorted by major, and a computer program randomly chooses 50 students from each major.	Representative of population.	May cost more. May be difficult to get full list of all members of any population of interest.
Cluster sampling	Two hundred clusters of psychology majors are identified at schools all over the United States. Out of these 200 clusters, 10 clusters are chosen randomly, and every psychology major in each cluster is sampled.	Researcher does not have to sample from lists of individuals in order to get a full, random sample.	May cost more. May be difficult to get full list of all members of any randomly chosen cluster.
Nonprobability sampling techniques			
Haphazard sampling	Ask students around you at lunch or in class to participate.	Inexpensive, efficient, convenient.	Likely to introduce bias into the sample; results may not generalize to intended population.
Purposive sampling	In an otherwise haphazard sample, select individuals who meet a criterion (e.g., an age group).	Sample includes only types of individuals you are interested in.	Likely to introduce bias into the sample; results may not generalize to intended population.
Quota sampling	Collect specific proportions of data representative of percentages of groups within population, then use haphazard techniques.	Inexpensive, efficient, convenient.	Likely to introduce bias into the sample; results may not generalize to intended population; no method for choosing individuals in subgroups.

prevents them from being at home when you are making calls. Also, if you are using the telephone directory to obtain numbers, you will exclude persons who have unlisted numbers. As another example, suppose you want to know what doctors think about the portrayal of the medical profession on television. A reasonable sampling frame would be all doctors listed in your telephone directory. Immediately you can see that you have limited your sample to a particular geographical area. More important, you have also limited the sample to doctors who have private practices—doctors who work only in clinics and hospitals have been excluded. When evaluating the results of the survey, you need to consider how well the sampling frame matches the population of interest. Often the biases introduced are quite minor; however, they could be consequential.

Response Rate

The **response rate** in a survey is simply the percentage of people in the sample who actually completed the survey. Thus, if you mail 1,000 questionnaires to a random sample of adults in your community and 500 are completed and returned to you, the response rate is 50%. Response rate is important because it indicates how much bias there might be in the final sample of respondents. Non-respondents may differ from respondents in any number of ways, including age, income, marital status, and education. The lower the response rate, the greater the likelihood that such biases may distort the findings and in turn limit the ability to generalize the findings to the population of interest.

In general, mail surveys have lower response rates than telephone surveys. With both methods, however, steps can be taken to maximize response rates. With mail surveys, an explanatory postcard or letter can be sent a week or so prior to mailing the survey. Follow-up reminders and even second mailings of the questionnaire are often effective in increasing response rates. It often helps to have a personally stamped return envelope rather than a business reply envelope. Even the look of the cover page of the questionnaire can be important (Dillman, 2000). With telephone surveys, respondents who aren't home can be called again and people who can't be interviewed today can be scheduled for a call at a more convenient time. Sometimes an incentive may be necessary to increase response rates. Such incentives can include cash, a gift, or a gift certificate for agreeing to participate. A crisp dollar bill "thank you" can be included with a mailed questionnaire. Another incentive is a chance to win a drawing for a prize. Finally, researchers should attempt to convince people that the survey's purposes are important and their participation will be a valuable contribution.

REASONS FOR USING CONVENIENCE SAMPLES

Much of the research in psychology uses nonprobability sampling techniques to obtain participants for either surveys or experiments. The advantage of these techniques is that the investigator can obtain research participants without spending a great deal of money or time on selecting the sample. For example, it is common practice to select participants from students in introductory psychology classes.

Often, these students are required to participate in studies being conducted by faculty and their students; the introductory psychology students can then choose which studies they wish to participate in.

Even in studies that do not use college students, the sample is often based on convenience rather than concern for obtaining a random sample. One of our colleagues studies children, but they are almost always from one particular elementary school. You can guess that this is because our colleague has established a good relationship with the teachers and administrators; thus, obtaining permission to conduct the research is fairly easy. Even though the sample is somewhat biased because it includes only children from one neighborhood that has certain social and economic characteristics, the advantages outweigh the sample concerns for the researcher.

Why aren't researchers more worried about obtaining random samples from the "general population" for their research? Most psychological research is focused on studying the relationships between variables even though the sample may be biased (e.g., the sample will have more college students, be younger, etc. than the general U.S. population). But to put this in perspective, remember that even a random sample of the general population of U.S. residents tells us nothing about citizens of other countries. So, our research findings provide important information even though the data cannot be strictly generalized beyond the population defined by the sample that was used. For example, the findings of Brown and Rahhal (1994) regarding experiences of younger and older adults when they hid an object but later forgot the location are meaningful even though the actual sample consisted of current students (younger adults) and alumni (older adults) of a particular university who received a mailed questionnaire. In Chapter 14, we will emphasize that generalization in science is dependent upon replicating the results. We do not need better samples of younger and older adults; instead, we should look for replications of the findings using multiple samples and multiple methods. The results of many studies can then be synthesized to gain greater insight into the findings (cf. Albright & Malloy, 2000).

These issues will be explored further in Chapter 14. For now, it is also important to recognize that some nonprobability samples are more representative than others. Introductory psychology students are fairly representative of college students in general, and most college student samples are fairly representative of young adults. There aren't many obvious biases, particularly if you are studying basic psychological processes. Other samples might be much less representative of an intended population. Not long ago, a public affairs program on a local public television station asked viewers to dial a telephone number or send e-mail to vote for or against a gun control measure being considered by the legislature; the following evening, the program announced that almost 90% of the respondents opposed the measure. The sampling problems here are obvious: Groups opposed to gun control could immediately contact members to urge them to vote, and there were no limits on how many times someone could respond. In fact, the show received about 100 times more votes than it usually receives when it does such surveys. It is likely, then, that this sample was not at all representative of the population of the city or even viewers of the program.

When local news programs, 24-hour news channels, or websites ask viewers to vote on a topic, the resulting samples are not representative of the population to which they are often trying to generalize. First, their viewers may be different from the U.S. population in meaningful ways (e.g., more Fox News viewers are conservative, more MSNBC viewers are liberal). Second, these programs and websites often ask about hot-button topics, things that people care passionately about, because that's what drives viewers and visitors to tune in. Questions about abortion, taxes, and wars tend to drive certain types of viewers to these informal "polls." The results, whatever they may be, are biased because the sample consists primarily of people who have chosen to watch the program or visit the website, and they have chosen to vote because they are deeply interested in a topic.

You now have a great deal of information about methods for asking people about themselves. If you engage in this type of research, you will often need to design your own questions by following the guidelines described in this chapter and consulting sources such as Groves, Fowler, Couper, and Lepkowski (2009) and Fowler (2008). However, you can also adapt questions and entire questionnaires that have been used in previous research. For example, Greenfield (1999) studied the phenomenon of Internet addiction by adapting questions from a large body of existing research on addiction to gambling. Consider using previously developed questions, particularly if they have proven useful in other studies (make sure you don't violate any copyrights, however). A variety of measures of social, political, and occupational attitudes developed by others have been compiled by Robinson and his colleagues (Robinson, Athanasiou, & Head, 1969; Robinson, Rusk, & Head, 1968; Robinson, Shaver, & Wrightsman, 1991, 1999).

We noted in Chapter 4 that both nonexperimental and experimental research methods are necessary to fully understand behavior. The previous chapters have focused on nonexperimental approaches. In the next chapter, we begin a detailed description of experimental research design.

ILLUSTRATIVE ARTICLE: SURVEY RESEARCH

Every year hundreds of thousands of U.S. college students travel to Florida, Mexico, or similar sunny locales for spring break. For the most part, everybody involved—students, their universities, their parents, and the communities that they are traveling to—realizes that spring break can also be a dangerous time for college students: Students consume more alcohol during spring break and the risks associated with over-consumption are more prevalent.

In a survey study conducted by Patrick, Morgan, Maggs, and Lefkowitz (2011), male and female college students completed a survey related to their perceptions of their friends' "understandings" of spring break behaviors. That is, students were surveyed to see if their friends would "have their back" during spring break.

First, acquire and read the following article:

> Patrick, M. E., Morgan, N., Maggs, J. L., & Lefkowitz, E. S., (2011). "I got your back": Friends' understandings regarding college student Spring Break behavior. *Journal of Youth and Adolescence, 40*, 108–120.

Then, after reading the article, consider the following:

1. What kinds of questions were included in the survey? Identify examples of each.
2. How and when was the survey administered? What are the potential problems with their administration strategy?
3. What was the nature of the sampling strategy? What was the final sample size?
4. What was the response rate for the survey?
5. Describe the demographic profile of the sample.
6. Do you think that these findings generalize to all college students? Why or why not?
7. Describe at least one finding that you found particularly interesting or surprising.

Study Terms

Computer-assisted telephone interview (CATI) (p. 141)

Closed-ended questions (p. 134)

Cluster sampling (p. 146)

Confidence interval (p. 144)

Face-to-face interview (p. 141)

Focus group (p. 141)

Graphic rating scale (p. 136)

Haphazard (convenience) sampling (p. 147)

Internet survey (p. 139)

Interviewer bias (p. 141)

Mail survey (p. 139)

Nonprobability sampling (p. 145)

Open-ended questions (p. 134)

Panel study (p. 142)

Population (p. 143)

Probability sampling (p. 145)

Purposive sampling (p. 147)

Quota sampling (p. 148)

Random sample (p. 146)

Rating scale (p. 135)

Response rate (p. 150)

Response set (p. 130)

Sampling (p. 143)

Sampling error (p. 144)

Sampling frame (p. 148)

Semantic differential scale (p. 136)

Simple random sampling (p. 145)

Stratified random sampling (p. 146)

Survey research (p. 129)

Telephone interview (p. 141)

Yea-saying and nay-saying (p. 133)

Review Questions

1. What is a survey? Describe some research questions you might address with a survey.

2. What are some factors to take into consideration when constructing questions for surveys (including both questions and response alternatives)?

3. What are the advantages and disadvantages of using questionnaires versus interviews in a survey?

4. Compare the different questionnaire, interview, and Internet survey administration methods.

5. Define interviewer bias.

6. What is a social desirability response set?

7. How does sample size affect the interpretation of survey results?

8. Distinguish between probability and nonprobability sampling techniques. What are the implications of each?

9. Distinguish between simple random, stratified random, and cluster sampling.

10. Distinguish between haphazard and quota sampling.

11. Why don't researchers who want to test hypotheses about the relationships between variables worry a great deal about random sampling?

Activity Questions

1. In the Chandra et al. (2008) study on television viewing and teen pregnancy (see page 142), exposure to television with sexual content was associated with a higher likelihood for teen pregnancy. Can you conclude that television viewing *causes* teen pregnancy? Why or why not? How might you expand the scope of this investigation through a panel study?

2. Select a topic for a survey. Write at least five closed-ended questions that you might include in the survey. For each question, write one "good" version and one "poor" version. For each poor question, state what elements make it poor and why the good version is an improvement.

3. As we noted at the beginning of the chapter, surveys are being conducted all the time. Many survey reports are not published in peer-reviewed journals. Identify a survey report of your own interest and answer the questions below. Survey reports can be found on the web. Here are some examples: Youth Risk Behavior Survey Surveillance, 2009: http://www.cdc.gov/mmwr/pdf/ss/ss5905.pdf; Pew U.S. Religious Landscape Survey: http://religions.pewforum.org/reports; National Crime Victimization Survey (NCVS): http://bjs.ojp.usdoj.gov/index.cfm?ty=dcdetail&iid=245; Behavioral Risk Factor Surveillance System: http://cdc.gov/brfss/

    a. What kinds of questions were included in the survey? Identify examples of each.

    b. How were the questions developed?

    c. How and when was the survey administered?

    d. What was the nature of the sampling strategy? What was the final sample size?

    e. What was the response rate for the survey?

    f. What was the confidence interval for the survey findings?

    g. Describe at least one survey finding that you found particularly interesting or surprising.

4. Suppose you want to know how many books in a bookstore have only male authors, only female authors, or both male and female authors (the "bookstore" in this case might be a large retail store, the textbook section of your college bookstore, or all the books in the stacks of your library). Because there are thousands of books in the store, you decide to study a sample of the books rather than examine every book there. Describe a possible sampling procedure using a nonprobability sampling technique. Then describe how you might sample books using a probability sampling technique. Now speculate on the ways that the outcomes of your research might differ using the two techniques.

Answers

TABLE 7.1:

    negative wording, double-barreled, loaded, double-barreled, simplicity, negative wording, loaded

8

Experimental Design

LEARNING OBJECTIVES

- Define confounding variable, and describe how confounding variables are related to internal validity.
- Describe the posttest-only design and the pretest-posttest design, including the advantages and disadvantages of each design.
- Contrast an independent groups (between-subjects) design with a repeated measures (within-subjects) design.
- Summarize the advantages and disadvantages of using a repeated measures design.
- Describe a matched pairs design, including reasons to use this design.

I n the experimental method, the researcher attempts to control all extraneous variables. Suppose you want to test the hypothesis that exercise affects mood. To do this, you might put one group of people through a 1-hour aerobics workout and put another group in a room where they are asked to watch a video of people exercising for an hour. All participants would then complete the same mood assessment. Now suppose that the people in the aerobics class rate themselves as happier than those in the video viewing condition. Can the difference in mood be attributed to the difference in the exercise? Yes, *if* there is no other difference between the groups. However, what if the aerobics group was given the mood assessment in a room with windows but the video only group was tested in a room without windows? In that case, it would be impossible to know whether the better mood of the participants in the aerobics group was due to the exercise or to the presence of windows.

CONFOUNDING AND INTERNAL VALIDITY

Recall from Chapter 4 that the experimental method has the advantage of allowing a relatively unambiguous interpretation of results. The researcher manipulates the independent variable to create groups and then compares the groups in terms of their scores on the dependent variable. All other variables are kept constant, either through direct *experimental control* or through *randomization*. If the scores of the groups are different, the researcher can conclude that the independent variable caused the results because the only difference between the groups is the manipulated variable.

Although the task of designing an experiment is logically elegant and exquisitely simple, you should be aware of possible pitfalls. In the hypothetical exercise experiment just described, the variables of exercise and window presence are confounded. The window variable was not kept constant. A **confounding variable** is a variable that varies along with the independent variable; confounding occurs when the effects of the independent variable and an uncontrolled variable are intertwined so you cannot determine which of the variables is responsible for the observed effect. If the window variable had been held constant, both the exercise and the video condition would have taken place in identical rooms. That way, the effect of windows would not be a factor to consider when interpreting the difference between the groups.

In short, both rooms in the exercise experiment should have had windows or both should have been windowless. Because one room had windows and one room did not, any difference in the dependent variable (mood) cannot be attributed solely to the independent variable (exercise). An alternative explanation can be offered: The difference in mood may have been caused, at least in part, by the window variable.

Good experimental design requires eliminating possible confounding variables that could result in alternative explanations. A researcher can claim that the independent variable caused the results only by eliminating competing, alternative explanations. When the results of an experiment can confidently be attributed to the effect of the independent variable, the experiment is said to have **internal validity** (remember that internal validity refers to the ability to draw conclusions about causal relationships from our data; see Chapter 4). To achieve internal validity, the researcher must design and conduct the experiment so that only the independent variable can be the cause of the results (Campbell & Stanley, 1966).

This chapter will focus on true experimental designs, which provide the highest degree of internal validity. In Chapter 11, we will turn to an examination of quasi-experimental designs, which lack the crucial element of random assignment while attempting to infer that an independent variable had an effect on a dependent variable. Internal validity is discussed further in Chapter 11. External validity, the extent to which findings may be generalized, is discussed in Chapter 14.

BASIC EXPERIMENTS

The simplest possible experimental design has two variables: the independent variable and the dependent variable. The independent variable has a minimum of two levels, an experimental group and a control group. Researchers must make every effort to ensure that the only difference between the two groups is the manipulated variable. Remember, the experimental method involves control over extraneous variables, through either keeping such variables constant (experimental control) or using randomization to make sure that any extraneous variables will affect both groups equally. The basic, simple experimental design can take one of two forms: a posttest-only design or a pretest-posttest design.

Posttest-Only Design

A researcher using a **posttest-only design** must (1) obtain two equivalent groups of participants, (2) introduce the independent variable, and (3) measure the effect of the independent variable on the dependent variable. The design looks like this:

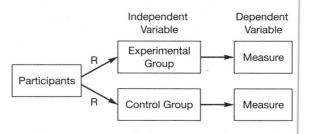

Thus, the first step is to choose the participants and assign them to the two groups. The procedures used must achieve equivalent groups to eliminate any potential **selection differences:** The people selected to be in the conditions cannot differ in any systematic way. For example, you cannot select high-income individuals to participate in one condition and low-income individuals for the other. The groups can be made equivalent by randomly assigning participants to the two conditions or by having the same participants participate in both conditions. Recall from Chapter 4 that random assignment is done in such a way that each participant is assigned to a condition randomly without regard to any personal characteristic of the individual. The R in the diagram means that participants were randomly assigned to the two groups.

Next, the researcher must choose two levels of the independent variable, such as an experimental group that receives a treatment and a control group that does not. Thus, a researcher might study the effect of reward on motivation by offering a reward to one group of children before they play a game and offering no reward to children in the control group. A study testing the effect of a treatment method for reducing smoking could compare a group that receives the treatment with a control group that does not. Another approach would be to use two different amounts of the independent variable—that is, to use more reward in one group than the other or to compare the effects of different amounts of relaxation training designed to help people quit smoking (e.g., 1 hour of training compared with 10 hours). Another approach would be to include two qualitatively different conditions; for example, one group of test-anxious students might write about their anxiety and the other group could participate in a meditation exercise prior to a test. All of these approaches would provide a basis for comparison of the two groups. (Of course, experiments may include more than two groups; for example we might compare two different smoking cessation treatments along with a no-treatment control group—these types of experimental designs will be described in Chapter 10).

Finally, the effect of the independent variable is measured. The same measurement procedure is used for both groups, so that comparison of the two groups is possible. Because the groups were equivalent prior to the introduction of the independent variable and there were no confounding variables, any difference between the groups on the dependent variable must be attributed to the effect of the independent variable. This elegant experimental design has a high degree of internal validity. That is, we can confidently conclude that the independent variable caused the dependent variable. In actuality, a statistical significance test would be used to assess the difference between the groups. However, we don't need to be concerned with statistics at this point. An experiment must be well designed, and confounding variables must be eliminated before we can draw conclusions from statistical analyses.

Pretest-Posttest Design

The only difference between the posttest-only design and the **pretest-posttest design** is that in the latter a pretest is given before the experimental manipulation is introduced:

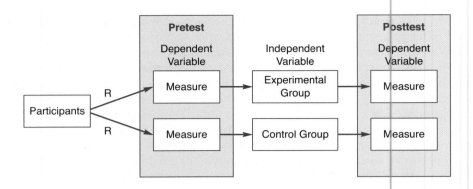

This design makes it possible to ascertain that the groups were, in fact, equivalent at the beginning of the experiment. However, this precaution is usually not necessary if participants have been randomly assigned to the two groups. With a sufficiently large sample of participants, random assignment will produce groups that are virtually identical in all respects.

You are probably wondering how many participants are needed in each group to make sure that random assignment has made the groups equivalent. The larger the sample, the less likelihood there is that the groups will differ in any systematic way prior to the manipulation of the independent variable. In addition, as sample size increases, so does the likelihood that any difference between the groups on the dependent variable is due to the effect of the independent variable. There are formal procedures for determining the sample size needed to detect a statistically significant effect, but as a rule of thumb you will probably need a minimum of 20 to 30 participants per condition. In some areas of research, many more participants may be necessary. Further issues in determining the number of participants needed for an experiment are described in Chapter 13.

Advantages and Disadvantages of the Two Designs

Each design has advantages and disadvantages that influence the decision whether to include or omit a pretest. The first decision factor concerns the equivalence of the groups in the experiment. Although randomization is likely to produce equivalent groups, it is possible that, with small sample sizes, the groups will not be equal. Thus, a pretest enables the researcher to assess whether the groups are in fact equivalent to begin with.

Sometimes, a pretest is necessary to select the participants in the experiment. A researcher might need to give a pretest to find the lowest or highest scorers on a smoking measure, a math anxiety test, or a prejudice measure. Once identified, the participants would be randomly assigned to the experimental and control groups.

The pretest-posttest design immediately makes us focus on the *change* from pretest to posttest. This emphasis on change is incorporated into the analysis of the group differences. Also, the extent of change in each individual can be examined. If a smoking reduction program appears to be effective for some individuals but not others, attempts can be made to find out why.

A pretest is also necessary whenever there is a possibility that participants will drop out of the experiment; this is most likely to occur in a study that lasts over a long time period. The dropout factor in experiments is called **attrition** or **mortality.** People may drop out for reasons unrelated to the experimental manipulation, such as illness; sometimes, however, attrition is related to the experimental manipulation. Even if the groups are equivalent to begin with, different attrition rates can make them nonequivalent. How might mortality affect a treatment program designed to reduce smoking? One possibility is that the heaviest smokers in the experimental group might leave the program. Therefore, when the posttest is given, only the light smokers would remain, so that a comparison of the experimental and control groups would show less smoking in the experimental group even if the program had no effect. In this way, attrition (mortality) becomes an alternative explanation for the results. Use of a pretest enables you to assess the effects of attrition; you can look at the pretest scores of the dropouts and know whether their scores differed from the scores of the individuals completing the study. Thus, with the pretest, it is possible to examine whether attrition is a plausible alternative explanation—an advantage in the experimental design.

One disadvantage of a pretest, however, is that it may be time-consuming and awkward to administer in the context of the particular experimental procedures being used. Perhaps most important, a pretest can sensitize participants to what you are studying, enabling them to figure out your hypothesis. They may then react differently to the manipulation than they would have without the pretest. When a pretest affects the way participants react to the manipulation, it is very difficult to generalize the results to people who have not received a pretest. That is, the independent variable may not have an effect in the real world, where pretests are rarely given. We will examine this issue more fully in Chapter 14.

If awareness of the pretest is a problem, the pretest can be disguised. One way to do this is by administering it in a completely different situation with a different experimenter. Another approach is to embed the pretest in a set of irrelevant measures so it is not obvious that the researcher is interested in a particular topic.

It is also possible to assess the impact of the pretest directly with a combination of both the posttest-only and the pretest-posttest design. In this design, half the participants receive only the posttest, and the other half receive both the pretest and the posttest (see Table 8.1). This is formally called a *Solomon four-group design.* If there is no impact of the pretest, the posttest scores will be the same in the two control groups (with and without the pretest) and in the two experimental groups. Garvin and Damson (2008) employed a Solomon four-group design to study the effect of viewing female fitness magazine models on a measure of depressed mood. Female college students spent 30 minutes viewing either

TABLE 8.1   Solomon four-group design

	Independent variable	
Pretest condition	Control group	Experimental group
No pretest (posttest only)		
Pretest and posttest		

Note: If there is no pretest effect, the posttest mean scores in the two control group conditions will be equal, and the two experimental posttest means will be equal as well. If there is a pretest effect, the pattern of results will differ in the posttest only and the pretest plus posttest conditions.

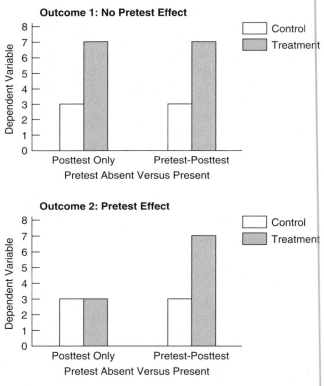

FIGURE 8.1
Examples of outcomes of Solomon four-group design

the fitness magazines or magazines such as *National Geographic*. Two possible outcomes of this study are shown in Figure 8.1. The top graph illustrates an outcome in which the pretest has no impact: The fitness magazine viewing results in higher depression in both the posttest-only and the pretest-posttest condition. This is what was found in the study. The lower graph shows an outcome in which there is a difference between the treatment and control groups when there is a pretest, but there is no group difference when the pretest is absent.

ASSIGNING PARTICIPANTS TO EXPERIMENTAL CONDITIONS

Recall that there are two basic ways of assigning participants to experimental conditions. In one procedure, participants are randomly assigned to the various conditions so that each participates in only one group. This is called an **independent groups design.** It is also known as a **between-subjects design** because comparisons are made between different groups of participants. In the other procedure, participants are in all conditions. In an experiment with two conditions, for example, each participant is assigned to both levels of the independent variable. This is called a **repeated measures design,** because each participant is measured after receiving each level of the independent variable. You will also see this called a **within-subjects design;** in this design, comparisons are made within the same group of participants (subjects). In the next two sections, we will examine each of these designs in detail.

INDEPENDENT GROUPS DESIGN

In an independent groups design, different participants are assigned to each of the conditions using **random assignment.** This means that the decision to assign an individual to a particular condition is completely random and beyond the control of the researcher. For example, you could ask for the participant's month of birth; individuals born in odd-numbered months would be assigned to one group and those born in even-numbered months would be assigned to the other group. In practice, researchers use a sequence of random numbers to determine assignment. Such numbers come from a random number generator computer program such as Research Randomizer, available online at http://www.randomizer.org or QuickCalcs at http://www.graphpad.com/quickcalcs/randomize1.cfm; Excel can also generate random numbers. These programs allow you to randomly determine the assignment of each participant to the various groups in your study. Random assignment will prevent any systematic biases, and the groups can be considered equivalent in terms of participant characteristics such as income, intelligence, age, personality, and political attitudes. In this way, participant differences cannot be an explanation for results of the experiment. As we noted in Chapter 4, in an experiment on the effects of exercise on anxiety, lower levels of anxiety in the exercise group than in the no-exercise group cannot be explained by saying that people in the groups are somehow different on characteristics such as income, education, or personality.

An alternative procedure is to have the *same* individuals participate in all of the groups. This is called a repeated measures experimental design.

REPEATED MEASURES DESIGN

Consider an experiment investigating the relationship between the meaningfulness of material and the learning of that material. In an independent groups design, one group of participants is given highly meaningful material to learn and another group receives less meaningful material. In a repeated measures design, the same individuals will participate in both conditions. Thus, participants might first read low-meaningful material and take a recall test to measure learning; the same participants would then read high-meaningful material and take the recall test. You can see why this is called a repeated measures design; participants are repeatedly measured on the dependent variable after being in each condition of the experiment.

Advantages and Disadvantages of Repeated Measures Design

The repeated measures design has several advantages. An obvious one is that fewer research participants are needed, because each individual participates in all conditions. When participants are scarce or when it is costly to run each individual in the experiment, a repeated measures design may be preferred. In much research on perception, for instance, extensive training of participants is necessary before the actual experiment can begin. Such research often involves only a few individuals who participate in all conditions of the experiment.

An additional advantage of repeated measures designs is that they are extremely sensitive to finding statistically significant differences between groups. This is because we have data from the same people in both conditions. To illustrate why this is important, consider possible data from the recall experiment. Using an independent groups design, the first three participants in the high-meaningful condition had scores of 68, 81, and 92. The first three participants in the low-meaningful condition had scores of 64, 78, and 85. If you calculated an average score for each condition, you would find that the average recall was a bit higher when the material was more meaningful. However, there is a lot of variability in the scores in both groups. You certainly are not finding that everyone in the high-meaningful condition has high recall and everyone in the other condition has low recall. The reason for this variability is that people differ—there are individual differences in recall abilities, so there is a range of scores in both conditions. This is part of "random error" in the scores that we cannot explain.

However, if the same scores were obtained from the first three participants in a repeated measures design, the conclusions would be much different. Let's line up the recall scores for the two conditions:

	High meaning	Low meaning	Difference
Participant 1	68	64	+4
Participant 2	81	78	+3
Participant 3	92	85	+7

With a repeated measures design, the individual differences can be seen and explained. It is true that some people score higher than others because of individual differences in recall abilities, but now you can much more clearly see the effect of the independent variable on recall scores. It is much easier to separate the systematic individual differences from the effect of the independent variable: Scores are higher for every participant in the high-meaningful condition. As a result, we are much more likely to detect an effect of the independent variable on the dependent variable.

The major problem with a repeated measures design stems from the fact that the different conditions must be presented in a particular sequence. Suppose that there is greater recall in the high-meaningful condition. Although this result could be caused by the manipulation of the meaningfulness variable, the result could also simply be an **order effect**—the order of presenting the treatments affects the dependent variable. Thus, greater recall in the high-meaningful condition could be attributed to the fact that the high-meaningful task came second in the order of presentation of the conditions. Performance on the second task might improve merely because of the practice gained on the first task. This improvement is in fact called a **practice effect,** or **learning effect.** It is also possible that a **fatigue effect** could result in a deterioration in performance from the first to the second condition as the research participant becomes tired, bored, or distracted.

It is also possible for the effect of the first treatment to carry over to influence the response to the second treatment—this is known as a **carryover effect.** Suppose the independent variable is severity of a crime. After reading about the less severe crime, the more severe one might seem much worse to participants than it normally would. In addition, reading about the severe crime might subsequently cause participants to view the less severe crime as much milder than they normally would. In both cases, the experience with one condition carried over to affect the response to the second condition. In this example, the carryover effect was a psychological effect of the way that the two situations contrasted with one another.

A carryover effect may also occur when the first condition produces a change that is still influencing the person when the second condition is introduced. Suppose the first condition involves experiencing failure at an important task. This may result in a temporary increase in stress responses. How long does it take before the person returns to a normal state? If the second condition is introduced too soon, the stress may still be affecting the participant.

There are two approaches to dealing with order effects. The first is to employ counterbalancing techniques. The second is to devise a procedure in which the interval between conditions is long enough to minimize the influence of the first condition on the second.

Counterbalancing

Complete counterbalancing In a repeated measures design, it is very important to counterbalance the order of the conditions. With complete **counterbalancing,** all possible orders of presentation are included in the experiment. In the example of a study on learning high- and low-meaningful material, half of the participants would be randomly assigned to the low-high order, and the other half would be assigned to the high-low order. This design is illustrated as follows:

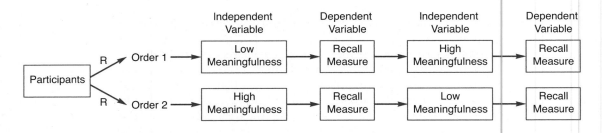

By counterbalancing the order of conditions, it is possible to determine the extent to which order is influencing the results. In the hypothetical memory study, you would know whether the greater recall in the high-meaningful condition is consistent for both orders; you would also know the extent to which a practice effect is responsible for the results.

Counterbalancing principles can be extended to experiments with three or more groups. With three groups, there are 6 possible orders ($3! = 3 \times 2 \times 1 = 6$). With four groups, the number of possible orders increases to 24 ($4! = 4 \times 3 \times 2 \times 1 = 24$); you would need a minimum of 24 participants to represent each order, and you would need 48 participants to have only two participants per order. Imagine the number of orders possible in an experiment by Shepard and Metzler (1971). In their basic experimental paradigm, each participant is shown a three-dimensional object along with the same figure rotated at one of 10 different angles ranging from 0 degrees to 180 degrees (see the sample objects illustrated in Figure 8.2). Each time, the participant presses a button when it is determined that the two figures are the same or different. The dependent variable is reaction time—the amount of time it takes to decide whether the figures are the same or different. The results show that reaction time becomes longer as

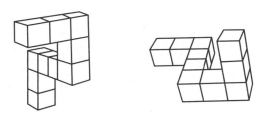

FIGURE 8.2
Three-dimensional figures used by Shepard and Metzler (1971)
Adapted from "Mental Rotation of Three-Dimensional Objects," by R. N. Shepard and J. Metzler, 1971, *Science*, 171, pp. 701–703.

the angle of rotation increases away from the original. In this experiment with 10 conditions, there are 3,628,800 possible orders! Fortunately, there are alternatives to complete counterbalancing that still allow researchers to draw valid conclusions about the effect of the independent variable without running some 3.6 million tests.

Latin squares A technique to control for order effects without having all possible orders is to construct a **Latin square:** a limited set of orders constructed to ensure that (1) each condition appears at each ordinal position and (2) each condition precedes and follows each condition one time. Using a Latin square to determine order controls for most order effects without having to include all possible orders. Suppose you replicated the Shepard and Metzler (1971) study using only 4 of the 10 rotations: 0, 60, 120, and 180 degrees. A Latin square for these four conditions is shown in Figure 8.3. Each row in the square is one of the orders of the conditions (the conditions are labeled A, B, C, and D). The number of orders in a Latin square is equal to the number of conditions; thus, if there are four conditions, there are four orders. When you conduct your study using the Latin square to determine order, you need at least 1 participant per row. Usually, you will have 2 or more participants per row; the number of participants tested in each order must be equal.

Time Interval Between Treatments

In addition to counterbalancing the order of treatments, researchers need to carefully determine the time interval between presentation of treatments and possible activities between them. A rest period may counteract a fatigue effect;

Order of Conditions

	1	2	3	4
Row 1	A (60)	B (0)	D (120)	C (180)
Row 2	B (0)	C (180)	A (60)	D (120)
Row 3	C (180)	D (120)	B (0)	A (60)
Row 4	D (120)	A (60)	C (180)	B (0)

FIGURE 8.3
A Latin square with four conditions

Note: The four conditions were randomly given letter designations. A = 60 degrees, B = 0 degrees, C = 180 degrees, and D = 120 degrees. Each row represents a different order of running the conditions.

attending to an unrelated task between treatments may reduce the possibility that participants will contrast the first treatment with the second. If the treatment is the administration of a drug that takes time to wear off, the interval between treatments may have to be a day or more. Wilson, Ellinwood, Mathew, and Johnson (1994) examined the effects of three doses of marijuana on cognitive and motor task performance. Each participant was tested before and after smoking a marijuana cigarette. Because of the time necessary for the effects of the drug to wear off, the three conditions were run on separate days. A similarly long time interval would be needed with procedures that produce emotional changes, such as heightened anxiety or anger. You may have noted that introduction of an extended time interval may create a separate problem: Participants will have to commit to the experiment for a longer period of time. This can make it more difficult to recruit volunteers, and if the study extends over two or more days, some participants may drop out of the experiment altogether.

Choosing Between Independent Groups and Repeated Measures Designs

Repeated measures designs have two major advantages over independent groups designs: (1) a reduction in the number of participants required to complete the experiment and (2) greater control over participant differences and thus greater ability to detect an effect of the independent variable. As noted previously, in certain areas of research, these advantages are very important. However, the disadvantages of repeated measures designs and the precautions required to deal with them are usually sufficient reasons for researchers to use independent groups designs.

A very different consideration in whether to use a repeated measures design concerns generalization to conditions in the "real world." Greenwald (1976) has pointed out that in actual everyday situations, we sometimes encounter independent variables in an independent groups fashion: We encounter only one condition without a contrasting comparison. However, some independent variables are most frequently encountered in a repeated measures fashion: Both conditions appear, and our responses occur in the context of exposure to both levels of the independent variable. Thus, for example, if you are interested in how a defendant's characteristics affects jurors, an independent groups design may be most appropriate because actual jurors focus on a single defendant in a trial. However, if you are interested in the effects of a job applicant's characteristics on employers, a repeated measures design would be reasonable because employers typically consider several applicants at once. Whether to use an independent groups or repeated measures design may be partially determined by these generalization issues.

Finally, any experimental procedure that produces a relatively permanent change in an individual cannot be used in a repeated measures design. Examples include a psychotherapy treatment or a surgical procedure such as the removal of brain tissue.

MATCHED PAIRS DESIGN

A somewhat more complicated method of assigning participants to conditions in an experiment is called a **matched pairs design.** Instead of simply randomly assigning participants to groups, the goal is to first match people on a participant variable (see Chapter 4). The matching variable will be either the dependent measure or a variable that is strongly related to the dependent variable. For example, in a learning experiment, participants might be matched on the basis of scores on a cognitive ability measure or even grade point average. If cognitive ability is not related to the dependent measure, however, matching would be a waste of time. The goal is to achieve the same equivalency of groups that is achieved with a repeated measures design without the necessity of having the same participants in both conditions. The design looks like this:

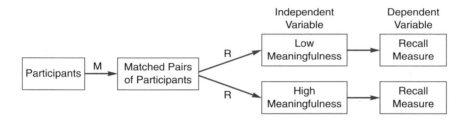

When using a matched pairs design, the first step is to obtain a measure of the matching variable from each individual. The participants are then rank ordered from highest to lowest based on their scores on the matching variable. Now the researcher can form matched pairs that are approximately equal on the characteristic (the highest two participants form the first pair, the next two form the second pair, and so on). Finally, the members of each pair are randomly assigned to the conditions in the experiment. (Note that there are methods of matching pairs of individuals on the basis of scores derived from multiple variables; these methods are described briefly in Chapter 11.)

A matched pairs design ensures that the groups are equivalent (on the matching variable) prior to introduction of the independent variable manipulation. This assurance could be particularly important with small sample sizes, because random assignment procedures are more likely to produce equivalent groups as the sample size increases. Matching, then, is most likely to be used when only a few participants are available or when it is very costly to run large numbers of individuals in the experiment—as long as there is a strong relationship between a dependent measure and the matching variable. The result is a greater ability to detect a statistically significant effect of the independent variable because it is possible to account for individual differences in responses to the independent variable, just as we saw with a repeated measures design. (The issues of variability and statistical significance are discussed further in Chapter 13 and Appendix B.)

However useful they are, matching procedures can be costly and time-consuming, because they require measuring participants on the matching variable prior to the experiment. Such efforts are worthwhile only when the matching variable is strongly related to the dependent measure and you know that the relationship exists prior to conducting your study. For these reasons, matched pairs is not a commonly used experimental design. However, we will discuss matching again in Chapter 11 when describing quasi-experimental designs that do not have random assignment to conditions. You now have a fundamental understanding of the design of experiments. In the next chapter, we will consider issues that arise when you decide how to actually conduct an experiment.

ILLUSTRATIVE ARTICLE: EXPERIMENTAL DESIGN

We are constantly connected. We can be reached by cell phone almost anywhere, at any time. Text messages compete for our attention. E-mail and Internet messaging (IM) can interrupt our attention whenever we use a computer. Is this a problem? Most people like to think of themselves as experts at multitasking. Is that true?

A study conducted by Bowman, Levine, Waite, and Gendron (2010) attempted to determine whether IMing during a reading session affected test performance. In this study, participants were randomly assigned to one of three conditions: one where they were asked to IM prior to reading, one in which they were asked to IM during reading, and one in which IMing was not allowed at all. Afterward, all participants completed a brief test on the material presented in the reading.

First, acquire and read the article:

Bowman, L. L., Levine, L. E., Waite, B. M., & Gendron, M. (2010). Can students really multitask? An experimental study of instant messaging while reading. *Computers & Education, 54,* 927–931. doi:10.1016/j.compedu.2009.09.024

After reading the article, answer the following questions:

1. This experiment used a posttest-only design. How could the researchers have used a pretest-posttest design? What would the advantages and disadvantages be of using a pretest-posttest design?

2. This experiment used an independent groups design.

   a. How could they have used a repeated measures design? What would have been the advantages and disadvantages of using a repeated measures design?

   b. How could they have used a matched pairs design? What variables do you think would have been worthwhile to match participants on? What would have been the advantages and disadvantages of using a matched pairs design?

3. What potential confounding variables can you think of?

4. In what way does this study reflect—or not reflect—the reality of studying and test taking in college? That is, how would you evaluate the external validity of this study?

5. How good was the internal validity of this experiment?

6. What were the researchers' key conclusions of this experiment?

7. Would you have predicted the results obtained in this experiment? Why or why not?

Study Terms

Attrition (also mortality) (p. 161)

Between-subjects design (also independent groups design) (p. 163)

Carryover effect (p. 165)

Confounding variable (p. 157)

Counterbalancing (p. 165)

Fatigue effect (p. 165)

Independent groups design (also between-subjects design) (p. 163)

Internal validity (p. 158)

Latin square (p. 167)

Learning effect (also practice effect) (p. 165)

Matched pairs design (p. 169)

Mortality (also attrition) (p. 161)

Order effect (p. 165)

Posttest-only design (p. 158)

Practice effect (also learning effect) (p. 165)

Pretest-posttest design (p. 159)

Random assignment (p. 163)

Repeated measures design (also within-subjects design) (p.163)

Selection differences (p. 159)

Within-subjects design (also repeated measures design) (p. 163)

Review Questions

1. What is confounding of variables?

2. What is meant by the internal validity of an experiment?

3. How do the two true experimental designs eliminate the problem of selection differences?

4. Distinguish between the posttest-only design and the pretest-posttest design. What are the advantages and disadvantages of each?

5. What is a repeated measures design? What are the advantages of using a repeated measures design? What are the disadvantages?

6. What are some of the ways of dealing with the problems of a repeated measures design?

7. When would a researcher decide to use the matched pairs design? What would be the advantages of this design?

8. The procedure used to obtain your sample (i.e., random or nonrandom sampling) is not the same as the procedure for assigning participants to conditions; distinguish between random sampling and random assignment.

Activity Questions

1. Design an experiment to test the hypothesis that single-gender math classes are beneficial to adolescent females. Construct operational definitions of both the independent and dependent variables. Your experiment should have two groups and use the matched pairs procedure. Make a good case for your selection of the matching variable. In addition, defend your choice of either a posttest-only design or a pretest-posttest design.

2. Design a repeated measures experiment that investigates the effect of report presentation style on the grade received for the report. Use two levels of the independent variable: a "professional style" presentation (high-quality paper, consistent use of margins and fonts, carefully constructed tables and charts) and a "nonprofessional style" (average-quality paper, frequent changes in the margins and fonts, tables and charts lacking proper labels). Discuss the necessity for using counterbalancing. Create a table illustrating the experimental design.

3. Professor Foley conducted a cola taste test. Each participant in the experiment first tasted 2 ounces of Coca-Cola, then 2 ounces of Pepsi, and finally 2 ounces of Sam's Choice Cola. A rating of the cola's flavor was made after each taste. What are the potential problems with this experimental design and the procedures used? Revise the design and procedures to address these problems. You may wish to consider several alternatives and think about the advantages and disadvantages of each.

9

Conducting Experiments

LEARNING OBJECTIVES

- Distinguish between straightforward and staged manipulations of an independent variable.
- Describe the three types of dependent variables: self-report, behavioral, and physiological.
- Discuss sensitivity of a dependent variable, contrasting floor effects and ceiling effects.
- Describe ways to control participant expectations and experimenter expectations.
- List the reasons for conducting pilot studies.
- Describe the advantages of including a manipulation check in an experiment.

The previous chapters have laid the foundation for planning a research investigation. In this chapter, we will focus on some very practical aspects of conducting research. How do you select the research participants? What should you consider when deciding how to manipulate an independent variable? What should you worry about when you measure a variable? What do you do when the study is completed?

SELECTING RESEARCH PARTICIPANTS

The focus of your study may be children, college students, elderly adults, employees, rats, pigeons, or even cockroaches or flatworms; in all cases, the participants or subjects must somehow be selected. The method used to select participants can have a profound impact on external validity. Remember that external validity is defined as the extent to which results from a study can be generalized to other populations and settings.

Recall from Chapter 7 that most research projects involve sampling research participants from a population of interest. The population is composed of all of the individuals of interest to the researcher. Samples may be drawn from the population using probability sampling or nonprobability sampling techniques. When it is important to accurately describe the population, you must use probability sampling. This is why probability sampling is so crucial when conducting scientific polls. Much research, on the other hand, is more interested in testing hypotheses about behavior: attempting to detect whether X causes Y rather than describing a population. Here, the two focuses of the study are the relationships between the variables being studied and tests of predictions derived from theories of behavior. In such cases, the participants may be found in the easiest way possible using nonprobability sampling methods, also known as haphazard or "convenience" methods. You may ask students in introductory psychology classes to participate, knock on doors in your dorm to find people to be tested, or choose a class in which to test children simply because you know the teacher. Nothing is wrong with such methods as long as you recognize that they affect the ability to generalize your results to some larger population. In Chapter 14, we examine the issues of generalizing from the rather atypical samples of college students and other conveniently obtained research participants.

You will also need to determine your sample size. How many participants will you need in your study? In general, increasing your sample size increases the likelihood that your results will be statistically significant, because larger samples provide more accurate estimates of population values (see Table 7.2). Most researchers take note of the sample sizes in the research area being studied and select a sample size that is typical for studies in the area. A more formal approach to selecting a sample size, called power analysis, is discussed in Chapter 13.

MANIPULATING THE INDEPENDENT VARIABLE

To manipulate an independent variable, you have to construct an operational definition of the variable (see Chapter 4). That is, you must turn a conceptual variable into a set of operations—specific instructions, events, and stimuli to be presented to the research participants. The manipulation of the independent variable, then, is when a researcher changes the conditions to which participants are exposed. In addition, the independent and dependent variables must be introduced within the context of the total experimental setting. This has been called *setting the stage* (Aronson, Brewer, & Carlsmith, 1985).

Setting the Stage

In setting the stage, you usually have to supply the participants with the information necessary for them to provide their informed consent to participate (informed consent is covered in Chapter 3). This generally includes information about the underlying rationale of the study. Sometimes, the rationale given is completely truthful, although only rarely will you want to tell participants the actual hypothesis. For example, you might say that you are conducting an experiment on memory when, in fact, you are studying a specific aspect of memory (your independent variable). If participants know what you are studying, they may try to confirm the hypothesis, or they may try to look good by behaving in the most socially acceptable way. If you find that deception is necessary, you have a special obligation to address the deception when you debrief the participants at the conclusion of the experiment.

There are no clear-cut rules for setting the stage, except that the experimental setting must seem plausible to the participants, nor are there any clear-cut rules for translating conceptual variables into specific operations. Exactly how the variable is manipulated depends on the variable and the cost, practicality, and ethics of the procedures being considered.

Types of Manipulations

Straightforward manipulations
Researchers are usually able to manipulate an independent variable with relative simplicity by presenting written, verbal, or visual material to the participants. Such **straightforward manipulations** manipulate variables with instructions and stimulus presentations. Stimuli may be presented verbally, in written form, via videotape, or with a computer. Let's look at a few examples.

Goldstein, Cialdini, and Griskevicius (2008) were interested in the influence of signs that hotels leave in their bathrooms encouraging guests to reuse their towels. In their research, they simply printed signs that were hooked on towel shelves in the rooms of single guests staying at least two nights. In a standard message, the sign read "HELP SAVE THE ENVIRONMENT. You can show your respect of nature and help save the environment by reusing towels during your stay." In this case, 35% of the guests reused their towels on the second day. Another condition invoked a social norm that other people are reusing towels: "JOIN YOUR FELLOW GUESTS IN HELPING TO SAVE THE ENVIRONMENT. Almost 75% of guests who are asked to participate in our new resource savings program do help by using their towels more than once. You can join your fellow guests in this program to save the environment by reusing your towels during your stay." This sign resulted in 44% reusing their towels. As you might expect, the researchers have extended this research to study ways that the sign can be even more effective in increasing conservation.

Studies on jury decisions often ask participants to read a description of a jury trial in which a crucial piece of information is varied. Bornstein (1998) studied the effect of the severity of injury on product liability judgments. In the low-severity condition, participants read about a case in which a woman taking birth control pills had been diagnosed with cancer. In a low-severity condition, the cancer was detected early, one ovary was removed, the woman could still have children, and future prognosis was good. In the high-severity condition, the cancer was detected late, both ovaries were removed so pregnancy would not be possible, and the future prognosis was poor. The evidence on whether the pills could be responsible for the cancer was the same in both conditions, thus product liability judgments should be the same in both conditions. Nevertheless, the severity information affected liability judgments: The pill manufacturer was found liable by 40% of the participants in the high-severity condition versus 21% in the low-severity condition.

Most memory research relies on straightforward manipulations. For example, Coltheart and Langdon (1998) displayed lists of words to participants and later measured recall. The word lists differed on phonological similarity: Some lists had words that sounded similar, such as *cat, map,* and *pat,* and other lists had dissimilar words such as *mop, pen,* and *cow.* They found that lists with dissimilar words are recalled more accurately. In a more complex memory study, Reeve and Aggleton (1998) presented a script of a future episode of a British soap opera called *The Archers* to both fans ("experts") and people unfamiliar with the show. In one condition, the script was typical of an actual episode of the program—the Archers visit a livestock market. In the other condition, the script was atypical—the Archers visit a boat show. The characters and basic structure of the show were identical in the two conditions. After reading the script, the participants were given a measure of retention of the details of the episode. They found that being an expert aided retention only when the story was a typical one. In the atypical condition, both fans and nonfans had equal retention. Reeve and Aggleton concluded that the benefits of being an expert are limited.

As a final example of a straightforward manipulation, consider a study by Mazer, Murphy, and Simonds (2009) on the effect of college teacher self-disclosure (via Facebook) on perceptions of teacher effectiveness. For this study, students read one of three Facebook profiles that were created for a volunteer teacher, one for each of the high-, medium-, and low-disclosure conditions. Level of disclosure was manipulated by changing the number and nature of photographs, biographical information, favorite movies/books/quotes, campus groups, and posts on "the wall." After viewing the profile to which they were assigned, participants rated the teacher on several dimensions. Higher disclosure resulted in perceptions of greater caring and trustworthiness; however, disclosure was not related to perceptions of teacher competence.

You will find that most manipulations of independent variables in all areas of research are straightforward. Researchers vary the difficulty of material to be learned, motivation levels, the way questions are asked, characteristics of people to be judged, and a variety of other factors in a straightforward manner.

Staged manipulations

Other manipulations are less straightforward. Sometimes, it is necessary to stage events during the experiment in order to manipulate the independent variable successfully. When this occurs, the manipulation is called a **staged manipulation** or *event manipulation*.

Staged manipulations are most frequently used for two reasons. First, the researcher may be trying to create some psychological state in the participants, such as frustration, anger, or a temporary lowering of self-esteem. For example, Zitek and her colleagues studied what is termed a *sense of entitlement* (Zitek, Jordan, Monin, & Leach, 2010). Their hypothesis is that the feeling of being unfairly wronged leads to a sense of entitlement and, as a result, the tendency to be more selfish with others. In their study, all participants played a computer game. The researchers programmed the game so that some participants would lose when the game crashed. This is an unfair outcome, because the participants lost for no good reason. Participants in the other condition also lost, but they thought it was because the game itself was very difficult. The participants experiencing the broken game did in fact behave more selfishly after the game; they later allocated themselves more money than deserved when competing with another participant.

Second, a staged manipulation may be necessary to simulate some situation that occurs in the real world. Recall the Milgram obedience experiment that was described in Chapter 3. In that study, an elaborate procedure—ostensibly to study learning—was constructed to actually study obedience to an authority. Or consider a study on computer multitasking conducted by Bowman, Levine, Waite, and Gendron (2009), wherein students read academic material presented on a computer screen. In one condition, the participants received and responded to instant messages while they were reading. Other participants did not receive any messages. Student performance on a test was equal in the two conditions. However, students in the instant message condition took longer to read the material (after the time spent on the message was subtracted from the total time working on the computer).

Staged manipulations frequently employ a **confederate** (sometimes termed an "accomplice"). Usually, the confederate appears to be another participant in an experiment but is actually part of the manipulation (we discussed the use of confederates in Chapter 3). A confederate may be useful to create a particular social situation. For example, Hermans, Herman, Larsen, and Engels (2010) studied whether food intake by males is affected by the amount of food consumed by a companion. Participants were recruited for a study on evaluation of movie trailers. The participant and a confederate sat in a comfortable setting in which they viewed and evaluated three trailers. They were then told that they needed a break before viewing the next trailers; snacks were available if they were interested. In one condition, the confederate took a large serving of snacks. A small serving was taken in another condition, and the confederate did not eat in the third condition. The researchers then measured the amount consumed by the actual participants; they did model the amount consumed by the confederate but only when they were hungry.

The classic Asch (1956) conformity experiment provides another example of how confederates may be used. Asch gathered people into groups and asked them to respond to a line judgment task such as the one in Figure 9.1. Which of the three test lines matches the standard? Although this appears to be a simple task, Asch made it more interesting by having several confederates announce the same incorrect judgment prior to asking the actual participant; this procedure was repeated over a number of trials with different line judgments. Asch was able to demonstrate how easy it is to produce conformity—participants conformed to the unanimous majority on many of the trials even though the correct answer was clear. Finally, confederates may be used in field experiments as well as laboratory research. As described in Chapter 4, Lee, Schwarz, Taubman, and Hou (2010) studied the impact of public sneezing on the perception of unrelated risks by having an accomplice either sneeze or not sneeze (control condition) while walking by someone in a public area of a university. A researcher then approached those people with a request to complete a questionnaire, which they described as a "class project." The questionnaire measured participants' perceptions of average Americans' risk of contracting a serious disease. The researchers found that, indeed, being around a person who sneezes increases self-reported perception of risk.

As you can see, staged manipulations demand a great deal of ingenuity and even some acting ability. They are used to involve the participants in an ongoing social situation that the individuals perceive not as an experiment but as a real experience. Researchers assume that the result will be natural behavior that truly

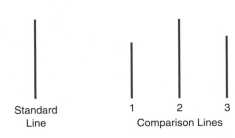

FIGURE 9.1
Example
of the
Asch line
judgment
task

Standard
Line

1   2   3
Comparison Lines

TABLE 9.1   Straightforward and staged manipulations

Straightforward manipulation	Staged or event manipulation
• Written, verbal, or visual instructions and/or stimulus presentation	• Necessary to create some psychological state in the participants OR to simulate a situation that occurs in the real world
• Can also use videos or computers	• May use confederate(s)

Test yourself: Read each statement and then circle the appropriate letter: T (true) or F (false). (Answers are provided on the last page of the chapter.)

1. Most manipulations are straightforward.	T	F
2. Staged manipulations are designed to get participants involved in the situation and to make them think that it is a real experience.	T	F
3. A staged experiment may be difficult to replicate by other researchers.	T	F
4. Straightforward manipulations are often difficult to interpret.	T	F

reflects the feelings and intentions of the participants. However, such procedures allow for a great deal of subtle interpersonal communication that is hard to put into words; this may make it difficult for other researchers to replicate the experiment. Also, a complex manipulation is difficult to interpret. If many things happened during the experiment, what *one* thing was responsible for the results? In general, it is easier to interpret results when the manipulation is relatively straightforward. However, the nature of the variable you are studying sometimes demands complicated procedures. A comparison of staged and straightforward manipulations is shown in Table 9.1.

Strength of the Manipulation

The simplest experimental design has two levels of the independent variable. In planning the experiment, the researcher has to choose these levels. A general principle to follow is to make the manipulation as strong as possible. A strong manipulation maximizes the differences between the two groups and increases the chances that the independent variable will have a statistically significant effect on the dependent variable.

To illustrate, suppose you think that there is a positive linear relationship between attitude similarity and liking ("birds of a feather flock together"). In conducting the experiment, you could arrange for participants to encounter another person, a confederate. In one group, the confederate and the participant would share similar attitudes; in the other group, the confederate and the participant would be dissimilar. Similarity, then, is the independent variable, and liking is the dependent variable. Now you have to decide on the amount of similarity. Figure 9.2 shows the hypothesized relationship between attitude similarity and liking at 10 different levels of similarity. Level 1 represents the

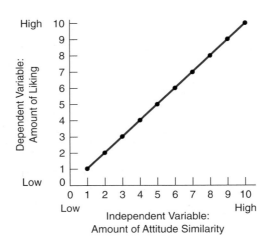

FIGURE 9.2
Relationship between attitude similarity and liking

least amount of similarity with no common attitudes, and level 10 the greatest (all attitudes are similar). To achieve the strongest manipulation, the participants in one group would encounter a confederate of level 1 similarity; those in the other group would encounter a confederate of level 10 similarity. This would result in the greatest difference in the liking means—a 9-point difference. A weaker manipulation—using levels 4 and 7, for example—would result in a smaller mean difference.

A strong manipulation is particularly important in the early stages of research, when the researcher is most interested in demonstrating that a relationship does, in fact, exist. If the early experiments reveal a relationship between the variables, subsequent research can systematically manipulate the other levels of the independent variable to provide a more detailed picture of the relationship.

The principle of using the strongest manipulation possible should be tempered by at least two considerations. The first concerns the external validity of a study: The strongest possible manipulation may entail a situation that rarely, if ever, occurs in the real world. For example, an extremely strong crowding manipulation might involve placing so many people in a room that no one could move—a manipulation that might significantly affect a variety of behaviors. However, we wouldn't know if the results were similar to those occurring in more common, less crowded situations, such as many classrooms or offices.

A second consideration is ethics: A manipulation should be as strong as possible within the bounds of ethics. A strong manipulation of fear or anxiety, for example, might not be possible because of the potential physical and psychological harm to participants.

Cost of the Manipulation

Cost is another factor in the decision about how to manipulate the independent variable. Researchers who have limited monetary resources may not be able to afford expensive equipment, salaries for confederates, or payments to participants in long-term experiments. Also, a manipulation in which participants must be run individually requires more of the researcher's time than a manipulation that allows running many individuals in a single setting. In this respect, a manipulation that uses straightforward presentation of written or verbal material is less costly than a complex, staged experimental manipulation. Some government and private agencies offer grants for research; because much research is costly, continued public support of these agencies is very important.

MEASURING THE DEPENDENT VARIABLE

In previous chapters, we have discussed various aspects of measuring variables including reliability, validity, and reactivity of measures; observational methods; and the development of self-report measures for questionnaires and interviews. In this section, we will focus on measurement considerations that are particularly relevant to experimental research.

Types of Measures

The dependent variable in most experiments is one of three general types: self-report, behavioral, or physiological.

Self-report measures   **Self-reports** can be used to measure attitudes, liking for someone, judgments about someone's personality characteristics, intended behaviors, emotional states, attributions about why someone performed well or poorly on a task, confidence in one's judgments, and many other aspects of human thought and behavior. Rating scales with descriptive anchors (endpoints) are most commonly used. For example, Labranche, Helweg-Larsen, Byrd, and Choquette (1997) studied the impact of health promotion brochures by asking women to read a brochure on breast self-examinations and then asking them to respond to several questions on a 7-point scale, which included the following:

> I feel I could properly give myself a breast self-examination.

Strongly disagree _____ _____ _____ _____ _____ _____ _____ Strongly agree

Behavioral measures   **Behavioral measures** are direct observations of behaviors. As with self-reports, measurements of an almost endless number of behaviors are possible. Sometimes, the researcher may record whether a given behavior occurs—for example, whether an individual responds to a request for help, makes an error on a test, or chooses to engage in one activity rather than another. Often, the researcher must decide whether to record the number of times a behavior occurs in a given time period—the *rate* of a behavior; how quickly a response occurs after a stimulus—a *reaction time;* or how long a behavior lasts— a measure of *duration.* The decision about which aspect of behavior to measure depends on which is most theoretically relevant for the study of a particular problem or which measure logically follows from the independent variable manipulation.

An example of a behavioral measure can be found in a study of adult couples' attachment behavior at an airport. Fraley and Shaver (1998) observed attachment behavior in adult couples that were either separating, or not separating, at an airport. In observing couples' behavior, Fraley and Shaver coded specific behaviors into categories. For example, crying was coded as sadness and holding hands until the last possible minute was coded as contact seeking.

Physiological measures
Physiological measures are recordings of responses of the body. Many such measurements are available; examples include the **galvanic skin response** (GSR), **electromyogram** (EMG), and **electroencephalogram** (EEG). The GSR is a measure of general emotional arousal and anxiety; it measures the electrical conductance of the skin, which changes when sweating occurs. The EMG measures muscle tension and is frequently used as a measure of tension or stress. The EEG is a measure of electrical activity of brain cells. It can be used to record general brain arousal as a response to different situations, such as activity in certain parts of the brain as learning occurs or brain activity during different stages of sleep.

The GSR, EMG, and EEG have long been used as physiological indicators of important psychological variables. Many other physiological measures are available, including temperature, heart rate, and analysis of blood or urine (see Cacioppo & Tassinary, 1990). In recent years, magnetic resonance imaging (MRI) has become an increasingly important tool for researchers in behavioral neuroscience. An **MRI** provides an image of an individual's brain structure. It allows scientists to compare the brain structure of individuals with a particular condition (e.g., a cognitive impairment, schizophrenia, or attention deficit hyperactivity disorder) with the brain structure of people without the condition. In addition, a **functional MRI** (fMRI) allows researchers to scan areas of the brain while a research participant performs a physical or cognitive task. The data provide evidence for what brain processes are involved in these tasks. For example, a researcher can see which areas of the brain are most active when performing different memory tasks. In one study using fMRI, elderly adults with higher levels of education not only performed better on memory tasks than their less educated peers, but they also used areas of their frontal cortex that were not used by other elderly and younger individuals (Springer, McIntosh, Winocur, & Grady, 2005).

Multiple Measures

Although it is convenient to describe single dependent variables, most studies include more than one dependent measure. One reason to use multiple measures stems from the fact that a variable can be measured in a variety of concrete ways (recall the discussion of operational definitions in Chapter 4). In a study on health-related behaviors, for example, researchers measured the number of work days missed because of ill health, the number of doctor visits, and the use of aspirin and tranquilizers (Matteson & Ivancevich, 1983). Physiological measures such as blood pressure might have been taken as well. If the independent variable has the same effect on several measures of the same dependent variable, our confidence in the results is increased. It is also useful to know whether the same independent variable affects some measures but not others. For example, an independent variable designed to affect liking might have an effect on some measures of liking (e.g., desirability as a person to work with) but not others (e.g., desirability as a dating partner). Researchers also may be interested in studying the effects of an independent variable on several different behaviors. For example, an experiment on the effects of a new classroom management technique might examine academic performance, interaction rates among classmates, and teacher satisfaction.

When you have more than one dependent measure, the question of *order* arises. Does it matter which measures are made first? Is it possible that the results for a particular measure will be different if the measure comes early rather than later? The issue is similar to the order effects that were discussed in Chapter 8 in the context of repeated measures designs. Perhaps responding to the first measures will somehow affect responses on the later measures; or perhaps the participants attend more closely to first measures than to later measures. There are two possible ways of responding to this issue. If it appears that the problem is serious, the order of presenting the measures can be counterbalanced using the techniques described in Chapter 8. Often there are no indications from previous research that order is a serious problem. In this case, the prudent response is to present the most important measures first and the less important ones later. With this approach, order will not be a problem in interpreting the results on the most important dependent variables. Even though order may be a potential problem for some of the measures, the overall impact on the study is minimized.

Making multiple measurements in a single experiment is valuable when it is feasible to do so. However, it may be necessary to conduct a separate series of experiments to explore the effects of an independent variable on various behaviors.

Sensitivity of the Dependent Variable

The dependent variable should be sensitive enough to detect differences between groups. A measure of liking that asks, "Do you like this person?" with only a simple "yes" or "no" response alternative is less sensitive than one that asks, "How much do you like this person?" on a 5- or 7-point scale. With the first measure, people may tend to be nice and say yes even if they have some negative feelings about the person. The second measure allows for a gradation of liking; such a scale would make it easier to detect differences in amount of liking.

The issue of **sensitivity** is particularly important when measuring human performance. Memory can be measured using recall, recognition, or reaction time; cognitive task performance might be measured by examining speed or number of errors during a proofreading task; physical performance can be measured through various motor tasks. Such tasks vary in their difficulty. Sometimes a task is so easy that everyone does well regardless of the conditions that are manipulated by the independent variable. This results in what is called a **ceiling effect**—the independent variable appears to have no effect on the dependent measure only because participants quickly reach the maximum performance level. The opposite problem occurs when a task is so difficult that hardly anyone can perform well; this is called a **floor effect.**

The need to consider sensitivity of measures is nicely illustrated in the Freedman et al. (1971) study of crowding mentioned in Chapter 4. The study examined the effect of crowding on various measures of cognitive task performance and found that crowding did not impair performance. You could conclude that crowding has no effect on performance; however, it is also possible that the measures were either too easy or too difficult to detect an effect of crowding. In fact, subsequent research showed that the tasks may have been too easy; when participants were asked to perform more complex tasks, crowding did result in lower performance (Paulus, Annis, Seta, Schkade, & Matthews, 1976).

Cost of Measures

Another consideration is cost—some measures may be more costly than others. Paper-and-pencil self-report measures are generally inexpensive; measures that require trained observers or elaborate equipment can become quite costly. A researcher studying nonverbal behavior, for example, might have to use a video camera to record each participant's behaviors in a situation. Two or more observers would then have to view the tapes to code behaviors such as eye contact, smiling, or self-touching (two observers are needed to ensure that the observations are reliable). Thus, there would be expenses for both equipment and personnel. Physiological recording devices are also expensive. Researchers need resources from the university or outside agencies to carry out such research.

ADDITIONAL CONTROLS

The basic experimental design has two groups: in the simplest case, an experimental group that receives the treatment and a control group that does not. Use of a control group makes it possible to eliminate a variety of alternative explanations for the results, thus improving internal validity. Sometimes additional control procedures may be necessary to address other types of alternative explanations. Two general control issues concern expectancies on the part of both the participants in the experiment and the experimenters.

Controlling for Participant Expectations

Demand characteristics   We noted previously that experimenters generally do not wish to inform participants about the specific hypotheses being studied or the exact purpose of the research. The reason for this lies in the problem of **demand characteristics** (Orne, 1962), which is any feature of an experiment that might inform participants of the purpose of the study. The concern is that when participants form expectations about the hypothesis of the study, they will then do whatever is necessary to confirm the hypothesis. For example, if you were studying the relationship between political orientation and homophobia, participants might figure out the hypothesis and behave according to what they think you want, rather than according to their true selves.

One way to control for demand characteristics is to use deception—to make participants think that the experiment is studying one thing when actually it is studying something else. The experimenter may devise elaborate cover stories to explain the purpose of the study and to disguise what is really being studied. The researcher may also attempt to disguise the dependent variable by using an unobtrusive measure or by placing the measure among a set of unrelated **filler items** on a questionnaire. Another approach is simply to assess whether demand characteristics are a problem by asking participants about their perceptions of the purpose of the research. It may be that participants do not have an accurate view of the purpose of the study; or if some individuals do guess the hypotheses of the study, their data may be analyzed separately.

Demand characteristics may be eliminated when people are not aware that an experiment is taking place or that their behavior is being observed. Thus, experiments conducted in field settings and observational research in which the observer is concealed or unobtrusive measures are used minimize the problem of demand characteristics.

Placebo groups   A special kind of participant expectation arises in research on the effects of drugs. Consider an experiment that is investigating whether a drug such as Prozac reduces depression. One group of people diagnosed as depressive receives the drug and the other group receives nothing. Now suppose that the drug group shows an improvement. We do not know whether the improvement was caused by the properties of the drug or by the participants' expectations about the effect of the drug—what is called a *placebo effect*. In other words, just administering a pill or an injection may be sufficient to cause an observed improvement in behavior. To control for this possibility, a **placebo group** can be added. Participants in the placebo group receive a pill or injection containing an inert, harmless substance; they do not receive the drug given to members of the experimental group. If the improvement results from the active properties of the drug, the participants in the experimental group should show greater improvement than those in the placebo group. If the placebo group improves as much as the experimental group, all improvement could be caused by a placebo effect.

Sometimes, participants' expectations are the primary focus of an investigation. For example, Marlatt and Rohsenow (1980) conducted research to determine which behavioral effects of alcohol are due to alcohol itself as opposed to the psychological impact of believing one is drinking alcohol. The experimental design to examine these effects had four groups: (1) expect no alcohol–receive no alcohol, (2) expect no alcohol–receive alcohol, (3) expect alcohol–receive no alcohol, and (4) expect alcohol–receive alcohol. This design is called a *balanced placebo design*. Marlatt and Rohsenow's research suggests that the belief that one has consumed alcohol is a more important determinant of behavior than the alcohol itself. That is, people who believed they had consumed alcohol (Groups 3 and 4) behaved very similarly, although those in Group 3 were not actually given any alcohol.

In some areas of research, the use of placebo control groups has ethical implications. Suppose you are studying a treatment that does have a positive effect on people (for example, by reducing migraine headaches or alleviating symptoms of depression). It is important to use careful experimental procedures to make sure that the treatment does have an impact and that alternative explanations for the effect, including a placebo effect, are eliminated. However, it is also important to help those people who are in the control conditions; this aligns with the concept of beneficence that was covered in Chapter 3. Thus, participants in the control conditions must be given the treatment as soon as they have completed their part in the study in order to maximize the benefits of participation.

Placebo effects are real and must receive serious study in many areas of research. A great deal of current research and debate focuses on the extent to which any beneficial effects of antidepressant medications such as Prozac are due to placebo effects (e.g., Kirsch, 2010; Wampold, Minami, Tierney, Baskin, & Bhati, 2005).

Controlling for Experimenter Expectations

Experimenters are usually aware of the purpose of the study and thus may develop expectations about how participants should respond. These expectations can in turn bias the results. This general problem is called **experimenter bias** or **expectancy effects** (Rosenthal, 1966, 1967, 1969).

Expectancy effects may occur whenever the experimenter knows which condition the participants are in. There are two potential sources of experimenter bias. First, the experimenter might unintentionally treat participants differently in the various conditions of the study. For example, certain words might be emphasized when reading instructions to one group but not the other, or the experimenter might smile more when interacting with people in one of the conditions. The second source of bias can occur when experimenters record the behaviors of the participants; there may be subtle differences in the way the experimenter interprets and records the behaviors.

Research on expectancy effects Expectancy effects have been studied in a variety of ways. Perhaps the earliest demonstration of the problem is the case of Clever Hans, a horse whose alleged brilliance was revealed by Pfungst (1911) to be an illusion. Robert Rosenthal describes Clever Hans:

Hans, it will be remembered, was the clever horse who could solve problems of mathematics and musical harmony with equal skill and grace, simply by tapping out the answers with his hoof. A committee of eminent experts testified that Hans, whose owner made no profit from his horse's talents, was receiving no cues from his questioners. Of course, Pfungst later showed that this was not so, that tiny head and eye movements were Hans' signals to begin and to end his tapping. When Hans was asked a question, the questioner looked at Hans' hoof, quite naturally so, for that was the way for him to determine whether Hans' answer was correct. Then, it was discovered that when Hans approached the correct number of taps, the questioner would inadvertently move his head or eyes upward—just enough that Hans could discriminate the cue, but not enough that even trained animal observers or psychologists could see it.[1]

If a clever horse can respond to subtle cues, it is reasonable to suppose that clever humans can too. In fact, research has shown that experimenter expectancies can be communicated to humans by both verbal and nonverbal means (Duncan, Rosenberg, & Finklestein, 1969; Jones & Cooper, 1971). An example of more systematic research on expectancy effects is a study by Rosenthal (1966). In this experiment, graduate students trained rats that were described as coming from either "maze bright" or "maze dull" genetic strains. The animals actually came from the same strain and had been randomly assigned to the bright and dull categories; however, the "bright" rats *did* perform better than the "dull" rats. Subtle differences in the ways the students treated the rats or recorded their behavior must have caused this result. A generalization of this particular finding is called "teacher expectancy." Research has shown that telling a teacher that a pupil will bloom intellectually over the next year results in an increase in the pupil's IQ score (Rosenthal & Jacobson, 1968). In short, teachers' expectations can influence students' performance.

The problem of expectations influencing ratings of behavior is nicely illustrated in an experiment by Langer and Abelson (1974). Clinical psychologists were shown a videotape of an interview in which the person interviewed was described as either an applicant for a job or a patient; in reality, all saw the same tape. The psychologists later rated the person as more "disturbed" when they thought the person was a patient than when the person was described as a job applicant.

Solutions to the expectancy problem
Clearly, experimenter expectations can influence the outcomes of research investigations. How can this problem be solved? Fortunately, there are a number of ways to minimize expectancy effects. First, experimenters should be well trained and should practice behaving consistently with all participants. The benefit of training was illustrated in the Langer and Abelson study with clinical psychologists. The bias of rating

---

1. From Rosenthal, R. (1967). Covert communication in the psychological experiment. *Psychological Bulletin, 67,* 356–367. Copyright 1967 by the American Psychological Association. Reprinted by permission.

the "patient" as disturbed was much less among behavior-oriented therapists than among traditional ones. Presumably, the training of the behavior-oriented therapists led them to focus more on the actual behavior of the person, so they were less influenced by expectations stemming from the label of "patient."

Another solution is to run all conditions simultaneously so that the experimenter's behavior is the same for all participants. This solution is feasible only under certain circumstances, however, such as when the study can be carried out with the use of printed materials or the experimenter's instructions to participants are the same for everyone.

Expectancy effects are also minimized when the procedures are automated. As noted previously, it may be possible to manipulate independent variables and record responses using computers; with automated procedures, the experimenter's expectations are less likely to influence the results.

A final solution is to use experimenters who are unaware of the hypothesis being investigated. In these cases, the person conducting the study or making observations is blind regarding what is being studied or which condition the participant is in. This procedure originated in drug research using placebo groups. In a **single-blind experiment,** the participant is unaware of whether a placebo or the actual drug is being administered; in a **double-blind experiment,** neither the participant nor the experimenter knows whether the placebo or actual treatment is being given. To use a procedure in which the experimenter or observer is unaware of either the hypothesis or the group the participant is in, you must hire other people to conduct the experiment and make observations.

Because researchers are aware of the problem of expectancy effects, solutions such as the ones just described are usually incorporated into the procedures of the study. The procedures used in scientific research must be precisely defined so they can be replicated by others. This allows other researchers to build on previous research. If a study does have a potential problem of expectancy effects, researchers are bound to notice and will attempt to replicate the experiment with procedures that control for them. It is also a self-correcting mechanism that ensures that methodological flaws will be discovered. The importance of replication will be discussed further in Chapter 14.

ADDITIONAL CONSIDERATIONS

So far, we have discussed several of the factors that a researcher considers when planning a study. Actually conducting the study and analyzing the results is a time-consuming process. Before beginning the research, the investigator wants to be as sure as possible that everything will be done right. And once the study has been designed, there are some additional procedures that will improve it.

Research Proposals

After putting considerable thought into planning the study, the researcher writes a research proposal. The proposal will include a literature review that provides a background for the study. The intent is to clearly explain why the research is being done—what questions the research is designed to answer. The details of the procedures that will be used to test the idea are then given. The plans for analysis of the data are also provided. A research proposal is very similar to the introduction and method sections of a journal article. Such proposals must be included in applications for research grants; ethics review committees require some type of proposal as well (see Chapter 3 for more information on Institutional Review Boards).

Preparing a proposal is a good idea in planning any research project because simply putting your thoughts on paper helps to organize and systematize ideas. In addition, you can show the proposal to friends, colleagues, professors, and other interested parties who can provide useful feedback about the adequacy of your procedures. They may see problems that you didn't recognize, or they may offer ways of improving the study.

Pilot Studies

When the researcher has finally decided on all the specific aspects of the procedure, it is possible to conduct a **pilot study** in which the researcher does a trial run with a small number of participants. The pilot study will reveal whether participants understand the instructions, whether the total experimental setting seems plausible, whether any confusing questions are being asked, and so on.

Sometimes participants in the pilot study are questioned in detail about the experience following the experiment. Another method is to use the think aloud protocol (described in Chapter 7) in which the participants in the pilot study are instructed to verbalize their thoughts about everything that is happening during the study. Such procedures provide the researcher with an opportunity to make any necessary changes in the procedure before doing the entire study. Also, a pilot study allows the experimenters who are collecting the data to become comfortable with their roles and to standardize their procedures.

Manipulation Checks

A **manipulation check** is an attempt to directly measure whether the independent variable manipulation has the intended effect on the participants. Manipulation checks provide evidence for the construct validity of the manipulation (construct validity was discussed in Chapter 4). If you are manipulating anxiety, for example, a manipulation check will tell you whether participants in the high-anxiety group really were more anxious than those in the low-anxiety condition. The manipulation check might involve a self-report of anxiety, a behavioral measure (such as number of arm and hand movements), or a physiological measure. All manipulation checks, then, ask whether the independent variable manipulation was in fact a successful operationalization of the conceptual variable being studied. Consider, for example, a manipulation of physical attractiveness as an independent variable. In an experiment, participants respond to someone who is supposed to be perceived as attractive or unattractive. The manipulation check in this case would determine whether participants do rate the highly attractive person as more physically attractive.

Manipulation checks are particularly useful in the pilot study to decide whether the independent variable manipulation is in fact having the intended effect. If the independent variable is not effective, the procedures can be changed. However, it is also important to conduct a manipulation check in the actual experiment. Because a manipulation check in the actual experiment might distract participants or inform them about the purpose of the experiment, it is usually wise to position the administration of the manipulation check measure near the end of the experiment; in most cases, this would be after measuring the dependent variables and prior to the debriefing session.

A manipulation check has two advantages. First, if the check shows that your manipulation was not effective, you have saved the expense of running the actual experiment. You can turn your attention to changing the manipulation to make it more effective. For instance, if the manipulation check shows that neither the low- nor the high-anxiety group was very anxious, you could change your procedures to increase the anxiety in the high-anxiety condition.

Second, a manipulation check is advantageous if you get nonsignificant results—that is, if the results indicate that no relationship exists between the independent and dependent variables. A manipulation check can identify whether the nonsignificant results are due to a problem in manipulating the independent variable. If your manipulation is not successful, it is only reasonable that you will obtain nonsignificant results. If both groups are equally anxious after you manipulate anxiety, anxiety can't have any effect on the dependent measure. What if the check shows that the manipulation was successful, but you still get nonsignificant results? Then you know at least that the results were not due to a problem with the manipulation; the reason for not finding a relationship lies elsewhere. Perhaps you had a poor dependent measure, or perhaps there really is no relationship between the variables.

Debriefing

The importance of debriefing was discussed in Chapter 3 in the context of ethical considerations. After all the data are collected, a debriefing session is usually held. This is an opportunity for the researcher to interact with the participants to discuss the ethical and educational implications of the study.

The debriefing session can also provide an opportunity to learn more about what participants were thinking during the experiment. Researchers can ask participants what they believed to be the purpose of the experiment, how they interpreted the independent variable manipulation, and what they were thinking when they responded to the dependent measures. Such information can prove useful in interpreting the results and planning future studies.

Finally, researchers may ask the participants to refrain from discussing the study with others. Such requests are typically made when more people will be participating and they may talk with one another in classes or residence halls.

People who have already participated are aware of the general purposes and procedures; it is important that these individuals not provide expectancies about the study to potential future participants.

ANALYZING AND INTERPRETING RESULTS

After the data have been collected, the next step is to analyze them. Statistical analyses of the data are carried out to allow the researcher to examine and interpret the pattern of results obtained in the study. The statistical analysis helps the researcher decide whether there really is a relationship between the independent and dependent variables; the logic underlying the use of statistical tests is discussed in Chapter 13. It is not the purpose of this book to teach statistical methods; however, the calculations involved in several statistical tests are provided in Appendix B.

COMMUNICATING RESEARCH TO OTHERS

The final step is to write a report that details why you conducted the research, how you obtained the participants, what procedures you used, and what you found. A description of how to write such reports is included in Appendix A. After you have written the report, what do you do with it? How do you communicate the findings to others? Research findings are most often submitted as journal articles or as papers to be read at scientific meetings. In either case, the submitted paper is evaluated by two or more knowledgeable reviewers who decide whether the paper is acceptable for publication or presentation at the meeting.

Professional Meetings

Meetings sponsored by professional associations are important opportunities for researchers to present their findings to other researchers and the public. National and regional professional associations such as the American Psychological Association (APA) and the Association for Psychological Science (APS) hold annual meetings at which psychologists and students present their own research and learn about the latest research being done by their colleagues. Sometimes, verbal presentations are delivered to an audience. However, poster sessions are more common; here, researchers display posters that summarize the research and are available to discuss the research with others.

Journal Articles

As we noted in Chapter 2, many journals publish research papers. Nevertheless, the number of journals is small compared to the number of reports written; thus, it is not easy to publish research. When a researcher submits a paper to a journal, two or more reviewers read the paper and recommend acceptance (often with the stipulation that revisions be made) or rejection. This process is called *peer review* and it is very important in making sure that research has careful external review before it is published. As many as 90% of papers submitted to the more prestigious journals are rejected. Many rejected papers are submitted to other journals and eventually accepted for publication, but much research is never published. This is not necessarily bad; it simply means that selection processes separate high-quality research from that of lesser quality.

Many of the decisions that must be made when planning an experiment were described in this chapter. The discussion focused on experiments that use the simplest experimental design with a single independent variable. In the next chapter, more complex experimental designs are described.

ILLUSTRATIVE ARTICLE: CONDUCTING EXPERIMENTS

Many people behave superstitiously. That is, they may believe that their lucky shirt helps them with an exam, or that washing a uniform after a game removes the "luck," or that winning the lottery is dependent on playing one's lucky numbers. Many of us believe that, indeed, these superstitions do not really affect outcomes. Superstition has been studied in psychology for some time. B.F. Skinner (1947) demonstrated that superstitious behavior could be seen in a pigeon! More recently, Damisch, Stoberock, and Mussweiler (2010) decided to see if they could observe any effect that superstitious behaviors had on several different performance measures, including putting in golf, motor dexterity, memory, and performance on a word jumble puzzle.

Over four different experiments, the researchers varied participants' perceptions of "luck" and then measured performance. In the first experiment, university students were randomly assigned to conditions wherein they were asked to putt using either a "lucky ball" (condition 1) or a "neutral ball" (condition 2). Participants in the "lucky ball" condition were statistically better putters than those in the "neutral ball" condition.

First, acquire and read the article:

Damisch, L., Stoberock, B., and Mussweiler, T. (2010), Keep your fingers crossed! How superstition improves performance. *Psychological Science, 21*, 1014–1020. doi:10.1177/0956797610372631

Then, after reading the article, consider the following:

1. For each of the four experiments, describe how the manipulation of the independent variable was straightforward or staged.
2. In this chapter, we discuss three types of dependent measures: self-report, behavioral, and physiological. In the experiments presented in this paper,

what types of dependent measures were used? Could other types of dependent measures have been used? How so?

3. Was the dependent measure used in Experiment 1 sensitive? How so?

4. Did these researchers use any manipulation checks in their experiments? Design a manipulation check for Experiment 2.

5. This paper includes four experiments. Given that these researchers were interested in superstition, why was using multiple studies a good thing for the internal validity of the study?

6. How good was the internal validity of this series of studies?

7. How would you extend the study?

Study Terms

Behavioral measure (p. 181)

Ceiling effect (p. 184)

Confederate (p. 177)

Demand characteristics (p. 185)

Double-blind experiment (p. 188)

Electroencephalogram (p. 182)

Electromyogram (p. 182)

Expectancy effects
(experimenter bias) (p. 186)

Filler items (p. 185)

Floor effect (p. 184)

Functional MRI (p. 182)

Galvanic skin response (p. 182)

Manipulation check (p. 189)

Manipulation strength (p. 179)

MRI (p. 182)

Physiological measure (p. 182)

Pilot study (p. 189)

Placebo group (p. 185)

Self-report (p. 181)

Sensitivity (p. 184)

Single-blind experiment (p. 188)

Staged manipulation (p. 177)

Straightforward manipulation (p. 175)

Review Questions

1. What is the difference between staged and straightforward manipulations of an independent variable?

2. What are the general types of dependent variables?

3. What is meant by the sensitivity of a dependent measure? What are ceiling and floor effects?

4. What are demand characteristics? Describe ways to minimize demand characteristics.

5. What is the reason for a placebo group?

6. What are experimenter expectancy effects? What are some solutions to the experimenter bias problem?

7. What is a pilot study?

8. What is a manipulation check? How does it help the researcher interpret the results of an experiment?

9. Describe the value of a debriefing following the study.

10. What does a researcher do with the findings after completing a research project?

Activity Questions

1. Dr. Turk studied the relationship between age and reading comprehension, specifically predicting that older people will show lower comprehension than younger ones. Turk was particularly interested in comprehension of material that is available in the general press. Groups of participants who were 20, 30, 40, and 50 years of age read a chapter from a book by theoretical physicist Stephen W. Hawking (1988) entitled *A Brief History of Time: From the Big Bang to Black Holes*. After reading the chapter, participants were given a comprehension measure. The results showed that there was no relationship between age and comprehension scores; all age groups had equally low comprehension scores. Why do you think no relationship was found? Identify at least two possible reasons.

2. Recall the experiment on facilitated communication by children with autism that was described on p. 24 in Chapter 2 (Montee, Miltenberger, & Wittrock, 1995). Interpret the findings of that study in terms of experimenter expectancy effects.

3. Your lab group has been assigned the task of designing an experiment to investigate the effect of time spent studying on a recall task. Thus far, your group has come up with the following plan: "Participants will be randomly assigned to two groups. Individuals in one group will study a list of 5 words for 5 minutes, and those in the other group will study the same list for 7 minutes. Immediately after studying, the participants will read a list of 10 words and circle those that appeared on the original study list." Improve this experiment, giving specific reasons for any changes.

4. If you were investigating variables that affect helping behavior, would you be more likely to use a straightforward or staged manipulation? Why?

5. Design an experiment using a staged manipulation to test the hypothesis that when people are in a good mood, they are more likely to contribute to a charitable cause. Include a manipulation check in your design.

6. In a pilot study, Professor Mori conducted a manipulation check and found no significant difference between the experimental conditions. Should she continue with the experiment? What should she do next? Explain your recommendations for Professor Mori.

7. Write a debriefing statement that you would read to participants in the Asch line judgment study (p. 178).

Answers

TABLE 9.1:

    1. T, 2. T, 3. T, 4. F

10

Complex Experimental Designs

LEARNING OBJECTIVES

- Define *factorial design* and discuss reasons a researcher would use this design.
- Describe the information provided by main effects and interaction effects in a factorial design.
- Describe an IV × PV design.
- Discuss the role of simple main effects in interpreting interactions.
- Compare the assignment of participants in an independent groups design, a repeated measures design, and a mixed factorial design.

Thus far we have focused primarily on the simplest experimental design, in which one independent variable is manipulated and one dependent variable is measured. However, researchers often investigate problems that demand more complicated designs. These complex experimental designs are the subject of this chapter.

We begin by discussing the idea of increasing the number of levels in an independent variable in an experiment. Then, we describe experiments that expand the number of independent variables. Both of these changes impact the complexity of an experiment.

INCREASING THE NUMBER OF LEVELS OF AN INDEPENDENT VARIABLE

In the simplest experimental design, there are only two levels of the independent variable. However, a researcher might want to design an experiment with three or more levels for several reasons. First, a design with only two levels of the independent variable cannot provide very much information about the exact form of the relationship between the independent and dependent variables. For example, Figure 10.1 is based on the outcome of an experiment on the relationship between amount of "mental practice" and performance on a motor task: dart throwing score (Kremer, Spittle, McNeil, & Shinners, 2009). Mental practice consisted of imagining practice throws prior to an actual dart throwing task. Does mental practice improve dart performance? The solid line describes the results when only two levels were used—no mental practice throws and 100 mental practice throws.

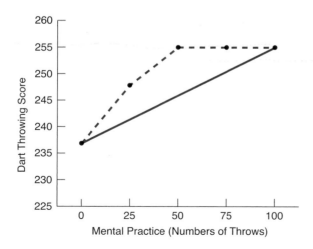

FIGURE 10.1
Linear versus positive monotonic functions
Note: Data based on an experiment conducted by Kremer, Spittle, McNeil, and Shinners (2009); that experiment did not include a 75-practice-throws condition.

Because there are only two levels, the relationship can be described only with a straight line. We do not know what the relationship would be if other practice amounts were included as separate levels of the independent variable. The broken line in Figure 10.1 shows the results when 25, 50, and 75 mental practice throws are also included. This result is a more accurate description of the relationship between amount of mental practice and performance. The amount of practice is very effective in increasing performance up to a point, after which further practice is not helpful. Thus, the relationship is a monotonic positive relationship rather than a strictly linear relationship (see Chapter 4). An experiment with only two levels cannot yield such exact information.

Recall from Chapter 4 that variables are sometimes related in a curvilinear or nonmonotonic fashion; that is, the direction of relationship changes. Figure 10.2 shows an example of a curvilinear relationship; this particular form is called an *inverted-U* because the wide range of levels of the independent variable produces an inverted U shape (recall our discussion of inverted-U relationships in Chapter 4). An experimental design with only two levels of the independent variable cannot detect curvilinear relationships between variables. If a curvilinear relationship is predicted, at least three levels must be used. As Figure 10.2 shows, if only levels 1 and 3 of the independent variable had been used, no relationship between the variables would have been detected. Many such curvilinear relationships exist in psychology. The relationship between fear arousal and attitude change is one example—we can be scared into changing an attitude, but if we think that a message is "over the top," attitude change does not occur. In other words, increasing the amount of fear aroused by a persuasive message increases attitude change up to a moderate level of fear; further increases in fear arousal actually reduce attitude change.

Finally, researchers frequently are interested in comparing more than two groups. Suppose you want to know whether playing with an animal has beneficial effects on nursing home residents. You could have two conditions, such as a no-animal control group and a group in which a dog is brought in for play each day.

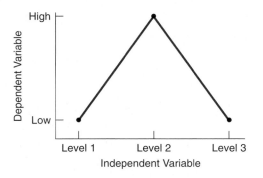

FIGURE 10.2
Curvilinear relationship

Note: At least three levels of the independent variable are required to show curvilinear relationships.

However, you might also be interested in knowing the effect of a cat and a bird, and so you could add these two groups to your study. Or you might be interested in comparing the effect of a large versus a small dog in addition to a no-animal control condition. In an actual study with four groups, Strassberg and Holty (2003) compared responses to women's Internet personal ads. The researchers first devised a control ad portraying a woman with generally positive attributes, such as liking painting and hiking. The other ads each added a more specific characteristic: (1) slim and attractive, (2) sensual and passionate, or (3) financially independent and ambitious. Contrary to the researchers' initial expectations, the independent/ambitious woman received many more responses than the other three.

INCREASING THE NUMBER OF INDEPENDENT VARIABLES: FACTORIAL DESIGNS

Researchers often manipulate more than one independent variable in a single experiment. Typically, two or three independent variables are operating simultaneously. This type of experimental design is a closer approximation of real-world conditions, in which independent variables do not exist by themselves. Researchers recognize that in any given situation a number of variables are operating to affect behavior. Recall the exercise and mood experiment that was described in Chapter 8. An actual experiment on the relationship between exercise and depression was conducted by Dunn, Trivedi, Kampert, Clark, and Chambliss (2005). The participants were randomly assigned to one of two exercise conditions—a low or high amount, with energy expenditure of either 7.0 or 17.5 kcal per kilogram per week. The dependent variable was the score on a standard depression measure after 12 weeks of exercise. You might be wondering how often the participants exercised each week. Indeed, the researchers did wonder if frequency of exercising would be important, so they scheduled some subjects to exercise 3 days per week and others to exercise 5 days per week. Thus, the researchers designed an experiment with two independent variables—in this case, amount of exercise and frequency of exercise.

Factorial designs are designs with more than one independent variable (or *factor*). In a factorial design, all levels of each independent variable are combined with all levels of the other independent variables. The simplest factorial design—known as a 2 × 2 (two by two) factorial design—has two independent variables, each having two levels.

An experiment by Smith and Ellsworth (1987) illustrates a 2 × 2 factorial design. Smith and Ellsworth studied the effects of asking misleading questions on the accuracy of eyewitness testimony. Participants in the experiment first viewed a videotape of a robbery and then were asked questions about what they saw. One independent variable was the type of question—misleading or unbiased. The second independent variable was the questioner's knowledge of the crime: The person asking the questions had either viewed the tape only once (a "naïve" questioner) or had seen the tape a number of times (a "knowledgeable" questioner).

	Type of Question: Independent Variable A	
Questioner Type: Independent Variable B	Unbiased	Misleading
Knowledgeable	Unbiased/ Knowledgeable	Misleading/ Knowledgeable
Naive	Unbiased/Naive	Misleading/Naive

FIGURE 10.3
2 × 2 factorial design: Setup of eyewitness testimony experiment

This 2 × 2 design results in four experimental conditions: (1) knowledge-able questioner–misleading questions, (2) knowledgeable questioner–unbiased questions, (3) naive questioner–misleading questions, and (4) naive questioner–unbiased questions. A 2 × 2 design always has four groups. Figure 10.3 shows how these experimental conditions are created.

The general format for describing factorial designs is

$$\underset{\text{of first IV}}{\text{Number of levels}} \times \underset{\text{of second IV}}{\text{Number of levels}} \times \underset{\text{of third IV}}{\text{Number of levels}}$$

and so on. A design with two independent variables, one having two levels and the other having three levels, is a 2 × 3 factorial design; there are six conditions in the experiment. A 3 × 3 design has nine conditions.

Interpretation of Factorial Designs

Factorial designs yield two kinds of information. The first is information about the effect of each independent variable taken by itself: the **main effect** of an independent variable. In a design with two independent variables, there are two main effects—one for each independent variable. The second type of information is called an **interaction.** If there is an interaction between two independent variables, the effect of one independent variable depends on the particular level of the other variable. In other words, the effect that an independent variable has on the dependent variable depends on the level of the other independent variable. Interactions are a new source of information that cannot be obtained in a simple experimental design in which only one independent variable is manipulated.

To illustrate main effects and interactions, we can look at the results of the Smith and Ellsworth study on accuracy of eyewitness testimony. Table 10.1 illustrates a common method of presenting outcomes for the various groups in a factorial design. The number in each cell represents the mean percent of errors made in the four conditions.

TABLE 10.1   2 × 2 factorial design: Results of the eyewitness testimony experiment

Questioner type (independent variable B)	Type of question (independent variable A)		Overall means (main effect of B)
	Unbiased	Misleading	
Knowledgeable	13.0	41.0	27.0
Naive	13.0	18.0	15.5
Overall means (main effect of A)	13.0	29.5	

Main effects

A main effect is the effect each variable has by itself. The main effect of independent variable A, type of question, is the overall effect of the variable on the dependent measure. Similarly, the main effect of independent variable B, type of questioner, is the effect of the different types of questioners on accuracy of recall.

The main effect of each independent variable is the overall relationship between that independent variable and the dependent variable. For independent variable A, is there a relationship between type of question and recall errors? We can find out by looking at the overall means in the unbiased and misleading questions conditions. These overall main effect means are obtained by averaging across all participants in each group, irrespective of the type of questioner (knowledgeable or naive). These means are shown in the rightmost column and bottom row (called the margins of the table) of Table 10.1. The overall percent of errors made by participants in the misleading questions condition is 29.5, and the error percent in the unbiased questions condition is 13.0. Note that the overall mean of 29.5 in the misleading questions condition is the average of 41 in the knowledgeable–misleading group and 18 in the naive–misleading group (this calculation assumes equal numbers of participants in each group). You can see that overall, more errors are made when the questions are misleading than when they are unbiased. Statistical tests would enable us to determine whether this is a significant main effect.

The main effect for independent variable B (questioner type) is the overall relationship between that independent variable, by itself, and the dependent variable. You can see in Table 10.1 that the overall score in the knowledgeable questioner condition is 27.0, and the overall score in the naive questioner group is 15.5. Thus, in general, more errors result when the questioner is knowledgeable.

Interactions

These main effects tell us that, overall, there are more errors when the questioner is knowledgeable and when the questions are misleading. There is also the possibility that an interaction exists; if so, the main effects of the independent variables must be qualified. This is because an interaction between independent variables indicates that the effect of one independent

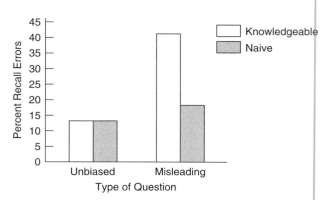

FIGURE 10.4
Interaction between type of question and type of questioner
(Based on data from Smith and Ellsworth, 1987)

variable is different at different levels of the other independent variable. That is, an interaction tells us that the effect of one independent variable depends on the particular level of the other.

We can see an interaction in the results of the Smith and Ellsworth study. The effect of the type of question is different depending on whether the questioner is knowledgeable or naive. When the questioner is knowledgeable, misleading questions result in more errors (41% in the misleading question condition versus 13% in the unbiased condition). However, when the questioner is naive, the type of question has little effect (18% for misleading questions and 13% for unbiased questions). Thus, the relationship between type of question and recall errors is best understood by considering both independent variables: We must consider whether the questions are misleading *and* whether the questioner is knowledgeable or naive.

Interactions can be seen easily when the means for all conditions are presented in a graph. Figure 10.4 shows a bar graph of the results of Smith and Ellsworth's eyewitness testimony experiment. Note that all four means have been graphed. Two bars compare the types of questioner in the unbiased question condition; the same comparison is shown for the misleading question condition. You can see that questioner knowledge is not a factor when an unbiased question is asked; however, when the question is misleading, the knowledgeable questioner has a greater ability to create bias than does the naive questioner.

The concept of interaction is a relatively simple one that you probably use all the time. When we say "it depends," we are usually indicating that some sort of interaction is operating—it depends on some other variable. Suppose, for example, that a friend has asked you if you want to go to a movie. Whether you want to go may reflect an interaction between two variables: (1) Is an exam coming up? and (2) Who stars in the movie? If there is an exam coming up, you won't go under any circumstance. If you do not have an exam to worry about, your decision will depend on whether you like the actors in the movie; that is, you will go only if a favorite star is in the movie.

You might try graphing the movie example in the same way we graphed the eyewitness testimony example in Figure 10.4. The dependent variable (going to the movie) is always placed on the vertical axis. One independent variable is placed on the horizontal axis. Bars are then drawn to represent each of the levels of the other independent variable. Graphing the results in this manner is a useful method of visualizing interactions in a factorial design.

Factorial Designs with Manipulated and Nonmanipulated Variables

One common type of factorial design includes both experimental (manipulated) and nonexperimental (measured or nonmanipulated) variables. These designs—sometimes called **IV × PV designs** (i.e., independent variable by participant variable)—allow researchers to investigate how different types of individuals (i.e., participants) respond to the same manipulated variable. These "participant variables" are personal attributes such as gender, age, ethnic group, personality characteristics, and clinical diagnostic category. You will sometimes see participant variables described as *subject variables* or *attribute variables*. This is only a difference of terminology.

The simplest IV × PV design includes one manipulated independent variable that has at least two levels and one participant variable with at least two levels. The two levels of the subject variable might be two different age groups, groups of low and high scorers on a personality measure, or groups of males and females. An example of this design is a study by Furnham, Gunter, and Peterson (1994). Do you ever try to study in the presence of a distraction such as a television program? Furnham et al. showed that the ability to study with such a distraction depends on whether you are more extraverted or introverted. The manipulated variable was distraction. College students read material in silence and within hearing range of a TV drama. Thus, a repeated measures design was used and the order of the conditions was counterbalanced. After they read the material, the students completed a reading comprehension measure. The participant variable was extraversion: Participants completed a measure of extraversion and then were classified as extraverts or introverts. The results are shown in Figure 10.5. There was a main effect of distraction and an interaction.

Overall, students had higher comprehension scores when they studied in silence. In addition, there was an interaction between extraversion and distraction. Without a distraction, the performance of extraverts and introverts was almost the same. However, extraverts performed better than introverts when the TV was on. If you are an extravert, be more understanding when your introverted friends want things quiet when studying!

Factorial designs with both manipulated independent variables and participant variables offer a very appealing method for investigating many interesting

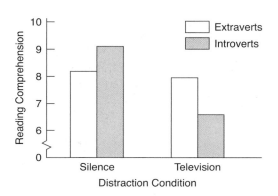

FIGURE 10.5
Interaction in IV × PV design

research questions. Such experiments recognize that full understanding of behavior requires knowledge of both situational variables and the personal attributes of individuals.

Interactions and Moderator Variables

In many research studies, interactions are discussed in terms of the operation of a **moderator variable.** A moderator variable influences the relationship between two other variables (Baron & Kenny, 1986). In the study of eyewitness testimony, we can begin with a general statement of the relationship between the type of question and recall errors, for example, *misleading questions result in more errors than do unbiased questions.* What if we then make a qualifying statement that the type of questioner influences this relationship: *Misleading questions result in more errors only when the questioner is believed to be knowledgeable; no increase in errors will occur when the questioner is naive.* The questioner variable is a moderator variable because it *moderates* the relationship between the other variables. Moderator variables may be particular situations, as in the study of eyewitness testimony by Smith and Ellsworth (1987), or they may be characteristics of people, as in the study on reading comprehension of extraverts and introverts.

Outcomes of a 2 × 2 Factorial Design

A 2 × 2 factorial design has two independent variables, each with two levels. When analyzing the results, researchers deal with several possibilities: (1) There may or may not be a significant main effect for independent variable A, (2) there may or may not be a significant main effect for independent variable B, and (3) there may or may not be a significant interaction between the independent variables.

Figure 10.6 illustrates the eight possible outcomes in a 2 × 2 factorial design. For each outcome, the means are given and then graphed using line graphs. In addition, for each graph in Figure 10.6, the main effect for each variable (A and B) is indicated by a Yes (indicating the presence of a main effect) or No (no main effect). Similarly, the A × B interaction is either present ("Yes" on the figure) or

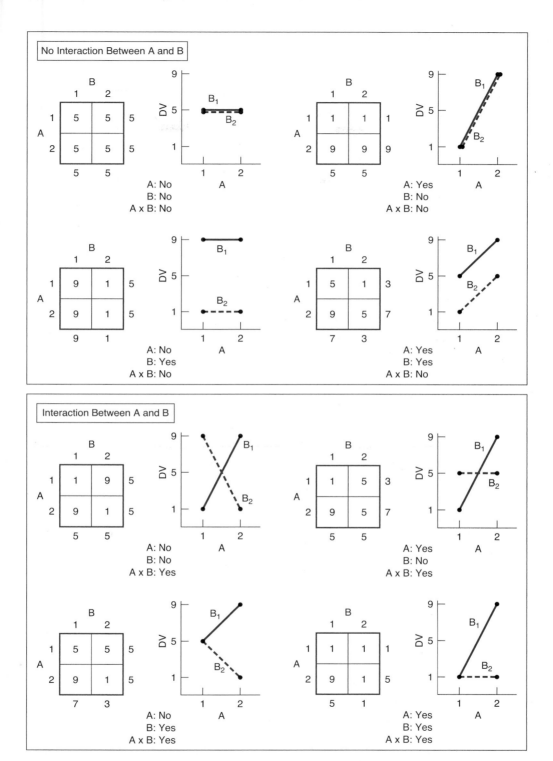

FIGURE 10.6
Outcomes of a factorial design with two independent variables

not present ("No" on the figure). The means that are given in the figure are idealized examples; such perfect outcomes rarely occur in actual research. Nevertheless, you should study the graphs to determine for yourself why, in each case, there is or is not a main effect for A, a main effect for B, and an A × B interaction. Before you begin studying the graphs, it will help to think of concrete variables to represent the two independent variables and the dependent variable. You might want to think about the example of the effect of amount and frequency of exercise on depression. Suppose that independent variable A is amount of exercise per week (A_1 is low exercise—fewer calories per week; A_2 is higher amount of exercise—more calories per week) and independent variable B is frequency of exercise (B_1 is 3 times per week and B_2 is 5 times per week). The dependent variable ("DV") is the score on a depression measure, with higher numbers indicating greater depression.

The top four graphs illustrate outcomes in which there is no A × B interaction, and the bottom four graphs depict outcomes in which there is an interaction. When there is a statistically significant interaction, you need to carefully examine the means to understand why the interaction occurred. In some cases, there is a strong relationship between the first independent variable and the dependent variable at one level of the second independent variable; however, there is no relationship or a weak relationship at the other level of the second independent variable. In other outcomes, the interaction may indicate that one independent variable has opposite effects on the dependent variable, depending on the level of the second independent variable.

The independent and dependent variables in the figure do not have concrete variable labels. As an exercise, interpret each of the graphs using actual variables from three different hypothetical experiments, using the scenarios suggested below. This works best if you draw the graphs, including labels for the variables, on a separate sheet of paper for each experiment. You can try depicting the data as either line graphs or bar graphs. The data points in both types of graphs are the same and both have been used in this chapter. In general, line graphs are used when the levels of the independent variable on the horizontal axis (independent variable A) are quantitative—low and high amounts. Bar graphs are more likely to be used when the levels of the independent variable represent different categories, such as one type of therapy compared with another type.

Hypothetical experiment 1: Effect of age of defendant and type of substance use during an offense on months of sentence. A male, age 20 or 50, was found guilty of causing a traffic accident while under the influence of either alcohol or marijuana.

Independent variable A: Type of Offense—Alcohol versus Marijuana

Independent variable B: Age of Defendant—20 versus 50 years of age

Dependent variable: Months of sentence (range from 0 to 10 months)

Hypothetical experiment 2: Effect of gender and violence on recall of advertising. Participants (males and females) viewed a video on a computer screen that was either violent or not violent. They were then asked to read print ads for 8 different products over the next 3 minutes. The dependent variable was the number of ads correctly recalled.

> Independent variable A: Exposure to Violence—Nonviolent versus Violent Video
>
> Independent variable B: Participant Gender—Male versus Female
>
> Dependent variable: Number of ads recalled (range from 0 to 8)

Hypothetical experiment 3: Devise your own experiment with two independent variables and one dependent variable.

Interactions and Simple Main Effects

A procedure called *analysis of variance* is used to assess the statistical significance of the main effects and the interaction in a factorial design. When a significant interaction occurs, the researcher must statistically evaluate the individual means. If you take a look at Table 10.1 and Figure 10.4 once again, you see a clear interaction. When there is a significant interaction, the next step is to look at the **simple main effects.** A simple main effect analysis examines mean differences at *each level* of the independent variable. Recall that the main effect of an independent variable averages across the levels of the other independent variable; with simple main effects, the results are analyzed as if we had separate experiments at each level of the other independent variable.

Simple main effect of type of questioner In Figure 10.4, we can look at the simple main effect of type of questioner. This will tell us whether the difference between the knowledgeable and naive questioner is significant when the question is (1) unbiased and (2) misleading. In this case, the simple main effect of type of questioner is significant when the question is misleading (means of 41 versus 18), but the simple main effect of questioner type is not significant when the question is unbiased (means of 13 and 13).

Simple main effect of type of question We could also examine the simple main effect of type of question; here, we would compare the two questions when the questioner is (1) knowledgeable and (2) naive. The simple main effect that you will be most interested in will depend on the predictions that you made when you designed the study. The exact statistical procedures do not concern us; the point here is that the pattern of results with all the means must be examined when there is a significant interaction in a factorial design.

Assignment Procedures and Factorial Designs

The considerations of assigning participants to conditions that were discussed in Chapter 8 can be generalized to factorial designs. There are two basic ways of assigning participants to conditions: (1) In an independent groups design, different participants are assigned to each of the conditions in the study; (2) in a repeated measures design, the *same* individuals participate in all conditions in the study. These two types of assignment procedures have implications for the number of participants necessary to complete the experiment. We can illustrate this fact by looking at a 2 × 2 factorial design. The design can be completely independent groups, completely repeated measures, or a **mixed factorial design**—that is, a combination of the two.

Independent groups (between-subjects) design
In a 2 × 2 factorial design, there are four conditions. If we want a completely **independent groups (between-subjects) design**, a different group of participants will be assigned to each of the four conditions. The Smith and Ellsworth (1987) study on eyewitness testimony illustrates a factorial design with different individuals in each of the conditions. Suppose that you have planned a 2 × 2 design and want to have 10 participants in each condition; you will need a total of 40 *different* participants, as shown in the first table in Figure 10.7.

Repeated measures (within-subjects) design
In a completely **repeated measures (within-subjects) design**, the same individuals will participate in *all* conditions. Suppose you have planned a study on the effects of marijuana: One factor is marijuana (marijuana treatment versus placebo control) and the other factor is task difficulty (easy versus difficult). In a 2 × 2 completely repeated measures design, each individual would participate in all of the conditions

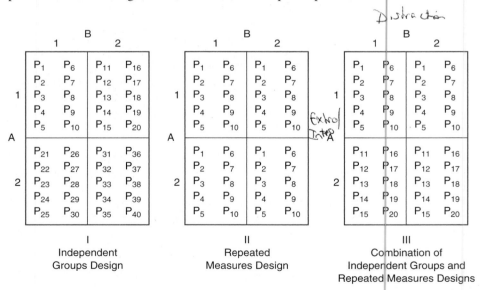

FIGURE 10.7
Number of participants (P) required to have 10 observations in each condition

by completing both easy and difficult tasks under both marijuana treatment conditions. If you wanted 10 participants in each condition, a total of 10 subjects would be needed, as illustrated in the second table in Figure 10.7. This design offers considerable savings in the number of participants required. In deciding whether to use a completely repeated measures assignment procedure, however, the researcher would have to consider the disadvantages of repeated measures designs.

Mixed factorial design using combined assignment

The Furnham, Gunter, and Peterson (1994) study on television distraction and extraversion illustrates the use of both independent groups and repeated measures procedures in a mixed factorial design. The participant variable, extraversion, is an independent groups variable. Distraction is a repeated measures variable; all participants studied with both distraction and silence. The third table in Figure 10.7 shows the number of participants needed to have 10 per condition in a 2 × 2 mixed factorial design. In this table, independent variable A is an independent groups variable. Ten participants are assigned to level 1 of this independent variable, and another 10 participants are assigned to level 2. Independent variable B is a repeated measures variable, however. The 10 participants assigned to A_1 receive both levels of independent variable B. Similarly, the other 10 participants assigned to A_2 receive both levels of the B variable. Thus, a total of 20 participants are required.

Increasing the Number of Levels of an Independent Variable

The 2 × 2 is the simplest factorial design. With this basic design, the researcher can arrange experiments that are more and more complex. One way to increase complexity is to increase the number of levels of one or more of the independent variables. A 2 × 3 design, for example, contains two independent variables: Independent variable A has two levels, and independent variable B has three levels. Thus, the 2 × 3 design has six conditions. Table 10.2 shows a 2 × 3 factorial design with the independent variables of task difficulty (easy, hard) and anxiety level (low, moderate, high). The dependent variable is performance on the task. The numbers in each of the six cells of the design indicate the mean performance score of the group. The overall means in the margins (rightmost column and bottom row) show the main effects of each of the independent variables. The results in Table 10.2 indicate a main effect of task difficulty because the *overall* performance score in the easy-task group is higher than the hard-task mean. However, there is no main effect of anxiety because the mean performance score is the same in each of the three anxiety groups. Is there an interaction between task difficulty and anxiety? Note that increasing the amount of anxiety has the effect of increasing performance on the easy task but *decreasing* performance on the hard task. The effect of anxiety is different, depending on whether the task is easy or hard; thus, there is an interaction.

This interaction can be easily seen in a graph. Figure 10.8 is a line graph in which one line shows the effect of anxiety for the easy task and a second line represents the effect of anxiety for the difficult task. As noted previously, line

TABLE 10.2   2 × 3 factorial design

Task difficulty	Anxiety level			Overall means (main effect)
	Low	Moderate	High	
Easy	4	7	10	7.0
Hard	7	4	1	4.0
Overall means (main effect)	5.5	5.5	5.5	

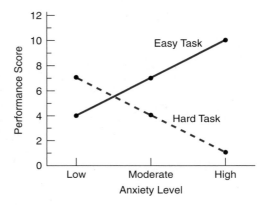

FIGURE 10.8
Line graph of data from 3 (anxiety level) × 2 (task difficulty) factorial design

graphs are used when the independent variable represented on the horizontal axis is quantitative—that is, the levels of the independent variable are increasing amounts of that variable (not differences in category).

Increasing the Number of Independent Variables in a Factorial Design

We can also increase the number of variables in the design. A 2 × 2 × 2 factorial design contains three variables, each with two levels. Thus, there are eight conditions in this design. In a 2 × 2 × 3 design, there are 12 conditions; in a 2 × 2 × 2 × 2 design, there are 16. The rule for constructing factorial designs remains the same throughout.

A 2 × 2 × 2 factorial design is constructed in Table 10.3. The independent variables are (1) instruction method (lecture, discussion), (2) class size (10, 40), and (3) student gender (male, female). Note that gender is a nonmanipulated variable and the other two variables are manipulated variables. The dependent variable is performance on a standard test.

TABLE 10.3   2 × 2 × 2 factorial design

Instruction method	Class size	
	10	40
	Male	
Lecture		
Discussion		
	Female	
Lecture		
Discussion		

Notice that the 2 × 2 × 2 design can be seen as two 2 × 2 designs, one for the males and another for the females. The design yields main effects for each of the three independent variables. For example, the overall mean for the lecture method is obtained by considering all participants who experience the lecture method, irrespective of class size or gender. Similarly, the discussion method mean is derived from all participants in this condition. The *two* means are then compared to see whether there is a significant main effect: Is one method superior to the other *overall*?

The design also allows us to look at interactions. In the 2 × 2 × 2 design, we can look at the interaction between (1) method and class size, (2) method and gender, and (3) class size and gender. We can also look at a three-way interaction that involves all three independent variables. Here, we want to determine whether the nature of the interaction between two of the variables differs depending on the particular level of the other variable. Three-way interactions are rather complicated; fortunately, you will not encounter too many of these in your explorations of behavioral science research.

Sometimes students are tempted to include in a study as many independent variables as they can think of. A problem with this is that the design may become needlessly complex and require enormous numbers of participants. The design previously discussed had 8 groups; a 2 × 2 × 2 × 2 design has 16 groups; adding yet another independent variable with two levels means that 32 groups would be required. Also, when there are more than three or four independent variables, many of the particular conditions that are produced by the combination of so many variables do not make sense or could not occur under natural circumstances.

The designs described thus far all use the same logic for determining whether the independent variable did in fact cause a change on the dependent variable measure. In the next chapter, we will consider alternative designs that use somewhat different procedures for examining the relationship between independent and dependent variables.

ILLUSTRATIVE ARTICLE: COMPLEX EXPERIMENTAL DESIGNS

As the saying goes, "money can't buy happiness." Mogilner (2010) put this idea to an empirical test in a series of three experiments that examined the impact of our thinking on how we spend our time.

Participants in the first experiment were given a scrambled-word task that included words that either primed them to think about money ("sheets the change price"), time ("sheets the change clock"), or nothing in particular ("sheets the change socks"). Then participants were given a list of activities and were asked to indicate their own plans for the day as well as the plans of a typical American. The author concluded that participants primed to think about money (based on the scrambled-word task) focused more on plans to work; in contrast, the participants primed to think about time indicated that they were motivated to engage in social connections.

First, acquire and read the article:

Mogilner, C. (2010). The pursuit of happiness: Time, money, and social connection. *Psychological Science, 21*, 1348–1354. doi:10.1177/0956797610380696

Then, after reading the article, consider the following:

1. Identify each independent variable in Experiment 1a.
2. Identify each dependent variable in Experiment 1a.
3. What type of assignment procedure was used for Experiment 1a?
4. The author attempted to improve the external validity of the study in Experiment 1b and Experiment 2. Do you think that she was successful? Why or why not?
5. Create a graph for the dependent variable of *socializing*, with the independent variable *prime* on the *x*-axis and separate lines for one's own plans and plans of others. Describe what you see: Do you see a main effect for either of the independent variables? Do you see the interaction?
6. Create a graph for the dependent variable of *work*, with the independent variable *prime* with prime on *x*-axis. Describe what you see: Do you see a main effect for either of the independent variables? Do you see the interaction?

Study Terms

Factorial design (p. 199)

Independent groups design (Between-subjects design) (p. 208)

Interaction (p. 200)

IV × PV design (p. 203)

Main effect (p. 200)

Mixed factorial design (p. 208)

Moderator variable (p. 204)

Repeated measures design (Within-subjects design) (p. 208)

Simple main effect (p. 207)

Review Questions _____

1. Why would a researcher have more than two levels of the independent variable in an experiment?
2. What is a factorial design? Why would a researcher use a factorial design?
3. What are main effects in a factorial design? What is an interaction?
4. Describe an IV × PV factorial design.
5. Identify the number of conditions in a factorial design on the basis of knowing the number of independent variables and the number of levels of each independent variable.

Activity Questions _____

1. In a study by Chaiken and Pliner (1987), research participants read an "eating diary" of either a male or female stimulus person. The information in the diary indicated that the person ate either large meals or small meals. After reading this information, participants rated the person's femininity and masculinity.
   a. Identify the design of this experiment.
   b. How many conditions are in the experiment?
   c. Identify the independent variable(s) and dependent variable(s).
   d. Is there a participant variable in this experiment? If so, identify it. If not, can you suggest a participant variable that might be included?
2. Chaiken and Pliner reported the following mean femininity ratings (higher numbers indicate greater femininity): male–small meals (2.02), male–large meals (2.05), female–small meals (3.90), and female–large meals (2.82). Assume there are equal numbers of participants in each condition.
   a. Are there any main effects?
   b. Is there an interaction?
   c. Graph the means.
   d. Describe the results in a brief paragraph.
3. Assume that you want 15 participants in each condition of your experiment, which uses a 3 × 3 factorial design. How many *different* participants do you need for (a) a completely independent groups assignment, (b) a completely repeated measures assignment, and (c) a mixed factorial design with both independent groups assignment and repeated measures variables?
4. Practice graphing the results of the experiment on the effect of amount and frequency of exercise on depression. In the actual experiment, there was a main effect of amount of exercise: Participants in the 17.5 kcal/kg/week condition had lower depression scores after 12 weeks than the participants in the 7.0 kcal condition. There was no main effect of amount of

exercise: It did not matter whether exercise was scheduled for 3 or 5 times per week. There was no interaction effect. For this activity, higher scores on the depression measure indicate greater depression. Scores on this measure can range from 0 to 16.

5. Read each of the following research scenarios and then fill in the correct answer in each column of the table.

Scenario	Number of independent variables	Number of experimental conditions	Number of possible main effects	Number of possible interactions
a. Participants were randomly assigned to read a short story printed in either 12-point or 14-point font in one of three font style conditions: Courier, Times Roman, or Arial. Afterwords they answered several questions designed to measure memory recall.				
b. Researchers conducted an experiment to examine gender and physical attractiveness biases in juror behavior. Participants were randomly assigned to read a scenario describing a crime committed by either an attractive or unattractive woman or an attractive or unattractive man who was described as overweight or average weight.				

Answers

a. 2 IVs (font size and font style); 6 conditions; 2 possible main effects; one possible interaction

b. 3 IVs (gender, attractiveness, weight level); 8 conditions; 3 possible main effects; 4 possible interactions (three two-way interactions and one three-way interaction)

11

Single-Case, Quasi-Experimental, and Developmental Research

LEARNING OBJECTIVES

- Describe single-case experimental designs and discuss reasons to use this design.

- Describe the five types of evaluations involved in program evaluation research: needs assessment, program assessment, process evaluation, outcome evaluation, and efficiency assessment.

- Describe the one-group posttest-only design.

- Describe the one-group pretest-posttest design and the associated threats to internal validity that may occur: history, maturation, testing, instrument decay, and regression toward the mean.

- Describe the nonequivalent control group design and nonequivalent control group pretest-posttest design, and discuss the advantages of having a control group.

- Distinguish between the interrupted time series design and control series design.

- Describe cross-sectional, longitudinal, and sequential research designs, including the advantages and disadvantages of each design.

- Define *cohort effect*.

I n the classic experimental design described in Chapter 8, participants are randomly assigned to the independent variable conditions, and a dependent variable is measured. The responses on the dependent measure are then compared to determine whether the independent variable had an effect. Because all other variables are held constant, differences on the dependent variable must be due to the effect of the independent variable. This design has high internal validity—we are very confident that the independent variable caused the observed responses on the dependent variable. You will frequently encounter this experimental design when you explore research in the behavioral sciences. However, other research designs have been devised to address special research problems.

This chapter focuses on three types of special research situations. The first is the instance in which the effect of an independent variable must be inferred from an experiment with only one participant—single-case experimental designs. Second, we will describe pre-experimental and quasi-experimental designs that may be considered if it is not possible to use one of the true experimental designs described in Chapter 8. Third, we consider research designs for studying changes that occur with age.

SINGLE-CASE EXPERIMENTAL DESIGNS

Single-case experimental designs have traditionally been called *single-subject* designs; both terms are currently used and are equivalent. Much of the early interest in single-case designs in psychology came from research on operant conditioning pioneered by B. F. Skinner (e.g., Skinner, 1953). Today, research using single-case designs is often seen in clinical, counseling, educational, and other applied settings (Kazdin, 2011).

Single-case experiments were developed from a need to determine whether an experimental manipulation had an effect on a single research participant. In a single-case design, the subject's behavior is measured over time during a **baseline** control period. The manipulation is then introduced during a treatment period, and the subject's behavior continues to be observed. A change in the subject's behavior from baseline to treatment periods is evidence for the effectiveness of the manipulation. The problem, however, is that there could be many explanations for the change other than the experimental treatment (i.e., alternative explanations). For example, some other event may have coincided with the introduction of the treatment. The single-case designs described in the following sections address this problem.

Reversal Designs

As noted, the basic issue in single-case experiments is how to determine that the manipulation of the independent variable had an effect. One method is to demonstrate the reversibility of the manipulation. A simple **reversal design** takes the following form:

A (baseline period) ⟶ B (treatment period) ⟶ A (baseline period)

This basic reversal design is called an ABA design; it requires observation of behavior during the baseline control (A) period, again during the treatment (B) period, and also during a second baseline (A) period after the experimental treatment has been removed. (Sometimes this is called a *withdrawal design,* in recognition of the fact that the treatment is removed or withdrawn.) For example, the effect of a reinforcement procedure on a child's academic performance could be assessed with an ABA design. The number of correct homework problems could be measured each day during the baseline. A reinforcement treatment procedure would then be introduced in which the child received stars for correct problems; the stars could be accumulated and exchanged for toys or candy. Later, this treatment would be discontinued during the second baseline (A) period. Hypothetical data from such an experiment are shown in Figure 11.1. The fact that behavior changed when the treatment was introduced and reversed when the treatment was withdrawn is evidence for its effectiveness.

Figure 11.1 depicts a treatment that had a relatively dramatic impact on behavior. Some treatments do produce an immediate change in behavior, but many other variables may require a longer time to show an impact.

The ABA design can be greatly improved by extending it to an ABAB design, in which the experimental treatment is introduced a second time, or even to an ABABAB design that allows the effect of the treatment to be tested a third time. This is done to address two problems with the ABA reversal design. First, a single reversal is not extremely powerful evidence for the effectiveness of the treatment. The observed reversal might have been due to a random fluctuation in the child's behavior; perhaps the treatment happened to coincide with some other event, such as the child's upcoming birthday, that caused the change (and the post-birthday reversal). These possibilities are much less likely if the treatment

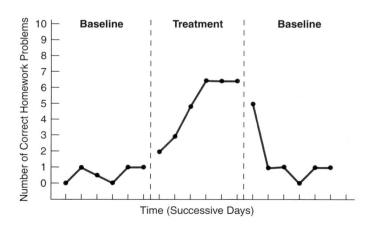

FIGURE 11.1
Hypothetical data from ABA reversal design

has been shown to have an effect two or more times; random or coincidental events are unlikely to be responsible for both reversals. The second problem is ethical. As Barlow, Nock, and Hersen (2009) point out, it doesn't seem right to end the design with the withdrawal of a treatment that may be very beneficial for the participant. Using an ABAB design provides the opportunity to observe a second reversal when the treatment is introduced again. The sequence ends with the treatment rather than the withdrawal of the treatment.

The logic of the reversal design can also be applied to behaviors observed in a single setting. For example, Kazbour and Bailey (2010) examined the effectiveness of a procedure designed to increase use of designated drivers in a bar. The percentage of bar patrons either serving as or being with a designated driver was recorded over a baseline period of 2 weeks. A procedure to increase the use of designated drivers was then implemented during the treatment phase. Designated drivers received a $5 gas card, and the driver and passengers received free pizza on their way out of the bar. The pizza and gas incentive was discontinued during the final phase of the study. The percentage of bar patrons engaged in designated driver arrangements increased substantially during the treatment phase but returned to baseline levels when the incentive was withdrawn.

Multiple Baseline Designs

It may have occurred to you that a reversal of some behaviors may be impossible or unethical. For example, it would be unethical to reverse treatment that reduces dangerous or illegal behaviors, such as indecent exposure or alcoholism, even if the possibility exists that a second introduction of the treatment might be effective. Other treatments might produce a long-lasting change in behavior that is not reversible. In such cases, multiple measures over time can be made before and after the manipulation. If the manipulation is effective, a change in behavior will be immediately observed, and the change will continue to be reflected in further measures of the behavior. In a **multiple baseline design,** the effectiveness of the treatment is demonstrated when a behavior changes only after the manipulation is introduced. To demonstrate the effectiveness of the treatment, such a change must be observed under *multiple* circumstances to rule out the possibility that other events were responsible.

There are several variations of the multiple baseline design (Barlow et al., 2009). In the multiple baseline *across subjects,* the behavior of several subjects is measured over time; for each subject, though, the manipulation is introduced at a different point in time. Figure 11.2 shows data from a hypothetical smoking reduction experiment with 3 subjects. Note that introduction of the manipulation was followed by a change in behavior for each subject. However, because this change occurred across all individuals and the manipulation was introduced at a different time for each subject, we can rule out explanations based on chance, historical events, and so on.

In a multiple baseline *across behaviors,* several different behaviors of a single subject are measured over time. At different times, the same manipulation is

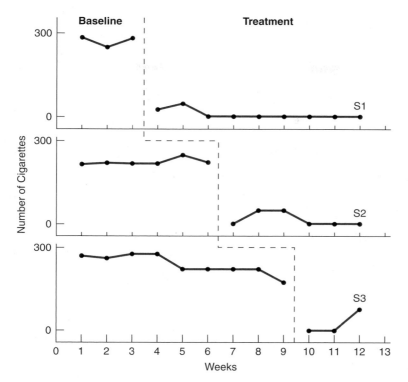

FIGURE 11.2
Hypothetical data from multiple baseline design across three subjects
(S1, S2, and S3)

applied to each of the behaviors. For example, a reward system could be instituted to increase the socializing, grooming, and reading behaviors of a psychiatric patient. The reward system would be applied to each of these behaviors at different times. Demonstrating that each behavior increased when the reward system was applied would be evidence for the effectiveness of the manipulation.

The third variation is the multiple baseline *across situations*, in which the same behavior is measured in different settings, such as at home and at work. Again, a manipulation is introduced at a different time in each setting, with the expectation that a change in the behavior in each situation will occur only after the manipulation.

Replications in Single-Case Designs

The procedures for use with a single subject can, of course, be replicated with other subjects, greatly enhancing the generalizability of the results. Usually, reports of research that employs single-case experimental procedures do present the results from several subjects (and often in several settings). The tradition in single-case research has been to present the results from each subject individually rather than as group data with overall means. Sidman (1960), a leading spokesperson for this tradition, has pointed out that grouping the data from a number of subjects by using group means can sometimes give a misleading picture of individual responses to the manipulation. For example, the manipulation may be effective in changing the behavior of some subjects but not others. This was true in a study conducted by Ryan and Hemmes (2005) that investigated the impact of rewarding college students with course grade points for submitting homework. For half of the 10 chapters, students received points for submitting homework; however, there were no points given if they submitted homework for the other chapters (to control for chapter topic, some students had points for odd-numbered chapters only and others received points for the even-numbered chapters). Ryan and Hemmes found that on average students submitted more homework assignments and performed better on chapter-based quizzes that were directly associated with point rewards. However, some individual participants performed about the same regardless of condition. Because the emphasis of the study was on the individual subject, this pattern of results was quickly revealed.

Single-case designs are useful for studying many research problems and should be considered a powerful alternative to more traditional research designs. They can be especially valuable for someone who is applying some change technique in a natural environment—for example, a teacher who is trying a new technique in the classroom. In addition, complex statistical analyses are not required for single-case designs.

PROGRAM EVALUATION

As we noted in Chapter 1, researchers frequently investigate applied research questions and conduct evaluation research. This research may use true experimental designs, surveys, observational techniques, and other methods available to researchers. Such research is often very difficult because numerous practical problems can prevent researchers from using the best practices for conducting research. True experiments are frequently not possible, and the researchers may be called in too late to decide on the best measurement technique, or the budget rules out many data collection possibilities (Bamberger, Rugh, Church, & Fort, 2004). Still, the research needs to be done. We will only focus on the use of quasi-experimental designs as a methodological tool in applied research settings. Before doing so, it will be helpful to discuss program evaluation research.

Program evaluation is research on programs that are implemented to achieve some positive effect on a group of individuals. Such programs may be implemented in schools, work settings, or entire communities. In schools, an example is the DARE (Drug Abuse Resistance Education) program designed to reduce drug use. This program is conducted in conjunction with local police departments and has become extremely popular since it was developed in the early 1980s—over 36 million children worldwide have participated in the program. Program evaluation applies many research approaches to investigate these types of programs.

Donald Campbell (1969) urged a culture of evaluation in which all such programs are honestly evaluated to determine whether they are effective. Thus, the initial focus of evaluation research was "outcome evaluation": Did the program result in the positive outcome for which it was designed (e.g., reductions in drug abuse, higher grades, lower absenteeism, or lower recidivism)? However, as the field of program evaluation has progressed since Campbell's 1969 paper, evaluation research has become concerned with much more than outcome evaluation (Rossi, Freeman, & Lipsey, 2004).

Rossi et al. (2004) identify five types of evaluations; each attempts to answer a different question about the program. These are depicted in Figure 11.3 as the five phases of the evaluation process. The first, is the evaluation of need. **Needs assessment** studies ask whether there are, in fact, problems that need to be addressed in a target population. For example, is there drug abuse by children and adolescents in the community? If so, what types of drugs are being used? What services do homeless individuals need most? Do repeat juvenile offenders have particular personal and family problems that could be addressed by an intervention program? Once a need has been established, programs can be planned to address the need. The data for the needs assessment may come from surveys, interviews, and statistical data maintained by public health, criminal justice, and other agencies.

The second type of program evaluation question addresses program theory. After identifying needs, a program can be designed to address them. Rossi et al. (2004) emphasize that the program must be based on valid assumptions about the causes of the problems and the rationale of the proposed program.

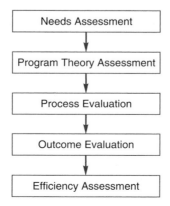

FIGURE 11.3 Phases of program evaluation research

Program theory assessment may involve the collaboration of researchers, service providers, and prospective clients of the program to determine that the proposed program does in fact address the needs of the target population in appropriate ways. Rossi et al. describe a study that assessed the needs of homeless men and women in New York City (Herman, Struening, & Barrow, 1994). The most important overall needs were help with finding a place to live, finding a job, and improving job skills. Men in particular needed help with drinking or drug problems, handling money, and getting along with others. Women were more likely to need help with health and medical problems. A program designed to address these needs should take this information into account and have a rationale for how homeless individuals will in fact benefit from the program.

The third type of program evaluation question is **process evaluation** or program monitoring. When the program is under way, the evaluation researcher monitors it to determine whether it is reaching the target population, whether it is attracting enough clients, and whether the staff is providing the planned services. Sometimes, the staff has not received adequate training, or the services are being offered in a location that is undesirable or difficult to find. In sum, the researcher wants assurance that the program is doing what it is supposed to do. This research is extremely important because we would not want to conclude that a program itself is ineffective if, in fact, it is the *implementation* of the program that is not working. Such research may involve questionnaires and interviews, observational studies, and analysis of records kept by program staff.

The fourth question concerns **outcome evaluation** or impact assessment: Are the intended outcomes of the program being realized? Is the goal—to reduce drug use, increase literacy, decrease repeat offenses by juveniles, or provide job skills—being achieved? To determine this, the evaluation researcher must devise a way of measuring the outcome and then study the impact of the program on the outcome measure. We need to know what participants of the program are like, and we need to know what they would be like if they had not completed the program. Ideally, a true experimental design with random assignment to conditions would be carried out to answer questions about outcomes. However, other research approaches, such as the quasi-experimental and single-case designs described in this chapter, are very useful ways of assessing the impact of an intervention program.

The final program evaluation question addresses **efficiency assessment.** Once it is shown that a program does have its intended effect, researchers must determine whether it is worth the resources it consumes. The cost of the program must be weighed against its benefits. Also, the researchers must determine whether the resources used to implement the program might be put to some better use.

QUASI-EXPERIMENTAL DESIGNS

Quasi-experimental designs address the need to study the effect of an independent variable in settings in which the control features of true experimental designs cannot be achieved. Thus, a quasi-experimental design allows us to examine the impact of an independent variable on a dependent variable, but causal inference is much more difficult because quasi-experiments lack important features of true experiments such as random assignment to conditions. In this chapter, we will examine several quasi-experimental designs that might be used in situations in which a true experiment is not possible.

There are many types of quasi-experimental designs—see Campbell (1968, 1969), Campbell and Stanley (1966), Cook and Campbell (1979), Shadish, Cook, and Campbell (2002). Only six designs will be described. As you read about each design, compare the design features and problems with the randomized true experimental designs described in Chapter 8. We start out with the simplest and most problematic of the designs. In fact, the first three designs we describe are sometimes called "pre-experimental" to distinguish them from other quasi-experimental designs. This is because of the problems associated with these designs. Nevertheless, all may be used in different circumstances, and it is important to recognize the internal validity issues raised by each design.

One-Group Posttest-Only Design

Suppose you want to investigate whether sitting close to a stranger will cause the stranger to move away. You might try sitting next to a number of strangers and measure the number of seconds that elapse before they leave. Your design would look like this:

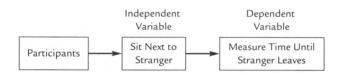

Now suppose that the average amount of time before the people leave is 9.6 seconds. Unfortunately, this finding is not interpretable. You don't know whether they would have stayed longer if you had not sat down or whether they would have stayed for 9.6 seconds anyway. It is even possible that they would have left sooner if you had not sat down—perhaps they liked you!

This **one-group posttest-only design**—called a "one-shot case study" by Campbell and Stanley (1966)—lacks a crucial element of a true experiment: a control or comparison group. There must be some sort of comparison condition to enable you to interpret your results. The one-group posttest-only design with its missing comparison group has serious deficiencies in the context of designing an internally valid experiment that will allow us to draw causal inferences about the effect of an independent variable on a dependent variable.

You might wonder whether this design is ever used. In fact, you may see this type of design used as evidence for the effectiveness of a program. For example, employees in a company might participate in a 4-hour information session on emergency procedures. At the conclusion of the program, they complete a knowledge test on which their average score is 90%. This result is then used to conclude that the program is successfully educating employees. Such studies lack internal validity—our ability to conclude that the independent variable had an effect on the dependent variable. With this design, we do not even know if the score on the dependent variable would have been equal, lower, or even higher without the program. The reason why results such as these are sometimes accepted is because we may have an implicit idea of how a control group would perform. Unfortunately, we need that comparison data.

One-Group Pretest-Posttest Design

One way to obtain a comparison is to measure participants before the manipulation (a pretest) and again afterward (a posttest). An index of change from the pretest to the posttest could then be computed. Although this **one-group pretest-posttest design** sounds fine, there are some major problems with it.

To illustrate, suppose you wanted to test the hypothesis that a relaxation training program will result in a reduction in cigarette smoking. Using the one-group pretest-posttest design, you would select a group of people who smoke, administer a measure of smoking, have them go through relaxation training, and then re-administer the smoking measure. Your design would look like this:

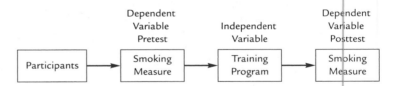

If you did find a reduction in smoking, you could not assume that the result was due to the relaxation training program. This design has failed to take into account several alternative explanations. These alternative explanations are threats to the internal validity of studies using this design and include history, maturation, testing, instrument decay, and regression toward the mean.

History
History refers to any event that occurs between the first and second measurements but is not part of the manipulation. Any such event is confounded with the manipulation. For example, suppose that a famous person dies of lung cancer during the time between the first and second measures. This event, and not the relaxation training, could be responsible for a reduction in smoking. Admittedly, the celebrity death example is dramatic and perhaps unlikely. However, **history effects** can be caused by virtually any confounding event that occurs at the same time as the experimental manipulation.

Maturation
People change over time. In a brief period they become bored, fatigued, perhaps wiser, and certainly hungrier; over a longer period, children become more coordinated and analytical. Any changes that occur systematically over time are called **maturation effects.** Maturation could be a problem in the

smoking reduction example if people generally become more concerned about health as they get older. Any such time-related factor might result in a change from the pretest to the posttest. If this happens, you might mistakenly attribute the change to the treatment rather than to maturation.

Testing

Testing becomes a problem if simply taking the pretest changes the participant's behavior—the problem of **testing effects.** For example, the smoking measure might require people to keep a diary in which they note every cigarette smoked during the day. Simply keeping track of smoking might be sufficient to cause a reduction in the number of cigarettes a person smokes. Thus, the reduction found on the posttest could be the result of taking the pretest rather than of the program itself. In other contexts, taking a pretest may sensitize people to the purpose of the experiment or make them more adept at a skill being tested. Again, the experiment would not have internal validity.

Instrument decay

Sometimes, the basic characteristics of the measuring instrument change over time; this is called **instrument decay.** Consider sources of instrument decay when human observers are used to measure behavior: Over time, an observer may gain skill, become fatigued, or change the standards on which observations are based. In our example on smoking, participants might be highly motivated to record all cigarettes smoked during the pretest when the task is new and interesting, but by the time the posttest is given they may be tired of the task and sometimes forget to record a cigarette. Such instrument decay would lead to an apparent reduction in cigarette smoking.

Regression toward the mean

Sometimes called *statistical regression,* **regression toward the mean** is likely to occur whenever participants are selected because they score extremely high or low on some variable. When they are tested again, their scores tend to change in the direction of the mean. Extremely high scores are likely to become lower (closer to the mean), and extremely low scores are likely to become higher (again, closer to the mean).

Regression toward the mean would be a problem in the smoking experiment if participants were selected because they were initially found to be extremely heavy smokers. By choosing people for the program who scored highest on the pretest, the researcher may have selected many participants who were, for whatever reason, smoking much more than usual at the particular time the measure was administered. Those people who were smoking much more than usual will likely be smoking less when their smoking is measured again. If we then compare the overall amount of smoking before and after the program, it will appear that people are smoking less. The alternative explanation is that the smoking reduction is due to statistical regression rather than the effect of the program.

Regression toward the mean will occur whenever you gather a set of extreme scores taken at one time and compare them with scores taken at another point in time. The problem is actually rooted in the reliability of the measure. Recall from Chapter 5 that any given measure reflects a true score plus measurement error.

If there is perfect reliability, the two measures will be the same (if nothing happens to lower or raise the scores). If the measure of smoking is perfectly reliable, a person who reports smoking 20 cigarettes today will report smoking 20 cigarettes 2 weeks from now. However, if the two measures are not perfectly reliable and there is measurement error, most scores will be close to the true score but some will be higher and some will be lower. Thus, one smoker with a true score of 20 cigarettes per day might sometimes smoke 5 and sometimes 35; however, most of the time, the number is closer to 20 than the extremes. Another smoker might have a true score of 35 but on occasion smokes as few as 20 and as many as 50; again, most of the time, the number is closer to the true score than to the extremes. Now suppose that you select two people who said they smoked 35 cigarettes on the previous day, and that both of these people are included in the group—you picked the first person on a very unusual day and the second person on a very ordinary day. When you measure these people two weeks later, the first person is probably going to report smoking close to 20 cigarettes and the second person close to 35. If you average the two, it will appear that there is an overall reduction in smoking.

What if the measure were perfectly reliable? In this case, the person with a true score of 20 cigarettes would always report this amount and therefore would not be included in the heavy smoker (35+) group at all. Only people with true scores of 35 or more would be in the group, and any reduction in smoking would be due to the treatment program. The point here is that regression toward the mean is a problem if there is measurement error.

Statistical regression occurs when we try to explain events in the "real world" as well. Sports columnists often refer to the hex that awaits an athlete who appears on the cover of *Sports Illustrated*. The performances of a number of athletes have dropped considerably after they were the subjects of *Sports Illustrated* cover stories. Although these cover stories might cause the lower performance (perhaps the notoriety results in nervousness and reduced concentration), statistical regression is also a likely explanation. An athlete is selected for the cover of the magazine because he or she is performing at an exceptionally high level; the principle of regression toward the mean states that very high performance is likely to deteriorate. We would know this for sure if *Sports Illustrated* also did cover stories on athletes who were in a slump and this became a good omen for them!

All these problems can be eliminated by the use of an appropriate control group. A group that does not receive the experimental treatment provides an adequate control for the effects of history, statistical regression, and so on. For example, outside historical events would have the same effect on both the experimental and the control groups. If the experimental group differs from the control group on the dependent measure administered after the manipulation, the difference between the two groups can be attributed to the effect of the experimental manipulation.

Given these problems, is the one-group pretest-posttest design ever used? This design may in fact be used in many applied settings. Recall the example of the evaluation of a program to teach emergency procedures to employees. With a one group pretest-posttest design, the knowledge test would be given before and after the training session. The ability to observe a change from the pretest to the posttest does represent an improvement over the posttest-only design, even with the threats to internal validity that we identified. In addition, the ability to use data from this design can be enhanced if the study is replicated at other times with other participants. However, formation of a control group is always the best way to strengthen this design.

In any control group, the participants in the experimental condition and the control condition must be equivalent. If participants in the two groups differ *before* the manipulation, they will probably differ *after* the manipulation as well. The next design illustrates this problem.

Nonequivalent Control Group Design

The **nonequivalent control group design** employs a separate control group, but the participants in the two conditions—the experimental group and the control group—are not equivalent. The differences become a confounding variable that provides an alternative explanation for the results. This problem, called **selection differences** or selection bias, usually occurs when participants who form the two groups in the experiment are chosen from existing natural groups. If the relaxation training program is studied with the nonequivalent control group design, the design will look like this:

The participants in the first group are given the smoking frequency measure after completing the relaxation training. The people in the second group do not participate in any program. In this design, the researcher does not have any control over which participants are in each group. Suppose, for example, that the study is conducted in a division of a large company. All of the employees who smoke are identified and recruited to participate in the training program. The people who volunteer for the program are in the experimental group, and the people in the control group are simply the smokers who did not sign up for the training. The problem of selection differences arises because smokers who choose to participate may differ in some important way from those who do not. For instance, they may already be light smokers compared with the others and more confident that a program can help them. If so, any difference between the groups on the smoking measure would reflect preexisting differences rather than the effect of the relaxation training.

It is important to note that the problem of selection differences arises in this design even when the researcher apparently has successfully manipulated the independent variable using two similar groups. For example, a researcher might have all smokers in the engineering division of a company participate in the relaxation training program and smokers who work in the marketing division serve as a control group. The problem here, of course, is that the smokers in the two divisions may have differed in smoking patterns *prior* to the relaxation program.

Nonequivalent Control Group Pretest-Posttest Design

The nonequivalent control group posttest-only design can be greatly improved if a pretest is given. When this is done, we have a **nonequivalent control group pretest-posttest design,** one of the most useful quasi-experimental designs. It can be diagrammed as follows:

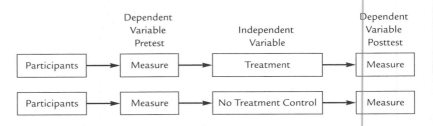

This is not a true experimental design because assignment to groups is not random; the two groups may not be equivalent. We have the advantage, however, of knowing the pretest scores. Thus, we can see whether the groups were the same on the pretest. Even if the groups are not equivalent, we can look at *changes* in scores from the pretest to the posttest. If the independent variable has an effect, the experimental group should show a greater change than the control group (see Kenny, 1979). Strategies for statistical analysis of such change scores are discussed by Shadish, Cook, and Campbell (2002) and Trochim (2006).

An evaluation of National Alcohol Screening Day (NASD) provides an example of the use of a nonequivalent control group pretest-posttest design (Aseltine, Schilling, James, Murray, & Jacobs, 2008). NASD is a community-based program that provides free access to alcohol screening, a private meeting with a health professional to review the results, educational materials, and referral information if necessary. For the evaluation, NASD attendees at five community locations completed a baseline (pretest) measure of their recent alcohol consumption. This measure was administered as a posttest 3 months later. A control group was formed 1 week following NASD at the same locations using displays that invited people to take part in a health survey. These individuals completed the same pretest measure and were contacted in 3 months for the posttest. The data analysis focused on participants identified as at-risk drinkers; the NASD participants showed a significant decrease in alcohol consumption from pretest to posttest when compared with similar individuals in the control group.

Propensity Score Matching of Nonequivalent Treatment and Control Groups

The nonequivalent control group designs lack random assignment to conditions and so the groups may in fact differ in important ways. For example, people who decide to attend an alcohol screening event may differ from those who are interested in a health screening. Perhaps the people at the health screening are in fact healthier than the alcohol screening participants.

One approach to making the groups equivalent on a variable such as health is to match participants in the conditions on a measure of health (this is similar to matched pairs designs, covered in Chapter 8). The health measure can be administered to everyone in the treatment condition and all individuals who are included in the control condition. Now, each person in the treatment condition would be matched with a control individual who possesses an identical or highly similar health score. Once this has been done, the analysis of the dependent measure can take place. This procedure is most effective when the measure used for the matching is highly reliable and the individuals in the two conditions are known to be very similar. Nonetheless, it is still possible that the two groups are different on other variables that were not measured.

Advances in statistical methods have made it possible to simultaneously match individuals on multiple variables. Instead of matching on just one variable such as health, the researcher can obtain measures of other variables thought to be important when comparing the groups. The scores on these variables are combined to produce what is called a *propensity score* (the statistical procedure is beyond the scope of the book). Individuals in the treatment and control groups can then be matched on propensity scores—this process is called **propensity score matching** (Guo & Fraser, 2010; Shadish, Cook, & Campbell, 2002).

Interrupted Time Series Design and Control Series Design

Campbell (1969) discusses at length the evaluation of one specific legal reform: the 1955 crackdown on speeding in Connecticut. Although seemingly an event in the distant past, the example is still a good illustration of an important methodological issue. The crackdown was instituted after a record high number of traffic fatalities occurred in 1955. The easiest way to evaluate this reform is to compare the number of traffic fatalities in 1955 (before the crackdown) with the number of fatalities in 1956 (after the crackdown). Indeed, the number of traffic deaths fell from 324 in 1955 to 284 in 1956. This single comparison is really a one-group pretest-posttest design with all of that design's problems of internal validity; there are many other reasons that traffic deaths might have declined. One alternative is to use an **interrupted time series design** that would examine the traffic fatality rates over an extended period of time, both before and after the reform was instituted. Figure 11.4 shows this information for the years 1951–1959. Campbell (1969) argues that the drop from 1955 to 1956 does not look particularly impressive, given the great fluctuations in previous years, but there is a steady downward trend in fatalities after the crackdown. Even here,

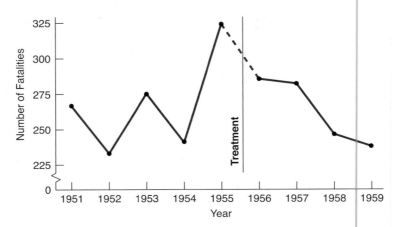

FIGURE II.4
Connecticut traffic fatalities, 1951–1959

however, Campbell sees a problem in interpretation. The drop could be due to statistical regression: Because 1955 was a record high year, the probability is that there would have been a drop anyway. Still, the data for the years extending before and after the crackdown allow for a less ambiguous interpretation than would be possible with data for only 1955 and 1956.

One way to improve the interrupted time series design is to find some kind of control group—a **control series design.** In the Connecticut speeding crackdown, this was possible because other states had not instituted the reform. Figure 11.5 shows the same data on traffic fatalities in Connecticut plus the fatality figures of four comparable states during the same years. The fact that the fatality rates in the control states remained relatively constant while those in Connecticut consistently declined led Campbell to conclude that the crackdown did indeed have some effect.

Conclusion

Earlier, we described the need to evaluate programs such as DARE. Many researchers have, in fact, conducted outcome evaluation studies using quasi-experimental designs to examine both short-term and long-term effects. Most studies compare students in schools that have DARE programs with students from schools that do not. The general conclusion is that DARE has very small effects on the participants (cf. Ennett, Tobler, Ringwalt, & Flewelling, 1994; West & O'Neal, 2004). Moreover, studies that have examined long-term effects conclude that there are no long-term benefits of the program (Rosenbaum & Hanson, 1998); for example, college students who had participated in DARE as a child or teenager had the same amount of substance use as students never exposed to the program (Thombs, 2000). These results have led to the development of revised DARE programs that will be evaluated.

As noted above, there are other quasi-experimental designs that are beyond the scope of this book. Researchers such as Bamberger et al. (2004) are also

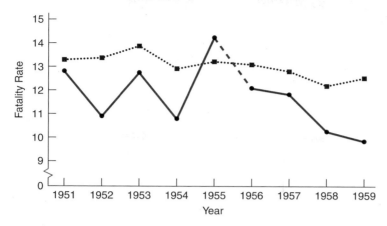

FIGURE 11.5
Control series design comparing Connecticut traffic fatality rate (solid color line) with the fatality rate of four comparable states (dotted black line)

developing systematic approaches to respond to specific challenges that arise when doing evaluation research—they refer to doing "shoestring evaluation" when there are restraints of time, budget, and data collection options.

DEVELOPMENTAL RESEARCH DESIGNS

Developmental psychologists often study the ways that individuals change as a function of age. A researcher might test a theory concerning changes in reasoning ability as children grow older, the age at which self-awareness develops in young children, or the global values people have as they move from adolescence through old age. In all cases, the major variable is age. Developmental researchers face an interesting choice in designing their studies because there are two general methods for studying individuals of different ages: the cross-sectional method and the longitudinal method. You will see that the cross-sectional method shares similarities with the independent groups design whereas the longitudinal method is similar to the repeated measures design. We will also examine a hybrid approach called the sequential method. The three approaches are illustrated in Figure 11.6.

Cross-Sectional Method

In a study using the **cross-sectional method,** persons of different ages are studied at only one point in time. Suppose you are interested in examining how the ability to learn a computer application changes as people grow older. Using the cross-sectional method, you might study people who are currently 20, 30, 40, and 50 years of age. The participants in your study would be given the same computer learning task, and you would compare the groups on their performance.

Cross-Sectional Method

	Year of Birth (cohort)	Time 1: 2005
Group 1:	1950	55 years old
Group 2:	1945	60 years old
Group 3:	1940	65 years old

Longitudinal Method

	Year of Birth (cohort)	Time 1: 2005	Time 2: 2010	Time 3: 2015
Group 1:	1950	55 years old →	60 years old →	65 years old

Sequential Method

	Year of Birth (cohort)	Time 1: 2005	Time 2: 2010	Time 3: 2015
Group 1:	1950	55 years old →	60 years old →	65 years old
Group 2:	1940	65 years old →	70 years old →	75 years old

FIGURE 11.6
Three designs for developmental research

Longitudinal Method

In the **longitudinal method,** the same group of people is observed at different points in time as they grow older. Perhaps the most famous longitudinal study is the Terman Life Cycle Study that was begun by Stanford psychologist Lewis Terman in 1921. Terman studied 1,528 California schoolchildren who had intelligence test scores of at least 135. The participants, who called themselves "Termites," were initially measured on numerous aspects of their cognitive and social development in 1921 and 1922. Terman and his colleagues continued studying the Termites during their childhood and adolescence and throughout their adult lives (cf. Terman, 1925; Terman & Oden, 1947, 1959). Terman's successors at Stanford continue to track the Termites until each one dies. The study has provided a rich description of the lives of highly intelligent individuals and disconfirmed many negative stereotypes of high intelligence—for example, the Termites were very well adjusted both socially and emotionally. The data have now been archived for use by other researchers such as Friedman and Martin (2011), who used the Terman data to study whether personality and other factors are related to health and longevity. To complete their investigations, Friedman and Martin obtained death certificates of Terman participants to have precise data on both how long they lived and the causes of death. One strong pattern that emerged was that the personality dimension of "conscientiousness" (being self-disciplined, organized) that was measured in childhood was related to longevity. Of interest is that changes in personality qualities also affected longevity. Participants who had become less conscientious as adults had a reduction in longevity; those who became more conscientious as adults experienced longer lives. Another interesting finding concerned interacting with pets. Questions about animals were asked when participants were in their sixties; contrary to common beliefs, having or playing with pets was not related to longevity.

A unique longitudinal study on aging and Alzheimer's disease called the Nun Study illustrates a different approach (Snowden, 1997). In 1991, all members of a particular religious order born prior to 1917 were asked to participate by providing access to their archived records as well as various annual medical and psychological measures taken over the course of the study. The sample consisted of 678 women with a mean age of 83. One fascinating finding from this study was based on autobiographies that all sisters wrote in 1930 (Donner, Snowden, & Friesen, 2001). The researchers devised a coding system to measure positive emotional content in the autobiographies. Greater positive emotions were strongly related to actual survival rate during the course of the study. Other longitudinal studies may study individuals over only a few years. For example, a nine-year study of U.S. children found a variety of impacts—positive and negative—of early nonmaternal child care (NICHD Early Child Care Research Network, 2005).

Comparison of Longitudinal and Cross-Sectional Methods

The cross-sectional method is much more common than the longitudinal method primarily because it is less expensive and immediately yields results. Note that, with a longitudinal design, it would take 30 years to study the same group of individuals from age 20 to 50, but with a cross-sectional design, comparisons of different age groups can be obtained relatively quickly.

There are, however, some disadvantages to cross-sectional designs. Most important, the researcher must infer that differences among age groups are due to the developmental variable of age. The developmental change is not observed directly among the same group of people, but rather is based on comparisons among different cohorts of individuals. You can think of a **cohort** as a group of people born at about the same time, exposed to the same events in a society, and influenced by the same demographic trends such as divorce rates and family size. If you think about the hairstyles of people you know who are in their 30s, 40s, 50s, and 60s, you will immediately recognize the importance of cohort effects! More crucially, differences among cohorts reflect different economic and political conditions in society, different music and arts, different educational systems, and different child-rearing practices. In a cross-sectional study, a difference among groups of different ages may reflect developmental age changes; however, the differences may result from **cohort effects** (Schaie, 1986).

To illustrate this issue, let's return to our hypothetical study on learning to use computers. Suppose you found that age is associated with a decrease in ability such that the people in the 50-year-old group score lower on the learning measure than the 40-year-olds, and so on. Should you conclude that the ability to learn to use a computer application decreases with age? That may be an accurate conclusion; alternatively, the differences could be due to a cohort effect: The older people had less experience with computers while growing up. The key point here is that the cross-sectional method confounds age and cohort effects. (Review the discussion of confounding and internal validity at the beginning of Chapter 8.) Finally, you should note that cohort effects are most likely to be a problem when the researcher is examining age effects across a wide range of ages (e.g., adolescents through older adults).

The only way to conclusively study changes that occur as people grow older is to use a longitudinal design. Also, longitudinal research is the best way to study how scores on a variable at one age are related to another variable at a later age. For example, researchers at the National Children's Study (http://www.nationalchildrensstudy.gov) began collecting data in 2009 at 105 study locations across the United States. In each of those study sites, participants (new parents) are being recruited to participate in the study that will run from the birth of their child until the child is 21 years of age. The goal of the study is to better understand the interactions of the environment and genetics and their effects on child health and well-being. The alternative in this case would be to study samples of children of various ages and ask them or their parents about the earlier home environment; this *retrospective* approach has its own problems when one considers the difficulty of remembering events in the distant past.

Thus, the longitudinal approach, despite being expensive and difficult, has definite advantages. However, there is one major problem: Over the course of a longitudinal study, people may move, die, or lose interest in the study. Researchers who conduct longitudinal studies become adept at convincing people to continue, often travel anywhere to collect more data, and compare test scores of people who drop out with those who stay to provide better analyses of their results. In sum, a researcher shouldn't embark on a longitudinal study without considerable resources and a great deal of patience and energy!

Sequential Method

A compromise between the longitudinal and cross-sectional methods is to use the **sequential method.** This method, along with the cross-sectional and longitudinal method, is illustrated in Figure 11.6. In the figure, the goal of the study is to minimally compare 55- and 65-year-olds. The first phase of the sequential method begins with the cross-sectional method; for example, you could study groups of 55- and 65-year-olds. These individuals are then studied using the longitudinal method with each individual tested at least one more time.

Orth, Trzesniewski, and Robins (2010) studied the development of self-esteem over time using just such a sequential method. Using data from the Americans' Changing Lives study, Orth and his colleagues identified six different age cohorts (25–34, 35–44, 45–54, 55–64, 65–74, 75+) and examined their self-esteem ratings from 1986, 1989, 1994, and 2002. Thus, they were interested in changes in self-esteem for participants at various ages, over time. Their findings provide an interesting picture of how self-esteem changes over time: They found that self-esteem gradually increases from age 25 to around age 60 and then declines in later years. If this were conducted as a full longitudinal study, it would require 100 years to complete!

Clearly, this method takes fewer years and less effort to complete than a longitudinal study, and the researcher reaps immediate rewards because data on the different age groups are available in the first year of the study. On the other hand, the participants are not followed over the entire time span as they would be in a full longitudinal investigation; that is, no one in the Orth study was followed from age 25 to 100.

We have now described most of the major approaches to designing research. In the next two chapters, we consider methods of analyzing research data.

ILLUSTRATIVE ARTICLE: A QUASI-EXPERIMENT

Sexual violence on college and university campuses has been and continues to be a widespread problem. Programs designed to prevent sexual violence on campuses have shown mixed results: Some evidence suggests that they can be effective, but other evidence shows that they are not.

Banyard, Moynihan, and Crossman (2009) implemented a prevention program that utilized specific sub-groups of campus communities to "raise awareness about the problem of sexual violence and build skill that individuals can use to end it." They exposed dormitory resident advisors to a program called "Bringing in the Bystander" and assessed change in attitudes as well as a set of six outcome measures (e.g., willingness to help).

First, acquire and read the article:

Banyard, V. L., Moynihan, M. M., & Crossman, M. T. (2009). Reducing sexual violence on campus: The role of student leaders as empowered bystanders. *Journal of College Student Development, 50*, 446–457. doi:10.1353/csd.0.0083

Then, after reading the article, consider the following:

1. This study was a quasi-experiment. What is the specific design?
2. What are the potential weaknesses of the design?
3. Given that this study attempted to assess the overall effectiveness of a prevention program, it can also be thought of as program evaluation. In which phase of program evaluation research (shown in Figure 11.3) do you think this study belongs?
4. The discussion of this article begins with this statement: "The results of this study are promising." Do you agree or disagree? Support your position.

5. How would you determine if there is a need to address the problem of sexual violence on your campus? If you discover that there is a need, would the program described here be appropriate? Why or why not?

Study Terms

Baseline (p. 216)

Cohort (p. 233)

Cohort effects (p. 233)

Control series design (p. 230)

Cross-sectional method (p. 231)

Efficiency assessment (p. 222)

History effects (p. 224)

Instrument decay (p. 225)

Interrupted time series design (p. 229)

Longitudinal method (p. 232)

Maturation effects (p. 224)

Multiple baseline design (p. 218)

Needs assessment (p. 221)

Nonequivalent control group design (p. 227)

Nonequivalent control group pretest-posttest design (p. 228)

One-group posttest-only design (p. 223)

One-group pretest-posttest design (p. 224)

Outcome evaluation (p. 222)

Process evaluation (p. 222)

Program evaluation (p. 220)

Program theory assessment (p. 222)

Propensity score matching (p. 229)

Quasi-experimental design (p. 222)

Regression toward the mean (Statistical regression) (p. 225)

Reversal design (p. 216)

Selection differences (p. 227)

Sequential method (p. 234)

Single-case experimental design (p. 216)

Testing effects (p. 225)

Review Questions

1. Describe what a program evaluation researcher's goals would be when addressing each of the five types of evaluation research questions.

2. What is a reversal design? Why is an ABAB design superior to an ABA design?

3. What is meant by *baseline* in a single-case design?

4. What is a multiple baseline design? Why is it used? Distinguish between multiple baseline designs across subjects, across behaviors, and across situations.

5. Why might a researcher use a quasi-experimental design rather than a true experimental design?

6. Why does having a control group eliminate the problems associated with the one-group pretest-posttest design?

7. Describe the threats to internal validity discussed in the text: history, maturation, testing, instrument decay, regression toward the mean, and selection differences.

8. Describe the nonequivalent control group pretest-posttest design. Why is this a quasi-experimental design rather than a true experiment?

9. Describe the interrupted time series and the control series designs. What are the strengths of the control series design as compared with the interrupted time series design?

10. Distinguish between longitudinal, cross-sectional, and sequential methods.

11. What is a cohort effect?

Activity Questions

1. Your dog gets lonely while you are at work and consequently engages in destructive activities such as pulling down curtains or strewing wastebasket contents all over the floor. You decide that playing a radio while you are gone might help. How might you determine whether this "treatment" is effective?

2. Your best friend frequently suffers from severe headaches. You've noticed that your friend consumes a great deal of diet cola, and so you consider the hypothesis that the artificial sweetener in the cola is responsible for the headaches. Devise a way to test your hypothesis using a single-case design. What do you expect to find if your hypothesis is correct? If you obtain the expected results, what do you conclude about the effect of the artificial sweetener on headaches?

3. Dr. Smith learned that one sorority on campus had purchased several Macintosh computers and another sorority had purchased several Windows-based computers. Dr. Smith was interested in whether the type of computer affects the quality of students' papers, so he went to each of the sorority houses to collect samples of papers from the members. Two graduate students in the English department then rated the quality of the papers. Dr. Smith found that the quality of the papers was higher in one sorority than in the other. What are the independent and dependent variables in this study? Identify the type of design that Dr. Smith used. What variables are confounded with the independent variable? Design a true experiment that would address Dr. Smith's original question.

4. Gilovich (1991) described an incident that he read about during a visit to Israel. A very large number of deaths had occurred during a brief time period in one region of the country. A group of rabbis attributed the deaths to a recent change in religious practice that allowed women to attend funerals. Women were immediately forbidden to attend funerals in that region, and the number of deaths subsequently decreased. How would you explain this phenomenon?

5. The captain of each precinct of a metropolitan police department selected two officers to participate in a program designed to reduce prejudice by increasing sensitivity to racial and ethnic group differences and community issues. The training program took place every Friday morning for 3 months. At the first and last meetings, the officers completed a measure of prejudice. To assess the effectiveness of the program, the average prejudice score at the first meeting was compared with the average score at the last meeting; it was found that the average score was in fact lower following the training program. What type of design is this? What specific problems arise if you try to conclude that the training program was responsible for the reduction in prejudice?

6. A student club is trying to decide whether to implement a peer tutoring program for students who are enrolled in the statistics class in your department. Club members who have completed the statistics class would offer to provide tutoring to students currently enrolled in the class. You decide to take the lessons of program evaluation seriously, and so you develop a strategy to conduct evaluation research.

   a. How would you measure whether there is a need for such a program?

   b. Briefly describe how you might implement a tutoring program. How would you monitor the program?

   c. Propose a quasi-experimental design to evaluate whether the program is effective.

   d. How might you determine the economic efficiency of such a program?

7. Many elementary schools have implemented a daily "sustained silent reading" period during which students, faculty, and staff spend 15–20 minutes silently reading a book of their choice. Advocates of this policy claim that the activity encourages pleasure reading outside the required silent reading time. Design a nonequivalent control group pretest-posttest quasi-experiment to test this claim. Include a well-reasoned dependent measure as well.

8. For the preceding situation, discuss the advantages and disadvantages of using a quasi-experimental design in contrast to conducting a true experiment.

9. Dr. Cardenas studied political attitudes among different groups of 20-, 40-, and 60-year-olds. Political attitudes were found to be most conservative in the age-60 group and least conservative in the age-20 group.

   a. What type of method was used in this study?

   b. Can you conclude that people become more politically conservative as they get older? Why or why not?

   c. Propose alternative ways of studying this topic.

12

Understanding Research Results: Description and Correlation

LEARNING OBJECTIVES

- Contrast the three ways of describing results: comparing group percentages, correlating scores, and comparing group means.
- Describe a frequency distribution, including the various ways to display a frequency distribution.
- Describe the measures of central tendency and variability.
- Define a correlation coefficient.
- Define *effect size*.
- Describe the use of a regression equation and a multiple correlation to predict behavior.
- Discuss how a partial correlation addresses the third-variable problem.
- Summarize the purpose of structural equation models.

S tatistics help us understand the data collected in research investigations in two fundamental ways: First, statistics are used to describe the data. Second, statistics are used to make inferences and draw conclusions, on the basis of sample data, about a population. We examine descriptive statistics and correlation in this chapter; inferential statistics are discussed in Chapter 13. This chapter will focus on the underlying logic and general procedures for making statistical decisions. Specific calculations for a variety of statistics are provided in Appendix B.

SCALES OF MEASUREMENT: A REVIEW

Before looking at any statistics, we need to review the concept of scales of measurement. Whenever a variable is studied, the researcher must create an operational definition of the variable and devise two or more levels of the variable. Recall from Chapter 5 that the levels of the variable can be described using one of four scales of measurement: nominal, ordinal, interval, and ratio. The scale used determines the types of statistics that are appropriate when the results of a study are analyzed. Also recall that the meaning of a particular score on a variable depends on which type of scale was used when the variable was measured or manipulated.

The levels of **nominal scale** variables have no numerical, quantitative properties. The levels are simply different categories or groups. Most independent variables in experiments are nominal, for example, as in an experiment that compares behavioral and cognitive therapies for depression. Variables such as gender, eye color, hand dominance, college major, and marital status are nominal scale variables; left-handed and right-handed people differ from each other, but not in a quantitative way.

Variables with **ordinal scale** levels exhibit minimal quantitative distinctions. We can rank order the levels of the variable being studied from lowest to highest. The clearest example of an ordinal scale is one that asks people to make rank-ordered judgments. For example, you might ask people to rank the most important problems facing your state today. If education is ranked first, health care second, and crime third, you know the order but you do not know how strongly people feel about each problem: Education and health care may be very close together in seriousness with crime a distant third. With an ordinal scale, the intervals between each of the items are probably not equal.

Interval scale and ratio scale variables have much more detailed quantitative properties. With an **interval scale** variable, the intervals between the levels are equal in size. The difference between 1 and 2 on the scale, for example, is the same as the difference between 2 and 3. Interval scales generally have five or more quantitative levels. You might ask people to rate their mood on a 7-point scale ranging from a "very negative" to a "very positive" mood. There is no absolute zero point that indicates an "absence" of mood.

In the behavioral sciences, it is often difficult to know precisely whether an ordinal or an interval scale is being used. However, it is often useful to assume that the variable is being measured on an interval scale because interval scales allow for more sophisticated statistical treatments than do ordinal scales. Of course, if the measure is a rank ordering (for example, a rank ordering of students in a class on the basis of popularity), an ordinal scale clearly is being used.

Ratio scale variables have both equal intervals and an absolute zero point that indicates the absence of the variable being measured. Time, weight, length, and other physical measures are the best examples of ratio scales. Interval and ratio scale variables are conceptually different; however, the statistical procedures used to analyze data with such variables are identical. An important implication of interval and ratio scales is that data can be summarized using the mean, or arithmetic average. It is possible to provide a number that reflects the mean amount of a variable—for example, the "average mood of people who won a contest was 5.1" or the "mean weight of the men completing the weight loss program was 187.7 pounds."

ANALYZING THE RESULTS OF RESEARCH INVESTIGATIONS

Scales of measurement have important implications for the way that the results of research investigations are described and analyzed. Most research focuses on the study of relationships between variables. Depending on the way that the variables are studied, there are three basic ways of describing the results: (1) comparing group percentages, (2) correlating scores of individuals on two variables, and (3) comparing group means.

Comparing Group Percentages

Suppose you want to know whether males and females differ in their interest in travel. In your study, you ask males and females whether they like or dislike travel. To describe your results, you will need to calculate the percentage of females who like to travel and compare this with the percentage of males who like to travel. Suppose you tested 50 females and 50 males and found that 40 of the females and 30 of the males indicated that they like to travel. In describing your findings, you would report that 80% of the females like to travel in comparison with 60% of the males. Thus, a relationship between the gender and travel variables appears to exist. Note that we are focusing on percentages because the travel variable is nominal: Liking and disliking are simply two different categories. After describing your data, the next step would be to perform a statistical analysis to determine whether there is a statistically significant difference between the males and females. Statistical significance is discussed in Chapter 13; statistical analysis procedures are described in Appendix B.

Correlating Individual Scores

A second type of analysis is needed when you do not have distinct groups of subjects. Instead, individuals are measured on two variables, and each variable has a range of numerical values. For example, we will consider an analysis of data on the relationship between location in a classroom and grades in the class: Do people who sit near the front receive higher grades?

Comparing Group Means

Much research is designed to compare the mean responses of participants in two or more groups. For example, in an experiment designed to study the effect of exposure to an aggressive adult, children in one group might observe an adult "model" behaving aggressively while children in a control group do not. Each child then plays alone for 10 minutes in a room containing a number of toys, while observers record the number of times the child behaves aggressively during play. Aggression is a ratio scale variable because there are equal intervals and a true zero on the scale.

   In this case, you would be interested in comparing the mean number of aggressive acts by children in the two conditions to determine whether the children who observed the model were more aggressive than the children in the control condition. Hypothetical data from such an experiment in which there were 10 children in each condition are shown in Table 12.1; the scores in the table

TABLE 12.1   Scores on aggression measure in a hypothetical experiment on modeling and aggression

Model group	No-model group
3	1
4	2
5	2
5	3
5	3
5	3
6	4
6	4
6	4
7	5
$\Sigma X = 52$	$\Sigma X = 31$
$\overline{X} = 5.20$	$\overline{X} = 3.10$
$s^2 = 1.29$	$s^2 = 1.43$
$s = 1.14$	$s = 1.20$
$n = 10$	$n = 10$

represent the number of aggressive acts by each child. In this case, the mean aggression score in the model group is 5.20 and the mean score in the no-model condition is 3.10. In the next chapter, we will conduct a statistical test to determine whether this difference is statistically significant.

For all types of data, it is important to understand your results by carefully describing the data collected. We begin by constructing frequency distributions.

FREQUENCY DISTRIBUTIONS

When analyzing results, researchers start by constructing a frequency distribution of the data. A **frequency distribution** indicates the number of individuals who receive each possible score on a variable. Frequency distributions of exam scores are familiar to most college students—they tell how many students received a given score on the exam. Along with the number of individuals associated with each response or score, it is useful to examine the percentage associated with this number.

Graphing Frequency Distributions

It is often useful to graphically depict frequency distributions. Let's examine several types of graphs: pie chart, bar graph, and frequency polygon.

Pie charts   **Pie charts** divide a whole circle, or "pie," into "slices" that represent relative percentages. Figure 12.1 shows a pie chart depicting a frequency distribution in which 70% of people like to travel and 30% dislike travel. Because there are two pieces of information to graph, there are two slices in this pie. Pie charts are particularly useful when representing nominal scale information. In the figure, the number of people who chose each response has been converted to a percentage—the simple number could have been displayed instead, of course. Pie charts are most commonly used to depict simple descriptions of categories for a single variable. They are useful in applied research reports and articles written for the general public. Articles in scientific journals require more complex information displays.

Bar graphs   **Bar graphs** use a separate and distinct bar for each piece of information. Figure 12.2 represents the same information about travel using a bar graph. In this graph, the *x* or horizontal axis shows the two possible

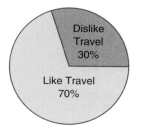

FIGURE 12.1
Pie chart

FIGURE 12.2
Bar graph
displaying
data
obtained in
two groups

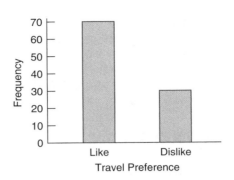

responses. The y or vertical axis shows the number who chose each response, and so the height of each bar represents the number of people who responded to the "like" and "dislike" options.

Frequency polygons
Frequency polygons use a line to represent the distribution of frequencies of scores. This is most useful when the data represent interval or ratio scales as in the modeling and aggression data shown in Table 12.1. Here we have a clear numeric scale of the number of aggressive acts during the observation period. Figure 12.3 graphs the data from the hypothetical experiment using two frequency polygons—one for each group. The solid line represents the no-model group, and the dotted line stands for the model group.

Histograms
A **histogram** uses bars to display a frequency distribution for a quantitative variable. In this case, the scale values are continuous and show increasing amounts on a variable such as age, blood pressure, or stress. Because the values are continuous, the bars are drawn next to each other. A histogram is shown in Figure 12.4 using data from the model group in Table 12.1.

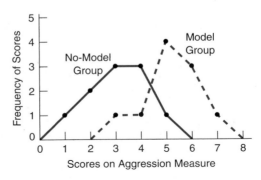

FIGURE 12.3
Frequency polygons illustrating the distributions of scores in Table 12.1

Note: Each frequency polygon is anchored at scores that were not obtained by anyone (0 and 6 in the no-model group; 2 and 8 in the model group).

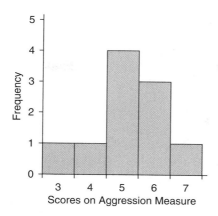

FIGURE 12.4
Histogram
showing
frequency
of
responses in
the model
group

What can you discover by examining frequency distributions? First, you can directly observe how your participants responded. You can see what scores are most frequent, and you can look at the shape of the distribution of scores. You can tell whether there are any outliers—scores that are unusual, unexpected, or very different from the scores of other participants. In an experiment, you can compare the distribution of scores in the groups.

DESCRIPTIVE STATISTICS

In addition to examining the distribution of scores, you can calculate descriptive statistics. **Descriptive statistics** allow researchers to make precise statements about the data. Two statistics are needed to describe the data. A single number can be used to describe the central tendency, or how participants scored overall. Another number describes the variability, or how widely the distribution of scores is spread. These two numbers summarize the information contained in a frequency distribution.

Central Tendency

A **central tendency** statistic tells us what the sample as a whole, or on the average, is like. There are three measures of central tendency—the mean, the median, and the mode. The **mean** of a set of scores is obtained by adding all the scores and dividing by the number of scores. It is symbolized as $\overline{X}$; in scientific reports, it is abbreviated as M. The mean is an appropriate indicator of central tendency only when scores are measured on an interval or ratio scale, because the actual values of the numbers are used in calculating the statistic. In Table 12.1, the mean score for the no-model group is 3.10 and for the model group is 5.20. Note that the Greek letter Σ (sigma) in Table 12.1 is statistical notation for summing a set of numbers. Thus, ΣX is shorthand for "sum of the values in a set of scores."

The **median** is the score that divides the group in half (with 50% scoring below and 50% scoring above the median). In scientific reports, the median is abbreviated as *Mdn*. The median is appropriate when scores are on an ordinal scale because it takes into account only the rank order of the scores. It is also useful with interval and ratio scale variables, however. The median for the no-model group is 3 and for the model group is 5.

The **mode** is the most frequent score. The mode is the only measure of central tendency that is appropriate if a nominal scale is used. The mode does not use the actual values on the scale, but simply indicates the most frequently occurring value. There are two modal values for the no-model group—3 and 4 occur equally frequently. The mode for the model group is 5.

The median or mode can be a better indicator of central tendency than the mean if a few unusual scores bias the mean. For example, the median family income of a county or state is usually a better measure of central tendency than the mean family income. Because a relatively small number of individuals have extremely high incomes, using the mean would make it appear that the "average" person makes more money than is actually the case.

Variability

We can also determine how much **variability** exists in a set of scores. A measure of variability is a number that characterizes the amount of spread in a distribution of scores. One such measure is the **standard deviation,** symbolized as s, which indicates the average deviation of scores from the mean. Income is a good example. The Census Bureau reports that the median U.S. household income in 2009 was $50,229 (http://quickfacts.census.gov/qfd/index.html). Suppose that you live in a community that matches the U.S median and there is very little variation around that median (i.e., every household earns something close to $50,229); your community would have a smaller standard deviation in household income compared to another community in which the median income is the same but there is a lot more variation (e.g., where many people earn $15,000 per year and many others $5 million per year). It is possible for measures of central tendency in two communities to be close with the variability differing substantially.

In scientific reports, it is abbreviated as *SD*. The standard deviation is derived by first calculating the **variance,** symbolized as s^2 (the standard deviation is the square root of the variance). The standard deviation of a set of scores is small when most people have similar scores close to the mean. The standard deviation becomes larger as more people have scores that lie farther from the mean value. For the model group, the standard deviation is 1.14, which tells us that most scores in that condition lie 1.14 units above and below the mean—that is, between 4.06 and 6.34. Thus, the mean and the standard deviation provide a great deal of information about the distribution. Note that, as with the mean, the calculation of the standard deviation uses the actual values of the scores; thus, the standard deviation is appropriate only for interval and ratio scale variables.

Another measure of variability is the **range,** which is simply the difference between the highest score and the lowest score. The range for both the model and no-model groups is 4.

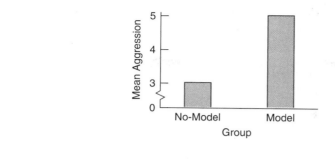

FIGURE 12.5
Graph of
the results
of the
modeling
experiment
showing
mean
aggression
scores

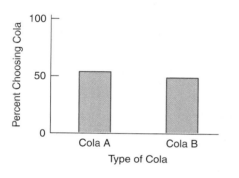
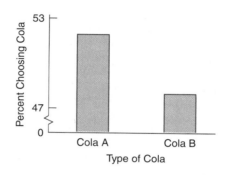

FIGURE 12.6
Two ways
to graph
the same
data

GRAPHING RELATIONSHIPS

Graphing relationships between variables was discussed briefly in Chapter 4. A common way to graph relationships between variables is to use a bar graph or a line graph. Figure 12.5 is a bar graph depicting the means for the model and no-model groups. The levels of the independent variable (no-model and model) are represented on the horizontal x axis, and the dependent variable values are shown on the vertical y axis. For each group, a point is placed along the y axis that represents the mean for the groups, and a bar is drawn to visually represent the mean value. Bar graphs are used when the values on the x axis are nominal categories (e.g., a no-model and a model condition). Line graphs are used when the values on the x axis are numeric (e.g., marijuana use over time, as shown in Figure 7.1). In line graphs, a line is drawn to connect the data points to represent the relationship between the variables.

Choosing the scale for a bar graph allows a common manipulation that is sometimes used by scientists and all too commonly used by advertisers. The trick is to exaggerate the distance between points on the measurement scale to make the results appear more dramatic than they really are. Suppose, for example, that a cola company (cola A) conducts a taste test that shows 52% of the participants prefer cola A and 48% prefer cola B. How should the cola company present these results? The two bar graphs in Figure 12.6 show the most honest method, as well as one that is considerably more dramatic. It is always wise to look carefully at the numbers on the scales depicted in graphs.

CORRELATION COEFFICIENTS: DESCRIBING THE STRENGTH OF RELATIONSHIPS

It is important to know whether a relationship between variables is relatively weak or strong. A **correlation coefficient** is a statistic that describes how strongly variables are related to one another. You are probably most familiar with the **Pearson product-moment correlation coefficient,** which is used when both variables have interval or ratio scale properties. The Pearson product-moment correlation coefficient is called the Pearson r. Values of a Pearson r can range from 0.00 to ± 1.00. Thus, the Pearson r provides information about the strength of the relationship and the direction of the relationship. A correlation of 0.00 indicates that there is no relationship between the variables. The nearer a correlation is to 1.00 (plus or minus), the stronger is the relationship. Indeed, a 1.00 correlation is sometimes called a perfect relationship because the two variables go together in a perfect fashion. The sign of the Pearson r tells us about the direction of the relationship; that is, whether there is a positive relationship or a negative relationship between the variables.

Data from studies examining similarities of intelligence test scores among siblings illustrate the connection between the magnitude of a correlation coefficient and the strength of a relationship. The relationship between scores of monozygotic (identical) twins reared together is .86 and the correlation for monozygotic twins reared apart is .74, demonstrating a strong similarity of test scores in these pairs of individuals. The correlation for dizygotic (fraternal) twins reared together is less strong, with a correlation of .59. The correlation among non-twin siblings raised together is .46, and the correlation among non-twin siblings reared apart is .24. Data such as these allow researchers to draw inferences about the heritability of intelligence (Devlin, Daniels, & Roeder, 1997).

There are many different types of correlation coefficients. Each coefficient is calculated somewhat differently depending on the measurement scale that applies to the two variables. As noted, the Pearson r correlation coefficient is appropriate when the values of both variables are on an interval or ratio scale. We will now focus on the details of the Pearson product-moment correlation coefficient.

Pearson r Correlation Coefficient

To calculate a correlation coefficient, we need to obtain pairs of observations from each subject. Thus, each individual has two scores, one on each of the variables. Table 12.2 shows fictitious data for 10 students measured on the variables of classroom seating pattern and exam grade. Students in the first row receive a seating score of 1, those in the second row receive a 2, and so on. Once we have made our observations, we can see whether the two variables are related. Do the variables go together in a systematic fashion?

The Pearson r provides two types of information about the relationship between the variables. The first is the strength of the relationship; the second is the direction of the relationship. As noted previously, the values of r can range from

TABLE 12.2   Pairs of scores for 10 participants on seating pattern and exam scores (fictitious data)

Subject identification number	Seating	Exam score
01	2	95
02	5	50
03	1	85
04	4	75
05	3	75
06	5	60
07	2	80
08	3	70
09	1	90
10	4	70

0.00 to ±1.00. The absolute size of r is the coefficient that indicates the strength of the relationship. A value of 0.00 indicates that there is no relationship. The nearer r is to 1.00 (plus or minus), the stronger is the relationship. The plus and minus signs indicate whether there is a positive linear or negative linear relationship between the two variables. It is important to remember that it is the size of the correlation coefficient, not the sign, that indicates the strength of the relationship. Thus, a correlation coefficient of $-.54$ indicates a stronger relationship than does a coefficient of $+.45$.

Scatterplots.   The data in Table 12.2 can be visualized in a **scatterplot** in which each pair of scores is plotted as a single point in a diagram. Figure 12.7 shows two scatterplots. The values of the first variable are depicted on the x axis,

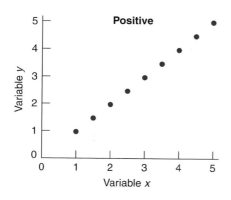
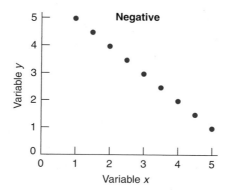

FIGURE 12.7 Scatterplots of perfect (±1.00) relationships

FIGURE 12.8
Scatterplots
depicting
patterns of
correlation

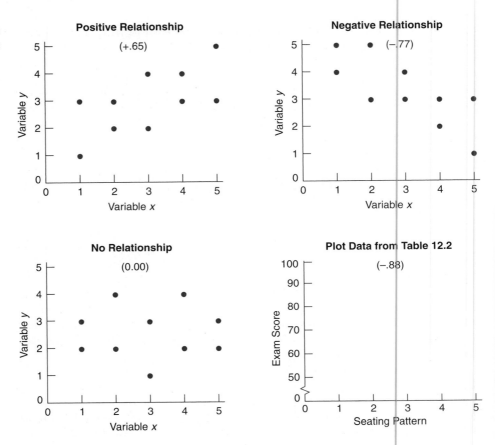

and the values of the second variable are shown on the y axis. These scatterplots show a perfect positive relationship (+1.00) and a perfect negative relationship (−1.00). You can easily see why these are perfect relationships: The scores on the two variables fall on a straight line that is on the diagonal of the diagram. Each person's score on one variable correlates precisely with his or her score on the other variable. If we know an individual's score on one of the variables, we can predict exactly what his or her score will be on the other variable. Such "perfect" relationships are rarely observed in reality.

The scatterplots in Figure 12.8 show patterns of correlation you are more likely to encounter in exploring research findings. The first diagram shows pairs of scores with a positive correlation of +.65; the second diagram shows a negative relationship, −.77. The data points in these two scatterplots reveal a general pattern of either a positive or negative relationship, but the relationships are not perfect. You can make a general prediction in the first diagram, for instance, that the higher the score on one variable, the higher the score on the second variable. However, even if you know a person's score on the first variable, you cannot perfectly predict what that person's score will be on the second variable. To confirm this, take a look at value 1 on variable x (the horizontal axis) in the positive scatterplot. Looking along the vertical y axis, you will see that two individuals had a score of 1. One of these had a score of 1 on variable y, and the other had a score of 3. The data points do not fall on the perfect diagonal shown in Figure 12.7. Instead, there is a variation (scatter) from the perfect diagonal line.

The third diagram shows a scatterplot in which there is absolutely no correlation ($r = 0.00$). The points fall all over the diagram in a completely random pattern. Thus, scores on variable x are not related to scores on variable y.

The fourth diagram has been left blank so that you can plot the scores from the data in Table 12.2. The x (horizontal) axis has been labeled for the seating pattern variable, and the y (vertical) axis for the exam score variable. To complete the scatterplot, you will need to plot the 10 pairs of scores. For each individual in the sample, find the score on the seating pattern variable; then go up from that point until you are level with that person's exam score on the y axis. A point placed there will describe the score on both variables. There will be 10 points on the finished scatterplot.

The correlation coefficient calculated from these data shows a negative relationship between the variables ($r = -.88$). In other words, as the seating distance from the front of the class increases, the exam score decreases. Although these data are fictitious, the negative relationship is consistent with actual research findings (Brooks & Rebata, 1991).

Important Considerations

Restriction of range
It is important that the researcher sample from the full range of possible values of both variables. If the range of possible values is restricted, the magnitude of the correlation coefficient is reduced. For example, if the range of seating pattern scores is restricted to the first two rows, you will not get an accurate picture of the relationship between seating pattern and exam score. In fact, when only scores of students sitting in the first two rows are considered, the correlation between the two variables is exactly 0.00. With a restricted range comes restricted variability in the scores and thus less variability that can be explained.

The problem of **restriction of range** occurs when the individuals in your sample are very similar on the variable you are studying. If you are studying age as a variable, for instance, testing only 6- and 7-year-olds will reduce your chances of finding age effects. Likewise, trying to study the correlates of intelligence will be almost impossible if everyone in your sample is very similar in intelligence (e.g., the senior class of a prestigious private college).

Curvilinear relationship
The Pearson product-moment correlation coefficient (r) is designed to detect only linear relationships. If the relationship is curvilinear, as in the scatterplot shown in Figure 12.9, the correlation coefficient will not indicate the existence of a relationship. The Pearson r correlation

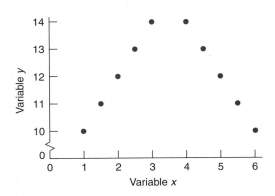

FIGURE 12.9
Scatterplot of a curvilinear relationship (Pearson product-moment correlation coefficient = 0.00)

coefficient calculated from these data is exactly 0.00, even though the two variables clearly are related.

Because a relationship may be curvilinear, it is important to construct a scatterplot in addition to looking at the magnitude of the correlation coefficient. The scatterplot is valuable because it gives a visual indication of the shape of the relationship. Computer programs for statistical analysis will usually display scatterplots and can show you how well the data fit to a linear or curvilinear relationship. When the relationship is curvilinear, another type of correlation coefficient must be used to determine the strength of the relationship.

EFFECT SIZE

We have presented the Pearson *r* correlation coefficient as the appropriate way to describe the relationship between two variables with interval or ratio scale properties. Researchers also want to describe the strength of relationships between variables in all studies. **Effect size** refers to the strength of association between variables. The Pearson *r* correlation coefficient is one indicator of effect size; it indicates the strength of the linear association between two variables. In an experiment with two or more treatment conditions, other types of correlation coefficients can be calculated to indicate the magnitude of the effect of the independent variable on the dependent variable. For example, in our experiment on the effects of witnessing an aggressive model on children's aggressive behavior, we compared the means of two groups. In addition to knowing the means, it is valuable to know the effect size. An effect size correlation coefficient can be calculated for the modeling and aggression experiment. In this case, the effect size correlation value is .69. As with all correlation coefficients, the values of this effect size correlation can range from 0.00 to 1.00 (we don't need to worry about the direction of relationship, so plus and minus values are not used). The formula used for calculating the correlation is discussed in Chapter 13.

The advantage of reporting effect size is that it provides us with a scale of values that is consistent across all types of studies. The values range from 0.00 to 1.00, irrespective of the variables used, the particular research design selected, or the number of participants studied. You might be wondering what correlation coefficients should be considered indicative of small, medium, and large effects. A general guide is that correlations near .15 (about .10 to .20) are considered small, those near .30 are medium, and correlations above .40 are large.

It is sometimes preferable to report the squared value of a correlation coefficient; instead of r, you will see r^2. Thus, if the obtained $r = .50$, the reported $r^2 = .25$. Why transform the value of r? This reason is that the transformation changes the obtained r to a percentage. The percentage value represents the percent of variance in one variable that is accounted for by the second variable. The range of r^2 values can range from 0.00 (0%) to 1.00 (100%). The r^2 value is sometimes referred to as the *percent of shared variance between the two variables*. What does this mean, exactly? Recall the concept of variability in a set of scores—if you measured the weight of a random sample of American adults, you would observe variability in that weights would range from relatively low weights to relatively high weights. If you are studying factors that contribute to people's weight, you would want to examine the relationship between weights and scores on the contributing variable. One such variable might be gender: In actuality, the correlation between gender and weight is about .70 (with males weighing more than females). That means that 49% (squaring .70) of the variability in weight is accounted for by variability in gender. You have therefore explained 49% of the variability in the weights, but there is still 51% of the variability that is not accounted for. This variability might be accounted for by other variables, such as the weights of the biological mother and father, prenatal stress, diet, and exercise. In an ideal world, you could account for 100% of the variability in weights if you had enough information on all other variables that contribute to people's weights: Each variable would make an incremental contribution until all the variability is accounted for.

REGRESSION EQUATIONS

Regression equations are calculations used to predict a person's score on one variable when that person's score on another variable is already known. They are essentially "prediction equations" that are based on known information about the relationship between the two variables. For example, after discovering that seating pattern and exam score are related, a regression equation may be calculated that predicts anyone's exam score based only on information about where the person sits in the class. The general form of a regression equation is

$$Y = a + bX$$

where Y is the score we wish to predict, X is the known score, a is a constant, and b is a weighting adjustment factor that is multiplied by X (it is the slope of the line created with this equation). In our seating–exam score example, the following regression equation is calculated from the data:

$$Y = 99 + (-8)X$$

Thus, if we know a person's score on X (seating), we can insert that into the equation and predict what that person's exam score (Y) will be. If the person's X score is 2 (by sitting in the second row), we can predict that $Y = 99 + (-16)$, or that the person's exam score will be 83. Through the use of regression equations such as these, colleges can use SAT scores to predict college grades.

When researchers are interested in predicting some future behavior (called the **criterion variable**) on the basis of a person's score on some other variable (called the **predictor variable**), it is first necessary to demonstrate that there is a reasonably high correlation between the criterion and predictor variables. The regression equation then provides the method for making predictions on the basis of the predictor variable score only.

MULTIPLE CORRELATION/REGRESSION

Thus far we have focused on the correlation between two variables at a time. Researchers recognize that a number of different variables may be related to a given behavior (this is the same point noted above in the discussion of factors that contribute to weight). A technique called **multiple correlation** is used to combine a number of predictor variables to increase the accuracy of prediction of a given criterion or outcome variable.

A multiple correlation (symbolized as R to distinguish it from the simple r) is the correlation between a combined set of predictor variables and a single criterion variable. Taking all of the predictor variables into account usually permits greater accuracy of prediction than if any single predictor is considered alone. For example, applicants to graduate school in psychology could be evaluated on a combined set of predictor variables using multiple correlation. The predictor variables might be (1) college grades, (2) scores on the Graduate Record Exam Aptitude Test, (3) scores on the Graduate Record Exam Psychology Test, and (4) favorability of letters of recommendation. No one of these factors is a perfect predictor of success in graduate school, but this combination of variables can yield a more accurate prediction. The multiple correlation is usually higher than the correlation between any one of the predictor variables and the criterion or outcome variable.

In actual practice, predictions would be made with an extension of the regression equation technique discussed previously. A multiple regression equation can be calculated that takes the following form:

$$Y = a + b_1X_1 + b_2X_2 + \ldots + b_nX_n$$

where Y is the criterion variable, X_1 to X_n are the predictor variables, a is a constant, and b_1 to b_n are weights that are multiplied by scores on the predictor variables. For example, a regression equation for graduate school admissions would be

Predicted grade point average $= a + b_1$ (college grades)

$+\ b_2$ (score on GRE Aptitude Test)

$+\ b_3$ (score on GRE Psychology Test)

$+\ b_4$ (favorability of recommendation letters)

Researchers use multiple regression to study basic research topics. For example, Ajzen and Fishbein (1980) developed a model called the "theory of reasoned action" that uses multiple correlation and regression to predict specific behavioral intentions (e.g., to attend church on Sunday, buy a certain product, or join an alcohol recovery program) on the basis of two predictor variables. These are (1) attitude toward the behavior and (2) perceived normative pressure to engage in the behavior. Attitude is one's own evaluation of the behavior, and normative pressure comes from other people such as parents and friends. In one study, Codd and Cohen (2003) found that the multiple correlation between college students' intention to seek help for alcohol problems and the combined predictors of attitude and norm was .35. The regression equation was as follows:

$$\text{Intention} = .29(\text{attitude}) + .18(\text{norm})$$

This equation is somewhat different from those described previously. In basic research, you are not interested in predicting an exact score (such as an exam score or GPA), and so the mathematical calculations can assume that all variables are measured on the same scale. When this is done, the weighting factor reflects the magnitude of the correlation between the criterion variable and each predictor variable. In the help-seeking example, the weight for the attitude predictor is somewhat higher than the weight for the norm predictor; this shows that, in this case, attitudes are more important as a predictor of intention than are norms. However, for other behaviors, attitudes may be less important than norms.

It is also possible to visualize the regression equation. In the help-seeking example, the relationships among variables could be diagrammed as follows:

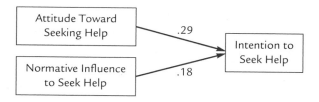

You should note that the squared multiple correlation coefficient (R^2) is interpreted in much the same way as the squared correlation coefficient (r^2). That is, R^2 tells you the percentage of variability in the criterion variable that is accounted for by the combined set of predictor variables. Again, this value will be higher than that of any of the single predictors by themselves.

PARTIAL CORRELATION AND THE THIRD-VARIABLE PROBLEM

Researchers face the third-variable problem in nonexperimental research when some uncontrolled third variable may be responsible for the relationship between the two variables of interest. The problem doesn't exist in experimental research, because all extraneous variables are controlled either by keeping the variables constant or by using randomization. A technique called **partial correlation** provides a way of statistically controlling third variables. A partial correlation is a correlation between the two variables of interest, with the influence of the third variable removed from, or "partialed out of," the original correlation. This provides an indication of what the correlation between the primary variables would be if the third variable were held constant. This is not the same as actually keeping the variable constant, but it is a useful approximation.

Suppose a researcher is interested in a measure of number of bedrooms per person as an index of household crowding—a high number indicates that more space is available for each person in the household. After obtaining this information, the researcher gives a cognitive test to children living in these households. The correlation between bedrooms per person and test scores is .50. Thus, children in more spacious houses score higher on the test. The researcher suspects that a third variable may be operating. Social class could influence both housing and performance on this type of test. If social class is measured, it can be included in a partial correlation calculation that looks at the relationship between bedrooms per person and test scores with social class held constant. To calculate a partial correlation, you need to have scores on the two primary variables of interest and the third variable that you want to examine.

When a partial correlation is calculated, you can compare the partial correlation with the original correlation to see if the third variable did have an effect. Is our original correlation of .50 substantially reduced when social class is held constant? Figure 12.10 shows two different partial correlations. In both, there is a .50 correlation between bedrooms per person and test score. The first partial correlation between bedrooms per person and test scores drops to .09 when social class is held constant because social class is so highly correlated with the primary variables. However, the partial correlation in the second example remains high at .49 because the correlations with social class are relatively small. Thus, the outcome of the partial correlation depends on the magnitude of the correlations between the third variable and the two variables of primary interest.

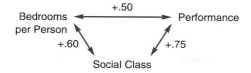
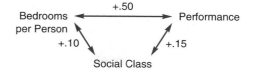

Partial correlation between bedrooms
per person and performance is +.09.

Partial correlation between bedrooms
per person and performance is +.49.

FIGURE 12.10
Two partial correlations between bedrooms per person and performance

STRUCTURAL EQUATION MODELING

Advances in statistical methods have resulted in a set of techniques to examine models that specify a set of relationships among variables using quantitative nonexperimental methods (see Raykov & Marcoulides, 2000; Ullman, 2007). **Structural equation modeling (SEM)** is a general term to refer to these techniques. The methods of SEM are beyond the scope of this book but you will likely encounter some research findings that use SEM; thus, it is worthwhile to provide an overview. A model is an expected pattern of relationships among a set of variables. The proposed model is based on a theory of how the variables are causally related to one another. After data have been collected, statistical methods can be applied to examine how closely the proposed model actually "fits" the obtained data.

Researchers typically present path diagrams to visually represent the models being tested. Such diagrams show the theoretical causal paths among the variables. The multiple regression diagram on attitudes and intentions shown previously is a path diagram of a very simple model. The theory of reasoned action evolved into a more complex "theory of planned behavior" that has an additional construct to predict behavior. Huchting, Lac, and LaBrie (2008) studied alcohol consumption among 247 sorority members at a private university. They measured four variables at the beginning of the study: (1) attitude toward alcohol consumption based on how strongly the women believed that consuming alcohol had positive consequences, (2) subjective norm or perceived alcohol consumption of other sorority members, (3) perceived lack of behavioral control based on beliefs about the degree of difficulty in refraining from drinking alcohol, and (4) intention to consume alcohol based on the amount that the women expected to consume during the next 30 days. The sorority members were contacted one month later to provide a measure of actual behavior—the amount of alcohol consumed during the previous 30 days.

The theory of planned behavior predicts that attitude, subjective norm, and behavior control will each predict the behavioral intention to consume alcohol. Intention will in turn predict actual behavior. The researchers used structural equation modeling techniques to study this model. It is easiest to visualize the

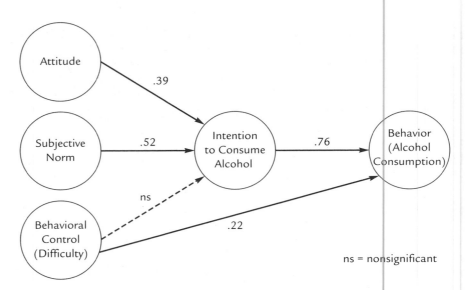

FIGURE 12.11
Structural model based on data from Huchting, Lac, and LaBrie (2008)

results using the path diagram shown in Figure 12.11. In the path diagram, arrows leading from one variable to another depict the paths that relate the variables in the model. The arrows indicate a causal sequence. Note that the model specifies that attitude, subjective norm, and behavioral control are related to intention and that intention in turn causes actual behavior. The statistical analysis provides what are termed *path coefficients*—these are similar to the standardized weights derived in the regression equations described previously. They indicate the strength of a relationship on our familiar −1.00 to 1.00 scale.

In Figure 12.11, you can see that both attitude and subjective norm were significant predictors of intention to consume alcohol. However, the predicted relationship between behavioral control and intention was not significant (therefore, the path is depicted as a dashed line). Intention was strongly related to actual behavior. Note also that behavioral control had a direct path to behavior; this indicates that difficulty in controlling alcohol consumption is directly related to actual consumption.

Besides illustrating how variables are related, a final application of SEM in the Huchting et al. study was to evaluate how closely the obtained data fit the specified model. The researchers concluded that the model did in fact closely fit the data. The lack of a path from behavioral control to intention is puzzling and will lead to further research.

There are many other applications of SEM. For example, researchers can compare two competing models in terms of how well each fits obtained data. Researchers can also examine much more complex models that contain many more variables. These techniques allow us to study nonexperimental data in more complex ways. This type of research leads to a better understanding of the complex networks of relationships among variables.

In the next chapter we turn from description of data to making decisions about statistical significance. These two topics are of course related. The topic of effect size that was described in this chapter is also very important when evaluating statistical significance.

Study Terms

Bar graph (p. 243)

Central tendency (p. 245)

Correlation coefficient (p. 248)

Criterion variable (p. 254)

Descriptive statistics (p. 245)

Effect size (p. 252)

Frequency distribution (p. 243)

Frequency polygons (p. 244)

Histogram (p. 244)

Interval scales (p. 240)

Mean (p. 245)

Median (p. 246)

Mode (p. 246)

Multiple correlation (p. 254)

Nominal scales (p. 240)

Ordinal scales (p. 240)

Partial correlation (p. 256)

Pearson product-moment correlation coefficient (p. 248)

Pie chart (p. 243)

Predictor variable (p. 254)

Range (p. 246)

Ratio scales (p. 241)

Regression equations (p. 253)

Restriction of range (p. 251)

Scatterplot (p. 249)

Standard deviation (p. 246)

Structural equation modeling (SEM) (p. 257)

Variability (p. 246)

Variance (p. 246)

Review Questions

1. Distinguish among comparing percentages, comparing means, and correlating scores.
2. What is a frequency distribution?
3. Distinguish between a pie chart, bar graph, and frequency polygon. Construct one of each.
4. What is a measure of central tendency? Distinguish between the mean, median, and mode.
5. What is a measure of variability? Distinguish between the standard deviation and the range.

6. What is a correlation coefficient? What do the size and sign of the correlation coefficient tell us about the relationship between variables?

7. What is a scatterplot?

8. What happens when a scatterplot shows the relationship to be curvilinear?

9. What is a regression equation? How might an employer use a regression equation?

10. How does multiple correlation increase accuracy of prediction?

11. What is the purpose of partial correlation?

12. When a path diagram is shown, what information is conveyed by the arrows leading from one variable to another?

Activity Questions

1. Your favorite newspaper, newsmagazine, or news-related website is a rich source of descriptive statistics on a variety of topics. Examine the past week's news; describe at least five instances of actual data presented. These can include surveys, experiments, business data, and even sports information.

2. Hill (1990) studied the correlations between final exam score in an introductory sociology course and several other variables such as number of absences. The following Pearson r correlation coefficients with final exam score were obtained:

Overall college GPA	.72
Number of absences	−.51
Hours spent studying on weekdays	−.11 (not significant)
Hours spent studying on weekends	.31

Describe each correlation and draw graphs depicting the general shape of each relationship. Why might hours spent studying on weekends be correlated with grades but weekday studying not be?

3. Ask 20 students on campus how many units (credits) they are taking, as well as how many hours per week they work in paid employment. Create a frequency distribution and find the mean for each data set. Construct a scatterplot showing the relationship between class load and hours per week employed. Does there appear to be a relationship between the variables? (Note: There might be a restriction of range problem on your campus because few students work or most students take about the same number of units. If so, ask different questions, such as the number of hours spent studying and watching television each week.)

4. Prior to the start of the school year, Mr. King reviewed the cumulative folders of the students in his fourth-grade class. He found that the standard deviation of the students' scores on the reading comprehension test was exactly 0.00. What information does this provide him? How might that information prove useful?

5. Refer to the figure below, then select the correct answer to questions a, b, and c.

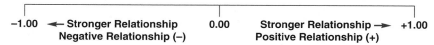

−1.00 ◄— **Stronger Relationship**   **0.00**   **Stronger Relationship** —► **+1.00**
            Negative Relationship (–)   **Positive Relationship (+)**

The size (value) of the coefficient indicates the strength of the relationship.
The sign (plus or minus) of the coefficient indicates the direction of the linear relationship.

  a. Which one of the following numbers could *not* be a correlation coefficient?

     −.99   +.71   +1.02   +.01   +.38

  b. Which one of the following correlation coefficients indicates the strongest relationship?

     +.23   −.89   −.10   −.91   +.77

  c. Which of the following correlation coefficients indicates the weakest negative relationship?

     −.28   +.08   −.42   +.01   −.29

Answers _____

  a. +1.02   b. −.91   c. −.28

13

Understanding Research Results: Statistical Inference

LEARNING OBJECTIVES

■ Explain how researchers use inferential statistics to evaluate sample data.

■ Distinguish between the null hypothesis and the research hypothesis.

■ Discuss probability in statistical inference, including the meaning of statistical significance.

■ Describe the *t* test and explain the difference between one-tailed and two-tailed tests.

■ Describe the *F* test, including systematic variance and error variance.

■ Describe what a confidence interval tells you about your data.

■ Distinguish between Type I and Type II errors.

■ Discuss the factors that influence the probability of a Type II error.

■ Discuss the reasons a researcher may obtain nonsignificant results.

■ Define *power* of a statistical test.

■ Describe the criteria for selecting an appropriate statistical test.

In the previous chapter, we examined ways of describing the results of a study using descriptive statistics and a variety of graphing techniques. In addition to descriptive statistics, researchers use inferential statistics to draw more general conclusions about their data. In short, inferential statistics allow researchers to (a) assess just how confident they are that their results reflect what is true in the larger population, and (b) assess the likelihood that their findings would still occur if their study was repeated over and over. In this chapter, we examine methods for doing so.

SAMPLES AND POPULATIONS

Inferential statistics are necessary because the results of a given study are based only on data obtained from a single sample of research participants. Researchers rarely, if ever, study entire populations; their findings are based on sample data. In addition to describing the sample data, we want to make statements about populations. Would the results hold up if the experiment were conducted repeatedly, each time with a new sample?

In the hypothetical experiment described in Chapter 12 (see Table 12.1), mean aggression scores were obtained in model and no-model conditions. These means are different: Children who observe an aggressive model subsequently behave more aggressively than children who don't see the model. **Inferential statistics** are used to determine whether the results match what would happen if we were to conduct the experiment again and again with multiple samples. In essence, we are asking whether we can infer that the difference in the *sample means* shown in Table 12.1 reflects a true difference in the *population means*.

Recall our discussion of this issue in Chapter 7 on the topic of survey data. A sample of people in your state might tell you that 57% prefer the Democratic candidate for an office and that 43% favor the Republican candidate. The report then says that these results are accurate to within 3 percentage points, with a 95% confidence level. This means that the researchers are very (95%) confident that, if they were able to study the entire population rather than a sample, the actual percentage who preferred the Democratic candidate would be between 60% and 54% and the percentage preferring the Republican would be between 46% and 40%. In this case, the researcher could predict with a great deal of certainty that the Democratic candidate will win because there is no overlap in the projected population values. Note, however, that even when we are very (in this case, 95%) sure, we still have a 5% chance of being wrong.

Inferential statistics allow us to arrive at such conclusions on the basis of sample data. In our study with the model and no-model conditions, are we confident that the means are sufficiently different to infer that the difference would be obtained in an entire population?

INFERENTIAL STATISTICS

Much of the previous discussion of experimental design centered on the importance of ensuring that the groups are equivalent in every way except the independent variable manipulation. Equivalence of groups is achieved by experimentally controlling all other variables or by randomization. The assumption is that if the groups are equivalent, any differences in the dependent variable must be due to the effect of the independent variable.

This assumption is usually valid. However, it is also true that the difference between any two groups will almost never be zero. In other words, there will be some difference in the sample means, even when all of the principles of experimental design are rigorously followed. This happens because we are dealing with samples, rather than populations. Random or chance error will be responsible for some difference in the means, even if the independent variable had no effect on the dependent variable.

Therefore, the difference in the sample means does show any true difference in the population means (i.e., the effect of the independent variable) *plus* any random error. Inferential statistics allow researchers to make inferences about the true difference in the population on the basis of the sample data. Specifically, inferential statistics give the probability that the difference between means reflects random error rather than a real difference.

NULL AND RESEARCH HYPOTHESES

Statistical inference begins with a statement of the null hypothesis and a research (or alternative) hypothesis. The **null hypothesis** is simply that the population means are equal—the observed difference is due to random error. The **research hypothesis** is that the population means are, in fact, not equal. The null hypothesis states that the independent variable had no effect; the research hypothesis states that the independent variable did have an effect. In the aggression modeling experiment, the null and research hypotheses are

H_0 (null hypothesis): The population mean of the no-model group is equal to the population mean of the model group.

H_1 (research hypothesis): The population mean of the no-model group is not equal to the population mean of the model group.

The logic of the null hypothesis is this: If we can determine that the null hypothesis is incorrect, then we accept the research hypothesis as correct. Acceptance of the research hypothesis means that the independent variable had an effect on the dependent variable.

The null hypothesis is used because it is a very precise statement—the population means are exactly equal. This permits us to know precisely the probability of obtaining our results if the null hypothesis is correct. Such precision isn't possible with the research hypothesis, so we infer that the research hypothesis is correct only by rejecting the null hypothesis. We reject the null hypothesis when we find a very low probability that the obtained results could be due to random error. This is what is meant by **statistical significance:** A significant result is one that has a very low probability of occurring if the population means are equal. More simply, significance indicates that there is a low probability that the difference between the obtained sample means was due to random error. Significance, then, is a matter of probability.

PROBABILITY AND SAMPLING DISTRIBUTIONS

Probability is the likelihood of the occurrence of some event or outcome. We all use probabilities frequently in everyday life. For example, if you say that there is a high probability that you will get an A in this course, you mean that this outcome is likely to occur. Your probability statement is based on specific information, such as your grades on examinations. The weather forecaster says there is a 10% chance of rain today; this means that the likelihood of rain is very low. A gambler gauges the probability that a particular horse will win a race on the basis of the past records of that horse.

Probability in statistical inference is used in much the same way. We want to specify the probability that an event (in this case, a difference between means in the sample) will occur if there is no difference in the population. The question is: What is the probability of obtaining this result if only random error is operating? If this probability is very low, we reject the possibility that only random or chance error is responsible for the obtained difference in means.

Probability: The Case of ESP

The use of probability in statistical inference can be understood intuitively from a simple example. Suppose that a friend claims to have ESP (extrasensory perception) ability. You decide to test your friend with a set of five cards commonly used in ESP research; a different symbol is presented on each card. In the ESP test, you look at each card and think about the symbol, and your friend tells you which symbol you are thinking about. In your actual experiment, you have 10 trials; each of the five cards is presented two times in a random order. Your task is to know whether your friend's answers reflect random error (guessing) or whether they indicate that something more than random error is occurring. The null hypothesis in your study is that only random error is operating. In this case, the research hypothesis is that the number of correct answers shows more than random or chance guessing. (Note, however, that accepting the research hypothesis could mean that your friend has ESP ability, but it could also mean that the cards were marked, that you had somehow cued your friend when thinking about the symbols, and so on.)

You can easily determine the number of correct answers to expect if the null hypothesis is correct. Just by guessing, 1 out of 5 answers (20%) should be correct. On 10 trials, 2 correct answers are expected under the null hypothesis. If, in the actual experiment, more (or less) than 2 correct answers are obtained, would you conclude that the obtained data reflect random error or something more than merely random guessing?

Suppose that your friend gets 3 correct. Then you would probably conclude that only guessing is involved, because you would recognize that there is a high probability that there would be 3 correct answers *even though only 2 correct are expected under the null hypothesis.* You expect that exactly 2 answers in 10 trials would be correct in the long run, if you conducted this experiment with this subject over and over again. However, small deviations away from the expected 2 are highly likely in a sample of 10 trials.

Suppose, though, that your friend gets 7 correct. You might conclude that the results indicate more than random error in this one sample of 10 observations. This conclusion would be based on your intuitive judgment that an outcome of 70% correct when only 20% is expected is very unlikely. At this point, you would decide to reject the null hypothesis and state that the result is significant. A significant result is one that is very unlikely if the null hypothesis is correct.

A key question then becomes: How unlikely does a result have to be before we decide it is significant? A decision rule is determined prior to collecting the data. The probability required for significance is called the **alpha level.** The most common alpha level probability used is .05. The outcome of the study is considered significant when there is a .05 or less probability of obtaining the results; that is, there are only 5 chances out of 100 that the results were due to random error in one sample from the population. If it is very unlikely that random error is responsible for the obtained results, the null hypothesis is rejected.

Sampling Distributions

You may have been able to judge intuitively that obtaining 7 correct on the 10 trials is very unlikely. Fortunately, we don't have to rely on intuition to determine the probabilities of different outcomes. Table 13.1 shows the probability of actually obtaining each of the possible outcomes in the ESP experiment with 10 trials and a null hypothesis expectation of 20% correct. An outcome of 2 correct answers has the highest probability of occurrence. Also, as intuition would suggest, an outcome of 3 correct is highly probable, but an outcome of 7 correct is highly unlikely.

The probabilities shown in Table 13.1 were derived from a probability distribution called the *binomial distribution;* all statistical significance decisions are based on probability distributions such as this one. Such distributions are called **sampling distributions.** The sampling distribution is based on the assumption that the null hypothesis is true; in the ESP example, the null hypothesis is that the person is only guessing and should therefore get 20% correct. Such a distribution assumes that if you were to conduct the study with the same number of observations over and over again, the most frequent finding would be 20%. However, because of the random error possible in each sample, there is a certain probability associated with other outcomes. Outcomes that are close to the expected null hypothesis value of 20% are very likely. However, outcomes farther from the

TABLE 13.1   Exact probability of each possible outcome
              of the ESP experiment with 10 trials

Number of correct answers	Probability
10	.00000+
9	.00000+
8	.00007
7	.00079
6	.00551
5	.02642
4	.08808
3	.20133
2	.30199
1	.26844
0	.10737

expected result are less and less likely if the null hypothesis is correct. When your obtained results are highly unlikely if you are, in fact, sampling from the distribution specified by the null hypothesis, you conclude that the null hypothesis is incorrect. Instead of concluding that your sample results reflect a random deviation from the long-run expectation of 20%, you decide that the null hypothesis is incorrect. That is, you conclude that you have not sampled from the sampling distribution specified by the null hypothesis. Instead, in the case of the ESP example, you decide that your data are from a different sampling distribution in which, if you were to test the person repeatedly, most of the outcomes would be near your obtained result of 7 correct answers.

All statistical tests rely on sampling distributions to determine the probability that the results are consistent with the null hypothesis. When the obtained data are very unlikely according to null hypothesis expectations (usually a .05 probability or less), the researcher decides to reject the null hypothesis and therefore to accept the research hypothesis.

Sample Size

The ESP example also illustrates the impact of sample size—the total number of observations—on determinations of statistical significance. Suppose you had tested your friend on 100 trials instead of 10 and had observed 30 correct answers. Just as you had expected 2 correct answers in 10 trials, you would now expect 20 of 100 answers to be correct. However, 30 out of 100 has a much lower likelihood of occurrence than 3 out of 10. This is because, with more observations sampled, you are more likely to obtain an accurate estimate of the true population value. Thus, as the size of your sample increases, you are more confident that your outcome is actually different from the null hypothesis expectation.

EXAMPLE: THE *t* AND *F* TESTS

Different statistical tests allow us to use probability to decide whether to reject the null hypothesis. In this section, we will examine the *t* test and the *F* test. The **t test** is commonly used to examine whether two groups are significantly different from each other. In the hypothetical experiment on the effect of a model on aggression, a *t* test is appropriate because we are asking whether the mean of the no-model group differs from the mean of the model group. The *F* test is a more general statistical test that can be used to ask whether there is a difference among three or more groups or to evaluate the results of factorial designs (discussed in Chapter 10).

To use a statistical test, you must first specify the null hypothesis and the research hypothesis that you are evaluating. The null and research hypotheses for the modeling experiment were described previously. You must also specify the significance level that you will use to decide whether to reject the null hypothesis; this is the alpha level. As noted, researchers generally use a significance level of .05.

t Test

The sampling distribution of all possible values of *t* is shown in Figure 13.1. (This particular distribution is for the sample size we used in the hypothetical experiment on modeling and aggression; the sample size was 20 with 10 participants in each group.) This sampling distribution has a mean of 0 and a standard deviation of 1. It reflects all the possible outcomes we could expect if we compare the means of two groups *and* the null hypothesis is correct.

To use this distribution to evaluate our data, we need to calculate a value of *t* from the obtained data and evaluate the obtained *t* in terms of the sampling distribution of *t* that is based on the null hypothesis. If the obtained *t* has a low probability of occurrence (.05 or less), then the null hypothesis is rejected.

The *t* value is a ratio of two aspects of the data, the difference between the group means and the variability within groups. The ratio may be described as follows:

$$t = \frac{\text{group difference}}{\text{within-group variability}}$$

The group difference is simply the difference between your obtained means; under the null hypothesis, you expect this difference to be zero. The value of *t* increases as the difference between your obtained sample means increases. Note that the sampling distribution of *t* assumes that there is no difference in the population means; thus, the expected value of *t* under the null hypothesis is zero. The within-group variability is the amount of variability of scores about the mean. The denominator of the *t* formula is essentially an indicator of the amount of random error in your sample. Recall from Chapter 12 that *s*,

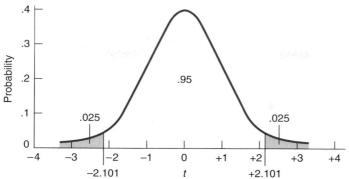

Critical Value for Two-Tailed Test with .05 Significance Level

FIGURE 13.1
Sampling dis-
tributions of
t values with
18 degrees of
freedom

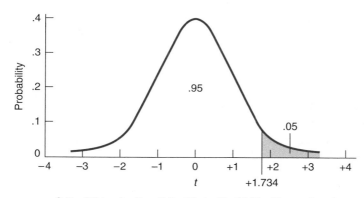

Critical Value for One-Tailed Test with .05 Significance Level

the standard deviation, and s^2, the variance, are indicators of how much scores deviate from the group mean.

A concrete example of a calculation of a *t* test should help clarify these concepts. The formula for the *t* test for two groups with equal numbers of participants in each group is

$$t = \frac{\overline{X}_1 - \overline{X}_2}{\sqrt{\dfrac{s_1^2}{n_1} + \dfrac{s_2^2}{n_2}}}$$

The numerator of the formula is simply the difference between the means of the two groups. In the denominator, we first divide the variance (s_1^2 and s_2^2) of each group by the number of subjects in that group (n_1 and n_2) and add these together. We then find the square root of the result; this converts the number from a squared score (the variance) to a standard deviation. Finally, we calculate our obtained t value by dividing the mean difference by this standard deviation. When the formula is applied to the data in Table 12.1, we find:

$$t = \frac{5.20 - 3.10}{\sqrt{\dfrac{1.29}{10} + \dfrac{1.43}{10}}}$$

$$= \frac{2.1}{\sqrt{.1289 + .1433}}$$

$$= 4.02$$

Thus, the t value calculated from the data is 4.02. Is this a significant result? A computer program analyzing the results would immediately tell you the probability of obtaining a t value of this size with a total sample size of 20. Without such a program, however, you can refer to a table of "critical values" of t, such as Table C.2 in Appendix C. We will discuss the use of the appendix tables in detail in Appendix B. Before going any farther, you should know that the obtained result is significant. Using a significance level of .05, the critical value from the sampling distribution of t is 2.101. Any t value greater than or equal to 2.101 has a .05 or less probability of occurring under the assumptions of the null hypothesis. Because our obtained value is larger than the critical value, we can reject the null hypothesis and conclude that the difference in means obtained in the sample reflects a true difference in the population.

Degrees of Freedom

You are probably wondering how the critical value was selected from the table. To use the table, you must first determine the **degrees of freedom** for the test (the term *degrees of freedom* is abbreviated as *df*). When comparing two means, you assume that the degrees of freedom are equal to $n_1 + n_2 - 2$, or the total number of participants in the groups minus the number of groups. In our experiment, the degrees of freedom would be $10 + 10 - 2 = 18$. The degrees of freedom are the number of scores free to vary once the means are known. For example, if the mean of a group is 6.0 and there are five scores in the group, there are 4 degrees of freedom; once you have any four scores, the fifth score is known because the mean must remain 6.0.

One-Tailed Versus Two-Tailed Tests

In the table, you must choose a critical t for the situation in which your research hypothesis either (1) specified a direction of difference between the groups (e.g., group 1 will be greater than group 2) or (2) did not specify a predicted direction of difference (e.g., group 1 will differ from group 2). Somewhat different critical values of t are used in the two situations: The first situation is called a one-tailed test, and the second situation is called a two-tailed test.

The issue can be visualized by looking at the sampling distribution of t values for 18 degrees of freedom, as shown in Figure 13.1. As you can see, a value of 0.00 is expected most frequently. Values greater than or less than zero are less likely to occur. The first distribution shows the logic of a two-tailed test. We used the value of 2.101 for the critical value of *t* with a .05 significance level because a direction of difference was not predicted. This critical value is the point beyond which 2.5% of the positive values and 2.5% of the negative values of *t* lie (hence, a total probability of .05 combined from the two "tails" of the sampling distribution). The second distribution illustrates a one-tailed test. If a directional difference had been predicted, the critical value would have been 1.734. This is the value beyond which 5% of the values lie in only one "tail" of the distribution. Whether to specify a one-tailed or two-tailed test will depend on whether you originally designed your study to test a directional hypothesis.

F Test

The **analysis of variance,** or **F test,** is an extension of the *t* test. The analysis of variance is a more general statistical procedure than the *t* test. When a study has only one independent variable with *two* groups, *F* and *t* are virtually identical—the value of *F* equals t^2 in this situation. However, analysis of variance is also used when there are more than two levels of an independent variable and when a factorial design with two or more independent variables has been used. Thus, the *F* test is appropriate for the simplest experimental design, as well as for the more complex designs discussed in Chapter 10. The *t* test was presented first because the formula allows us to demonstrate easily the relationship of the group difference and the within-group variability to the outcome of the statistical test. However, in practice, analysis of variance is the more common procedure. The calculations necessary to conduct an *F* test are provided in Appendix B.

The *F* statistic is a ratio of two types of variance: systematic variance and error variance (hence the term *analysis of variance*). **Systematic variance** is the deviation of the group means from the grand mean, or the mean score of all individuals in all groups. Systematic variance is small when the difference between group means is small and increases as the group mean differences increase. **Error variance** is the deviation of the individual scores in each group from their respective group means. Terms that you may see in research instead of systematic and error variance are *between-group variance* and *within-group variance*. Systematic variance is the variability of scores between groups, and error variance is the variability of scores within groups. The larger the *F* ratio is, the more likely it is that the results are significant.

Calculating Effect Size

The concept of effect size was discussed in Chapter 12. After determining that there was a statistically significant effect of the independent variable, researchers will want to know the magnitude of the effect. Therefore, we want to calculate an estimate of effect size. For a *t* test, the calculation is

$$\text{effect size } r = \sqrt{\frac{t^2}{t^2 + df}}$$

where *df* is the degrees of freedom. Thus, using the obtained value of *t*, 4.02, and 18 degrees of freedom, we find

$$\text{effect size } r = \sqrt{\frac{(4.02)^2}{(4.02)^2 + 18}} = \sqrt{\frac{16.201}{34.201}} = .69$$

This value is a type of correlation coefficient that can range from 0.00 to 1.00; as mentioned in Chapter 12, .69 is considered a large effect size. For additional information on effect size calculation, see Rosenthal (1991). The same distinction between *r* and *r²* that was made in Chapter 12 applies here as well.

Another effect size estimate used when comparing two means is called Cohen's *d*. Cohen's *d* expresses effect size in terms of standard deviation units. A *d* value of 1.0 tells you that the means are 1 standard deviation apart; a *d* of .2 indicates that the means are separated by .2 standard deviation.

You can calculate the value of Cohen's *d* using the means (*M*) and standard deviations (*SD*) of the two groups:

$$d = \frac{M_1 - M_2}{\sqrt{\dfrac{(SD_1^2 + SD_2^2)}{2}}}$$

Note that the formula uses *M* and *SD* instead of $\overline{X}$ and *s*. These abbreviations are used in APA style (see Appendix A)

The value of *d* is larger than the corresponding value of *r*, but it is easy to convert *d* to a value of *r*. Both statistics provide information on the size of the relationship between the variables studied. You might note that both effect size estimates have a value of 0.00 when there is no relationship. The value of *r* has a maximum value of 1.00, but *d* has no maximum value.

Confidence Intervals and Statistical Significance

Confidence intervals were described in Chapter 7. After obtaining a sample value, we can calculate a confidence interval. An interval of values defines the most likely range of actual population values. The interval has an associated confidence interval: A 95% confidence interval indicates that we are 95% sure that the population value lies within the range; a 99% interval would provide greater certainty but the range of values would be larger.

A confidence interval can be obtained for each of the means in the aggression experiment. The 95% confidence intervals for the two conditions are

	Obtained sample value	Low population value	High population value
Model group	5.20	4.39	6.01
No-model group	3.10	2.24	3.96

A bar graph that includes a visual depiction of the confidence interval can be very useful. The means from the aggression experiment are shown in Figure 13.2. The shaded bars represent the mean aggression scores in the two conditions.

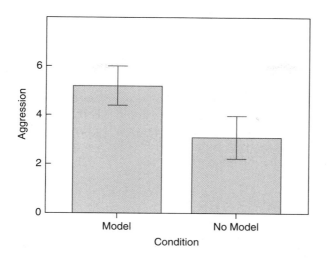

FIGURE 13.2
Mean aggression scores from the hypothetical modeling experiment including the 95% confidence intervals

The confidence interval for each group is shown with a vertical I-shaped line that is bounded by the upper and lower limits of the 95% confidence interval. It is important to examine confidence intervals to obtain a greater understanding of the meaning of your obtained data. Although the obtained sample means provide the best estimate of the population values, you are able to see the likely range of possible values. The size of the interval is related to both the size of the sample and the confidence level. As the sample size increases, the confidence interval narrows. This is because sample means obtained with larger sample sizes are more likely to reflect the population mean. Second, higher confidence is associated with a larger interval. If you want to be almost certain that the interval contains the true population mean (e.g., a 99% confidence interval), you will need to include more possibilities. Note that the 95% confidence intervals for the two means do not overlap. This should be a clue to you that the difference is statistically significant. Indeed, examining confidence intervals is an alternative way of thinking about statistical significance. The null hypothesis is that the difference in population means is 0.00. However, if you were to subtract all the means in the 95% confidence interval for the no-model condition from all the means in the model condition, none of these differences would include the value of 0.00. We can be very confident that the null hypothesis should be rejected.

Statistical Significance: An Overview

The logic underlying the use of statistical tests rests on statistical theory. There are some general concepts, however, that should help you understand what you are doing when you conduct a statistical test. First, the goal of the test is to allow you to make a decision about whether your obtained results are reliable; you want to be confident that you would obtain similar results if you conducted the study over and over again. Second, the significance level (alpha level) you choose indicates how confident you wish to be when making the decision. A .05 significance level says that you are 95% sure of the reliability of your findings; however, there is a 5%

chance that you could be wrong. There are few certainties in life! Third, you are most likely to obtain significant results when you have a large sample size because larger sample sizes provide better estimates of true population values. Finally, you are most likely to obtain significant results when the effect size is large, i.e., when differences between groups are large and variability of scores within groups is small.

In the remainder of the chapter, we will expand on these issues. We will examine the implications of making a decision about whether results are significant, the way to determine a significance level, and the way to interpret nonsignificant results. We will then provide some guidelines for selecting the appropriate statistical test in various research designs.

TYPE I AND TYPE II ERRORS

The decision to reject the null hypothesis is based on probabilities rather than on certainties. That is, the decision is made without direct knowledge of the true state of affairs in the population. Thus, the decision might not be correct; errors may result from the use of inferential statistics.

A decision matrix is shown in Figure 13.3. Notice that there are two possible decisions: (1) Reject the null hypothesis or (2) accept the null hypothesis. There are also two possible truths about the population: (1) The null hypothesis is true or (2) the null hypothesis is false. In sum, as the decision matrix shows, there are two kinds of correct decisions and two kinds of errors.

Correct Decisions

One correct decision occurs when we reject the null hypothesis and the research hypothesis is true in the population. Here, our decision is that the population means are not equal, and in fact, this is true in the population. This is the decision you hope to make when you begin your study.

The other correct decision is to accept the null hypothesis, and the null hypothesis is true in the population: The population means are in fact equal.

FIGURE 13.3
Decision matrix for Type I and Type II errors

		True State in Population	
		Null Hypothesis Is True	Null Hypothesis Is False
Decision	Reject the Null Hypothesis	Type I Error (α)	Correct Decision $(1 - \beta)$
	Accept the Null Hypothesis	Correct Decision $(1 - \alpha)$	Type II Error (β)

Type I Errors

A **Type I error** is made when we reject the null hypothesis but the null hypothesis is actually true. Our decision is that the population means are not equal when they actually are equal. Type I errors occur when, simply by chance, we obtain a large value of t or F. For example, even though a t value of 4.025 is highly improbable if the population means are indeed equal (less than 5 chances out of 100), this *can* happen. When we do obtain such a large t value by chance, we *incorrectly* decide that the independent variable had an effect.

The probability of making a Type I error is determined by the choice of significance or alpha level (alpha may be shown as the Greek letter alpha—α). When the significance level for deciding whether to reject the null hypothesis is .05, the probability of a Type I error (alpha) is .05. If the null hypothesis is rejected, there are 5 chances out of 100 that the decision is wrong. The probability of making a Type I error can be changed by either decreasing or increasing the significance level. If we use a lower alpha level of .01, for example, there is less chance of making a Type I error. With a .01 significance level, the null hypothesis is rejected only when the probability of obtaining the results is .01 or less if the null hypothesis is correct.

Type II Errors

A **Type II error** occurs when the null hypothesis is accepted although in the population the research hypothesis is true. The population means are not equal, but the results of the experiment do not lead to a decision to reject the null hypothesis.

Research should be designed so that the probability of a Type II error (this probability is called beta, or β) is relatively low. The probability of making a Type II error is related to three factors. The first is the significance (alpha) level. If we set a very low significance level to decrease the chances of a Type I error, we increase the chances of a Type II error. In other words, if we make it very difficult to reject the null hypothesis, the probability of incorrectly accepting the null hypothesis increases. The second factor is sample size. True differences are more likely to be detected if the sample size is large. The third factor is effect size. If the effect size is large, a Type II error is unlikely. However, a small effect size may not be significant with a small sample.

The Everyday Context of Type I and Type II Errors

The decision matrix used in statistical analyses can be applied to the kinds of decisions people frequently must make in everyday life. For example, consider the decision made by a juror in a criminal trial. As is the case with statistics, a decision must be made on the basis of evidence: Is the defendant innocent or guilty? However, the decision rests with individual jurors and does not necessarily reflect the true state of affairs: that the person really is innocent or guilty.

The juror's decision matrix is illustrated in Figure 13.4. To continue the parallel to the statistical decision, assume that the null hypothesis is the defendant is innocent (i.e., the dictum that a person is innocent until proven guilty). Thus, rejection of the null hypothesis means deciding that the defendant is guilty, and acceptance of the null hypothesis means deciding that the defendant is innocent. The decision matrix also shows that the null hypothesis may actually be true or false. There are two kinds of correct decisions and two kinds of errors like those described in statistical decisions. A Type I error is finding the defendant guilty when the person really is innocent; a Type II error is finding the defendant innocent when the person actually is guilty. In our society, Type I errors by jurors generally are considered to be more serious than Type II errors. Thus, before finding someone guilty, the juror is asked to make sure that the person is guilty "beyond a reasonable doubt" or to consider that "it is better to have a hundred guilty persons go free than to find one innocent person guilty."

The decision that a doctor makes to operate or not operate on a patient provides another illustration of how a decision matrix works. The matrix is shown in Figure 13.5. Here, the null hypothesis is that no operation is necessary. The decision is whether to reject the null hypothesis and perform the operation or

FIGURE 13.4
Decision matrix for a juror

	True State	
	Null Is True (Innocent)	Null Is False (Guilty)
Reject Null (Find Guilty)	Type I Error	Correct Decision
Accept Null (Find Innocent)	Correct Decision	Type II Error

FIGURE 13.5
Decision matrix for a doctor

	True State	
	Null Is True (No Operation Needed)	Null Is False (Operation Is Needed)
Reject Null (Operate on Patient)	Type I Error	Correct Decision
Accept Null (Don't Operate)	Correct Decision	Type II Error

to accept the null hypothesis and not perform surgery. In reality, the surgeon is faced with two possibilities: Either the surgery is unnecessary (the null hypothesis is true) or the patient will die without the operation (a dramatic case of the null hypothesis being false). Which error is more serious in this case? Most doctors would believe that not operating on a patient who really needs the operation—making a Type II error—is more serious than making the Type I error of performing surgery on someone who does not really need it.

One final illustration of the use of a decision matrix involves the important decision to marry someone. If the null hypothesis is that the person is "wrong" for you, and the true state is that the person is either "wrong" or "right," you must decide whether to go ahead and marry the person. You might try to construct a decision matrix for this particular problem. Which error is more costly: a Type I error or a Type II error?

CHOOSING A SIGNIFICANCE LEVEL

Researchers traditionally have used either a .05 or a .01 significance level in the decision to reject the null hypothesis. If there is less than a .05 or a .01 probability that the results occurred because of random error, the results are said to be significant. However, there is nothing magical about a .05 or a .01 significance level. The significance level chosen merely specifies the probability of a Type I error if the null hypothesis is rejected. The significance level chosen by the researcher usually is dependent on the consequences of making a Type I versus a Type II error. As previously noted, for a juror, a Type I error is more serious than a Type II error; for a doctor, however, a Type II error may be more serious.

Researchers generally believe that the consequences of making a Type I error are more serious than those associated with a Type II error. If the null hypothesis is rejected, the researcher might publish the results in a journal, and the results might be reported by others in textbooks or in newspaper or magazine articles. Researchers don't want to mislead people or risk damaging their reputations by publishing results that aren't reliable and so cannot be replicated. Thus, they want to guard against the possibility of making a Type I error by using a very low significance level (.05 or .01). In contrast to the consequences of publishing false results, the consequences of a Type II error are not seen as being very serious.

Thus, researchers want to be very careful to avoid Type I errors when their results may be published. However, in certain circumstances, a Type I error is not serious. For example, if you were engaged in pilot or exploratory research, your results would be used primarily to decide whether your research ideas were worth pursuing. In this situation, it would be a mistake to overlook potentially important data by using a very conservative significance level. In exploratory research, a significance level of .25 may be more appropriate for deciding whether to do more research. Remember that the significance level chosen and the consequences of a Type I or a Type II error are determined by what the results will be used for.

INTERPRETING NONSIGNIFICANT RESULTS

Although "accepting the null hypothesis" is convenient terminology, it is important to recognize that researchers are not generally interested in accepting the null hypothesis. Research is designed to show that a relationship between variables does exist, not to demonstrate that variables are unrelated.

More important, a decision to accept the null hypothesis when a single study does not show significant results is problematic, because negative or nonsignificant results are difficult to interpret. For this reason, researchers often say that they simply "fail to reject" or "do not reject" the null hypothesis. The results of a single study might be nonsignificant even when a relationship between the variables in the population does in fact exist. This is a Type II error. Sometimes, the reasons for a Type II error lie in the procedures used in the experiment. For example, a researcher might obtain nonsignificant results by providing incomprehensible instructions to the participants, by having a very weak manipulation of the independent variable, or by using a dependent measure that is unreliable and insensitive. Rather than concluding that the variables are not related, researchers may decide that a more carefully conducted study would find that the variables are related.

We should also consider the statistical reasons for a Type II error. Recall that the probability of a Type II error is influenced by the significance (alpha) level, sample size, and effect size. Thus, nonsignificant results are more likely to be found if the researcher is very cautious in choosing the alpha level. If the researcher uses a significance level of .001 rather than .05, it is more difficult to reject the null hypothesis (there is not much chance of a Type I error). However, that also means that there is a greater chance of accepting an incorrect null hypothesis (i.e., a Type II error is more likely). In other words, a meaningful result is more likely to be overlooked when the significance level is very low.

A Type II error may also result from a sample size that is too small to detect a real relationship between variables. A general principle is that the larger the sample size is, the greater the likelihood of obtaining a significant result. This is because large sample sizes give more accurate estimates of the actual population than do small sample sizes. In any given study, the sample size may be too small to permit detection of a significant result.

A third reason for a nonsignificant finding is that the effect size is small. Very small effects are difficult to detect without a large sample size. In general, the sample size should be large enough to find a real effect, even if it is a small one.

The fact that it is possible for a very small effect to be statistically significant raises another issue. A very large sample size might enable the researcher to find a significant difference between means; however, this difference, even though statistically significant, might have very little *practical* significance. For example, if an expensive new psychiatric treatment technique significantly reduces the average hospital stay from 60 days to 59 days, it might not be practical to use the technique despite the evidence for its effectiveness. The additional day of hospitalization costs less than the treatment. There are other circumstances, however, in which a treatment with a very small effect size has considerable practical significance. Usually this occurs when a very large population is affected by a fairly inexpensive treatment. Suppose a simple flextime policy for employees reduces employee turnover by 1% per year. This doesn't sound like a large effect. However, if a company normally has a turnover of 2,000 employees each year and the cost of training a new employee is $10,000, the company saves $200,000 per year with the new procedure. This amount may have practical significance for the company.

The key point here is that you should not accept the null hypothesis just because the results are nonsignificant. Nonsignificant results do not necessarily indicate that the null hypothesis is correct. However, there must be circumstances in which we can accept the null hypothesis and conclude that two variables are, in fact, not related. Frick (1995) describes several criteria that can be used in a decision to accept the null hypothesis. For example, we should look for well-designed studies with sensitive dependent measures and evidence from a manipulation check that the independent variable manipulation had its intended effect. In addition, the research should have a reasonably large sample to rule out the possibility that the sample was too small. Further, evidence that the variables are not related should come from multiple studies. Under such circumstances, you are justified in concluding that there is in fact no relationship.

CHOOSING A SAMPLE SIZE: POWER ANALYSIS

We noted in Chapter 9 that researchers often select a sample size based on what is typical in a particular area of research. An alternative approach is to select a sample size on the basis of a desired probability of correctly rejecting the null hypothesis. This probability is called the **power** of the statistical test. It is obviously related to the probability of a Type II error:

$$\text{Power} = 1 - p \,(\text{Type II error})$$

We previously indicated that the probability of a Type II error is related to significance level (alpha), sample size, and effect size. Statisticians such as Cohen (1988) have developed procedures for determining sample size based on these factors. Table 13.2 shows the total sample size needed for an experiment with two groups and a significance level of .05. In the table, effect sizes range from .10 to .50, and the desired power is shown at .80 and .90. Smaller effect sizes require larger samples to be significant at the .05 level. Higher desired power demands a greater sample size; this is because you want a more certain "guarantee" that your results will be statistically significant. Researchers usually use a power between .70 and .90 when using this method to determine sample size. Several computer programs have been developed to allow researchers to easily make the calculations

TABLE 13.2   Total sample size needed to detect a significant difference for a *t* test

Effect size *r*	Power = .80	Power = .90
.10	789	1052
.20	200	266
.30	88	116
.40	52	68
.50	26	36

Note: Effect sizes are correlations, based on two-tailed tests.

necessary to determine sample size based on effect size estimates, significance level, and desired power.

You may never need to perform a power analysis. However, you should recognize the importance of this concept. If a researcher is studying a relationship with an effect size correlation of .20, a fairly large sample size is needed for statistical significance at the .05 level. An inappropriately low sample size in this situation is likely to produce a nonsignificant finding.

THE IMPORTANCE OF REPLICATIONS

Throughout this discussion of statistical analysis, the focus has been on the results of a single research investigation. What were the means and standard deviations? Was the mean difference statistically significant? If the results are significant, you conclude that they would likely be obtained over and over again if the study were repeated. We now have a framework for understanding the results of the study. Be aware, however, that scientists do not attach too much importance to the results of a single study. A rich understanding of any phenomenon comes from the results of numerous studies investigating the same variables. Instead of inferring population values on the basis of a single investigation, we can look at the results of several studies that replicate previous investigations (see Cohen, 1994). The importance of replications is a central concept in Chapter 14.

SIGNIFICANCE OF A PEARSON *r* CORRELATION COEFFICIENT

Recall from Chapter 12 that the Pearson *r* correlation coefficient is used to describe the strength of the relationship between two variables when both variables have interval or ratio scale properties. However, there remains the issue of whether the correlation is statistically significant. The null hypothesis in this case is that the true population correlation is 0.00—the two variables are not related. What if you obtain a correlation of .27 (plus or minus)? A statistical significance test will allow you to decide whether to reject the null hypothesis and conclude that the true population correlation is, in fact, greater than 0.00. The technical way to do this is to perform a t test that compares the obtained coefficient with the null hypothesis correlation of 0.00. The procedures for calculating a Pearson r and determining significance are provided in Appendix B.

COMPUTER ANALYSIS OF DATA

Although you can calculate statistics with a calculator using the formulas provided in this chapter, Chapter 12, and Appendix B, most data analysis is carried out via computer programs. Sophisticated statistical analysis software packages make it easy to calculate statistics for any data set. Descriptive and inferential statistics are obtained quickly, the calculations are accurate, and information on statistical significance is provided in the output. Computers also facilitate graphic displays of data.

Some of the major statistical programs include SPSS, SAS, SYSTAT, and freely available R and MYSTAT. Other programs may be used on your campus. Many people do most of their statistical analyses using a spreadsheet program such as Microsoft Excel. You will need to learn the specific details of the computer system used at your college or university. No one program is better than another; they all differ in the appearance of the output and the specific procedures needed to input data and have the program perform the test. However, the general procedures for doing analyses are quite similar in all of the statistics programs.

The first step in doing the analysis is to input the data. Suppose you want to input the data in Table 12.1, the modeling and aggression experiment. Data are entered into columns. It is easiest to think of data for computer analysis as a matrix with rows and columns. Data for each research participant are the rows of the matrix. The columns contain each participant's scores on one or more measures, and an additional column may be needed to indicate a code to identify which condition the individual was in (e.g., Group 1 or Group 2). A data matrix in SPSS for Windows is shown in Figure 13.6. The numbers in the "group" column indicate whether the individual is in Group 1 (model) or Group 2 (no model), and the numbers in the "aggscore" column are the aggression scores from Table 12.1.

Other programs may require somewhat different methods of data input. For example, in Excel, it is usually easiest to set up a separate column for each group, as shown in Figure 13.6.

The next step is to provide instructions for the statistical analysis. Again, each program uses somewhat different steps to perform the analysis; most

	group	aggscore
1	1	3
2	1	4
3	1	5
4	1	5
5	1	5
6	2	1
7	2	2
8	2	2
9	2	3
10	2	3
11	1	5
12	1	6
13	2	3
14	2	4
15	2	4

Data Matrix in SPSS for Windows

	A	B
1	Model	No Model
2	3	1
3	4	2
4	5	2
5	5	3
6	5	3
7	5	3
8	6	4
9	6	4
10	6	4
11	7	5
12		
13		

Excel Method of Data Input

t Test: Two-Sample Assuming Equal Variances

	Model	No Model
Mean	5.200	3.100
Variance	1.289	1.433
Observations	10.000	10.000
Pooled Variance	1.361	
Hypothesized Mean Difference	0.000	
df	18.000	
t Stat	4.025	
P(T<=t) one-tail	0.000	
t Critical one-tail	1.734	
P(T<=t) two-tail	0.001	
t Critical two-tail	2.101	

Output for a *t* test using Excel

FIGURE 13.6
Sample computer input and output using data from Table 12.1 (modeling experiment)

require you to choose from various menu options. When the analysis is completed, you are provided with the output that shows the results of the statistical procedure you performed. You will need to learn how to interpret the output. Figure 13.6 shows the output for a t test using Excel.

When you are first learning to use a statistical analysis program, it is a good idea to practice with some data from a statistics text to make sure that you get the same results. This will ensure that you know how to properly input the data and request the statistical analysis.

SELECTING THE APPROPRIATE STATISTICAL TEST

We have covered several types of designs and the variables that we study may have nominal, ordinal, interval, or ratio scale properties. How do you choose the appropriate statistical test for analyzing your data? Fortunately, there are a number of online guides and tutorials such as http://www.socialresearchmethods.net/selstat/ssstart.htm and http://wise.cgu.edu/choosemod/opening.htm; SPSS even has its own Statistics Coach to help with the decision.

We cannot cover every possible analysis. Our focus will be on variables that have either (1) nominal scale properties—two or more discrete values such as male and female; or (2) interval/ratio scale properties with many values such as reaction time or rating scales (also called continuous variables). We will not address variables with ordinal scale values.

Research Studying Two Variables (Bivariate Research)

In these cases, the researcher is studying whether two variables are related. In general, we would refer to the first variable as the independent variable (IV) and the second variable as the dependent variable (DV). However, because it does not matter whether we are doing experimental or nonexperimental research, we could just as easily refer to the two variables as Variable X and Variable Y or Variable A and Variable B.

IV	DV	Statistical Test
Nominal *Male-female*	Nominal *Vegetarian—yes/no*	Chi-square
Nominal (2 groups) *Male-female*	Interval/ratio *Grade point average*	t test
Nominal (3 groups) *Study time (low, medium, high)*	Interval/ratio *Test score*	One-way analysis of variance
Interval/ratio *Optimism score*	Interval/ratio *Sick days last year*	Pearson correlation

Research with Multiple Independent Variables

In the following situations, we have more complex research designs with two or more independent variables that are studied with a single outcome or dependent variable.

IV	DV	Statistical Test
Nominal (2 or more variables)	Interval/ratio	Analysis of variance (factorial design)
Interval/ratio (2 or more variables)	Interval/ratio	Multiple regression

These research design situations have been described in previous chapters. There are of course many other types of designs. Designs with multiple variables (multivariate statistics) are described in detail by Tabachnick and Fidell (2007). Procedures for research using ordinal level measurement may be found in a book by Siegel and Castellan (1988).

You have now considered how to generate research ideas, conduct research to test your ideas, and evaluate the statistical significance of your results. In the final chapter, we will examine issues of generalizing research findings beyond the specific circumstances in which the research was conducted.

Study Terms

Alpha level (p. 266)

Analysis of variance (*F* test) (p. 271)

Confidence interval (p. 272)

Degrees of freedom (p. 270)

Error variance (p. 271)

Inferential statistics (p. 263)

Null hypothesis (p. 264)

Power (p. 279)

Probability (p. 265)

Research hypothesis (p. 264)

Sampling distribution (p. 266)

Statistical significance (p. 265)

Systematic variance (p. 271)

t test (p. 268)

Type I error (p. 275)

Type II error (p. 275)

Review Questions

1. Distinguish between the null hypothesis and the research hypothesis. When does the researcher decide to reject the null hypothesis?

2. What is meant by statistical significance?

3. What factors are most important in determining whether obtained results will be significant?

4. Distinguish between a Type I and a Type II error. Why is your significance level the probability of making a Type I error?

5. What factors are involved in choosing a significance level?

6. What influences the probability of a Type II error?

7. What is the difference between statistical significance and practical significance?

8. Discuss the reasons that a researcher might obtain nonsignificant results.

Activity Questions

1. In an experiment, one group of research participants is given 10 pages of material to proofread for errors. Another group proofreads the same material on a computer screen. The dependent variable is the number of errors detected in a 5-minute period. A .05 significance (alpha) level is used to evaluate the results.

   a. What statistical test would you use?

   b. What is the null hypothesis? The research hypothesis?

   c. What is the Type I error? The Type II error?

   d. What is the probability of making a Type I error?

2. In Professor Dre's study, the average number of errors detected in the print and computer conditions was 38.4 and 13.2, respectively; this difference was not statistically significant. When Professor Seuss conducted the same experiment, the means of the two groups were 21.1 and 14.7, but the difference was statistically significant. Explain how this could happen.

3. Suppose that you work for the child social services agency in your county. Your job is to investigate instances of possible child neglect or abuse. After collecting your evidence, which may come from a variety of sources, you must decide whether to leave the child in the home or place the child in protective custody. Specify the null and research hypotheses in this situation. What constitutes a Type I and a Type II error? Is a Type I or Type II error the more serious error in this situation? Why?

4. A researcher investigated attitudes toward individuals in wheelchairs. The question was: Would people react differently to a person they perceived as being temporarily confined to the wheelchair than to a person who had a permanent disability? Participants were randomly assigned to two groups. Individuals in one group each worked on various tasks with a confederate in a wheelchair; members of the other group worked with the same confederate in a wheelchair, but this time the confederate wore a leg cast. After

the session was over, participants filled out a questionnaire regarding their reactions to the study. One question asked, "Would you be willing to work with your test partner in the future on a class assignment?" with "yes" and "no" as the only response alternatives. What would be the appropriate significance test for this experiment? Can you offer a critique of the dependent variable? If you changed the dependent variable, would it affect your choice of significance tests? If so, how?

14

LEARNING OBJECTIVES

- Discuss the issues created by generalizing research results to other populations, including potential problems using college students as research participants.

- Discuss issues to consider regarding generalization of research results to other cultures and ethnic groups.

- Describe the potential problem of generalizing to other experimenters and suggest possible solutions.

- Discuss the importance of replications, distinguishing between exact replications and conceptual replications.

- Distinguish between narrative literature reviews and meta-analyses.

I n this chapter, we will consider the issue of generalization of research findings. When a single study is conducted with a particular sample and procedure, can the results then be generalized to other populations of research
participants, or to other ways of manipulating or measuring the variables? Recall
from Chapter 4 that internal validity refers to the ability to infer that there is a
causal relationship between variables. **External validity** is the extent to which
findings may be generalized.

GENERALIZING TO OTHER POPULATIONS OF RESEARCH PARTICIPANTS

Even though a researcher randomly assigns participants to experimental conditions, rarely are participants randomly selected from the general population. As
we noted in Chapters 7 and 9, the individuals who participate in psychological
research are usually selected because they are available, and the most available
population consists of college students—or more specifically, first-year students
and sophomores enrolled in the introductory psychology course to satisfy a
general education requirement. They may also be from a particular college or
university, may be volunteers, or may be mostly males or mostly females. Are
our research findings limited to these types of subjects, or can we generalize our
findings to a more general population? After considering these issues, we will
examine the larger issue of culture and how research findings can be generalized
to different cultural groups.

College Students (and Rats)

Smart (1966) found that college students were studied in over 70% of the articles
published between 1962 and 1964 in the *Journal of Experimental Psychology* and the
Journal of Abnormal and Social Psychology. Sears (1986) reported similar percentages
in 1980 and 1985 in a variety of social psychology journals; Arnett (2008) found
that 67% of the articles in the 2007 volume of the *Journal of Personality and Social
Psychology* used college student samples. The potential problem is that such studies use a highly restricted population. Sears points out that most of the students
are first-year students and sophomores taking the introductory psychology class.
They therefore tend to be young and to possess the characteristics of late adolescence: a sense of self-identity that is still developing, social and political attitudes
that are in a state of flux, a high need for peer approval, and unstable peer relationships. They are intelligent with high cognitive abilities. Thus, what we know
about "people in general" may actually be limited to a highly select and unusual
group. Indeed, Peterson (2001) found that students, as a group, are more homog-
enous than non-student samples. That is, students are more similar to each other
than adults are similar to other adults in the general population.

Research by Henry (2008) illustrates how the use of college students may
affect the external validity of research on prejudice. In his sample of articles from

1990 to 2005, an increasing percentage of studies used college students as participants. Further, in looking at the actual results of studies on prejudice that compared college students with adults, he reported a variety of differences among adults and college students. For example, college students were less conservative and rated women and ethnic minorities more favorably.

How are college students like white rats? A great deal of research with animals relies solely on the infamous white rat. Why? In part because, as Beach (1950) points out, "Rats are hardy, cheap, easy to rear, and well adapted to laboratory existence" (p. 119). Thus, like first-year students and sophomores, they are easy to obtain on a college campus.

Volunteers

Researchers usually must ask people to volunteer to participate in the research. At many colleges, introductory psychology students are required either to volunteer for research or to complete an alternative project. If you are studying populations other than college students, you are even more dependent on volunteers—for example, asking people at a homeowners' association meeting to participate in a study of marital interaction or conducting research on the Internet in which people must go to your web page and then agree to participate in the study, or conducting a telephone survey of county residents to determine health care needs. In all these cases, external validity of the findings may be limited because the data from volunteers may be different from what would be obtained with a more general sample. Some research indicates that volunteers differ in various ways from nonvolunteers. In their comprehensive study on the topic, Rosenthal and Rosnow (1975) reported that volunteers tend to be more highly educated, of a higher socioeconomic status, more in need of approval, and more social.

Further, different kinds of people volunteer for different kinds of experiments. In colleges, there may be a sign-up board with the titles of many studies listed. Different types of people may be drawn to the study titled "problem solving" than to the one titled "interaction in small groups." Available evidence indicates that the title does influence who signs up (Hood & Back, 1971; Silverman & Margulis, 1973).

Internet Research

Another important consideration arises when asking participants to volunteer via the Internet. Web-based surveys are very common: Everybody with an e-mail account has been asked at one time or another to complete a survey, and completing a web-based survey is an act of volunteering. This has important implications for external validity. First, although the Internet has become a fundamental and necessary part of our everyday lives, its use is still more common in a particular demographic. The Pew Research Center's Internet and American Life Project (Pew Internet, 2010) found that living in an urban/suburban area, being college educated, being younger, and having a higher income are all related to reporting more Internet use. Thus, by asking for volunteers for an Internet survey, researchers are sampling from a particular demographic that may not generalize well to the population of interest. Layer upon this issue the idea that even among Internet users, volunteers must be found, and it is easy to conclude that although Internet-based research is easier in some ways, it harbors potentially important trade-offs in terms of external validity.

Gender Considerations

Sometimes, researchers use only males or only females (or a very disproportionate ratio of males to females) simply because this is convenient or the procedures seem better suited to a particular gender. Given the possible differences between males and females, however, the results of such studies may not be generalizable (Denmark, Russo, Frieze, & Sechzer, 1988). Denmark et al. provide an example of studies on contraception practices that use only females because of stereotypical assumptions that only females are responsible for contraception. They also point out several other ways that gender bias may arise in psychological research, including confounding gender with age or job status and selecting response measures that are gender-stereotyped. The solution is to be aware of possible gender differences and include both males and females in our research investigations. Moreover, it is important to recognize the ways that males and females might differentially interpret independent variable manipulations or questions asked in a questionnaire.

Locale

The location that participants are recruited from can also have an impact on a study's external validity. Participants in one locale may differ from participants in another locale. For example, students at UCLA may differ from students at a nearby state university, who in turn may differ from students at a community college. People in Iowa may differ from people in New York City. Thus, a finding obtained with the students in one type of educational setting or in one geographic region may not generalize to people in other settings or regions. In fact, studies have explored how personality traits like extraversion (the tendency to seek social stimulation) and openness to new experiences vary across geographic areas. Rentfrow, Gosling, and Potter (2008) looked at geographic differences in personality traits among citizens of various U.S. states and found extraversion to vary by state. People in midwestern states tended to be more extraverted than people in northeastern states, and people in western states tended to be more open to new experiences. Thus, a study conducted in one location may not generalize well to another, particularly if the variables in question are related to location in some way.

Generalization as a Statistical Interaction

The problem of generalization can be thought of as an interaction in a factorial design (see Chapter 10). An interaction occurs when a relationship between variables exists under one condition but not another or when the nature of the relationship is different in one condition than in another. Thus, if you question the generalizability of a study that used only males, you are suggesting that there is an interaction between gender and the independent variable. Suppose, for example, that a study examines the relationship between crowding and aggression among males and reports that crowding is associated with higher levels of aggression. You might then question whether the results are generalizable to females.

Figure 14.1 shows four potential outcomes of a hypothetical study on crowding and aggression that tested both males and females. In each graph, the relationship between crowding and aggression for males has been maintained. In Graph A, there is no interaction—the behavior of males and females is virtually identical. Thus, the results of the original all-male study could be generalized to females. In Graph B, there is also no interaction; the effect of crowding is identical for males and females. However, in this graph, males are more aggressive than females. Although such a difference is interesting, it is not a factor in generalization because the overall relationship between crowding and aggression is present for both males and females.

Graphs C and D do show interactions. In both, the original results with males cannot be generalized to females. In Graph C, there is no relationship

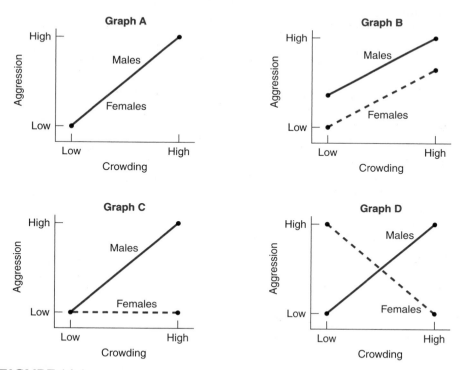

FIGURE 14.1
Outcomes of a hypothetical experiment on crowding and aggression
Note: The presence of an interaction indicates that the results for males cannot be generalized to females.

between crowding and aggression for females. In Graph D, the interaction tells us that a positive relationship between crowding and aggression exists for males but that a negative relationship exists for females. As it turns out, Graph D describes the results of several studies on this topic (cf. Freedman, Levy, Buchanan, & Price, 1972).

Researchers can address issues of external validity that stem from the use of different populations by including subject type as a variable in the study. By including variables such as gender, age, or ethnic group in the design of the study, the results may be analyzed to determine whether there are interaction effects like the ones illustrated in Figure 14.1.

In Defense of College Students (and Rats)

It is easy to criticize research on the basis of subject characteristics, yet criticism by itself does not mean that results cannot be generalized. Although we need to be concerned about the potential problems of generalizing from unique populations such as college students (cf. Sears, 1986), we should also keep several things in mind when thinking about this issue. First, criticisms of the use of any particular type of subject, such as college students, in a study should be backed with good reasons that a relationship would not be found with other types of subjects. College students, after all, *are* human, and researchers should not be blamed for not worrying about generalization to a particular type of subject if there is no good reason to do so. Moreover, college student bodies are increasingly diverse and increasingly representative of the society as a whole (although college students will always be characterized as having the ability and motivation to pursue a college degree). Second, replication of research studies provides a safeguard against the limited external validity of a single study. Studies are replicated at other colleges using different mixes of students, and many findings first established with college students are later applied to other populations, such as children, aging adults, and people in other countries. It is also worth noting that Internet samples are increasingly used in many types of studies. Although such studies raise their own issues of external validity, they frequently complement studies based on college student samples.

Finally, although rats are, in fact, hardy and inexpensive, the value of studying rats (and other animals such as pigeons) has been demonstrated by research that applies findings to humans. These applications include the biological bases of memory, food preferences, sexual behavior, choice behavior, and drug addictions.

CULTURAL CONSIDERATIONS

A broad external validity issue is the question of whether theories and research findings generalize across cultures. Some observers of current psychological research have been very critical of the types of samples employed in behavioral research. Based on analyses of published research by Arnett (2008) and others, Henrich, Heine, and Norenzayan (2010) contend that psychology is built on the study of WEIRD (Western, Educated, Industrialized, Rich, Democratic) people. In many cases, research samples consist primarily of college students from the United States, other English-speaking countries, and Europe. Ultimately, researchers wish to discover aspects of human behavior that have universal applications but in fact cannot generalize beyond their limited samples. This is, at its heart, a critique of the external validity of behavioral research: Does our human behavioral research generalize to all humans, or is it really a study of the WEIRD?

Clearly, if psychologists want to understand human behavior, they must understand human behavior across and among cultures (Henrich et al., 2010; Miller, 1999). Miller described research on self-concept by Kitayama, Markus, Matsumoto, and Norasakkunkit (1997) to illustrate the benefits of incorporating culture into psychological theory. Traditional theories of self-concept are grounded in the culture of the United States and Western Europe; the "self" is an individualistic concept where people are independent from others and self-enhancement comes from individual achievements. Kitayama and his colleagues take a broader, cultural perspective: In contrast to the U.S. meaning of self, in other cultures the "self" is a collective concept in which self-esteem is derived from relationships with others. Often, Japanese engage in self-criticism, which can be seen as relationship-maintaining, whereas Americans work to maintain and enhance self-esteem—thus, very different activities contribute to a positive self-concept in the two cultures (Kitayama et al., 1997). This is a very common theme in research that incorporates culture in psychological processes: "The significance of self-esteem, however, may be much more specific to a culture than has typically been supposed in the literature" (p. 1262).

Much of this cultural research centers on identifying similarities and differences that may exist in personality and other psychological characteristics, as well as ways that individuals from different cultures respond to the same environments (Matsumoto, 1994). Research by Kim, Sherman, and Taylor (2008) provides another example of the limits of external validity across cultural groups. This research focused on how people from different cultures use social support to cope with stress. In reviewing the research on the topic, they concluded that Asians and Asian Americans might benefit from different styles of social support as compared with European Americans. For example, Asian Americans are more likely to benefit from support that does not involve the sort of intense disclosure of personal stressful events and feelings that is the hallmark of support in many European American groups. Rather, they suggest that Asians and Asian Americans may benefit more from support that comes with the comforts of proximity (being with close friends) rather than sharing.

These examples all focused on differences among cultures. Many studies also find similarities across cultures. Evolutionary psychologists, for instance, often conduct studies in different cultural groups because they are looking for similarities across cultures in order to see if a particular behavior or attitude can be tied to our evolutionary past. For example, Singh, Dixson, Jessop, Morgon, and Dixson

(2010) wanted to see if a particular aspect of beauty that is tied to greater reproductive success—namely waist-to-hip ratio (e.g., the ratio for a 25-inch waist and 35-inch hips is .71), which is related to sex hormones and thus fertility—would be seen as attractive across cultures. Diverse groups from Africa, Samoa, Indonesia, and New Zealand evaluated photographs of females with small and large waist-to-hip ratios. The researchers found that indeed, low waist-to-hip ratio among females was seen as more attractive across all these groups. In this example, the results obtained in one culture do generalize to other cultures.

GENERALIZING TO OTHER EXPERIMENTERS

The person who actually conducts the experiment is the source of another external validity problem. In most research, only one experimenter is used, and rarely is much attention paid to the personal characteristics of the experimenter (McGuigan, 1963). The main goal is to make sure that any influence the experimenter has on subjects is constant throughout the experiment. There is always the possibility, however, that the results are generalizable only to certain types of experimenters.

Some of the important characteristics of experimenters have been discussed by Kintz and his colleagues (Kintz, Delprato, Mettee, Persons, & Schappe, 1965). These include the experimenter's personality and gender and the amount of practice in the role of experimenter. A warm, friendly experimenter will almost certainly produce different results from a cold, unfriendly experimenter. Participants also may behave differently with male and female experimenters. It has even been shown that rabbits learn faster when trained by experienced experimenters (Brogden, 1962)! The influence of the experimenter may depend as well on the characteristics of the participants. For example, participants seem to perform better when tested by an experimenter of the other sex (Stevenson & Allen, 1964).

One solution to the problem of generalizing to other experimenters is to use two or more experimenters. A fine example of the use of multiple experimenters is a study by Rubin (1975), who sent several male and female experimenters to the Boston airport to investigate self-disclosure. The experimenters revealed different kinds of information about themselves to both male and female travelers and recorded the passengers' self-disclosures in return. One interesting result was that women tended to reveal more about themselves to male experimenters, and men tended to reveal more about themselves to female experimenters.

PRETESTS AND GENERALIZATION

Researchers are often faced with the decision of whether to give a pretest. Intuitively, pretesting seems to be a good idea. The researcher can be sure that the groups are equivalent on the pretest, and it is often more satisfying to see that individuals changed their scores than it is to look only at group means on a posttest. Pretesting, however, may limit the ability to generalize to populations that did not receive a pretest. In the real world, people are rarely given a pretest—attitudes are not measured prior to listening to a political speech or viewing an advertisement, for example (cf. Lana, 1969).

An important reason for using a pretest is that it enables the researcher to assess mortality (attrition) effects when it is likely that some participants will withdraw from an experiment. If you give a pretest, you can determine whether the people who withdrew are different from those who completed the study. Recall from Chapter 8 that a Solomon four-group design (Solomon, 1949) can be used in situations in which a pretest is desirable but there is concern over the possible impact of taking the pretest. In the **Solomon four-group design,** half of the participants are given the pretest; the other half receive the posttest only. That is, the same experiment is conducted with and without the pretest. Mortality effects can be assessed in the pretest conditions. Also, the researcher can examine whether there is an interaction between the independent variable and the pretest: Are posttest scores on the dependent variable different depending on whether the pretest was given? Sometimes, researchers find that it is not feasible to conduct the study with all four groups in a single experiment. In this case, the first study can include the pretest; the study can be replicated later without the pretest.

GENERALIZING FROM LABORATORY SETTINGS

Research conducted in a laboratory setting has the advantage of allowing the experimenter to study the impact of independent variables under highly controlled conditions. The internal validity of the research is the primary consideration. The question arises, however, as to whether the artificiality of the laboratory setting limits the ability to generalize what is observed in the laboratory to real-life settings.

Mook (1983) articulated one response to the artificiality issue: Generalization to real-life settings is not relevant when the purpose of the study was to investigate causal relationships under carefully controlled conditions. Mook is concerned that a "knee-jerk" criticism of laboratory research on the basis of external validity is too common. Good research is what is most important.

Another response to the laboratory artificiality criticism is to examine the results of field experiments. Recall from Chapter 4 that in a field experiment, the researcher manipulates the independent variable in a natural setting—a factory, a school, or a street corner, for example.

Anderson, Lindsay, and Bushman (1999) asked whether laboratory and field experiments that examine the same variables do in fact produce the same results. To answer this question, they found 38 pairs of studies for which a laboratory investigation had a field experiment counterpart. The studies were drawn from a variety of research areas including aggression, helping, memory, leadership style, and depression. Results of the laboratory and field experiments were in fact very similar—the effect size of the independent variable on the dependent variable was very similar in the two types of studies. Thus, even though lab and field experiments are conducted in different settings, the results are complementary rather than contradictory. When findings are replicated using multiple methods, our confidence in the external validity of the findings increases.

THE IMPORTANCE OF REPLICATIONS

Replication of research is a way of overcoming any problems of generalization that occur in a single study. There are two types of replications to consider: exact replications and conceptual replications.

Exact Replications

An **exact replication** is an attempt to replicate precisely the procedures of a study to see whether the same results are obtained. A researcher who obtains an unexpected finding will frequently attempt a replication to make sure that the finding is reliable. If you are starting your own work on a problem, you may try to replicate a crucial study to make sure that you understand the procedures and can obtain the same results. Often, exact replications occur when a researcher builds on the findings of a prior study. For example, suppose you are intrigued by Singh et al.'s (2010) research on waist-to-hip ratio that was mentioned previously. Singh reports that males rate females with a ratio of .70 as most attractive. In your research, you might replicate the procedures used in the original study and expand on the original research. For example, you might study this phenomenon with males similar to those in the original sample as well as males from different cultures or age groups. When you replicate the original research findings using very similar procedures, your confidence in the external validity of the original findings is increased.

The "Mozart effect" provides us with an interesting example of the importance of replications. In the original study by Rauscher, Shaw, and Ky (1993), college students listened to 10 minutes of a Mozart sonata. These students then showed better performance on a spatial-reasoning measure drawn from the Stanford-Binet Intelligence Scale than students exposed to a relaxation tape or simple silence. This finding received a great deal of attention in the press as people quickly generalized it to the possibility of increasing children's intelligence with Mozart sonatas. In fact, one state governor began producing Mozart CDs to distribute in maternity wards, and entrepreneurs began selling Mozart kits to parents over the Internet. Over the next few years, however, there were many failures to replicate the Mozart effect (see Steele, Bass, & Crook, 1999). We noted above that failures to replicate may occur because the exact conditions for producing the effect were not used. In this case, Rauscher and Shaw (1998) responded to the many replication failures by precisely describing the conditions necessary to produce the Mozart effect. However, Steele et al. (1999) and McCutcheon (2000) were unable to obtain the effect even though they followed the recommendations of Rauscher and Shaw. Research on the Mozart effect continues. Some recent findings suggest that the effect is limited to music that also increases arousal; it is this arousal that can cause better performance following exposure to the music (Thompson, Schellenberg, & Husain, 2001). Bangerter and Heath (2004) present a detailed analysis of the development of the research on the Mozart effect.

A single failure to replicate does not reveal much, though; it is unrealistic to assume, on the basis of a single failure to replicate, that the previous research is necessarily invalid. Failures to replicate share the same problems as nonsignificant results, discussed in Chapter 13. A failure to replicate could mean that the original results are invalid, but it could also mean that the replication attempt was flawed. For example, if the replication is based on the procedure as reported in a journal article, it is possible that the article omitted an important aspect of the procedure. For this reason, it is usually a good idea to write to the researcher to obtain detailed information on all of the materials that were used in the study.

On the other hand, as we saw in the case of the Mozart effect, attempts to replicate do not occur in isolation, as many researchers attempt replications. Repeated failures to replicate may lead to a conclusion that the original results were a fluke—a Type I error was made. Another possibility is that the research will demonstrate that the results can be obtained only under certain limited circumstances. In a few cases, it may turn out that the original researcher misrepresented the results in some way (see Chapter 3 for a discussion of the role of replications in detecting instances of fraud).

Conceptual Replications

A **conceptual replication** is the use of different procedures to replicate a research finding. In a conceptual replication, researchers attempt to understand the relationships among abstract conceptual variables by using new, or different, operational definitions of those variables. Conceptual replications are even more important than exact replications in furthering our understanding of behavior.

In most research, a key goal is to discover whether a relationship between conceptual variables exists. In the original Mozart effect study, researchers examined the effect of *exposure to classical music* on *spatial reasoning*. These are conceptual variables; in the actual study, specific operational definitions of the variables were used. *Exposure to classical music* was operationalized as 10 minutes of exposure to the Mozart Sonata for Two Pianos in D Major. *Spatial reasoning* was operationalized as performance on a particular spatial reasoning measure.

In a conceptual replication, the same independent variable is operationalized in a different way, and the dependent variable may be measured in a different way, too. Conceptual replications are extremely important in the social sciences because the variables used are complex and can be operationalized in different ways. Complete understanding of any variable involves studying the variable using a variety of operational definitions. A crucial generalization question is whether the relationship holds when other ways of manipulating or measuring the variables are studied. Sometimes the conceptual replication may involve an alternative stimulus (e.g., a different Mozart sonata, a selection by a different composer) or an alternative dependent measure (e.g., a different spatial-reasoning task). Or as we previously noted, the same variables are sometimes studied in both laboratory and field settings. When conceptual replications produce similar results, our confidence in the generalizability of relationships between variables is greatly increased.

This discussion should also alert you to an important way of thinking about research findings. The findings represent relationships between conceptual variables but are grounded in specific operations. You may read about the specific methods employed in a study conducted 20 years ago and question whether the study could be replicated today. You might also speculate that the methods used in a study are so unusual that they could never generalize to other situations. These concerns are not as serious when placed within the context of conceptual replications because although operational definitions can change over time, the underlying conceptual variable often remains more consistent. Admittedly, a specific method from a study conducted at one time might not be effective today, given changes in today's political and cultural climate. A conceptual replication of the manipulation, however, would demonstrate that the relationship between the conceptual theoretical variables is still present. Similarly, the narrow focus of a particular study is less problematic if the general finding is replicated with different procedures.

EVALUATING GENERALIZATIONS VIA LITERATURE REVIEWS AND META-ANALYSES

Researchers have traditionally drawn conclusions about the external validity of research findings by conducting literature reviews. In a **literature review,** a reviewer reads a number of studies that address a particular topic and then writes a paper that summarizes and evaluates the literature. The *Publication Manual of the American Psychological Association* provides the following description: "*Literature reviews*, including research syntheses and meta-analyses, are critical evaluations of material that has already been published. . . . By organizing, integrating, and evaluating previously published material, authors of literature reviews consider the progress of research toward clarifying a problem" (APA, 2010, p. 10). The literature review provides information that (1) summarizes what has been found, (2) tells the reader what findings are strongly supported and those that are only weakly supported in the literature, (3) points out inconsistent findings and areas in which research is lacking, and (4) discusses future directions for research.

Sometimes a review will be a narrative in which the author provides descriptions of research findings and draws conclusions about the literature. The conclusions in a narrative literature review are based on the subjective impressions of the reviewer. Another technique for comparing a large number of studies in an area is **meta-analysis** (Borenstein, Hedges, Higgins, & Rothstein, 2009). In a meta-analysis, the researcher combines the actual results of a number of studies. The analysis consists of a set of statistical procedures that employ effect sizes to compare a given finding across many different studies. Instead of relying on judgments obtained in a narrative literature review, you can draw statistical conclusions from this material. The statistical procedures need not concern you. They involve examining several features of the results of studies, including the effect sizes and significance levels obtained. The important point here is that meta-analysis is a method for determining the reliability of a finding by examining the results from many different studies.

Stewart and Chambless (2009) conducted a meta-analysis of research on the effectiveness of cognitive-behavioral therapy (CBT) for anxiety disorders. Both a traditional literature review and a meta-analysis begin with a body of previous research on a topic; in this case, Stewart and Chambless located 56 studies using CBT with adults diagnosed with an anxiety disorder (including panic disorder, social anxiety, post-traumatic stress disorder, generalized anxiety disorder, and obsessive-compulsive disorder). Studies that included an additional medication treatment were excluded. The researchers performed a statistical analysis of the results of these studies and concluded that CBT was effective in treating all of the types of anxiety disorders. In a traditional literature review, it can be difficult to provide the type of general conclusion that was reached with the meta-analysis because it is necessary to integrate information from many studies with different experimental designs, disorders, and measures of anxiety.

One of the most important reasons a meta-analysis can lead to clear conclusions is that meta-analysis studies focus on effect size (recall that an effect size represents the extent to which two variables are associated, see page 252). A typical table in a meta-analysis will show the effect size obtained in a number of studies along with a summary of the average effect size across the studies. More important, the analysis allows comparisons of the effect sizes in different types of studies to allow tests of hypotheses. For example, Miller and Downey (1999) analyzed the results of 71 studies that examined the relationship between weight and self-esteem. Table 14.1 shows a few of the findings. The effect size r averaged across all studies was $-.18$: Heavier weight is associated with lower self-esteem. However, several variables moderate the relationship between weight and self-esteem. Thus, the effect size is larger when the weight variable is a report of self-perceived rather than actual weight, and the relationship between weight and self-esteem is somewhat larger for females than for males. Finally, the effect is greater among individuals with a high socioeconomic background.

Both narrative reviews and meta-analyses provide valuable information and in fact are often complementary. A meta-analysis allows statistical, quantitative conclusions whereas a narrative review identifies trends in the literature and directions for future study—a more qualitative approach. A study by Bushman and Wells (2001) points to an interesting way in which knowledge of meta-analysis can improve the way that we interpret information for literature reviews.

TABLE 14.1   Some meta-analysis findings for weight and self-esteem

Variable	Effect size r
Overall relationship	−.18
Weight measure	
Actual weight	−.12
Self-perceived weight	−.34
Gender	
Females	−.23
Males	−.19
Socioeconomic status (SES)	
Low SES	−.16
Middle SES	−.19
High SES	−.31

Note: Adapted from Miller and Downey (1999).

The reviewers in their study were undergraduates who were provided with both titles and information about the findings of 20 studies dealing with the effect of attitude similarity on attraction. Sometimes the titles were salient with respect to the findings ("Birds of a Feather Flock Together") and others were nonsalient ("Research Studies Who Likes Whom"). Salient titles are obviously easier to remember. When asked to draw conclusions about the findings, naive reviewers with no knowledge of meta-analysis overestimated the size of the similarity–attraction relationship when provided with salient titles. Other reviewers were given brief training in meta-analysis; these reviewers drew accurate conclusions about the actual findings. That is, they were not influenced by the article title. Thus, even without conducting a meta-analysis, a background in meta-analysis can be beneficial when reviewing research findings.

USING RESEARCH TO IMPROVE LIVES

In a presidential address to the American Psychological Association, George Miller (1969) discussed "psychology as a means of promoting human welfare" and spoke of "giving psychology away." Miller was addressing the broadest issue of generalization, taking what we know about human behavior and allowing it to be applied by many people in all areas of everyday life. Zimbardo's (2004) presidential address to the American Psychological Association described many ways in which Miller's call to give psychology away is being honored. The impact of psychological research can be seen in areas such as health (programs to promote health-related behaviors related to stress, heart disease, and sexually transmitted diseases), law and criminal justice (providing data on the effects of 6- versus 12-person juries and showing how law enforcement personnel can improve the accuracy of eyewitness identification), education (providing methods for encouraging academic performance or reducing conflict among different ethnic groups), and work environments (providing workers with more control and improving the ways that people interact with computers and other machines in the workplace). In addition, psychologists are using the Internet to provide the public with information on parenting, education, mental health, and many other topics—for example, the websites of the American Psychological Association and the Association for Psychological Science (http://www.apa.org; http://www.psychologicalscience.org), National Mental Health Information Center (http://www.mentalhealth.samsha.gov), and many individual psychologists who are sharing their expertise with the public.

We have discussed only a few of the ways that basic research has been applied to improve people's lives. Despite all the potential problems of generalizing research findings that were highlighted in this chapter, the evidence suggests that we can generalize our findings to many aspects of our lives.

ILLUSTRATIVE ARTICLE: GENERALIZING RESULTS

Driving around in a 4,000-pound automobile is a dangerous thing. Motor vehicle accidents are among the leading preventable causes of death in the United States every year. Distraction is one of the most common causes of automobile accidents, and talking to another person is a very common distraction.

In an effort to observe the impact of conversation on driving, Drews, Pasupathi, and Strayer (2008) conducted a study using a driving simulator that tracks errors committed by drivers. The researchers varied the type of conversation. In one condition, participants had a conversation with a passenger; in another condition, participants talked on a cell phone. There was also a no-conversation, control condition. As you would expect, having any conversation resulted in more driving errors. However, the number of driving errors was highest in the cell phone condition.

For this exercise, acquire and read the article:

Drews, F., Pasupathi, M., & Strayer, D. (2008). Passenger and cell phone conversations in simulated driving. *Journal of Experimental Psychology: Applied, 14*, 392–400. doi:10.1037/a0013119

After reading the article, consider the following:

1. Describe how well you think the sample of participants in this study generalizes to other groups of people. What about age? What about sex?

2. In this study, participants were told to have a conversation about a time when "their lives were threatened." Do you think that the results of this

study would be different if the conversation were about something else? How so? Why?

3. Do you think that the findings from this study would generalize to other cultures? Do you think that a sample of college students in Mexico, Italy, and Germany would generate similar results? Why or why not?

4. How well do you think the driving simulator generalizes to real-world driving? What would you change to improve the generalizability of the simulator?

5. Evaluate the internal validity of this study. Explain your answer.

6. Evaluate the external validity of this study. Explain your answer.

Study Terms

Conceptual replication (p. 297)

Exact replication (p. 296)

External validity (p. 288)

Literature review (p. 298)

Meta-analysis (p. 299)

Replication (p. 296)

Solomon four-group design (p. 295)

Review Questions

1. What is external validity?

2. Why should a researcher be concerned about generalizing to other populations?

3. How can the fact that most studies are conducted with college students, volunteers, and individuals from a limited location and culture potentially impact external validity?

4. How does the use of the Internet to recruit subjects and collect data impact external validity?

5. What is the source of the problem of generalizing to other experimenters? How can this problem be solved?

6. Why is it important to pretest a problem for generalization? Discuss the reasons why including a pretest *may* affect the ability to generalize results.

7. Distinguish between an exact replication and a conceptual replication. What is the value of a conceptual replication?

8. What is a meta-analysis?

Activity Questions

1. It is easy to collect data for experiments and surveys on the Internet. Anyone in the world who is connected to the Internet can participate in an online experiment or survey. Use a search term such as "psychological research on the Internet" to find some studies that are being conducted. What issues of generalization might arise when interpreting the results of such studies? Does the computer aspect of the research make this research less generalizable than traditional research, or does the fact that people throughout the world can participate make it more generalizable? Could you empirically answer this question?

2. Use *PsycINFO* to find abstracts of articles that included race, ethnicity, gender, or nationality as a key variable. Consider topics such as body image, rumination, academic achievement, or identity development. What conclusions do the authors of these studies draw about generalization?

3. Find a meta-analysis published in a journal; two good sources are the *Review of Educational Research* and *Psychological Bulletin*. What conclusions were drawn from the meta-analysis? How were studies selected for the analysis? How was the concept of effect size discussed in the meta-analysis?

Appendix A
Writing Research Reports

INTRODUCTION

This appendix presents the information you will need to prepare a written report of your research for a course and for possible publication in a professional journal. In addition, an example article illustrates the stylistic features of a research report. We will consider the specific rules that should be followed in organizing and presenting research results. These rules are a great convenience for both the writer and the reader. They provide structure for the report and a uniform method of presentation, making it easier for the reader to understand and evaluate the report. In addition to discussing research report format, we will briefly summarize some guidelines for preparing a poster for presentation at a professional meeting.

Specific rules vary from one discipline to another. A rule for presenting research results in psychology may not apply to the same situation in, for example, sociology research. Also, the rules may vary depending on whether you are preparing the report for a class, a thesis, or submission to a journal. Fortunately, the variation is usually minor, and the general rules of presentation are much the same across disciplines and situations.

The format presented here for writing research reports is drawn from the *Publication Manual of the American Psychological Association* (Sixth Edition, 2010). APA style is used in many journals in psychology, child development, family relations, and education. If you are concerned about specific rules for a particular journal, consult a recent issue of that journal. APA has also published a book titled *Concise Rules of APA Style* (APA, 2010). You may purchase the *Publication Manual* through your college bookstore, at retail bookstores, or directly from the American Psychological Association. Useful online resources for APA style include http://www.apastyle.org and the Online Writing Lab at http://owl.english.purdue.edu/owl/resource/560/01/. Other recommended sources for preparing papers are Rosnow and Rosnow (2009), Sternberg (2003), Kazdin (1995), and Bem (2003).

The APA manual identifies five types of articles that students and professionals might prepare:

- Empirical studies are reports of research that have been conducted by the author(s) of the report.
- Literature reviews describe past research in a specific area of psychology. Reports integrate research findings, evaluate the current status of research on the topic, and point to new directions for research.
- Theoretical articles emphasize the status of existing theory and may propose changes in a theory or development of a new theory.
- Methodological articles focus on the methods of conducting research and analyzing data.
- Case studies present descriptions and interpretations of research with a specific individual, group, or organization.

Each type of article has a different emphasis in the way that information is presented. In this appendix, we will describe only procedures for reporting empirical studies. Further, we will simplify the discussion by focusing primarily on articles that present the results of a single study rather than multiple studies.

WRITING STYLE

In any format for preparing your report, writing style is important. A poorly written report that is difficult to understand is of no value (and almost certainly will bring you a poor grade!). Also, a good paper should be free of grammar, spelling, and typographical errors.

Clarity

Clarity in writing is essential. Be precise and clear in presenting ideas, and think about your intended audience. It is helpful to direct your paper to an audience that is unfamiliar with your general topic and the methods you used to study the topic. Eliminate jargon that most readers will not comprehend. Sometimes a researcher will develop an abbreviated notation for referring to a specific variable or procedure. Such abbreviations may be convenient when communicating with others who are directly involved in the research project, but they are confusing to the general reader. However, you should assume that the reader has a general familiarity with statistics and hypothesis testing. Statistical outcomes can usually be presented without defining terms such as the *mean, standard deviation,* or *significance.* These are only general guidelines, however. Rosnow and Rosnow (2009) point out that when your intended audience is your instructor you should pay close attention to what he or she has to say about expectations for the paper!

The entire report should have a coherent structure. Ideas should be presented in an orderly, logical progression to facilitate understanding. If you write your report for someone who is being introduced to your ideas and research findings for the first time, you will be more likely to communicate clearly with the reader.

One method of producing a more organized report is to use an outline. Many writers plan a paper by putting their thoughts and ideas into outline form. The outline then serves as a writing guide. This method forces writers to develop a logical structure before writing the paper. Other writers prefer to use a less structured approach for the first draft. They then try to outline what has been written. If the paper does not produce a coherent outline, the organization needs to be improved. Word processing programs usually have an outline feature to help you organize your paper; find this feature using the program's help menu.

Paragraphs should be well organized. It is a good idea for a paragraph to contain a topic sentence. Other sentences within a paragraph should be related to the topic sentence and develop the idea in this sentence by elaborating, expanding, explaining, or supporting the idea in the topic sentence. Also, avoid one-sentence paragraphs. If you find such paragraphs in your paper, expand the paragraph, include the idea in another paragraph, or delete the concept.

After completing the first draft of your paper, let it sit for a day or so before you reread it. Carefully proofread the paper, paying attention to grammar and spelling. Some grammatical considerations are described here; you can also use a word processor to check your spelling and grammar. After you make changes and corrections, you may want to get feedback from others. Find one or more people who will read your report critically and suggest improvements. Be prepared to write several drafts before you have a satisfactory finished product.

Acknowledging the Work of Others

It is extremely important to clearly separate your own words and ideas from those obtained from other sources. If you use a passage drawn from an article or book, make sure the passage is presented as a direct quotation. There is nothing wrong with quoting another author as long as you acknowledge your source. Never present another person's idea as your own. This is plagiarism and is inexcusable. You should cite your sources even if you are not using direct quotations. Indicating that your paper draws on the works of others actually strengthens your paper.

Sometimes writers are tempted to fill a paper with quotes from other sources or to quote another paper at great length (e.g., several paragraphs or more). This practice is distracting and counterproductive. Be direct and use your own descriptions and interpretations while acknowledging your sources. If you have any questions about how to properly include material from source articles in your own paper, consult your instructor.

Active Versus Passive Voice

Many writers rely too much on the passive voice in their reports, perhaps because they believe that the passive voice makes their writing seem more "scientific." Consider the following sentences:

> It was found by Yee and Johnson (1996) that adolescents prefer . . .
>
> Participants were administered the test after a 10-minute rest period.
>
> Participants were read the instructions by the experimenter.

Now try writing those sentences in a more active voice. For example:

> Yee and Johnson (1996) found that adolescents prefer . . .
>
> Participants took the test after a 10-minute rest period.
>
> I read the instructions to the participants.

Prose that seems stilted using the passive voice is much more direct when phrased in the active voice.

Although APA style allows the author to use "I" (or "we" when there are multiple authors), many authors are still uncomfortable with the use of the first person pronoun and refer to themselves in the third person. They might say "The experimenter distributed the questionnaires" instead of "I distributed the questionnaires" or "This researcher contacted the head administrators at five community mental health centers" instead of "I contacted the head administrators at five community mental health centers." Thus, when reading research papers, you should not be surprised to see this form of wording.

Avoiding Biased Language

The APA style manual describes several ways of reducing bias. One of the most important is to be specific when describing the participants in your study. The APA manual now allows the use of either *participants* or *subjects* when describing humans who take part in psychological research. (Guidelines for student papers in a class may call for one or the other term.). In addition, it is appropriate to describe participants as *respondents* in survey research. You may also use specific descriptors such as *children, patients, clients,* and so on if these terms more accurately describe the participants in your study. Moreover, you should make sure to provide specific information about your participants. Descriptors such as *toddlers* or *teenagers* or *young adults* are not sufficiently specific; you should also provide exact age ranges.

You must also be sensitive to the possibility that your writing might convey a bias, however unintentional, regarding gender, sexual orientation, and ethnic or racial group. As a general principle, be as specific as possible when referring to groups of people. For example, referring to the participants in your study as "Korean Americans and Vietnamese Americans" is more specific and accurate than describing them as "Asians." Also, be sensitive to the use of labels that might be offensive to members of certain groups. In practice, this means that you refer to people using the terms that these people prefer. Also, avoid implicit labels by saying, "The lesbian sample, in contrast to the sample of normal women" or "We tested groups of autistics and normals." The latter phrase could be written as "We tested people with autism and without autism."

The APA manual has numerous examples of ways of being sensitive to gender, racial and ethnic identity, age, sexual orientation, and disabilities. The term *gender* refers to males and females as social groups. Thus, gender is the proper term to use in a phrase such as "gender difference in average salary." The term *sex* refers to biological aspects of men and women; for example, "sex fantasies" or "sex differences in the size of certain brain structures." The use of gender pronouns can be problematic. Do not use *he, his, man, man's,* and so on when both males and females are meant. Sentences can usually be rephrased or specific pronouns deleted to avoid linguistic biases. For example, "The worker is paid according to his productivity" can be changed to "The worker is paid according to productivity" or "Workers are paid according to their productivity." In the first case, *his* was simply deleted; in the second case, the subject of the sentence was changed to plural. Do *not* try to avoid sexist language by simply substituting *s/he* whenever that might appear convenient.

There are certain rules to follow when referring to racial and ethnic groups. The names of these groups are capitalized and never hyphenated; for example, Black, White, African American, Latino, Asian, Asian American. The manual also reminds us that the terms that members of racial and ethnic groups use to describe themselves may change over time, and there may be a lack of consensus about a preferred term. Currently, for example, both *Black* and *African American* are generally acceptable. Depending on a number of factors, participants may prefer to be called Hispanic, Latino, Chicana, or Mexican American. You are urged to use the term most preferred by your participants.

The APA manual includes a great deal of information and numerous examples to encourage sensitivity in writing reports. The best advice is to review your papers for possible problems at least once prior to writing your final draft. If you have any questions about appropriate language, consult the manual and colleagues whose opinions you respect.

Word Processing

You will eventually have to prepare a typed copy of your paper. In APA style, the paper should be *entirely double-spaced.* The margins for text should be set to 1 inch on all four sides of the page. Page headers—the information that appears at the top of each page including the running head and page number—are set approximately .5 inch from the top of the page. All pages are numbered. Paragraphs are indented .5 inch (use the tab function, not the space bar). Make sure that hyphenation is turned off: Words should never be hyphenated at the end of a line.

Be sure to learn about and take advantage of the features of your word processing application. The software can automatically place a page header and a page number at the top of each page, double-space text, check spelling and grammar, and so on. Use the tabs and table functions to format text correctly; do not use the space bar to format text or tables.

Set the alignment of your text to the left margin. Set all text and tables in a 12-point size serif font (Times New Roman is the preferred serif font). Figures should be prepared with a sans serif font, either Arial or Helvetica font style. Serif fonts have short lines at the ends of the strokes that form the letters; sans serif literally means "without serif" and so does not have serif lines. Here are examples:

This is Times New Roman serif text.
This is Arial sans serif text.

There is a minor controversy about the number of spaces to insert between sentences or after a colon. In the fifth edition of the *APA Publication Manual*, APA joined the Associated Press, Modern Language Association, and *Chicago Manual of Style* in requiring one space between sentences. This practice improves the appearance of the paper when using modern fonts such as Times New Roman. However, the sixth edition of the *APA Publication Manual* states: "spacing twice after punctuation marks at the end of a sentence aids readers of draft manuscripts" (p. 88). This does not specifically mandate using two spaces but states that APA believes that there is a justification for using two spaces in draft manuscripts. Comments by professors on the APA Style website (www.apastyle.org) lead us to conclude that most professors will not care whether students use one or two spaces between sentences for class papers. However, some have very strong opinions about the issue, so it is worthwhile to note whether the number of spaces is mentioned in guidelines for papers. Finally, dissertations and theses are considered final publications and so most graduate programs will continue to require one space between sentences.

You will need to use italic and boldface fonts correctly. Use the italics feature of your word processor to create italics for (a) titles and volume numbers of periodicals, (b) titles of books, (c) some headings in your paper, (d) most statistical terms, (e) anchors of a scale, such as 1 (*strongly disagree*) to 5 (*strongly agree*), (f) emphasis of a particular word or phrase when first mentioned in the paper, and (g) words used as words, as in "Authors now routinely use the word *participants*." Pay attention to the use of italics in the examples used throughout this appendix. Boldface font is used for some of the headings of your paper (examples are shown below).

APA style uses a "hanging indent" for the reference list at the end of your paper. Here is an example:

Goldstein, N. J, Cialdini, R. B., & Griskevicius, V. (2008). A room
    with a viewpoint: Using social norms to motivate environmental
    conservation in hotels. *Journal of Consumer Research, 35,* 472–482.
    doi:10.1086/586910

Note that the first line of a reference begins flush with the left margin, but subsequent lines are indented .5 inch (you might want to think of the old "hangman" game to remember why this is called a hanging indent). Do not try to create a hanging indent using the space bar. This takes time and can cause problems when printing. Use the hanging indent feature of your word processor for correct, reliable formatting. It is very easy to learn how to do this through your Help menu or a search on your web browser.

APA Style and Student Paper Formats

APA style is intended to provide a manuscript to a typesetter who then prepares the paper for publication in a journal; several APA style requirements are for the convenience of the typesetter. When you prepare a paper for a class report, an honors project, or a thesis, however, your paper may be the "final product" for your readers. In such cases, many aspects of APA style may be ignored so that your paper will closely resemble a printed report. For example, APA style calls for placement of tables and figures at the end of the paper; the typesetter inserts the tables and figures in the body of the paper for the published article. However, if your report is the final version for your readers, you may need to (a) place tables and figures on separate pages in the body of your report, or (b) actually insert the tables and figures in the text. Some of the ways that a student report may differ from APA style are described below. When you are getting ready to prepare your own report, be sure to check the particular requirements of your instructor or college.

ORGANIZATION OF THE REPORT

A paper prepared using APA style has several major parts:

- Title page that includes the title, author name and affiliation, and author note
- Abstract
- Body of the paper including the Introduction, Method, Results, and Discussion
- References
- Footnotes (if any)
- Tables and figures

We will consider the parts of the paper in the order prescribed by APA style. Refer to the sample paper at the end of this appendix as you read the material that follows.

Title Page

Title   The first page of the paper is the title page. It is a separate page and is numbered page 1. The title should be fairly short (usually no more than 12 words) and should inform the reader of the nature of your research. A good way to do this is to include the names of your variables in the title. For example, the following titles are both short and informative:

    Effect of Anxiety on Mathematical Problem Solving

    Memory for Faces Among Elderly and Young Adults

Sometimes a colon in the title will help to convey the nature of your research or even add a bit of "flair" to your title, as in

    Cognitive Responses in Persuasion: Affective and Evaluative Determinants

    Comparing the Tortoise and the Hare: Gender Differences and Experience in

    Dynamic Spatial Reasoning Tasks

Another method of titling a paper is to pose the question that the research addresses. For example,

    Do Rewards in the Classroom Undermine Intrinsic Motivation?

    Does Occupational Stereotyping Still Exist?

One further consideration in the choice of a title is that computer literature searches are most likely to include your article if the title includes words and phrases that people are most likely to use when conducting the search. This consideration also applies to the abstract.

Note that the title is typed in upper- and lowercase. It is positioned in the top half of the page but is not at the very top of the page.

Author and affiliation
The author's name and affiliation are provided just below the title. This is sometimes called the byline. The name usually includes the full first name, middle initial, and last name. Some people adopt a professional name that has a first initial and full middle name. Do not use your initials only. The author name should not include any other descriptive information such as professional title (e.g., Dr.) or degree (e.g., M.A.).

The author's institutional affiliation where the research was conducted is typed below the byline. For student papers, the affiliation is the name of your college or university. Use the complete name of your college without abbreviations or shortened names. If in doubt, check how the college or university name is presented on its official website. If there are two or more authors, the order is determined by the relative contribution of each author to the research.

Following are examples of bylines with affiliation for one or two authors:

                    Amanda S. Reynolds
                New Mexico State University
            Jorge Orozco and Olivia R. Dunham
            University of Houston-Clear Lake

The APA manual also includes examples for other authorship possibilities with more authors, authors with multiple affiliations, and authors with no affiliation.

Author note   The author note, typed in the lower half of the title page, provides information on contacting the author, acknowledging the assistance of others, and specifying any funding sources that supported the research. Student research papers, theses, and dissertations will probably not require an author note; the example paper in this appendix therefore does not include one.

Begin the author note by typing "Author Note" centered several lines below the last author affiliation. The first paragraph (with first line indented) gives detailed department affiliations of the authors. Here you specify that an author is in the Department of Psychology, the Department of Human Development, or a special research laboratory or institute.

A second paragraph provides information on changes of affiliation of any authors if this is needed. Most commonly, an author publishing a master's thesis from one institution may describe a new affiliation in this paragraph.

The next paragraph contains acknowledgments and any special information that the author wishes to include with the paper. This would include sources of grant support, names of colleagues who assisted with the study in some way, and any details about authorship (e.g., that the order is alphabetical because contributions were equal).

A final paragraph begins with "Correspondence concerning this article should be addressed to . . ." followed by the mailing address of the person designated for that purpose. The e-mail address for correspondence is included as well.

Running head and page number   The last task in preparing the title page is to create a running head and page number in the header area of your page. The header is located between the page edge and the top margin, and the information that you type there will be printed at the top of the page. Use your word processor's Help feature or an Internet search to learn how to create a header; do not manually type the information at the top of each page of your paper. Your word processor may have a Header/Footer menu choice to facilitate this.

First you must decide on the wording of the running head, which should be a brief (up to 50 characters, including spaces) summary of your title. Thus, a title such as "Aging and Memory for Pictures of Faces" might use MEMORY FOR FACES as the running head. It will be printed on each page of your paper. In a published paper, it is printed at the top (or head) of the pages. It helps the reader identify your paper. Also, the title page with names is usually removed when the paper is sent for masked review; this allows the paper to be identified even if the pages become mixed with other papers.

The running head is typed against the left margin and will look like this:

```
Running head: MEMORY FOR FACES
```

Type the words "Running head:" and then type the actual running head with all words capitalized. (Note: You may not have to include this separate "Running head:" version for a student paper; check with your instructor.)

Next you need to activate the automatic page numbering feature of your word processing application. Move your cursor to the right margin of the header and insert the automatic page number command that will cause page numbers to appear throughout your paper.

When the title page is complete, insert a break to begin the second page (in Microsoft Word, insert a section break). Do not simply press the Enter key multiple times, or your page numbers may be incorrect.

Abstract

The abstract is a brief summary of the research report and is usually 150 to 250 words in length, depending on the rules specified by the publication or your college. The purpose of the abstract is to introduce the article, allowing readers to decide whether the article appears relevant to their own interests. The abstract should provide enough information so that the reader can decide whether to read the entire report, and it should make the report easier to comprehend when it is read.

Although the abstract appears at the beginning of your report, it is easiest to write the abstract last. Read a few abstracts and you will get some good ideas for how to condense a full-length research report down to 8 or 10 information-packed sentences. A very informative exercise is to write an abstract for a published article and then compare your abstract to the one written by the original authors.

Abstracts generally include a sentence or two about each of the four main sections in the body of the article. First, from the Introduction section, state the problem under study and the primary hypotheses. Second, from the Method section, include information on the characteristics of the participants (e.g., number, age, sex, and any special characteristics) and a brief summary of the procedure (e.g., self-report questionnaires, direct observation, repeated measurements on several occasions). Third, from the Results section, describe the pattern of findings for major variables. This is typically done by reporting the direction of differences without relying on numerical values. APA guidelines recommend including statistical significance levels, yet few authors comply (Ono, Phillips, & Leneman, 1996). Rely on guidelines provided by your instructor. Finally, the abstract will include implications of the study taken from the Discussion section. Informative comments about the findings are preferred to general statements such as "the implications of the study are addressed" (Kazdin, 1995).

The abstract is typed on a separate page and is numbered page 2. The word "Abstract" is centered at the top of the page. The abstract is always typed as a single paragraph with no paragraph indentation.

Depending upon your instructor's requirements, you may need to re-format the header at the top of the abstract page. Recall that the header on the title page includes the text "Running head:" followed by the actual running head text; for example,

```
Running head: OCCUPATIONAL STEREOTYPING                              1
```

On all the other pages, only the actual running head needs to appear; you do not include the words "Running head:" so all the remaining pages will show only this:

```
OCCUPATIONAL STEREOTYPING
```

and the page number in the header area. This means that you need to turn off the first header and start a new header on the abstract page. In Microsoft Word, you have to insert a section break at the bottom of the title page and specify that the new section starting on page 2 will have a different header. An Internet search for "page header changes" should lead you to information on doing this with your word processing software. When you have completed the abstract page, insert a page break to take you to the third page of your paper.

Body of the Paper

Begin the third page by typing the complete title of your paper, centered on the first line. Do not include your name or affiliation (this allows a masked review in which the reader cannot identify the author). You are now ready to type the body of your paper. For most research reports, the body of the paper will have four sections: Introduction, Method, Results, and Discussion. These are organized through the use of headings.

Introduction   The Introduction section begins after the title at the top of the page. It is not labeled "Introduction"—instead, you (and your readers) understand that the first part of the body of the paper is the Introduction. The Introduction has three components, although formal subsections introduced by headings are rarely used. The components are (1) the problem under study, (2) the literature review, and (3) the rationale and hypotheses of the study. After reading the Introduction, the reader should know why you decided to do the research and how you decided to go about doing it. In general, the Introduction progresses from broad theories and research findings to specific details and expectations of the current research.

The Introduction should begin with an opening statement of the problem under study. In one or two paragraphs, give the reader an appreciation of the broad context and significance of the topic being studied (Bem, 1981; Kazdin, 1995). Stating what problem is being investigated is worthwhile; it helps readers, even those who are unfamiliar with the topic, to understand and appreciate why the topic was studied in the first place.

Following the opening statement, the Introduction provides a description of past research and theory. This is called the *literature review*. An exhaustive review of past theory and research is not necessary. (If there are major literature reviews of the topic, you would of course refer the reader to the reviews.) Rather, you want to describe only the research and theoretical issues that are clearly related to your study. State explicitly how this previous work is logically connected to your research problem. This tells the reader why your research was conducted and shows the connection to prior research.

The final part of the Introduction tells the reader the rationale of the current study. Here you state what variables you are studying and what results you expect. The links between the research hypotheses, prior research, and the current research design are shown by explaining why the hypotheses are being examined by the study.

Method   As noted above, the body of the paper is organized using headings. The Method section begins immediately after you have completed the Introduction (on the same page if space permits). The heading for this section is the word *Method*, centered on the line using boldface type, as follows:

Method

The Method section provides the reader with detailed information about how your study was conducted. Ideally, there should be enough information in the Method section to allow a reader to replicate your study.

The Method section is typically divided into a number of subsections. Both the order of the subsections and the number of subsections vary in published articles. Decisions about which subsections to include are guided by the complexity of the investigation. The sample paper in this appendix uses three subsections: *Participants, Design and Materials,* and *Procedure.* Some of the most commonly used subsections are discussed next.

Overview   If the experimental design and procedures used in the research are complex, a brief overview of the method should be presented to help the reader understand the information that follows.

Participants   A subsection on the participants (or subjects or respondents) is always necessary. The number and nature of the participants should be described. Age, sex, ethnicity, and any other relevant characteristics should be described. Special characteristics of participants are described, such as firstborn children, adolescent children of alcoholics, student teachers, or parents of children being treated for ADHD. State explicitly how participants were recruited and what incentives for participation might have been used. The number of individuals in each experimental condition also can be included here.

Apparatus or Materials   An Apparatus or Materials subsection may be necessary to describe special equipment or materials used in the experiment. The apparatus or materials should be described in sufficient detail to allow other researchers to replicate the study.

Procedure   The Procedure subsection tells the reader exactly how the study was conducted. One way to report this information is to describe, step by step, what occurred in the experiment. Maintain the temporal sequence of events so the reader is able to visualize the sequence of events the participants experienced.

The Procedure subsection tells the reader what instructions were given to the participants, how the independent variables were manipulated, and how the dependent variables were measured. The methods used to control extraneous variables also should be described. These include randomization procedures, counterbalancing, and special means that were used to keep a variable constant across all conditions. Finally, the method of debriefing should be described.

If your study used a nonexperimental method, you would still provide details on exactly how you conducted the study and the measurement techniques you used.

It is up to you to decide how much detail to include here. Use your own judgment to determine the importance of a specific aspect of the procedure and the amount of detail that is necessary for the reader to clearly understand what was done in the study. Include any detail that might be important in a replication of the study.

Other subsections   Include other subsections if they are needed for clear presentation of the method. For example, a subsection on testing materials might be necessary instead of an Apparatus subsection. Other sections are customized by the authors to suit their study. If you glance through a recent issue of a journal, you will find that some studies have only two subsections and others have many more subsections. This reflects the varying complexity of the studies and the particular writing styles of the researchers.

Results

In the Results section, present the results as clearly as possible. The Results section is a straightforward description of your analyses. Although it is tempting to explain your findings in the Results section, save that discussion for the next section of the paper.

Be sure to state the alpha (probability) level that you used in making decisions about statistical significance: This will usually be .05 or .01 and requires only a simple sentence such as "An alpha level of .05 was used for statistical analyses."

Present your results in the same order that your predictions are stated in the Introduction section of the paper. If a manipulation check was made, present it before you describe the major results.

The content of your Results section will vary according to the type of statistical test performed and the number of analyses you conducted. However, every Results section includes some basic elements. If applicable, describe any scoring or coding procedures performed on the data to prepare them for analysis. This is particularly important when coding qualitative data. (Sometimes data transformations are included in a subsection of the Method section.) State which statistical test was performed on the data (t test, F test, correlation, etc.). Justify the selection of a particular statistical comparison to address your hypothesis. Be sure to summarize each finding in words as well as to include the results of statistical tests in the form of statistical phrases. The APA manual includes guidelines for reporting statistics that were recommended by an APA Task Force on Statistical Inference (Wilkinson, 1999). One major recommendation is to report exact probability values that are routinely provided by computer programs used to perform statistical analyses. In the past, most researchers reported probabilities as "less than" the standard probabilities shown in statistical tables, for example, $p < .10$, $p < .05$, or $p < .01$. It is now possible to report exact probabilities of the null hypothesis being correct, for example, $p = .09$, $p = .03$, or $p = .02$. This change allows readers to apply their own standards of statistical significance when evaluating the study.

Another recommendation is to report effect size. The manual recognizes that there are currently many indicators of effect size associated with different statistical procedures; the primary concern is to have an effect size in the published article.

A related APA guideline is to report statistical values (e.g., mean, standard deviation, t, F, or chi-square) using two decimal places. When you are reporting statistical significance, probabilities are rounded to two or three decimals (e.g., $p = .03$ or $p = .034$). If you are consistently using two decimals, any value less than .01 should be reported as $p < .01$. For three decimals, values less than .001 are reported as $p < .001$. Your instructor may specify a decimal place rule for your papers.

The results should be stated in simple sentences. For example, the results of the modeling and aggression experiment described in Chapter 12 might be expressed as follows:

> As predicted, children who viewed the aggressive model were significantly more aggressive than children in the no-model condition, $t(18) = 4.03$, $p < .01$. The mean aggression score in the model group was 5.20 ($SD = 1.14$) and the no-model mean was 3.10 ($SD = 1.20$). The effect size r associated with this finding was .69.

These brief sentences inform the reader of the general patterns of the results, the obtained means, statistical significance, and effect size. You should note the wording of the phrase that includes the symbol for the t test, degrees of freedom, and significance level (probability).

If the results are relatively straightforward, they can be presented entirely in sentence form. If the study involved a complex design, tables and figures may be needed to clarify presentation of the results.

Tables and figures

Tables are generally used to present large arrays of data. For example, a table might be useful in a design with several dependent measures; the means of the different groups for all dependent measures would be presented in the table. Tables are also convenient when a factorial design has been used. For example, in a $2 \times 2 \times 3$ factorial design, a table could be used to present all 12 means.

Figures are used when a visual display of the results would help the reader understand the outcome of the study. Figures may be used to illustrate a significant interaction or show trends over time. When preparing a figure, you will need to decide whether to present the information as a pie chart, a bar graph, or a line graph. Pie charts are used when showing percentages or proportions. The entire pie represents 100% and is divided into slices. In this way, the whole is divided into separate groups or responses. Bar graphs are used when describing the responses of two or more groups—for example, the mean aggression score of a model and a no-model group in an experiment. Line graphs are used when both the independent and dependent variables have quantitative properties, for example, the average response time of two groups on days 1, 2, 3, 4, and 5 of an experiment. Nicol and Pexman (2003) provide detailed information on creating figures and other visual displays of data.

In APA style, tables and figures are not presented in the main body of the manuscript. Rather, they are placed at the end of the paper. Each table and figure appears on a separate page. A table or figure is noted in the text by referring to a table or figure number and describing the content of the table or figure. Never make a reference to the placement of the figure because the placement is deter-mined by the typesetter. In the Results section, make a statement such as "As shown in Figure 2, the model group . . ." or "Table 1 presents the demographic characteristics of the survey respondents." Describe the important features of the table or figure rather than use a generic comment such as "See Figure 3."

Do not repeat the same data in more than one place. An informative table or figure supplements, not duplicates, the text. Using tables and figures does not diminish your responsibility to clearly state the nature of the results in the text of your report.

When you are writing a research report for a purpose other than publication—for example, to fulfill a course or degree requirement—it may be more convenient to place each figure and table on a separate page within the main body of the paper. Because rules about the placement of tables and figures may vary, check on the proper format before writing your report.

Discussion of the results   It is usually *not* appropriate to discuss the implica-tions of the results in the Results section. However, the Results and Discussion sections may be combined if the discussion is brief and greater clarity is achieved by the combination.

Discussion   The Discussion section is the proper place to discuss the im-plications of the results. One way to organize the Discussion is to begin by summarizing the original purpose and expectations of the study, then to state whether the results were consistent with your expectations. If the results do support your original ideas, you should discuss how your findings contribute to knowledge of the problem you investigated. You will want to consider the relationship between your results and past research and theory. If you did not obtain the expected results, discuss possible explanations. The explana-tions would be quite different, of course, depending on whether you obtained results that were the opposite of what you expected or the results were not significant.

It is often a good idea to include your own criticisms of the study. Many published articles include limitations of the study. Try to anticipate what a reader might find wrong with your methodology. For example, if you used a nonexperimental research design, you might point out problems of cause and effect and possible extraneous variables that might be operating. Sometimes there may be major or minor flaws that could be corrected in a subsequent study (if you had the time, money, and so on). You can describe such flaws and suggest corrections. If there are potential problems in generalizing your results, state the problems and give reasons why you think the results would or would not generalize.

The results will probably have implications for future research. If so, you should discuss the direction that research might take. It is also possible that the results have practical implications—for example, for childrearing or improving learning in the classroom. Discussion of these larger issues is usually placed at the end of the Discussion section. Finally, you will probably wish to have a brief concluding paragraph that provides "closure" to the entire paper.

References

The list of references begins on a new page. The References must contain complete citations for all sources mentioned in your report. Do not omit any sources from the list of references; also, do not include any sources that are not mentioned in your report. The exact procedures for citing sources within the body of your report and in your list of references are described later in Appendix A. Follow the examples in recent publications.

Appendix

An appendix is rarely provided in manuscripts submitted for publication. The APA *Publication Manual* notes that an appendix might be appropriate when necessary material would be distracting in the main body of the report. Examples of appendices include a sample of a questionnaire or survey instrument, a complex mathematical proof, or a long list of words used as stimulus items. An appendix (or several appendices) is much more appropriate for a student research project or a thesis. The appendix might include the entire questionnaire that was used, a new test that was developed, or other materials employed in the study. Check with your instructor concerning the appropriateness of an appendix for your paper. If an appendix is provided, it begins on a new page with the word "Appendix" centered at the top.

Footnotes

Footnotes, if used, are not typed in the body of the text. Instead, all footnotes in the paper are typed on one page at the end of the paper. Avoid using footnotes unless they are absolutely necessary. They tend to be distracting to readers, and the information can and should be integrated into the body of the paper.

Tables

Each table should be on a separate page. As noted previously, APA style requires placement of the table at the end of the paper, but for a class you may be asked to place your tables on separate pages within the body of the paper. In preparing your table, allow enough space so that the table does not appear cramped on a small portion of the page. Define areas of the table using typed horizontal lines (do not use vertical lines). Give some thought to the title so that it accurately and clearly describes the content of the table. You may wish to use an explanatory note in the table to show significance levels or the range of possible values on a variable. Before you make up your own tables, examine the tables in a recent issue of one of the journals published by the American Psychological Association as well as the examples in the *Publication Manual* and Nicol and Pexman (2003). Formats are provided for many types of tables, for example, tables of means, correlation coefficients, multiple regression analyses, and so on. For example, here is a table of correlations:

Table 1

Correlations Between Dependent Measures

Measure	1	2	3	4
1. Attractiveness	—	.52	.35	.29
2. Extraversion		—	.11	.23
3. Conscientiousness			—	.49
4. Starting salary				—

Note that the title of the table is typed in italics. Also, the areas of the table are separated by horizontal lines.

Figures

Figures consist of graphic displays of information including results depicted in graphs (e.g., a line graph or bar graph), drawings, or photographs. In APA style, figures are placed after any tables in your paper. However, when preparing a student report or thesis, you may be asked to include figures within the body of the paper.

Although it is sometimes tempting to draw a graph by hand, you will find it much easier to use a computer program to create graphs. Most spreadsheet, word processing, and statistical analysis programs have graphing features. Independent and predictor variables are placed on the horizontal axis; dependent and criterion variables are placed on the vertical axis. Both the horizontal and vertical axes must be labeled. Figures should be easy to read and should fit on the page along with the figure caption. Use a sans serif typeface such as Arial or Helvetica. Select font sizes no larger than 14 point and no smaller than 8 point. The figure number and figure caption appear below each figure.

Remember that the purpose of a figure is to increase comprehension of results by having a graphic display of data. If the graph is cluttered with information, it will confuse the reader and will not serve its purpose. Plan your graphs carefully to make sure that you are accurately and clearly informing the reader. If you become interested in the topic of how to display information in graphs and charts, Tufte's (1983, 1990, 1997, 2006) books are recommended. Tufte explores a variety of ways of presenting data, factors that lead to data clarity, and ways that graphs can deceive the reader.

Summary: Order of Pages

To summarize, the organization of your paper is as follows:

1. Title page, including Author Note if required (page 1)
2. Abstract (page 2)
3. Body of paper (start on page 3)
   a. Title at top of page 3 followed by the Introduction (no heading)
   b. Method (boldface type and centered)
   c. Results (boldface type and centered)
   d. Discussion (boldface type and centered)
4. References (start on new page)
5. Appendix (start on new page if included)
6. Footnotes (start on new page if included)
7. Tables, with table captions (each table on a separate page)
8. Figures, with figure captions (each figure on a separate page)

You should now have a general idea of how to structure and write your report. The remainder of Appendix A focuses on some of the technical rules that may be useful as you prepare your own research report.

THE USE OF HEADINGS

The body of the paper in APA style is organized through the use of headings. There are five levels of heading. Most commonly, you will use the first three levels. The five levels of heading are shown below:

Level 1:

`Centered Heading, Boldface, Upper and Lowercase`

Level 2:

`Margin Heading, Flush Left, Boldface, Upper and Lowercase`
`    The text begins indented on a new line.`

Level 3:

`    Paragraph heading. The heading is indented as is a new paragraph; it`
`is boldface, uses lowercase as in a sentence, and ends with a period. The`
`text begins on the same line.`

Level 4:

> ***Italicized boldface paragraph heading.*** This heading will usually not be needed in papers reporting a single study. See the APA manual for information on reporting the results of two or more studies in a single paper.

Level 5:

> *Italicized paragraph heading.* This additional paragraph heading will probably not be needed in student papers.

Recall that the headings for the main sections of the papers—Method, Results, Discussion—are centered using boldface type; these are level 1 headings. (The Introduction section does not require a level 1 heading; it is assumed that the text on page 3 of the paper is the beginning of the Introduction section.) Each of these sections can be further divided into subsections using level 2 headings. If needed, level 3 headings allow you to provide an organizational structure for any subsections. Figure A.1 shows an example of the use of headings in the body of your paper.

CITING AND REFERENCING SOURCES

Citation Style

Whenever you refer to information reported by other researchers, you *must* accurately identify the sources. APA journals use the author–date citation method: The author name(s) and year of publication are inserted at appropriate points. The citation style depends on whether the author names are part of the narrative or are in parentheses.

One author   When the author's name is part of the narrative, include the publication date in parentheses immediately after the name:

> Markman (1991) found that marital discord can lead to constructive resolution of conflict.

When the author's name is not part of the narrative, the name and date are cited in parentheses at the end of an introductory phrase or at the end of the sentence:

> In one study (Markman, 1991), couples learned to discuss ...

> Couples have lower rates of divorce and marital violence after problem-solving intervention (Markman, 1991).

Title of Paper Centered in Regular Type

The text for the Introduction section begins after the title. Your first paragraphs introduce your research. You may or may not wish to organize the Introduction using subsections.

Level 2 Heading for a Subsection

Text would continue here.

Level 2 Heading for Another Subsection

Text begins here for the second subsection.

Method

Begin the Method, Results, and Discussion sections with a centered and boldface Level 1 heading. Further subsections will have Level 2 and Level 3 headings as shown below.

Participants

Describe your participants and sampling procedures here.

Procedure

This is your description of how the study was conducted. Level 3 paragraph headings may be useful. These are only examples.

Stimuli. Here you might describe the stimuli that participants were given in various conditions. Note that this is a Level 3 heading.

Dependent measures. Describe the measures that were made after participants were presented with the stimuli. This is another Level 3 heading.

Results

An introduction to the results would go here.

Perceived Competence (Example of a Level 2 Heading)

This subsection would be a description of results for the first dependent measure.

Perceived Attractiveness (Example of a Level 2 Heading)

Here you would present the results for the second dependent variable.

Discussion

You may wish to divide the discussion into subsections. Begin with a discussion of the ways that your results supported or did not support your predictions. Explain what you found and relate your findings to past research. You may include additional subsections. The following are only examples.

Limitations

Future Research

Possible Applications

FIGURE A.1
Example of Headings in the Body of a Paper

Two authors   When the work has two authors, both names are included in each reference citation. The difference between narrative and parenthetical citations is in the use of the conjunction "and" and the ampersand "&" to connect authors' names. When the names are part of a sentence, use the word "and" to join the names of two authors. When the complete citation is in parentheses, use the "&" symbol:

> Harris and Marmer (1996) reported that fathers in poor families are less involved with their adolescent children than fathers in non-poor families.

> Fathers in poor families are less likely to spend time with their adolescent children than fathers in non-poor families (Harris & Marmer, 1996).

Three to five authors   When a report has three to five authors, all author names are cited the first time the reference occurs. Thereafter, cite the first author's surname followed by the abbreviation et al. ("and others") along with the publication date. The abbreviation may be used in narrative and parenthetical citations:

First citation

> Abernathy, Massad, and Romano-Dwyer (1995) reported that female adolescents with low self-esteem are more likely to smoke than their peers with high self-esteem.

> Research suggests that low self-esteem is one reason teenage girls are motivated to smoke (Abernathy, Massad, & Romano-Dwyer, 1995).

Subsequent citations

> Abernathy et al. (1995) also examined the relationship between smoking and self-esteem in adolescent males.

> For males, there is no relationship between smoking and self-esteem, suggesting gender-specific motivations for initiating smoking in adolescence (Abernathy et al., 1995).

Another question about subsequent citations is whether to include the publication date each time an article is referenced. Within a paragraph, you do *not* need to include the year in subsequent citations as long as the study cannot be confused with other studies cited in your report.

Citation within a paragraph

```
In a recent study of reaction times, Yokoi and Jones (2006) ...

Yokoi and Jones also reported that ...
```

When subsequent citations are in another paragraph or in another section of the report, the publication date should be included.

Six or more authors   Occasionally you will reference a report with six or more authors. In this case, use the abbreviation et al. after the first author's last name in *every* citation.

References with no author   When an article has no author (e.g., some newspaper or magazine articles), cite the first two or three words of the title in quotation marks, followed by the publication date:

Citation in reference list

```
Parental smoking kills 6,200 kids a year, study says. (1997, July 15).
    Orange County Register, p. 11.
```

Citation in text

```
In an article on smoking ("Parental Smoking," 1997), data obtained from ...
```

Multiple works within the same parentheses   A convenient way to cite several studies on the same topic or several studies with similar findings is to reference them as a series within the same parentheses. When two or more works are by the same author(s), report them in order of year of publication, using commas to separate citations:

```
Mio and Willis (2003, 2005) found ...

Past research (Mio & Willis, 2003, 2005) indicates ...
```

When two or more works by different authors are cited within the same parentheses, arrange them in alphabetical order and separate citations with semicolons:

```
Investigations of families in economic distress consistently report that

girls react with internalization problems whereas boys respond with
```

```
externalization problems (Conger, Ge, Elder, Lorenz, & Simons, 1994;
Flanagan & Eccles, 1993; Lempers, Clark-Lempers, & Simons, 1989).
```

Reference List Style

The APA *Publication Manual* provides examples of 77 different reference formats for journal articles, books, book chapters, technical reports, convention presentations, dissertations, web pages, and videos, among many others. Only a few of these are presented here. When in doubt about how to construct a reference, consult the APA manual. The general format for a reference list is as follows:

1. The references are listed in alphabetical order by the first author's last name. Do not categorize references by type (i.e., books, journal articles, and so on). Note the spacing in the typing of authors' names in the examples.
2. Elements of a reference (authors' names, article title, publication data) are separated by periods.

The first line of each reference is typed flush to the left margin; subsequent lines are indented. This is called a "hanging indent." When you type the reference, it will appear as follows:

```
Bushman, B. (2006). Effects of warning and information labels on
    attraction to television violence in viewers of different ages.
    Journal of Applied Social Psychology, 36, 2073–2078. doi:10.1111/
    j.0021-9029.2006.00094.x
```

Each reference begins on a new line (think of each reference as a separate paragraph). Most word processors will allow you to easily format the paragraph with a hanging indent so you do not have to manually insert spaces on the second and subsequent lines. Using Microsoft Word, for example, begin the paragraph with Ctrl-t (Control key and letter t pressed simultaneously).

Page numbers   APA recommends using the en-dash symbol between page numbers rather than a simple hyphen. To type an en dash in Microsoft Word for Windows, press Ctrl-numeric hyphen (the hyphen on the numeric keypad); or choose Symbol from the Insert menu, click the Special Characters tab, highlight En Dash, and click Insert. To type an en dash on a Macintosh, press Option-hyphen (not the hyphen on the numeric keypad). Check with your instructor to determine if using an en dash is necessary in your papers.

Inclusion of a URL or DOI   The new edition of the *Publication Manual* has incorporated changes that reflect the fact that we only rarely access printed sources; instead, we are much more likely to access sources using websites and library or publisher databases. It is therefore often necessary to provide readers with additional information on the source that you used.

The URL is used when your source was a website. This is the full web address of the location and file name of the document as it appears in your web browser. Examples will be provided below. An important rule about typing the URL (location) of the document you are citing concerns insertion of line breaks. It is acceptable to have the URL carry over two lines if it will not fit on a single line. However, never insert a hyphen because this is not part of the address. Instead, let the address carry over with no extra hyphen.

The DOI (Digital Object Identifier) was devised by publishers to provide a unique and consistent method of identifying and locating electronic sources of information. The DOI takes the form, doi:10.xxxx/xxxxxxxxx. The DOI always begins with 10 and a period. What follows is a "prefix" that identifies the publishing organization, a slash, and then a "suffix" that the publisher assigns to the article.

You will see the DOI when you access research articles using databases such as PsycINFO. The DOI also appears on the first page of the full-text version of the article, no matter where it appears (e.g., a printed journal article or a downloaded version that might be available in either PDF or HTML format). The *Publication Manual* now recommends including the DOI in the reference if it is available.

Format for journal articles   Most journals are organized by volume and year of publication (e.g., Volume 60 of *American Psychologist* consists of journal issues published in 2005). A common confusion is whether to include the journal issue number in addition to the volume number. The rule is simple: If the issues in a volume are paginated consecutively throughout the volume, *do not* include the journal issue number. If each issue in a volume begins with page 1, the issue number should be included.

In the reference list, both the name of the journal and the volume number are italicized. Also, only the first letter of the first word in article titles is capitalized (except for proper nouns and the first word after a colon or question mark).

Following are examples:

One author—no issue number, no DOI provided

```
Newby, T. J. (1991). Classroom motivation strategies: Strategies of
    first-year teachers. Journal of Educational Psychology, 83, 195–200.
```

Two authors—use of issue number, no DOI provided

```
Greenwald-Robbins, J., & Greenwald, R. (1994). Environmental attitudes
    conceptualized through developmental theory: A qualitative analysis.
    Journal of Social Issues, 50(3), 29–47.
```

Three to seven authors—DOI provided

Hammen, C., Brennan, P. A., & Le Brocque, R. (2011). Youth depression and
early childrearing: Stress generation and intergenerational transmission
of depression. *Journal of Consulting and Clinical Psychology, 79,*
353–363. doi:10.1037/a0023536

Eight or more authors—DOI provided

Note that only names of the first six authors and the last author are provided.

Duberstein, P. R., Chapman, B. P., Tindle, H. A., Sink, K. M.,
Bamonti, P., Robbins, J., . . . Franks, P. (2011). Personality and risk
for Alzheimer's disease in adults 72 years of age and older: A 6-year
follow-up. *Psychology and Aging,* 26, 351–362. doi:10.1037/a0021377

Format for books   When a book is cited, the title of the book is italicized.
Only the first word of the title is capitalized; however, proper nouns and the first
word after a colon or question mark are also capitalized. The city and state (and
country if outside the United States) of publication and the publishing company
follow the title. Use the U.S. Postal Service two-letter abbreviation for the state
(e.g., AZ, NY, MN, TX).

One-author book

Nisbett, R. E. (2003). *The geography of thought: How Asians and
Westerners think differently...and why.* New York, NY: Free Press.

Book retrieved from a website

James, W. (1929). *The varieties of religious experience: A study in human
nature.* New York, NY: Modern Library. Retrieved from http://books.
google.com/books?id=Qi4XAAAAIAAJ&printsec=frontcover&dq=william+james
&cd=1#v=onepage&q&f=false

One-author book—second or later edition

Regan, P. C. (2008). *The mating game: A primer on love, sex, and marriage*
(2nd ed.). Thousand Oaks, CA: Sage.

Edited book

Dass-Brailsford, P. (Ed.). (2010). *Crisis and disaster counseling: Lessons
learned from Hurricane Katrina and other disasters.* Thousand Oaks, CA: Sage.

Format for articles/chapters in edited books For edited books, the reference begins with the names of the authors of the article, not the book. The title of the article follows. The name(s) of the book editor(s), the book title, the inclusive page numbers for the article, and the publication data for the book follow, in that order. Only the book title is italicized, and only the first letters of the article and book titles are capitalized. Here are some examples:

One editor

Goldstein, N. J., & Cialdini, R. B. (2009). Normative influences on consumption and conservation behaviors. In M. Wänke (Ed.), *Social psychology of consumer behavior* (pp. 273–296). New York, NY: Psychology Press.

Two editors

Bartlett, A. (2010). Gender, crime, and violence. In A. Bartlett & G. McGauley (Eds.), *Forensic mental health: Concepts, systems, and practice* (pp. 53–65). New York, NY: Oxford University Press.

Chapter from book in multivolume series

Stors, T. J. (2006). Stressful experience and learning across the lifespan. In S. T. Fiske, A. E. Kazdin, & D. L. Schachter (Eds.), *Annual review of psychology: Vol. 57* (pp. 55–85). Palo Alto, CA: Annual Reviews, Inc. doi:10.1146/annurev.psych.57.102904.190205

Format for "popular" articles The reference styles shown below should be used for articles from popular magazines and newspapers appearing in print or on websites. As a general rule, popular press articles are used sparingly (e.g., when no scientific articles on a topic can be found or to provide an example of an event that is related to your topic).

Magazine—continuous pages

Begley, S. (1995, March 27). Gray matters. *Newsweek*, 125, 48–54.

Magazine—retrieved from website

Cullen, L. T. (2006, Jan. 6). How to get smarter, one breath at a time. *Time*. Retrieved from http://www.time.com/time/magazine/article/0,9171,1147167-2,00.html

Newspaper—retrieved from website

Parker-Pope, T. (2010, May 10). The science of a happy marriage. *The New York Times.* Retrieved from http://well.blogs.nytimes.com/2010/05/10/tracking-the-science-of-commitment/

Newspaper—discontinuous pages

Cole, K. C. (1995, May 1). Way the brain works may play role in bias, experts say. *Los Angeles Times,* pp. A1, A18.

No author—retrieved from website

Substitute the title for the author in the reference:

4-year-old shot in road rage incident (2011, April 6). Retrieved from http://www.wsbtv.com/news/27443049/detail.html

The citation in the body of the paper uses the first few words of the title in quotation marks along with the year:

Road rage can in fact have serious consequences ("4-year old shot," 2011).

Format for papers and posters presented at conferences

Occasionally you may need to cite an unpublished paper or poster that was presented at a professional meeting. Provide the year and month of the conference as well as the name and location of the conference.

Conference paper

Gates, K., & Rovine, M. (2009, April). Modeling mother-infant interactions as dynamic processes. *Paper presented at the meeting of the Society for Research on Child Development,* Denver, CO.

Poster presentation

Storm, B. C., & White, H. A. (2009, May). ADHD and retrieval-induced forgetting: Evidence for a deficit in inhibitory control. *Poster presented at the annual convention of the Association for Psychological Science,* Boston, MA.

Secondary sources   Sometimes you need to cite an article, book, or book chapter that you read about through a textbook, an abstract, or a book review. Although it is always preferable to read primary sources, sometimes you may have to cite a secondary source when the primary source cannot be found in a timely manner (with Internet searches, this is becoming less likely!).

Suppose you wish to cite an article that you read about in a book. When you refer to the article in your paper, you need to say that it was cited in the book. In the following example, a paper by Conway and Pleydell-Pearce is the secondary source:

> Conway and Pleydell-Pearce (as cited in Woll, 2002) suggested that auto-
> biographical memory . . .

In the reference list at the end of the paper, simply provide the reference for the primary source you used (in this case, the 2002 book by Woll).

Sometimes you may need to cite the abstract of an article that you found in a search of PsycINFO or another database. Although it is preferable to find the original article, the original article may not be available online or at any nearby libraries or is published in a foreign language with only the abstract available in English. Here is an example:

> King, Y., & Parker, D. (2008). Driving violations, aggression and perceived
> consensus. *European Review of Applied Psychology, 58,* 43–49. Abstract
> retrieved from PsycINFO database. (Accession No. 2007-19875-005)

In this example, the complete reference is given. However, you also provide the crucial information that you have only examined the abstract of the article and you found the abstract through a search of the PsycINFO database. The accession number is provided with the abstract.

Citing specific web documents/pages   Many web pages were written just for the web and should not be considered journal articles *or* books. For example, a document prepared by David Kenny provides information on mediating variables. Here you would cite the title of the document and retrieval information. To cite this document, your text might read as follows:

> Kenny (2009) describes a procedure for using multiple regression to
> examine causal models that include mediating variables.

Your actual reference to the document would be

> Kenny, D. A. (2009). *Mediation.* Retrieved from http://davidakenny.net/cm/
> mediate.htm

Note that the reference includes the author, a date that was provided in the document, and a title. Some web documents do not include a date; in this case, simply substitute n.d. in parentheses to indicate that there is no date. However, documents that may be regularly updated should include the date that you accessed the website. This will make it clear to others that you may have accessed a different version than the one that is currently available. Here is an example of how to do that using the Kenny reference:

Kenny, D. A. (2009). *Mediation.* Retrieved March 6, 2010 from http://davidakenny.net/cm/mediate.htm

ABBREVIATIONS

Abbreviations are not used extensively in APA-style papers. They can be distracting because the reader must constantly try to translate the abbreviation into its full meaning. However, APA style does allow for the use of abbreviations that are accepted as words in the dictionary (specifically, Webster's *Collegiate Dictionary*). These include IQ, REM, ESP, and AIDS.

Certain well-known terms may be abbreviated when it would make reading easier, but the full meaning should be given when first used in the paper. Examples of commonly used abbreviations are

MMPI	Minnesota Multiphasic Personality Inventory
STM	short-term memory
CS	conditioned stimulus
RT	reaction time
CVC	consonant-vowel-consonant
ANOVA	analysis of variance

Statistical terms are sometimes used in their abbreviated or symbol form. These are always italicized in a manuscript. For example,

M	mean
SD	standard deviation
Mdn	median
df	degrees of freedom
n	number of individuals in a group or experimental condition
N	total number of participants or respondents
p	probability (significance) level
SS	sum of squares

MS	mean square
F	value of *F* in analysis of variance
r	Pearson correlation coefficient
R	multiple correlation coefficient

The following scientific abbreviations for various measurement units are frequently used:

cm	centimeter
g	gram
hr	hour
in	inch
kg	kilogram
km	kilometer
m	meter
mg	milligram
min	minute
ml	milliliter
mm	millimeter
ms	millisecond
s	second

Finally, certain abbreviations of Latin and Middle English terms are regularly used in papers, although the APA manual states that they should be used only in parenthetical material. Some of these abbreviations and their meanings are given below:

cf.	compare	(from Latin *confer*)
e.g.,	for example	(from Latin *exempli gratia*)
etc.	and so forth	(from Latin *et cetera*)
i.e.,	that is	(from Latin *id est*)
viz.	namely	
vs.	versus	

SOME GRAMMATICAL CONSIDERATIONS

Transition Words and Phrases

One way to produce a clearly written research report is to pay attention to how you connect sentences within a paragraph and connect paragraphs within a section. The transitions between sentences and paragraphs should be smooth and consistent with the line of reasoning. Some commonly used transition words and phrases and their functions are described in this section.

Adverbs
Adverbs can be used as introductory words in sentences. However, you must use them to convey their implied meanings.

Adverb	*Implied meaning*
(Un)fortunately	It is (un)fortunate that . . .
Similarly	In a similar manner . . .
Certainly	It is certain that . . .
Clearly	It is clear that . . .

One adverb that is frequently misused as an introductory or transition word is *hopefully. Hopefully* means "in a hopeful manner," *not* "it is hoped that. . . ."

Incorrect: Hopefully, this is not the case.

Correct: I hope this is not the case.

Words suggesting contrast
Some words and phrases suggest a contrast or contradiction between what was written immediately before and what is now being written:

Between sentences	*Within sentences*
By contrast,	whereas
On the other hand,	although
However,	but

The words in the left list refer to the previous sentence. The words in the right list connect phrases within a sentence; that is, they refer to another point in the same sentence.

Words suggesting a series of ideas
The following words and phrases suggest that information after the transition word is related or similar to information in the sentence:

First	In addition	Last	Further
Second	Additionally	Finally	Moreover
Third	Then	Also	Another

Words suggesting implication
These words and phrases indicate that the information following the transition word is implied by or follows from the previous information:

Therefore	If . . . then
It follows that	Thus
In conclusion	Then

When you use transition words, be sure that they convey the meaning you intend. Sprinkling them around to begin sentences leads to confusion on the reader's part and defeats your purpose.

Troublesome Words and Phrases

"That" versus "which"   *That* and *which* are relative pronouns that introduce subordinate clauses and reflect the relationship of the subordinate clause to the main clause. *That* clauses are called restrictive clauses and are essential to the meaning of the sentence; *which* clauses are nonrestrictive and simply add more information. Note the different meanings of the same sentence using *that* and *which:*

> The mice that performed well in the first trial were used in the second trial.
>
> The mice, which performed well in the first trial, were used in the second trial.

The first sentence states that only mice that performed well in the first trial were used in the second. The second sentence states that all the mice were used in the second trial and they also happened to perform well in the first trial.

"While" versus "since"   *While* and *since* are subordinate conjunctions that also introduce subordinate clauses. To increase clarity in scientific writing, the APA manual suggests that *while* and *since* should be used only to refer to time. *While* is used to describe simultaneous events, and *since* is used to refer to a subsequent event:

> The participants waited together while their personality tests were scored.
>
> Since the study by Elder (1974), many studies have been published on this topic.

The APA manual suggests other conjunctions to use to link phrases that do not describe temporal events. *Although, whereas,* and *but* can be used in place of *while,* and *because* should be substituted for *since.*

> *Incorrect:* While the study was well designed, the report was poorly written.
>
> *Correct:* Although the study was well designed, the report was poorly written.

"Effect" versus "affect"   A common error in student reports is incorrect use of *effect* and *affect. Effect* is a noun that is used in scientific reports to mean "what is produced by a cause," as in the sentence: "The movie had a strong effect on me." *Affect* can be a noun or a verb. As a noun it means emotion, as in "The patient seemed depressed but she displayed very little affect." As a verb it means "to have an influence on," as in "The listeners' responses were affected by the music they heard."

Incorrect: The independent variable effected their responses.

Correct: The independent variable affected their responses.

Incorrect: The independent variable had only a weak affect on the participants' behavior.

Correct: The independent variable had only a weak effect on the participants' behavior.

Singular and plural

The following words are often misused. The left list shows singular nouns requiring singular verb forms. The right list contains plural nouns that must be used with plural verbs.

Singular	Plural
datum	data
stimulus	stimuli
analysis	analyses
phenomenon	phenomena
medium	media
hypothesis	hypotheses
schema	schemas

Probably the most frequently misused word is *data*.

Incorrect: The data *was* coded for computer analysis.

Correct: The data *were* coded for computer analysis.

Some spelling considerations

Here are words that are frequently misspelled or used with incorrect capitalization:

questionnaire
database
e-journal
e-mail
web
Internet
URL

REPORTING NUMBERS AND STATISTICS

Virtually all research papers report numbers: number of participants, number of groups, the values of statistics such as t, F, or r. Should you use numbers (e.g., *43*), or should you use words (e.g., *forty-three*)? The general rule is to use words when expressing the numbers zero through nine but to use numbers for 10 and above. There are some important qualifications, however.

If you start a sentence with a number, you should use words even if the number is 10 or larger (e.g., *Eighty-five student teachers participated in the study.*). Starting a sentence with a number is often awkward, especially with large numbers. Therefore, you should try to revise the sentence to avoid the problem (e.g., *The participants were 85 students enrolled in teaching credential classes.*).

When numbers both above and below 10 are being compared in the same sentence, use numerals for both (e.g., *Participants read either 8 or 16 paragraphs.*). However, this sentence contains an appropriate mix of numbers and words: *Participants read eight paragraphs and then answered 20 multiple-choice questions.* The sentence is correct because the paragraphs and the questions are different entities and so are not being compared.

When reporting a percentage, always use numerals followed by a percent sign except when beginning a sentence. This is true regardless of whether the number is less than 10 (e.g., *Only 6% of the computer games appealed to females.*) or greater than 10 (e.g., *When using this technique, 85% of the participants improved their performance.*).

Always use numbers when describing ages (e.g., *5-year-olds*), points on a scale (e.g., *a 3 on a 5-point scale*), units of measurement (e.g., *the children stood 2 m from the target*), sample size (e.g., *6 girls and 6 boys were assigned to each study condition*), and statistics (e.g., *the mean score in the no-model group was 3.10*). An odd but sensible exception to the word–number rule occurs when two different types of numbers must appear together. An example is *Teachers identified fifteen 7-year-olds as the most aggressive.* This sentence avoids an awkward juxtaposition of two numbers.

For a multiplication sign, use either a lowercase x or the multiplication symbol used by your word processor. This is true whether you are describing a mathematical operation or a factorial design (e.g., *a 2 × 2 design*). For a minus sign, use a hyphen with a space both before and after the hyphen.

Finally, you need to know about presenting statistical results within your paper. As noted previously, statistical terms are abbreviated and typed with italics (e.g., M, r, t, F). In addition, when reporting the results of a statistical significance test, provide the name of the test, the degrees of freedom, the value of the test statistic, and the probability level. Here are two examples of sentences that describe statistical results:

```
As predicted, participants in the high-anxiety condition took longer to
recognize the words (M = 2.63, SD = .42) than did the individuals in the
low-anxiety condition (M = 1.42, SD = .36), t(20) = 2.54, p = .02.
```

> Job satisfaction scores were significantly correlated with marital satis-
> faction, $r(50) = .48$, $p < .01$.

Recall that exact probabilities are reported using two or three decimal places. However, the computer printout may not indicate very small probabilities so you should use the $<$ (less than) symbol for probabilities less than .01, as follows: $p < .01$. Many researchers prefer to report probabilities using three decimal places (e.g., $p = .037$) because the major statistical software applications provide that level of precision. In that case, use $p < .001$ with very small probabilities.

Pay attention to the way statistics are described in the articles you read. You will find that you can vary your descriptions of results to best fit your data and presentation, as well as vary your sentence constructions.

Finalizing Your Paper

Use the APA Checklist (see inside back cover) to doublecheck that formats in your report are correct. Before printing your final copy, use your spelling and grammar checker; then give the paper one last look to find any possible errors.

CONCLUSION

When you have completed your research report, you should feel proud of your effort. You have considered past research on a problem, conducted a research project, analyzed the results, and reported the findings. Such a research effort may result in a publication or presentation at a convention. This is not the most important part of your research, however. What is most important is that you have acquired new knowledge and that your curiosity has been aroused so you will want to learn even more.

PAPER AND POSTER PRESENTATIONS

Students present their research findings in many different ways: in class, at regional and national meetings of psychology organizations, and at conferences specifically designed to highlight student research. Psi Chi, the International Honor Society in Psychology, maintains a list of such meetings at http://www.psichi.org/conventions.

The presentation may take the form of a talk to an audience or a poster presentation in which individuals may read the poster and engage in conversation with the presenter. The Psi Chi conventions web page includes guidelines for preparing papers and posters. We will explore the major points, but any student planning a presentation may wish to obtain more detailed advice.

Paper Presentations

Paper presentations are only about 10 to 12 minutes long, and people in attendance receive lots of information in many sessions of the meeting. The major thing to remember, then, is that you should attempt to convey only a few major ideas about why and how you conducted your research. You can avoid describing the details of past research findings, discussing exactly how you did your data analysis, or listing every step in your procedure. Remember that your audience wants the "big picture," so make sure that you do not use technical jargon. Instead, use clear language to convey the reason you conducted the research, the general methods used, and the major results. You should try to provide a summary at the end, along with the conclusions you have reached about the meaning of the results.

The Psi Chi guidelines also advise you to write the presentation in advance but not to read it to your actual audience. You can use the written version for practice and timing. Remember that many people in the audience would like a written summary to which they can refer later. It is a good idea to bring copies of a summary that includes your name, the title of the presentation, when and where it was presented, and how you can be contacted.

Posters

A poster session consists of a fairly large number of presenters who are provided with space to display poster material. During the poster session, members of the audience may stop to read the poster, and some may have questions or comments. The chance to have conversations about your research with people who find your work interesting is the most valuable feature of a poster session.

The conference organizers will provide information on the amount of space available for each poster. Typical dimensions are 3 to 4 feet high and 6 to 8 feet wide. The poster materials will usually be divided up into areas of (1) title, name, affiliation, (2) abstract, (3) introduction information, (4) method, (5) results, along with tables and figures, and (6) conclusions. An example poster layout is provided in Figure A.2. The Psi Chi website has other suggested layouts. The actual construction of the poster may consist of a series of separate pages or a single professionally printed poster using large format printing technology.

Avoid providing too much detail—often a bulleted list of major points will be most effective. One or two easy-to-read figures can also be very helpful. There are probably no more than two major points that you would like someone to remember after viewing your poster. Make sure those points are obvious. The font that you use should be large enough to be read from a distance (usually the text will be 18 point font). Color can be used to enhance the attractiveness of the display. Remember to bring copies of a summary that includes the date and location of the conference.

FIGURE A.2
A sample poster

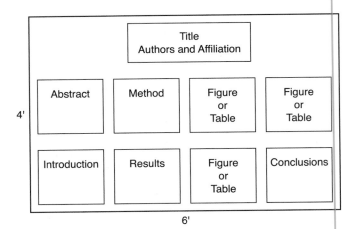

SAMPLE PAPER

The remainder of this appendix consists of a typed manuscript of a paper that was published in a professional journal. This is intended to be a useful guide when you write your own reports in APA style. Read through the manuscript, paying particular attention to the general format, and make sure you understand the rules concerning page numbering, section headings, reference citation, and the format of figures. Writing your first research report is always a challenging task. It will become easier as you read the research of others and gain practice by writing reports of your own.

The remainder of this appendix consists of a typed manuscript of a paper that was published in a professional journal. You can easily find other such manuscripts with an Internet search using a term such as *APA style example paper*. Example papers such as this are intended to help you write your own reports in APA style. Read through the manuscript, paying particular attention to the general format, and make sure you understand the rules concerning page numbering, section headings, reference citation, and formatting figures. Writing your first research report is always a challenging task. It will become easier as you read the research of others and gain practice by writing reports of your own.

Dr. Janet Polivy graciously gave permission to adapt the paper to illustrate elements of APA style. The comments at the side alert you to features of APA style that you will need to know about when writing your own papers. Be aware, though, that every paper will include slightly different types of information depending on the particular topic, method, and results. Your paper will follow the general guidelines of APA style, but many of the details will be determined by the needs of your study.

You may note that the title of this paper is longer than the 12 words recommended by APA style (many journals do not enforce the word length rule). A briefer title might be *Effects of Perceived Portion Size on Eating and Emotion*. A problem with this shorter title is that a search for articles with *restrained eaters* in the title would not find this article; a few extra words can often be useful to future researchers.

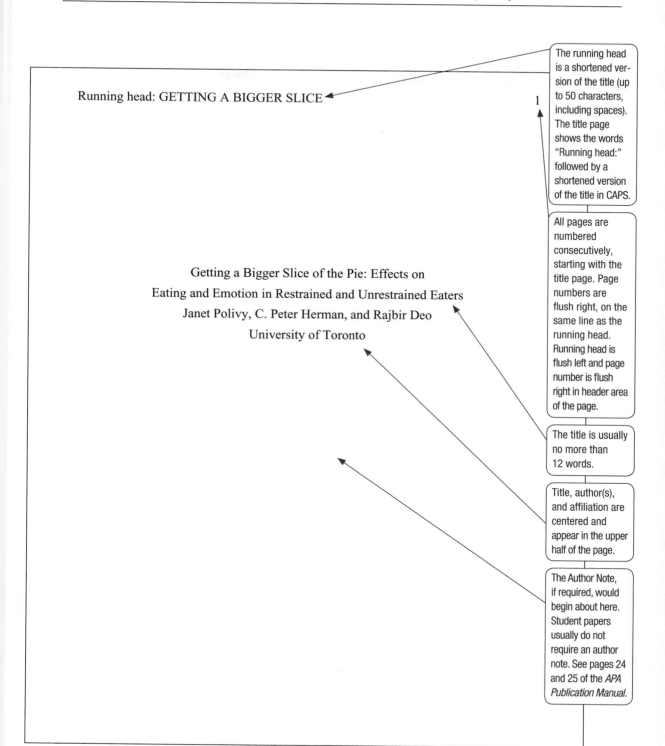

Running head: GETTING A BIGGER SLICE

1

Getting a Bigger Slice of the Pie: Effects on
Eating and Emotion in Restrained and Unrestrained Eaters
Janet Polivy, C. Peter Herman, and Rajbir Deo
University of Toronto

The running head
is a shortened ver-
sion of the title (up
to 50 characters,
including spaces).
The title page
shows the words
"Running head:"
followed by a
shortened version
of the title in CAPS.

All pages are
numbered
consecutively,
starting with the
title page. Page
numbers are
flush right, on the
same line as the
running head.
Running head is
flush left and page
number is flush
right in header area
of the page.

The title is usually
no more than
12 words.

Title, author(s),
and affiliation are
centered and
appear in the upper
half of the page.

The Author Note,
if required, would
begin about here.
Student papers
usually do not
require an author
note. See pages 24
and 25 of the *APA
Publication Manual.*

The running head identified on the title page should be carried forward on every subsequent page. It should remain flush left in all uppercase letters. The words "Running head" are deleted on subsequent pages.

There is no paragraph indentation in the abstract.

Abstract begins on a new page with the word "Abstract" centered.

The abstract is generally 150–250 words in length.

GETTING A BIGGER SLICE   2

Abstract

We investigated the influence of perceptions of the portion size of food on subsequent eating by restrained and unrestrained eaters. In the present study, all participants were served a same-sized slice of pizza. For one-third of participants, their slice appeared larger than the slice being served to another ostensible participant, another third perceived their slice as smaller, and the final third did not see a second slice. All participants then proceeded to "taste and rate" cookies in an ad lib eating opportunity. A significant interaction reflected the fact that when the pizza slice was perceived as large, restrained eaters tended to eat more cookies whereas unrestrained eaters tended to eat less cookies. Emotion data suggest that the differential responses of restrained and unrestrained eaters to the belief that they have overeaten relative to another eater influenced their subsequent dissimilar ad lib eating behavior.

GETTING A BIGGER SLICE   3

Getting a Bigger Slice of the Pie: Effects on Eating and Emotion in Restrained
and Unrestrained Eaters

We often eat one food followed by another (e.g., main course and then dessert).
How much we eat of the later food probably depends to a large extent on our intake
of the earlier food. In the laboratory, we refer to the earlier food as a "preload." The
effects of food preloads on subsequent eating are complex: Chronic dieters or restrained
eaters generally respond quite differently than nondieters or unrestrained eaters do.
Whereas unrestrained eaters typically compensate by eating less after a larger preload
than after a smaller one, restrained eaters often "counter-regulate," eating more after
a large preload than after a small preload or after no preload at all (Adams & Leary,
2007; Herman, Polivy, & Esses, 1987; Polivy, Heatherton, & Herman, 1988; Polivy,
Herman, Hackett, & Kuleshnyk, 1986). Presumably, the larger preload is more likely to
sabotage the restrained eater's diet for that day, undermining motivation for continued
restraint and unleashing disinhibited eating (possibly potentiated by chronic perceived
deprivation). If the preload is actually large and fattening, it is likely to produce
disinhibited eating by restrained eaters (Herman et al., 1987; McCann, Perri, Nezu,
& Lowe, 1992; Polivy et al., 1986, 1988), but disinhibition may be observed even
when the restrained eater is merely led to believe that the preload is high in calories or
otherwise forbidden (Polivy, 1976; Spencer & Fremouw, 1979) or when the restrained
eater draws that implication from the nature of the food itself (Knight & Boland, 1989).

Previous studies have manipulated the perceived size of the preload (holding
actual size or caloric content constant) by either telling participants that the
preloads are high in calories (Polivy, 1976; Spencer & Fremouw, 1979) or by
implication. For example, Knight and Boland (1989), served iso-caloric preloads
of milkshake or a cottage cheese and fruit mixture. Restrained eaters displayed
disinhibition only when served milkshake, because they regard milkshake as
inherently more caloric than the salad-like cottage cheese and fruit mixture. More

---

Marginal notes:

Punctuation such as periods and commas appear inside the quotes. Punctuation such as question marks, exclamation marks, colons, and semicolons that are not part of the quote appear outside the quotes.

Standard form: Citation of two authors, parenthetically (Author & Author, Year).

Standard form: Citation of three to five authors, first citation, parenthetically (Author, Author, & Author, Year).

When several references are cited together, alphabetize, and separate with a semicolon.

Standard form: Citation of three or more authors, after first citation in text, parenthetically (Author et al., Year).

Standard form: Citation of a single author, parenthetically (Author, Year).

GETTING A BIGGER SLICE   4

recently, Pliner and Zec (2007) showed that thinking about a preload as a meal (rather than as a snack) makes people perceive the preload as higher in calories and affects eating accordingly.

The present study was designed to further extend the exploration of the effects of perceived preload/portion size on eating and, moreover, to do this in a more externally valid meal setting. In order to understand the source of these effects, we included measures of affective responses, as it has been shown that affect influences eating differently for restrained and unrestrained eaters (Polivy & Herman, 1999), and eating, especially eating what is seen as a large amount, affects emotions differently in restrained and unrestrained eaters (Polivy & Herman, 2005).

We hypothesized that even with the preload/meal held constant, restrained eaters who regard the portion as larger will subsequently eat more than will those who regard it as normal sized or small, because the "large" portion is more likely to break their diets and lead to disinhibited eating. We also predicted that unrestrained eaters will eat less after a perceived large portion than after what they perceive to be a normal-sized meal, and less after a portion perceived as normal sized than after one perceived as small. In the present study, all participants received an identical, standard light lunch meal, but some were led to perceive the portion they received as large and some were led to perceive the portion as small simply by means of social comparison (or more accurately, perceptual contrast). If someone gets a larger portion than yours, your own portion may appear to be "small," whereas, if someone gets a portion that is smaller than yours, your own portion may appear to be "large."

Method

Participants

The participants were 106 female undergraduate students enrolled in an introductory psychology class at a large university. The participants were recruited via an experimental database, where they could sign up for a study entitled "Market Taste

---

Standard form for citation of two authors, in text: Name and Name (Year).

The Method section begins immediately after the Introduction (no new page). The word "Method" is centered and boldface.

*Subsection headings such as "Participants" are **boldface**, typed flush to the left margin, and set alone on the line.*

Use numerals to express numbers 10 and above.

GETTING A BIGGER SLICE   5

Test Study." Each experimental session lasted 1 hr; participants received credit toward a course requirement for their participation.

Materials

Food. Extra-large uncut cheese pizza was ordered from a local pizza chain for each day of experimentation. The slices were reheated in a microwave oven before they were served to the participants. Any leftover pizza was stored in a freezer for use on another day. Frozen cookie dough (from a manufacturer who supplies "fresh-baked" cookies to local restaurants) was stored in a freezer and used to bake bite-sized cookies regularly throughout the week. Three different types of cookies were baked as needed: oatmeal raisin, chocolate chip, and double chocolate chip.

Questionnaires. Pre- and post-pizza rating scales were completed by all participants immediately after the manipulation and again after the pizza but before the cookie taste test. The pizza rating scales included a section from the PANAS (Positive and Negative Affect Schedule; Watson, Clark, & Tellegen, 1988), which was designed to measure the participants' negative affect. Participants described their negative emotional states such as "guilty" and "angry" using rating scales ranging from 1 for *very slightly or not at all* to 5 for *extremely*. Other questions assessed hunger and various aspects of the pizza that they were about to eat or had just eaten using a 9-point Likert-type scale. These questions included a manipulation check that asked participants to rate the portion size (rating from 1 for *too small* to 5 for *just right* to 9 for *too big*). The questions were answered before and after eating the pizza (with wording changed appropriately). In addition, participants were asked at the end of the study to what extent they had noticed any difference in the size of the pizza slices ("How did your slice of pizza compare to the slice received by the other person in the study?" Response options were *smaller*, *the same*, and *larger*).

Restraint scale. The 10-item Herman and Polivy Revised Restraint Scale (Herman, Polivy, & Silver, 1979) was used to determine restraint status. Participants who scored 15 or less on the restraint scale were classified as unrestrained eaters, whereas participants who scored above 15 were classified as restrained eaters.

Use numerals to express numbers that are immediately followed by a unit of measurement (in this case, hr for hour). Also abbreviate min (minute), s (second), ms (millisecond). Do not abbreviate day, week, month, year.

This section describes the measures and materials used to conduct the study. They make up a sort of "ingredients" list for the study.

Define unfamiliar acronyms when they are first used.

This additional level of subheadings begins the paragraph. They are **boldface**, indented, and separated from the text of the paragraph with a period.

The anchors of scales (e.g., *very slightly or not at all*) are italicized.

GETTING A BIGGER SLICE   6

Procedure

Female participants were recruited for this study through a psychology experimental website advertisement that specified that the participants must have no food allergies, must not be lactose intolerant, and should refrain from eating for up to 3 hr prior to their experimental session.

Each participant was informed that she would be given a light vegetarian cheese-pizza lunch in order to ensure that each participant had the same taste experience and same level of fullness before completing taste ratings for market research. She was told that she would be sampling various food products that were being proposed for the market by a large food company that targeted the university-student population. The participant was also informed that she would be completing some questionnaires to assess her mood and other variables to ensure that these factors were not influencing her food ratings. Furthermore, the participant was told that she would be discussing her food ratings with another female participant in a brief discussion at the end of their session. She then signed the consent form.

Participants were randomly assigned to one of three pizza-slice conditions: smaller slice, larger slice, and no information. Regardless of which condition the participant was in, she always received a standard slice of pizza (1/6 of the pizza), but the size of the "other participant's" slice was varied. Each pizza was cut into six pieces consisting of four standard-sized slices (1/6 of the pizza), one larger slice (1/3 larger than a standard-sized slice), and one smaller slice (1/3 smaller than the standard slice). In order to ensure that each slice was consistently cut for all pizzas used in the study, the appropriate sized slices were drawn onto a piece of paper and cut out to be used as templates for all pizzas. Thus, in the "smaller" condition, the participant received a standard-sized slice of pizza, while the "other female participant" was supposedly receiving the slice 1/3 larger than the standard slice. Similarly, participants in the "larger" condition received the standard slice of pizza, while the "other female participant" appeared to be receiving the slice 1/3 smaller than the standard slice.

This section describes exactly how the study was conducted.

Numbers less than 10 are expressed as words.

GETTING A BIGGER SLICE 7

In the "no information" control condition, participants were given a standard-sized slice of pizza, with no indication of the "other female participant's" slice.

When the experimenter presented the participant with the pizza slices, the pizza slices were placed on a tray with a glass of water next to each slice and brought into the experimental room. Each participant in the "smaller" condition was presented with her standard-sized slice of pizza next to the 1/3 larger slice belonging to the "other female participant," which was identified as such as it was situated further away from her. Each participant in the "larger condition" saw her standard-sized slice along with the "other" female participant's smaller slice. In the "no information" control condition, the participant was presented only with her standard-sized slice, along with a glass of water. The experimenter then left the room, leaving the slices in the room and explaining that she had to retrieve a questionnaire for the participants. The experimenter left the room for exactly 1 min, allowing a sufficient amount of time for the participant to observe the slices and perceive the differences in their sizes. When the experimenter returned, the participant's slice and water were placed on the table in front of her and the pre-pizza rating scale was handed to the participant. She was asked to complete the questionnaire before eating her pizza slice. The experimenter then left the room with the "other participant's" slice.

The participant was given 7 min to complete the preeating questionnaire and to eat her entire pizza slice (supposedly to ensure equal fullness in all participants), after which time the experimenter returned to the experimental room and handed the participant another set of questionnaires (to maintain the cover story). These questionnaires included the post-pizza scales. The participant was instructed to ring a bell when she had completed the questionnaires. At that time, the experimenter returned with three heaping (preweighed) plates of each of three types of cookie and another glass of water, plus three cookie-rating sheets (one for each cookie type). Tasting these cookies was ostensibly the principal purpose of the experiment, but the cookies were actually provided as a measure of ad lib consumption. In order to

Numbers that are immediately followed by a unit of measurement are expressed as numerals, as are numbers that represent time.

measure how many cookies the participants ate, the cookies were weighed prior to the experimental session and again after the "taste-test task." A heaping amount of each cookie type (oatmeal raisin, chocolate chip, and double chocolate chip) was placed onto one of three separate plates and the weight of each plate was measured and recorded. The three plates of cookies were placed on the table in front of the participant, with oatmeal-raisin cookies always being first, chocolate-chip cookies second, and double chocolate-chip cookies third. The participant was instructed that she would now be participating in the taste-test portion of the study, wherein she would sample three different types of cookies that were about to be released on the market by a large food company that marketed its snack foods to the university-aged population. The participant was instructed to begin with the oatmeal-raisin cookies and take as many cookies as she required to be very sure of her taste ratings of the cookies. She was told to sample the oatmeal-raisin cookies first, followed by the chocolate-chip cookies, and finally the double chocolate-chip cookies. It was emphasized that once she had completed the ratings for one cookie type, she was not to go back and resample the previous cookie type and she was not to change her ratings once she had moved on to a "new taste." The water was provided to permit the participant to "cleanse her palate" as she moved from cookie to cookie. Moreover, the participant was reminded to be sure of her ratings since she would be comparing her food ratings with the "other female participant" at the end of the session. Finally, the participant was informed that once she was finished making her ratings, there were plenty of cookies and she was free to have as many more of any type as she liked, as long as she did not change any ratings. After the instructions were clear to the participant, the experimenter left the room for 10 min.

The experimenter reentered the room with the final set of questionnaires to be completed (including the restraint scale). The cookie plates were removed from the room, where they were reweighed without the participants' knowledge, in order to measure how many grams of cookies the participant had consumed. When the

GETTING A BIGGER SLICE   9

participant had completed the last set of questionnaires, her height and weight were measured and recorded. The participant was debriefed as to the purpose of the study. She was also asked if she had noticed the size difference in the pizza slices that had been presented, when she last ate, and what she ate at that time. She was thanked and asked some questions about the experiment so that she could receive credit for her psychology course before being dismissed. The study was thus conducted in accordance with ethical principles and had full institutional ethical review and approval.

Results

Participant Characteristics

A series of 2 (restrained versus unrestrained) $\times$ 3 (control, "small slice," "large slice") ANOVAs indicated the usual restraint main effect on BMI, $F(1,98) = 9.77$, $p = .002$, with restrained eaters having higher BMIs ($M = 24.27$) than unrestrained eaters ($M = 21.63$). There was no effect of condition and no significant interaction; as well, there were no restraint or condition differences in preeating hunger.

Manipulation Checks

On the pre- and post-pizza questionnaires, participants were asked about the quantity of pizza that they had been served. A 2 (restrained versus unrestrained) $\times$ 3 (control, "small slice," "large slice") ANOVA on each of these questions yielded only main effects for condition, preeating $F(2,97) = 5.25$, $p = .008$, and posteating $F(2,100) = 8.16$, $p < .001$. In both analyses, the "small" slice was rated as close to 5 (which corresponded to "just right") ($Mpre = 5.22$; $Mpost = 5.43$), the control/no information slice was seen as bigger than the small one ($Mpre = 5.69$; $Mpost = 6.03$), and the "large" slice was seen as bigger than either of the others ($Mpre = 6.33$; $Mpost = 6.80$). All differences were significant at the .05 level.

Cookie Intake

A 2 (Restraint: restrained, unrestrained) $\times$ 3 (Condition: control, "small slice," "large slice") ANOVA on the amount of cookies eaten (in grams) yielded no main effects of restraint or condition; however, there was a significant interaction, $F(2,100) =$

The Results section begins immediately following the Method section. The word "Results" is centered and **boldface**.

When the outcome of a statistical test is presented, the name of the test is italicized and followed by the degrees of freedom in parentheses. The *p* refers to the probability of obtaining the results if the null hypothesis is correct.

Generally, exact probabilities are shown except when *p* < .001. Sometimes it is appropriate to use "ns" to indicate that a result is nonsignificant.

Statistical symbols, such as *M* for the mean, are italicized.

3.51, $p = .034$, $\eta^2 = 0.066$. Post hoc t tests indicated that whereas neither restrained nor unrestrained participants in the "small slice" condition differed from those in the control condition or from each other, restrained and unrestrained eaters in the "large slice" condition differed significantly from each other, $t(100) = 2.98$, $p = .005$. In addition, although not significant, restrained eaters in the "large slice" condition ate marginally more than did restrained eaters in the control condition, $t(100) = 1.82$, $p = .075$, and unrestrained eaters in the "large slice" condition ate marginally less than did unrestrained eaters in the control condition, $t(100) = 1.66$, $p = .10$ (see Table 1 for all means and standard deviations).

Negative Affect

A 2 × 3 ANOVA on total negative affect before eating the pizza (but after the manipulation of perceived portion size) yielded no significant main effects, but there was a significant interaction between restraint and condition, $F(2,100) = 3.40$, $p = .037$, $\eta^2 = 0.066$ (see Figure 1). The only significant differences found in the post hoc t tests were between the "small" versus "large" conditions for the unrestrained eaters, with those receiving the large slice feeling more negative emotion than those receiving the small slice, $t(100) = 2.25$, $p = .026$, and between restrained and unrestrained eaters in the "small" condition, $t(100) = 2.03$, $p = .045$, with restrained eaters feeling more negative affect than did unrestrained eaters. The analysis comparing restrained and unrestrained participants in the "large" slice condition indicated a trend in the opposite direction, $t(100) = 1.49$, $p = .14$, as did the analysis comparing "small" versus "large" for restrained eaters, $t(100) = 1.41$, $p = .17$. The negative affect ratings made after eating the pizza were no longer significantly different. Also, there were no significant effects on hunger ratings either before or after eating the pizza.

Discussion

Participants clearly perceived the size of their portion of pizza differently as a function of whether they saw a comparison slice and what they saw in the comparison. When they saw their slice next to a larger one, they perceived their slice as smaller

---

Greek letter eta, an indicator of effect size (squared value).

Any figures or tables must be mentioned in the text.

The Discussion section is used to list and comment upon the implications of the results of the study. The Discussion section immediately follows the Results section. The word "Discussion" is centered and **boldface**.

GETTING A BIGGER SLICE   11

than did those who did not see a comparison slice; and when they saw their slice next to a smaller slice they perceived it as larger than did participants who saw only their own slice. The change in perception occurred despite the fact that not only were all participants given the same-sized slice, but this size is the standard slice sold on campus and at all other outlets of the major pizza chain that supplied the pizza.

Based simply on these different perceptions of the identical portion, participants went on to eat different amounts, as shown by the significant interaction between restraint and condition. Those who saw their pizza slice as smaller ate the same amount of cookies as did those who did not have a comparison (regardless of restraint status), but the cookie intake of those who thought that they had eaten a larger slice of pizza was affected by this perception (in different ways depending on restraint status). That the effect was more a matter of the "large slice" condition changing intake somewhat (relative to control) than of the "small slice" condition changing intake (relative to control) was probably due to the fact that in the "small slice" condition, the slice was seen as close to—indeed, slightly more than—"just right," but the "large slice" was seen as significantly larger than "just right." In other words, it was the pizza in the "large slice" condition that was seen as unusually large, rather than the pizza in the "small slice" condition being seen as unusually small.

> Quotation marks are placed after the period.

The direction of the effect in the "large slice" condition depended on restraint status, as was reflected in the significant interaction. Restrained and unrestrained eaters ate the same amount of cookies in the control and "small slice" conditions, but unrestrained eaters tended to eat less in the "large slice" condition, whereas restrained eaters tended to eat more in the "large slice" condition. (Restrained eaters ate significantly more than did unrestrained eaters in the "large slice" condition.) In other words, unrestrained eaters compensated by eating less cookies if they thought that they had eaten a lot of pizza, whereas restrained eaters counter-regulated and ate more cookies when they thought that they had already overeaten on pizza. This pattern corresponds to the effect obtained in previous research when preload size

GETTING A BIGGER SLICE   12

was actually manipulated or when perceived preload size was manipulated by telling participants that the preloads varied in caloric value (Polivy, 1976) or by implying that the preloads differed in caloric value because they were either "forbidden" or "allowed" foods (e.g., Knight & Boland, 1989). While subtle manipulations such as the smell of food have been shown to induce restrained eaters to eat more (Fedoroff, Polivy, & Herman, 1997, 2003; Jansen & Van den Hout, 1991), the present study involved arguably the subtlest manipulation yet. Nothing was said about size or caloric value of the preload, and the identical preload/meal was used in all conditions; only a visual comparison to someone else's smaller portion acted to render one's own portion relatively large, with predictable effects on subsequent intake. Moreover, the present "preload" was actually a meal ("light lunch") rather than extraneous eating. However, even simply perceiving one's meal as "larger than just right" seems to have been enough to push eating in opposite directions for restrained versus unrestrained eaters. Eating was thus more strongly influenced by social comparison and the perception this fostered (I'm eating more than she is) than by actual portion size.

> APA strongly encourages writers to use past tense when reporting procedures and results.

    The fact that restrained eaters ate somewhat more in the "large slice" condition is what we have come to expect from the literature in which restrained eaters typically overeat after a large preload (or a preload perceived as large). That they did not eat less in the "small slice" condition than in the control condition was consistent with the finding that restrained eaters' eating is "dichotomous": they ate either a small, reasonable amount, when they were not disinhibited (i.e., when the preload was not seen as large, or they were not disinhibited by food cues, negative emotion, or other factors) or they ate a large amount when they became disinhibited (i.e., when the preload—or in the present case, meal—was large or perceived as large). In the present study, the "large slice" condition was perceived as a large preload/meal whereas the other two conditions were seen as appropriate sized.

    The unrestrained eaters on the other hand did not compensate for receiving the smaller piece of pizza by eating more cookies, even though they perceived the smaller portion as smaller than the other portions. They did, however, rate the small slice as "just right" in size. They may possibly have simply responded to their internal signals of satiety and thus ate the same amount of cookies as did the unrestrained eaters who got no comparative information (and also saw their slice as close to the "right" size). Of course, unrestrained eaters in the large slice condition presumably had the same satiety signals, but unrestrained eaters may be more prepared to eat less (after a preload/meal that they consider to be large) than to eat more (after a preload/meal that they consider to be "just right").

Not surprisingly, because all participants were actually given and ate the same amount of pizza, there were no group or condition differences in hunger either before or after eating the pizza. There were, however, some potentially interesting differences in the extent of negative affect experienced upon realizing that one had been given a larger or smaller portion of pizza. For unrestrained eaters, getting a large slice made them more dysphoric, but for restrained eaters, dysphoria was higher when they received a smaller slice. Although small, these opposite emotional reactions may speak to the differential psychology of the restrained and unrestrained eaters. Unrestrained eaters may be responding to the prescriptive norm of not appearing to eat excessively (Herman, Roth, & Polivy, 2003), and feel worse if they think that they are violating the norm. Restrained eaters, on the other hand, may actually be more upset with being allowed to maintain their diets (by eating the smaller piece); apparently they feel somewhat better when "forced" by the experimenter to eat "more," break their diets, and indulge themselves with additional cookies. This interpretation comports with the assumption that fundamentally, people want to eat as much as possible, but are constrained by considerations of social propriety (not eating excessively so as not to look like a "pig") or their self-imposed dietary agendas (Herman et al., 2003). When forced by someone else to transgress against their diets, restrained eaters may well experience what we have called the "what the hell effect" (Herman & Polivy, 1984) and feel relieved to be pushed off their diets and allowed to unleash their eating.

GETTING A BIGGER SLICE   14

The present study shows that the mere perception that one's meal was excessively large acts the same as a gratuitous preload to disinhibit eating in restrained eaters. The data also show that restrained and unrestrained eaters alike judge the amount that they are served in comparison to what those around them are eating. Such perceptions about the social context or meaning of one's portion apparently outweigh feelings of hunger in influencing the amount eaten, particularly if one sees oneself as having overeaten relative to others. Restrained eaters, when they perceive themselves as having eaten excessively compared to others, continue to eat liberally rather than curtail their intake. This indulgence undermines their stated dietary goals, but the fact that they feel worse when they do not (get to) overindulge provides a hint as to why dieters so often find themselves breaking their diets.

GETTING A BIGGER SLICE   15

References

Adams, C., & Leary, M. (2007). Promoting self-compassionate attitudes toward eating
among restrictive and guilty eaters. *Journal of Social & Clinical Psychology, 26,*
1120–1144. doi:10.1521/jscp.2007.26.10.1120

Fedoroff, I., Polivy, J., & Herman, C. P. (1997). The effect of pre-exposure to food
cues on the eating behavior of restrained and unrestrained eaters. *Appetite, 28,*
33–47. doi:10.1006/appe.1996.0057

Fedoroff, I., Polivy, J., & Herman, C. P. (2003). The specificity of restrained versus
unrestrained eaters' responses to food cues: General desire to eat, or craving for
the cued food? *Appetite, 41,* 7–13. doi:10.1016/S0195-6663(03)00026-6

Jansen, A., & Van den Hout, M. (1991). On being led into temptation:
"Counterregulation" of dieters after smelling a preload. *Addictive Behaviors,*
16, 247–253. doi:10.1016/0306-4603(91)90017-C

Herman, C. P., & Polivy, J. (1984). A boundary model for the regulation of eating.
Psychiatric Annals, 13, 918–927.

Herman, C. P., Polivy, J., & Silver, R. (1979). Effects of an observer on eating
behavior: The induction of "sensible" eating. *Journal of Personality, 47,* 85–99.
doi:10.1111/j.1467-6494.1979.tb00616.x

Herman, C. P., Polivy, J., & Esses, V. M. (1987). The illusion of counter-regulation.
Appetite, 9, 161–169. doi:10.1016/S0195-6663(87)80010-7

Herman, C. P., Roth, D., & Polivy, J. (2003). Effects of the presence of others on
food intake. A normative interpretation. *Psychological Bulletin, 129,* 873–886.
doi:10.1037/0033-2909.129.6.873

Knight, L., & Boland, F. (1989). Restrained eating. An experimental disentanglement
of the disinhibiting variables of calories and food type. *Journal of Abnormal
Psychology, 98,* 412–420. doi:10.1037/0021-843X.98.4.412

References begin on a new page. The word "References" is centered at the top of the page and not boldface.

A comma always follows the first author's initial, even if only two authors are listed.

APA style recommends including the DOI (Digital Object Identifier) if it is available.

APA recommends using the en-dash symbol between page numbers rather than a simple hyphen. The Microsoft Word shortcut to insert the en dash is Control-hyphen. This is probably not necessary for student papers.

Each reference begins on a new line and is considered a paragraph.

The paragraph is a hanging indent, in which the first line is flush to the left margin and subsequent lines are indented.

GETTING A BIGGER SLICE   16

McCann, K. L., Perri, M. G., Nezu, A. M., & Lowe, M. R. (1992). An investigation of
    counterregulatory eating in obese clinic attenders. *International Journal of
    Eating Disorders, 12,* 161–169. doi:10.1002/1098-108X(199209)12:2<161::
    AID-EAT2260120206>3.0.CO;2-A

Pliner, P., & Zec, D. (2007). Meal schemas during a preload decrease subsequent
    eating. *Appetite, 48,* 278–288. doi:10.1016/j.appet.2006.04.009

Polivy, J. (1976). Perception of calories and regulation of intake in restrained and
    unrestrained subjects. *Addictive Behaviors, 1,* 237–243. doi:10.1016/
    0306-4603(76)90016-2

Polivy, J., Heatherton, T. F., & Herman, C. P. (1988). Self-esteem, restraint, and
    eating behavior. *Journal of Abnormal Psychology, 97,* 354–356. doi:10.1037/
    0021-843X.97.3.354

Polivy, J., & Herman, C. P. (1999). Distress and eating: Why do dieters overeat?
    International Journal of Eating Disorders, 26, 153–164. doi:10.1002/
    (SICI)1098-108X(199909)26.2<153::AID-EAT4>3.0.CO;2-R

Polivy, J., & Herman, C. P. (2005). Mental health and eating behaviours: A
    bi-directional relation. *Canadian Journal of Public Health, 96,* 43–48.

Polivy, J., Herman, C. P., Hackett, R., & Kuleshnyk, I. (1986). The effects of
    self-attention and public attention on eating in restrained and unrestrained
    subjects. *Journal of Personality and Social Psychology, 50,* 1203–1224.
    doi:10.1037/0022-3514.50.6.1253

Spencer, J. A., & Fremouw, W. J. (1979). Binge eating as a function of restraint
    and weight classification. *Journal of Abnormal Psychology, 88,* 262–267.
    doi:10.1037/0021-843X.88.3.262

Watson, D., Clark, L. A., & Tellegen, A. (1988). Development and validation of
    brief measures of positive and negative affect: The PANAS scale. *Journal
    of Personality and Social Psychology, 54,* 1063–1070. doi:10.1037/
    0022-3514.54.6.1063

Titles of books
and journals are
italicized, as are
the volume num-
bers of journals.

Note that "&" is
used for multiple
authors through-
out the Reference
section.

Note capitaliza-
tion: First word
and first word
following a colon,
plus any proper
nouns.

When the same
set of authors is
included multiple
times, the entries
are ordered by
date, from oldest
to newest.

GETTING A BIGGER SLICE   17

Table 1

Amount of Cookies Eaten (in grams) in the Pizza Size Conditions

	Larger slice			Control/no info			Smaller slice		
Restraint	*M*	*SD*	*n*	*M*	*SD*	*n*	*M*	*SD*	*n*
Unrestrained eaters	50.39	6.83	25	67.89	8.05	18	61.20	7.12	23
Restrained eaters	84.36	9.13	14	59.94	9.86	12	62.12	9.13	14

Note. The number of participants (*n*) in the unrestrained eaters group is higher than the number in the restrained group when using the standard cutoff score on the Restraint Scale.

The first line of the page should include the table number.

The next double-spaced line should include the table title, which should be *italicized*, with all major words capitalized. No period is required.

Only the first word of headings within the table are capitalized. Sections of the table are separated by horizontal lines. Do not use vertical lines.

A horizontal line should separate column headers from data presented in the table.

Include another horizontal line below the last row of information.

A note below the table is optional. The note may provide additional information such as an explanation of abbreviations or specific group differences.

GETTING A BIGGER SLICE   18

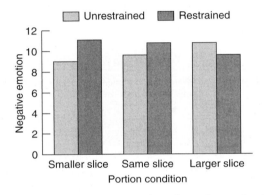

Figure 1. Total negative affect before eating pizza (but after seeing it). Post hoc *t* tests show a significant difference between the restrained and unrestrained eaters who were given the smaller slice. Unrestrained eaters getting the small slice felt better than those given the larger slice; restrained eaters given the small slice felt marginally worse than those given the large slice.

Figure caption. Note italics for figure number. Caption may include more than one sentence.

Appendix B

Statistical Tests

The purpose of this appendix is to provide the formulas and calculational procedures for analysis of data. Not all possible statistical tests are included, but a variety of tests are given that should be appropriate for many of the research designs you might use.

We will examine both descriptive and inferential statistics. Before you study the statistics, however, you should review the properties of measurement scales described in Chapter 5. Remember that there are four types of measurement scales: nominal, ordinal, interval, and ratio. Nominal scales have no numerical properties, ordinal scales provide rank-order information only, and interval and ratio scales have equal intervals between the points on the scale. In addition, ratio scales have a true zero point. You will also recall from Chapter 13 that the appropriate statistical analysis is determined by the type of design and by the measurement scale that was used in the study. As we proceed, the discussion of the various statistical tests will draw to your attention the relevant measurement scale restrictions that apply.

The examples here use small and simple data sets so the calculations can be easily done by hand using a calculator. You will probably use a computer program such as SPSS, SAS, R, or Excel for your analyses. However, a review of the underlying calculations will help you understand the output from these computer programs.

DESCRIPTIVE STATISTICS

With a knowledge of the types of measurement scales, we can turn to a consideration of statistical techniques. We can start with two ways of describing a set of scores: central tendency and variability.

Measures of Central Tendency

A measure of central tendency gives a single number that describes how an entire group scores as a whole, or on the average. Three different central tendency measures are available: the mode, the median, and the mean.

The Mode   The mode is the most frequently occurring score. Table B.1 shows a set of scores and the descriptive statistics that are discussed in this section. The most frequently occurring score in these data is 5. No calculations are necessary to find the mode. The mode can be used with any of the four types of measurement scales. However, it is the only measure of central tendency that can be used with nominal scale data. If you are measuring gender and find there are 100 females and 50 males, the mode is "female" because this is the most frequently occurring category on the nominal scale.

The Median   The median is the score that divides the group in half: 50% of the scores are below the median and 50% are above the median. When the scores have been ordered from lowest to highest (as in Table B.1), the median is easily found. If there are an odd number of scores, you simply find the middle score. (For example, if there are 11 scores, the sixth score is the median, because there are 5 lower and 5 higher scores.) If there are an even number of scores, the median is the midpoint between the two middle scores. In the data in Table B.1, there are 10 scores, so the fifth and sixth scores are the two middle scores. To find the median, we add the two middle scores and divide by 2. Thus, in Table B.1, the median is

$$\frac{5+5}{2} = 5$$

The median can be used with ordinal, interval, or ratio scale data. It is most likely to be used with ordinal data, however. This is because calculation of the median considers only the rank ordering of scores and not the actual size of the scores.

TABLE B.1   Descriptive statistics for a set of scores

Score	Descriptive statistic
1	Mode = 5
2	
4	Median = 5
4	
5	$\overline{X} = \frac{\Sigma X}{N} = 4.5$
5	
5	
6	Range = 6
6	
7	$s^2 = \frac{\Sigma(X - \overline{X})^2}{N-1} = \frac{\Sigma X^2 - N\overline{X}^2}{N-1} = \frac{233 - 202.5}{9} = 3.388$
$\Sigma X = 45$	
$\Sigma X^2 = 233$	$s = \sqrt{s^2} = 1.84$
$N = 10$	

The Mean The mean is based on more information about the scores than either the mode or the median. However, it is appropriate only for interval or ratio scale data.

The mean is the sum of the scores in a group divided by the number of scores. The calculational formula for the mean can be expressed as

$$\overline{X} = \frac{\Sigma X}{N}$$

where $\overline{X}$ is the symbol for the mean. In this formula, X represents a score obtained by an individual, and the Σ symbol indicates that scores are to be summed or added. The symbol ΣX can be read as "sum of the Xs" and simply is an indication that the scores are to be added. Thus, ΣX in the data from Table B.1 is

$$1 + 2 + 4 + 4 + 5 + 5 + 5 + 6 + 6 + 7 = 45$$

The N in the formula symbolizes the number of scores in the group. In our example, $N = 10$. Thus, we can now calculate the mean:

$$\overline{X} = \frac{\Sigma X}{N} = \frac{45}{10} = 4.5$$

Measures of Variability

In addition to describing the central tendency of the set of scores, we want to describe how much the scores vary. That is, how much spread is there in the set of scores?

The Range The range is the highest score minus the lowest score. In our example, the range is 6. The range is not a very useful statistic, however, because it is based on only two scores in the distribution. It does not take into account all of the information that is available in the entire set of scores.

The Variance and Standard Deviation The variance, and a related statistic called the standard deviation, use all the scores to yield a measure of variability. The variance indicates the degree to which scores vary about the group mean. The formula for the variance (symbolized as s^2) is

$$s^2 = \frac{\Sigma(X - \overline{X})^2}{N - 1}$$

where $(X - \overline{X})^2$ is an individual score, X, minus the mean, $\overline{X}$, and then squared. Thus $(X - \overline{X})^2$ is the squared deviation of each score from the mean. The Σ sign indicates that these squared deviation scores are to be summed. Finally, dividing by $N - 1$ gives the mean of the squared deviations. The variance, then, is the mean of the squared deviations from the group mean. (Squared deviations are used because simple deviations would add up to zero. $N - 1$ is used in most cases for statistical purposes because the scores represent a sample and not an entire population. As the sample size becomes larger, it makes little difference whether N or $N - 1$ is used.)

The data in Table B.1 can be used to illustrate calculation of the variance. $\Sigma (X - \overline{X})^2$ is equal to

$$(1 - 4.5)^2 + (2 - 4.5)^2 + (4 - 4.5)^2 + (4 - 4.5)^2 + (5 - 4.5)^2 + (5 - 4.5)^2$$
$$+ (5 - 4.5)^2 + (6 - 4.5)^2 + (6 - 4.5)^2 + (7 - 4.5)^2 = 30.50$$

The next step is to divide $\Sigma (X - \overline{X})^2$ by $N - 1$. The calculation for the variance, then, is

$$s^2 = \frac{\Sigma(X - \overline{X})^2}{N - 1} = \frac{30.50}{9} = 3.388$$

A simpler, and equivalent, calculational formula for the variance is

$$s^2 = \frac{\Sigma X^2 - N\overline{X}^2}{N - 1}$$

where ΣX^2 is the sum of the squared individual scores, and $\overline{X}^2$ is the mean squared. You can confirm that the two formulas are identical by computing the variance using this simpler formula. (Remember that ΣX^2 tells you to square each score and then sum the squared scores.)

The standard deviation is the square root of the variance. Because the variance uses squared scores, the variance does not describe the amount of variability in the same units of measurement as the original scale. The standard deviation (s) corrects this problem. Thus, the standard deviation is the average deviation of scores from the mean.

STATISTICAL SIGNIFICANCE AND EFFECT SIZE

This section describes several statistical significance tests. These tests are used to determine the probability that the outcome of the research was due to the operation of random error. All use the logic of the null hypothesis discussed in Chapter 13. We will consider two significance tests in this section: the chi-square test and the analysis of variance or F test.

Chi-Square (χ^2)

The chi-square (Greek letter chi, squared) test is used when dealing with nominal scale data. It is used when the data consist of frequencies—the number of subjects who fall into each of several categories.

Chi-square can be used with either experimental or nonexperimental data. The major requirement is that both variables are studied using nominal scales.

Example   Suppose you want to know whether there is a relationship between gender and hand dominance. To do this, you sample 50 males and
50 females and ask whether they are right-handed, left-handed, or ambidextrous (use both hands with equal skill). Your data collection involves clas-
sifying each person as male or female and as right-handed, left-handed, or
ambidextrous.

Fictitious data for such a study are presented in Table B.2. The frequencies
labeled as "O" in each of the six cells in the table refer to the *observed* number of
male and female subjects who fall into each of the three hand-dominance categories. The frequencies labeled "E" refer to frequencies that are *expected* if the
null hypothesis is correct. It is important that each subject falls into only one of
the cells when using chi-square (that is, no subject can be counted as both male
and female or both right- and left-handed).

The chi-square test examines the extent to which the frequencies that are
actually observed in the study differ from the frequencies that are expected if the
null hypothesis is correct. The null hypothesis states that there is no relationship between sex and hand dominance: Males and females do not differ on this
characteristic.

The formula for computing chi-square is

$$\chi^2 = \Sigma \frac{(O - E)^2}{E}$$

TABLE B.2   **Data for hypothetical study on hand dominance:
Chi-square test**

Sex of subject	Right	Left	Ambidextrous	Row totals
		Hand dominance		
Male	$O_1 = 15$	$O_2 = 30$	$O_3 = 5$	50
	$E_1 = 25$	$E_2 = 20$	$E_3 = 5$	
Female	$O_4 = 35$	$O_5 = 10$	$O_6 = 5$	50
	$E_4 = 25$	$E_5 = 20$	$E_6 = 5$	
Column totals	50	40	10	$N = 100$

Computations:	Cell number	$\frac{(O-E)^2}{E}$	
	1	4.00	
	2	5.00	
	3	0.00	
	4	4.00	$\chi^2 = \Sigma \frac{(O - E)^2}{E}$
	5	5.00	$= 18.00$
	6	0.00	
		$\Sigma = 18.00$	

where O is the *observed* frequency in each cell, E is the *expected* frequency in each cell, and the symbol Σ refers to summing over all cells. The steps in calculating the value of χ^2 are:

Step 1: Arrange the observed frequencies in a table such as Table B.2. Note that in addition to the observed frequencies in each cell, the table presents row totals, column totals, and the total number of observations (N).

Step 2: Calculate the expected frequencies for each of the cells in the table. The expected frequency formula is

$$E = \frac{\text{row total} \times \text{column total}}{N}$$

where the row total refers to the row total for the cell, and the column total refers to the column total for the cell. Thus, the expected frequency for cell 1 (male right-handedness) is

$$E_1 = \frac{50 \times 50}{100} = 25$$

The expected frequencies for each of the cells are shown in Table B.2 below the observed frequencies.

Step 3: Calculate the quantity $(O - E)^2/E$ for each cell. For cell 1, this quantity is

$$\frac{(15 - 25)^2}{25} = \frac{100}{25} = 4.00$$

Step 4: Find the value of χ^2 by summing the $(O - E)^2/E$ values found in step 3. The calculations for obtaining χ^2 for the example data are shown in Table B.2.

Significance of Chi-Square
The significance of the obtained χ^2 value can be evaluated by consulting a table of critical values of χ^2. A table of critical χ^2 values is presented as Table C.1 in Appendix C. The critical χ^2 values indicate the value that the *obtained* χ^2 must equal or exceed to be significant at the .10 level, the .05 level, and the .01 level.

To be able to use the table of critical values of χ^2 as well as most other statistical tables, you must understand the concept of *degrees of freedom* (df). The critical value of χ^2 for any given study depends on the degrees of freedom. Degrees of freedom refers to the number of scores that are free to vary. In the table of categories for a chi-square test, the number of degrees of freedom is the number of cells in which the frequencies are free to vary once we know the row totals and column totals. The degrees of freedom for chi-square is easily calculated:

$$df = (R - 1)(C - 1)$$

where R is the number of rows in the table and C is the number of columns. In our example in Table B.1, there are two rows and three columns, so there are 2 degrees of freedom. In a study with three rows and three columns, there are 4 degrees of freedom, and so on.

To use Table C.1, find the correct degrees of freedom and then determine the critical value of χ^2 necessary to reject the null hypothesis at the chosen significance level. With 2 degrees of freedom, the obtained χ^2 value must be *equal to* or *greater than* the critical value of 5.991 to be significant at the .05 level. There is only a .05 probability that a χ^2 of 5.991 would occur if only random error is operating. Because the obtained χ^2 from our example is 18.00, we can reject the null hypothesis that there is no relationship between sex and hand dominance. (The chi-square was based on fictitious data, but it would be relatively easy for you to determine for yourself whether there is in fact a relationship.)

Effect Size for the Chi-Square Statistic

Measures of effect size indicate the strength of association between variables. Results range from 0.00, which indicates no relationship, to 1.00. Correlations above .50 are considered to show very strong relationships. In much research, expect correlations between about .15 and .40. Correlations between about .10 and .20 are weaker, but can be statistically significant with large sample sizes. They can also be important for theoretical and even practical reasons.

The chi-square (χ^2) test was described previously. In addition to determining whether there is a significant relationship, you want an indicator of effect size to tell you the strength of association between the variables. For the sex difference in hand dominance example, a statistic called Cramer's V (or phi) is appropriate. The V coefficient is computed after obtaining the value of chi-square. The formula is

$$V = \sqrt{\frac{\chi^2}{N(k - 1)}}$$

In this formula, N is the total number of cases or subjects and k is the smaller of the rows or columns in the table (thus, in our example with 3 columns [hand dominance] and 2 rows [sex], the value of k is 2, the lower value).

The value of V for the sex and hand dominance example in Table B.2 is

$$V = \sqrt{\frac{18}{100(2 - 1)}} = \sqrt{.18} = .42$$

Because the significance of the chi-square value has already been determined, no further significance testing is necessary.

Concluding Remarks
The chi-square test is extremely useful and is used frequently in all of the behavioral sciences. The calculational formula described is generalizable to expanded studies in which there are more categories on either of the variables. One note of caution, however: When both variables have only two categories, so that there are only two rows and two columns, the formula for calculating chi-square changes slightly. In such cases, the formula is

$$\chi^2 = \Sigma \frac{(|O - E|) - .5)^2}{E}$$

where $|O - E|$ is the absolute value of $O - E$, and .5 is a constant that is subtracted for each cell.

Analysis of Variance (F Test)

The analysis of variance, or F test, is used to determine whether there is a significant difference between groups that have been measured on either interval or ratio scales. The groups may have been formed using either the experimental or the correlational method; the important thing is that at least an interval scale measure was used. The analysis of variance may be used with either independent groups or repeated measures designs. Procedures for calculating F for both types of designs are presented.

Analysis of Variance: One Independent Variable

To illustrate the use of the analysis of variance, let's consider a hypothetical experiment on physical distance and self-disclosure. You think that people will reveal more about themselves to an interviewer when they are sitting close to the interviewer than they will when sitting farther away. To test this idea, you conduct an experiment on interviewing. Participants are told that interviewing techniques are being studied. Each participant is seated in a room; the interviewer comes into the room and sits at one of three distances from the participant: close (2 feet, or .61 meter), medium (4 feet, or 1.22 meters), or far (6 feet, or 1.83 meters). The distance chosen by the interviewer is the independent variable manipulation. Participants are randomly assigned to the three distance conditions, and the interviewer's behavior is constant in all conditions. The interview consists of a number of questions, and the dependent variable is the number of personal, revealing statements made by the participant during the interview.

Fictitious data for such an experiment are shown in Table B.3. Note that this is an independent groups design with five subjects in each group. The calculations of the systematic variance and error variance involve computing the *sum of squares* for the different types of variance.

Sum of Squares   Sum of squares stands for the *sum of squared deviations from the mean*. Computing an analysis of variance for the data in Table B.3 involves three sums of squares: (1) SS_{TOTAL}, the sum of squared deviations of each individual score from the grand mean; (2) SS_A, the sum of squared deviations of each of the group means from the grand mean; and (3) SS_{ERROR}, the sum of squared deviations of the individual scores from their respective group means. The "A" in SS_A is used to indicate that we are dealing with the systematic variance associated with independent variable A.

The three sums of squares are deviations from a mean. (Recall that we calculated such deviations earlier when discussing the variance in a set of scores.) We could calculate the deviations directly with the data in Table B.3, but such calculations are hard to work with, so we will use simplified formulas for computational purposes. The computational formulas are

$$SS_{TOTAL} = \Sigma X^2 - \frac{G^2}{N}$$

$$SS_A = \Sigma \frac{T_a^2}{n_a} - \frac{G^2}{N}$$

$$SS_{ERROR} = \Sigma X^2 - \Sigma \frac{T_a^2}{n_a}$$

You might note here that $SS_{TOTAL} = SS_A + SS_{ERROR}$. The actual computations are shown in Table B.3.

SS_{TOTAL}   The formula for SS_{TOTAL} is

$$\Sigma X^2 - \frac{G^2}{N}$$

TABLE B.3   Data for hypothetical experiment on distance and self-disclosure: Analysis of variance

	Distance (A)	
Close (A1)	Medium (A2)	Far (A3)
33	21	20
24	25	13
31	19	15
29	27	10
34	26	14
$T_{A1} = 151$	$T_{A2} = 118$	$T_{A3} = 72$
$n_{A1} = 5$	$n_{A2} = 5$	$n_{A3} = 5$
$X_{A1} = 30.20$	$X_{A2} = 23.60$	$X_{A3} = 14.40$
$\Sigma X_{A1}^2 = 4623$	$\Sigma X_{A2}^2 = 2832$	$\Sigma X_{A3}^2 = 1090$
$T_{A1}^2 = 22801$	$T_{A2}^2 = 13924$	$T_{A3}^2 = 5184$

$$SS_{TOTAL} = \Sigma X^2 - \frac{G^2}{N} = (4623 + 2832 + 1090) - \frac{(151 + 118 + 72)^2}{15}$$
$$= 8545 - 7752.07 = 792.93$$

$$SS_A = \Sigma \frac{T_a^2}{n_a} - \frac{G^2}{N} = \left[\frac{(151)^2}{5} + \frac{(118)^2}{5} + \frac{(72)^2}{5}\right] - 7752.07$$
$$= 8381.80 - 7752.07 = 629.73$$

$$SS_{ERROR} = \Sigma X^2 - \Sigma \frac{T_a^2}{n_a} = 8545 - 8381.80 = 163.20$$

ΣX^2 is the sum of the squared scores of all subjects in the experiment. Each of the scores is squared first and then added. Thus, for the data in Table B.3, ΣX^2 is $33^2 + 24^2 + 31^2$ and so on until all of the scores have been squared and added. If you are doing the calculations by hand or with a pocket calculator, it may be convenient to find the ΣX^2 for the scores in each group and then add these up for your final computation. This is what I did for the data in the table. The G in the formula stands for the grand total of all of the scores. This involves adding up the scores for all subjects. The grand total is then squared and divided by N, the total number of subjects in the experiment. When computing the sum of squares, you should always keep the calculations clearly labeled, because you can simplify later calculations by referring to these earlier ones. Once you have computed SS_{TOTAL}, SS_A can be calculated.

SS_A The formula for SS_A is

$$\Sigma \frac{T_a^2}{n_a} - \frac{G^2}{N}$$

The T_a in this formula refers to the total of the scores in Group a of independent variable A. (T_a is a shorthand notation for ΣX in each group. [Recall the computation of ΣX from our discussion of the mean.] The T_a symbol is used to avoid having to deal with too many Σ signs in our calculation procedures.) The a is used to symbolize the particular group number; thus, T_a is a general symbol for T_1, T_2, and T_3. Looking at our data in Table B.3, $T_1 = 151$, $T_2 = 118$, and $T_3 = 72$. These are the sums of the scores in each of the groups. After T_a has been calculated, T_a^2 is found by squaring T_a. Now, T_a^2 is divided by n_a, the number of subjects in Group a. Once the quantity T_a^2/n_a has been computed for each group, the quantities are summed as indicated by the Σ symbol.

Note that the second part of the formula, G^2/N, was calculated when SS_{TOTAL} was obtained. Because we already have this quantity, it need not be calculated again when computing SS_A. After obtaining SS_A, we can now compute SS_{ERROR}.

SS_{ERROR} The formula for SS_{ERROR} is

$$\Sigma X^2 - \Sigma \frac{T_a^2}{n_a}$$

Both of these quantities were calculated above in obtaining SS_{TOTAL} and SS_A. To obtain SS_{ERROR}, we merely have to find these quantities and perform the proper subtraction.

As a check on the calculations, we can make sure that $SS_{TOTAL} = SS_A + SS_{ERROR}$.

The next step in the computation of the analysis of variance is to find the *mean square* for each of the sums of squares. We can then find the value of F. The necessary computations are shown in an analysis of variance summary table in Table B.4. Constructing a summary table is the easiest way to complete the computations.

TABLE B.4   Analysis of variance summary table

Source of variance	Sum of squares	df	Mean square	F
A	SS_A	$a - 1$	SS_A/df_A	MS_A/MS_{ERROR}
Error	SS_{ERROR}	$N - a$	SS_{ERROR}/df_{ERROR}	
Total	SS_{TOTAL}	$N - 1$		
A	629.73	2	314.87	23.15
Error	163.20	12	13.60	
Total	792.93	14		

Mean Squares   After obtaining the sum of squares, it is necessary to compute the mean squares. Mean square stands for the *mean of the sum of the squared deviations from the mean* or, more simply, the mean of the sum of squares. The mean square (MS) is the sum of squares divided by the degrees of freedom. The degrees of freedom are determined by the number of scores in the sum of squares that are free to vary. The mean squares are the variances that are used in computing the value of F.

From Table B.4, you can see that the mean squares that concern us are the mean square for A (systematic variance) and the mean square for error (error variance). The formulas are

$$MS_A = SS_A/df_A$$
$$MS_{ERROR} = SS_{ERROR}/df_{ERROR}$$

where $df_A = a - 1$ (the number of groups minus one) and $df_{ERROR} = N - a$ (the total number of subjects minus the number of groups).

Obtaining the F Value   The obtained F is found by dividing MS_A by MS_{ERROR}. If only random error is operating, the expected value of F is 1.0. The greater the F value, the lower the probability that the results of the experiment were due to chance error.

Significance of F   To determine the significance of the obtained F value, it is necessary to compare the obtained F to a critical value of F. Table C.3 in Appendix C shows critical values of F for significance levels of .10, .05, and .01. To find the critical value of F, locate on the table the degrees of freedom for the numerator of the ratio (the systematic variance) and the degrees of freedom for the denominator of the F ratio (the error variance). The intersection of these two degrees of freedom on the table is the critical F value.

The appropriate degrees of freedom for our sample data are 2 and 12 (see Table B.4). The critical F value from Table C.3 is 3.89 for a .05 level of significance. For the results to be significant, the obtained F value must be equal to or greater than the critical value. Because the obtained value of F in Table B.4 (23.15) is greater than the critical value, we conclude that the results are significant and reject the null hypothesis that the means of the groups are equal in the population.

Effect Size for the F Statistic

After computing an analysis of variance and evaluating the significance of the F statistic, you need to examine effect size. *Eta* is a type of correlation coefficient that can be calculated easily. The formula is

$$\text{eta} = \sqrt{\frac{\text{between group (systematic) variance}}{\text{total variance}}}$$

In the experiment on interpersonal distance and disclosure previously described, the SS_A was 629.73, and the SS_{TOTAL} was 792.93. The value of eta then would be

$$\text{eta} = \sqrt{\frac{629.73}{792.93}}$$
$$= .89$$

This is a very high correlation, reflecting the fact that the data were all manufactured for ease of computation.

Concluding Remarks   The analysis of variance for one independent variable with an independent groups design can be used when there are two or more groups in the experiment. The general formulas described are appropriate for all such designs. Also, the calculations are the same whether the experimental or the correlational method is used to form the groups. The formulas are also applicable to cases in which the number of subjects in each group is not equal (although you should have approximately equal numbers of subjects in the groups).

When the design of the experiment includes more than two levels of the independent variable (as in our example experiment, which had three groups), the obtained F value does not tell us whether any two specific groups are significantly different from one another. One way to examine the difference between two groups in such a study is to use the formula for SS_A to compute the sum of squares and the mean square for the two groups (the df in this case is $2 - 1$). When doing this, the previously calculated MS_{ERROR} should be used as the error variance term for computing F. More complicated procedures for evaluating the difference between two groups in such designs are available, and easily calculated with statistical software.

Analysis of Variance: Two Independent Variables

In this section, we will describe the computations for analysis of variance with a factorial design containing two independent variables. The formulas apply to an $A \times B$ factorial design with any number of levels of the independent variables.

The formulas apply only to a completely independent groups design with different subjects in each group, and the number of subjects in each group must be equal. Once you understand this analysis, however, you should have little trouble understanding the analysis for more complicated designs with repeated measures or unequal numbers of subjects. With these limitations in mind, let's consider example data from a hypothetical experiment.

The experiment uses a 2 × 2 IV × PV factorial design. Variable *A* is the type of instruction used in a course, and variable *B* is the intelligence level of the students. The students are classified as of either "low" or "high" intelligence on the basis of intelligence test scores and are randomly assigned to one of two types of classes. One class uses the traditional lecture method; the other class uses an individualized learning approach with frequent testing over small amounts of material, proctors to help individual students, and a stipulation that students master each section of material before going on to the next section. The information presented to students in the two classes is identical. At the end of the course, all students take the same test, which covers all of the material presented in the course. The score on this examination is the dependent variable.

Table B.5 shows fictitious data for such an experiment, with five subjects in each condition. This design allows us to evaluate three effects—the main effect of *A*, the main effect of *B*, and the *A* × *B* interaction. The main effect of *A* is whether one type of instruction is superior to the other; the main effect of *B* is whether high-intelligence students score differently on the test than do low-intelligence students; the *A* × *B* interaction examines whether the effect of one independent variable is different depending on the particular level of the other variable.

The computation of the analysis of variance starts with calculation of the sum of squares for the following sources of variance in the data: SS_{TOTAL}, SS_A, SS_B, $SS_{A\times B}$, and SS_{ERROR}. The procedures for calculation are similar to the calculations performed for the analysis of variance with one independent variable. The numerical calculations for the example data are shown in Table B.6. We can now consider each of these calculations.

SS_{TOTAL}   The SS_{TOTAL} is computed in the same way as the previous analysis formula. The formula is

$$SS_{TOTAL} = \Sigma X^2 - \frac{G^2}{N}$$

where ΣX^2 is the sum of the squared scores of all subjects in the experiment, *G* is the grand total of all of the scores, and *N* is the total number of subjects. It is usually easiest to calculate ΣX^2 and *G* in smaller steps by calculating subtotals separately for each group in the design. The subtotals are then added. This is the procedure followed in Tables B.5 and B.6.

SS_A   The formula for SS_A is

$$SS_A = \frac{\Sigma T_a^2}{n_a} - \frac{G^2}{N}$$

TABLE B.5   Data for hypothetical experiment on the effect of type of instruction and intelligence level on exam score: Analysis of variance

	Intelligence (B)		
	Low (B1)	High (B2)	
Traditional lecture (A1)	75	90	
	70	95	
	69	89	
	72	85	
	68	91	
	$T_{A1B1} = 354$	$T_{A1B2} = 450$	$T_{A1} = 804$
	$\Sigma X^2_{A1B1} = 25094$	$\Sigma X^2_{A1B2} = 40552$	$n_{A1} = 10$
	$n_{A1B1} = 5$	$n_{A1B2} = 5$	$\overline{X}_{A1} = 80.40$
	$\overline{X}_{A1B1} = 70.80$	$\overline{X}_{A1B2} = 90.00$	
Individualized method (A2)	85	87	
	87	94	
	83	93	
	90	89	
	89	92	
	$T_{A2B1} = 434$	$T_{A2B2} = 455$	$T_{A2} = 889$
	$\Sigma X^2_{A2B1} = 37704$	$\Sigma X^2_{A2B2} = 41439$	$n_{A2} = 10$
	$n_{A2B1} = 5$	$n_{A2B2} = 5$	$\overline{X}_{A2} = 88.90$
	$\overline{X}_{A2B1} = 86.80$	$\overline{X}_{A2B2} = 91.00$	
	$T_{B1} = 788$	$T_{B2} = 905$	
	$n_{B1} = 10$	$n_{B2} = 10$	
	$\overline{X}_{B1} = 78.80$	$\overline{X}_{B2} = 90.50$	

where ΣT^2_a is the sum of the squared totals of the scores in each of the groups of independent variable A, and n_a is the number of subjects in each level of independent variable A. When calculating SS_A, we consider only the groups of independent variable A without considering the particular level of B. In other words, the totals for each group of the A variable are obtained by considering all subjects in that level of A, irrespective of which condition of B the subject may be in. The quantity of G^2/N was previously calculated for SS_{TOTAL}.

TABLE B.6   Computations for analysis of variance with two independent variables

$$SS_{TOTAL} = \Sigma X^2 - \frac{G^2}{N}$$

$$= (25094 + 40552 + 37704 + 41439)$$
$$- \frac{(354 + 450 + 434 + 455)^2}{20}$$
$$= 144789 - 143312.45$$
$$= 1476.55$$

$$SS_A = \frac{\Sigma T_a^2}{n_a} - \frac{G^2}{N}$$

$$= \frac{(804)^2 + (889)^2}{10} - 143312.45$$
$$= 143673.70 - 143312.45$$
$$= 361.25$$

$$SS_B = \frac{\Sigma T_b^2}{n_b} - \frac{G^2}{N}$$

$$= \frac{(788)^2 + (905)^2}{10} - 143312.45$$
$$= 143996.90 - 143312.45$$
$$= 684.45$$

$$SS_{A\times B} = \frac{\Sigma T_{ab}^2}{n_{ab}} - \frac{G^2}{N} - SS_A - SS_B$$

$$= \frac{(354)^2 + (450)^2 + (434)^2 + (455)^2}{5}$$
$$- 143312.45 - 361.25 - 684.45$$
$$= 144639.40 - 143312.45 - 361.25 - 684.45$$
$$= 281.25$$

$$SS_{ERROR} = \Sigma X^2 - \frac{\Sigma T_{ab}^2}{n_{ab}}$$

$$= 144789 - 144639.40$$
$$= 149.60$$

SS_B The formula for SS_B is

$$SS_B = \frac{\Sigma T_b^2}{n_b} - \frac{G^2}{N}$$

SS_B is calculated in the same way as SS_A. The only difference is that we are calculating totals of the groups of independent variable B.

$SS_{A\times B}$ The formula for $SS_{A\times B}$ is

$$SS_{A\times B} = \frac{\Sigma T_{ab}^2}{n_{ab}} - \frac{G^2}{N} - SS_A - SS_B$$

The sum of squares for the $A \times B$ interaction is computed by first calculating the quantity ΣT_{ab}^2. This involves squaring the total of the scores in each of the ab conditions in the experiment. In our example experiment in Table B.5, there are four conditions; the interaction calculation considers *all* of the groups. Each of the group totals is squared, and then the sum of the squared totals is obtained. This sum is divided by n_{ab}, the number of subjects in each group. The other quantities in the formula for $SS_{A\times B}$ have already been calculated, so the computation of $SS_{A\times B}$ is relatively straightforward.

TABLE B.7 Analysis of variance summary table: Two independent variables

Source of variance	Sum of squares	df	Mean square	F
A	SS_A	$a - 1$	SS_A/df_A	MS_A/MS_{ERROR}
B	SS_B	$b - 1$	SS_B/df_B	MS_B/MS_{ERROR}
$A \times B$	$SS_{A \times B}$	$(a - 1)(b - 1)$	$SS_{A \times B}/df_{A \times B}$	$MS_{A \times B}/MS_{ERROR}$
Error	SS_{ERROR}	$N - ab$	SS_{ERROR}/df_{ERROR}	
Total	SS_{TOTAL}			
A	361.25	1	361.25	38.64
B	684.45	1	684.45	73.20
$A \times B$	281.25	1	281.25	30.08
Error	149.60	16	9.35	
Total	1476.55	19		

SS_{ERROR} The quantities involved in the SS_{ERROR} formula have already been calculated. The formula is

$$SS_{ERROR} = \Sigma X^2 - \frac{\Sigma T_{ab}^2}{n_{ab}}$$

These quantities were calculated previously, so we merely have to perform the proper subtraction to complete the computation of SS_{ERROR}.

At this point, you may want to practice calculating the sums of squares using the data in Table B.5. As a check on the calculations, make sure that $SS_{TOTAL} = SS_A + SS_B + SS_{A \times B} + SS_{ERROR}$.

After obtaining the sums of squares, the next step is to find the mean square for each of the sources of variance. The easiest way to do this is to use an analysis of variance summary table like Table B.7.

Mean Square

The mean square for each of the sources of variance is the sum of squares divided by the degrees of freedom. The formulas for the degrees of freedom and the mean square are shown in the top portion of Table B.7, and the computed values are shown in the bottom portion of the table.

Obtaining the F Value

The F value for each of the three sources of systematic variance (main effects for A and B, and the interaction) is obtained by dividing the appropriate mean square by the MS_{ERROR}. We now have three obtained F values and can evaluate the significance of the main effects and the interaction.

Significance of F

To determine whether an obtained F is significant, we need to find the critical value of F from Table C.3 in Appendix C. For all of the

*F*s in the analysis of variance summary table, the degrees of freedom are 1 and 16. Let's assume that a .01 significance level for rejecting the null hypothesis was chosen. The critical *F* at .01 for 1 and 16 degrees of freedom is 8.53. If the obtained *F* is larger than 8.53, we can say that the results are significant at the .01 level. By referring to the obtained *F*s in Table B.7, you can see that the main effects and the interaction are all significant. I will leave it to you to interpret the main effect means and to graph the interaction. If you do not recall how to do this, you should review the material in Chapter 10.

Analysis of Variance: Repeated Measures

The analysis of variance computations considered thus far have been limited to independent groups (between-subjects) designs. This section considers the computations for analysis of variance of a repeated measures (within-subjects) design with one independent variable.

Fictitious data for a hypothetical experiment using a repeated measures design are presented in Table B.8. The experiment examines the effect of a job candidate's physical attractiveness on judgments of the candidate's competence. The independent variable is the candidate's physical attractiveness; the dependent variable is judged competence on a 10-point scale. Participants in the experiment view two videotapes of different females performing a mechanical aptitude task that involved piecing together a number of parts. Both females do equally well, but one is physically attractive and the other is unattractive. The order of presentation of the two tapes is counterbalanced to control for order effects.

The main difference between the repeated measures analysis of variance and the independent groups analysis described earlier is that the effect of subject differences becomes a source of variance. There are four sources of variance in the repeated measures analysis of variance, and so four sums of squares are calculated:

$$SS_{TOTAL} = \Sigma X^2 - \frac{G^2}{N}$$

$$SS_A = \frac{\Sigma T_a^2}{n_a} - \frac{G^2}{N}$$

$$SS_{SUBJECTS} = \frac{\Sigma T_s^2}{n_s} - \frac{G^2}{N}$$

$$SS_{ERROR} = SS_{TOTAL} - SS_A - SS_{SUBJECTS}$$

The calculations for these sums of squares are shown in the lower portion of Table B.8. The quantities in the formula should be familiar to you by now. The only new quantity involves the calculation of $SS_{SUBJECTS}$. The term T_s^2 refers to the squared total score of each subject—that is, the squared total of the scores that each subject gives when measured in the different groups in the experiment. The quantity ΣT_s^2 refers to the sum of these squared totals for all subjects. The calculation of $SS_{SUBJECTS}$ is completed by dividing ΣT_s^2 by n_s and then subtracting by G^2/N. The term n_s refers to the number of scores that each subject gives. Because

TABLE B.8 Data for hypothetical experiment on attractiveness and judged competence: Repeated measures analysis of variance

| Subjects (or subject pairs) | Condition (A) | | T_s | T_s^2 |
	Unattractive candidate (A_1)	Attractive candidate (A_2)		
#1	6	8	14	196
#2	5	6	11	121
#3	5	9	14	196
#4	7	6	13	169
#5	4	6	10	100
#6	3	5	8	64
#7	5	5	10	100
#8	4	7	11	121

$$T_{A1} = 39 \qquad T_{A2} = 52 \qquad \Sigma T_s^2 = 1067$$

$$\Sigma X_{A1}^2 = 201 \qquad \Sigma X_{A2}^2 = 352$$

$$n_{A1} = 8 \qquad n_{A2} = 8$$

$$\overline{X}_{A1} = 4.88 \qquad \overline{X}_{A2} = 6.50$$

$$SS_{TOTAL} = \Sigma X^2 - \frac{G^2}{N} = (201 + 352) - \frac{(39 + 52)^2}{16}$$
$$= 553 - 517.56$$
$$= 35.44$$

$$SS_A = \frac{\Sigma T_a^2}{n_a} - \frac{G^2}{N} = \frac{(39)^2 + (52)^2}{8} - 517.56$$
$$= 528.13 - 517.56$$
$$= 10.57$$

$$SS_{SUBJECTS} = \frac{\Sigma T_s^2}{n_s} - \frac{G^2}{N} = \frac{1067}{2} - 517.56$$
$$= 533.50 - 517.56$$
$$= 15.94$$

$$SS_{ERROR} = SS_{TOTAL} - SS_A - SS_{SUBJECTS} = 35.44 - 10.57 - 15.94$$
$$= 8.93$$

our hypothetical experiment has two groups, $n_s = 2$, the total for each subject is based on two scores.

An analysis of variance summary table is shown in Table B.9. The procedures for computing the mean squares and obtaining F are similar to our previous calculations. Note that the mean square and F for the subjects' source of variance are not computed. There is usually no reason to know or care whether subjects differ significantly from one another. The ability to calculate this source of variance does have the advantage of reducing the amount of error variance—in an

TABLE B.9   Analysis of variance summary table:
Repeated measures design

Source of variance	Sum of squares	df	Mean square	F
A	SS_A	$a - 1$	SS_A/df_A	MS_A/MS_{ERROR}
Subjects	$SS_{SUBJECTS}$	$s - 1$	—	
Error	SS_{ERROR}	$(a - 1)(s - 1)$	SS_{ERROR}/df_{ERROR}	
Total	SS_{TOTAL}	$N - 1$		
A	10.57	1	10.57	8.26
Subjects	15.94	7	—	
Error	8.93	7	1.28	
Total	35.44	15		

independent groups design, subject differences are part of the error variance. Because there is only one score per subject in the independent groups design, it is impossible to estimate the influence of subject differences.

You can use the summary table and the table of critical F values to determine whether the difference between the two groups is significant. The procedures are identical to those discussed previously.

Analysis of Variance: Conclusion

The analysis of variance is a very useful test that can be extended to any type of factorial design, including those that use both independent groups and repeated measures in the same design. The method of computing analysis of variance is much the same regardless of the complexity of the design. A section on analysis of variance as brief as this cannot hope to cover all of the many aspects of such a general statistical technique. However, you should now have the background to compute an analysis of variance and to understand the more detailed discussions of analysis of variance in advanced statistics texts.

Pearson Product-Moment Correlation Coefficient

The Pearson product–moment correlation coefficient (r) is used to find the strength of the relationship between two variables that have been measured on interval or ratio scales.

Example   Suppose you want to know whether travel experiences are related to knowledge of geography. In your study, you give a 15-item quiz on North American geography, and you also ask how many states and Canadian provinces participants have visited. After obtaining the pairs of observations from each participant, a Pearson r can be computed to measure the strength of the relationship between travel experience and knowledge of geography.

TABLE B.10 Data for hypothetical study on travel and knowledge of geography: Pearson r

Subject identification number	Travel score (X)	Knowledge score (Y)	XY
01	4	10	40
02	6	15	90
03	7	8	56
04	8	9	72
05	8	7	56
06	12	10	120
07	14	15	210
08	15	13	195
09	15	15	225
10	17	14	238
	$\Sigma X = 106$	$\Sigma Y = 116$	$\Sigma XY = 1302$
	$\Sigma X^2 = 1308$	$\Sigma Y^2 = 1434$	
	$(\Sigma X)^2 = 11236$	$(\Sigma Y)^2 = 13456$	

Computation:
$$r = \frac{N\Sigma XY - \Sigma X \Sigma Y}{\sqrt{N\Sigma X^2 - (\Sigma X)^2}\sqrt{N\Sigma Y^2 - (\Sigma Y)^2}}$$

$$= \frac{10(1302) - (106)(116)}{\sqrt{10(1308) - 11236}\sqrt{10(1434) - 13456}}$$

$$= \frac{13020 - 12296}{\sqrt{13080 - 11236}\sqrt{14340 - 13456}}$$

$$= \frac{724}{\sqrt{1844}\sqrt{884}}$$

$$= \frac{724}{1276.61}$$

$$= .567$$

Table B.10 presents fictitious data from such a study along with the calculations for r. The calculational formula for r is

$$r = \frac{N\Sigma XY - \Sigma X \Sigma Y}{\sqrt{N\Sigma X^2 - (\Sigma X)^2}\sqrt{N\Sigma Y^2 - (\Sigma Y)^2}}$$

where X refers to a subject's score on variable X, and Y is a subject's score on variable Y. In Table B.10, the travel experience score is variable X, and the geography knowledge score is variable Y. In the formula, N is the number of paired observations (that is, the number of participants measured on both variables).

The calculation of r requires a number of arithmetic operations on the X and Y scores. ΣX is simply the sum of the scores on variable X. ΣX^2 is the sum of the squared scores on X (each score is first squared and then the sum of the squared scores is obtained). The quantity $(\Sigma X)^2$ is the square of the sum of the scores: The total of the X scores (ΣX) is first calculated and then this total is squared. It is important not to confuse the two quantities, ΣX^2 and $(\Sigma X)^2$. The same calculations are made, using the Y scores, to obtain ΣY, ΣY^2, and $(\Sigma Y)^2$. To find ΣXY, each participant's X score is multiplied by the score on Y; these values are then summed for all subjects. When these calculations have been made, r is computed using the formula for r given above.

At this point, you may wish to examine carefully the calculations shown in Table B.10 to familiarize yourself with the procedures for computing r. You might then try calculating r from another set of data, such as the seating pattern and exam score study shown in Table 12.2.

Significance of r   To test the null hypothesis that the population correlation coefficient is in fact 0.00, we consult a table of critical values of r. Table C.4 in Appendix C shows critical values of r for .10, .05, and .01 levels of significance. To find the critical value, you first need to determine the degrees of freedom. The df for the significance test for r is $N - 2$. In our example study on travel and knowledge, the number of paired observations is 10, so the $df = 8$. For 8 degrees of freedom, the critical value of r at the .05 level of significance is .632 (plus or minus). The obtained r must be greater than the critical r to be significant. Because our obtained r (from Table B.10) of .567 is less than the critical value, we do not reject the null hypothesis.

Notice that we do not reject the null hypothesis in this case, even though the magnitude of r is fairly large. Recall the discussion of nonsignificant results from Chapter 13. It is possible that you would obtain a significant correlation if you used a larger sample size or more sensitive and reliable measures of the variables.

Appendix C

Statistical Tables

TABLE C.1 Critical values of chi-square

Degrees of freedom	Probability level		
	.10	.05	.01
1	2.706	3.841	6.635
2	4.605	5.991	9.210
3	6.251	7.815	11.345
4	7.779	9.488	13.277
5	9.236	11.070	15.086
6	10.645	12.592	16.812
7	12.017	14.067	18.475
8	13.362	15.507	20.090
9	14.684	16.919	21.666
10	15.987	18.307	23.209
11	17.275	19.675	24.725
12	18.549	21.026	26.217
13	19.812	22.362	27.688
14	21.064	23.685	29.141
15	22.307	24.996	30.578
16	23.542	26.296	32.000
17	24.769	27.587	33.409
18	25.989	28.869	34.805
19	27.204	30.144	36.191
20	28.412	31.410	37.566

Source: Table adapted from Fisher and Yates, *Statistical Tables for Biological, Agricultural, and Medical Research* (1963, 6th ed.), London: Longman. Reprinted by permission.

TABLE C.2 Critical values of *t*

	Significance level*			
	.05	.025	.01	.005
df	.10	.05	.02	.01
1	6.314	12.706	31.821	63.657
2	2.920	4.303	6.965	9.925
3	2.353	3.182	4.541	5.841
4	2.132	2.776	3.747	4.604
5	2.015	2.571	3.365	4.032
6	1.943	2.447	3.143	3.707
7	1.895	2.365	2.998	3.499
8	1.860	2.306	2.896	3.355
9	1.833	2.262	2.821	3.250
10	1.812	2.228	2.764	3.169
11	1.796	2.201	2.718	3.106
12	1.782	2.179	2.681	3.055
13	1.771	2.160	2.650	3.012
14	1.761	2.145	2.624	2.977
15	1.753	2.131	2.602	2.947
16	1.746	2.120	2.583	2.921
17	1.740	2.110	2.567	2.898
18	1.734	2.101	2.552	2.878
19	1.729	2.093	2.539	2.861
20	1.725	2.086	2.528	2.845
21	1.721	2.080	2.518	2.831
22	1.717	2.074	2.508	2.819
23	1.714	2.069	2.500	2.807
24	1.711	2.064	2.492	2.797
25	1.708	2.060	2.485	2.787
26	1.706	2.056	2.479	2.779
27	1.703	2.052	2.473	2.771
28	1.701	2.048	2.467	2.763
29	1.699	2.045	2.462	2.756
30	1.697	2.042	2.457	2.750
40	1.684	2.021	2.423	2.704
60	1.671	2.000	2.390	2.660
120	1.658	1.980	2.358	2.617
∞	1.645	1.960	2.326	2.576

*Use the top significance level when you have predicted a specific directional difference (a one-tailed test; e.g., Group 1 will be greater than Group 2). Use the bottom significance level when you have predicted only that Group 1 will differ from Group 2 without specifying the direction of the difference (a two-tailed test).

TABLE C.3   Critical values of F

df for denominator (error)	α	*df* for numerator (systematic)											
		1	2	3	4	5	6	7	8	9	10	11	12
1	.10	39.9	49.5	53.6	55.8	57.2	58.2	58.9	59.4	59.9	60.2	60.5	60.7
	.05	161	200	216	225	230	234	237	239	241	242	243	244
2	.10	8.53	9.00	9.16	9.24	9.29	9.33	9.35	9.37	9.38	9.39	9.40	9.41
	.05	18.5	19.0	19.2	19.2	19.3	19.3	19.4	19.4	19.4	19.4	19.4	19.4
	.01	98.5	99.0	99.2	99.2	99.3	99.3	99.4	99.4	99.4	99.4	99.4	99.4
3	.10	5.54	5.46	5.39	5.34	5.31	5.28	5.27	5.25	5.24	5.23	5.22	5.22
	.05	10.1	9.55	9.28	9.12	9.01	8.94	8.89	8.85	8.81	8.79	8.76	8.74
	.01	34.1	30.8	29.5	28.7	28.2	27.9	27.7	27.5	27.3	27.2	27.1	27.1
4	.10	4.54	4.32	4.19	4.11	4.05	4.01	3.98	3.95	3.94	3.92	3.91	3.90
	.05	7.71	6.94	6.59	6.39	6.26	6.16	6.09	6.04	6.00	5.96	5.94	5.91
	.01	21.2	18.0	16.7	16.0	15.5	15.2	15.0	14.8	14.7	14.5	14.4	14.4
5	.10	4.06	3.78	3.62	3.52	3.45	3.40	3.37	3.34	3.32	3.30	3.28	3.27
	.05	6.61	5.79	5.41	5.19	5.05	4.95	4.88	4.82	4.77	4.74	4.71	4.68
	.01	16.3	13.3	12.1	11.4	11.0	10.7	10.5	10.3	10.2	10.1	9.96	9.89
6	.10	3.78	3.46	3.29	3.18	3.11	3.05	3.01	2.98	2.96	2.94	2.92	2.90
	.05	5.99	5.14	4.76	4.53	4.39	4.28	4.21	4.15	4.10	4.06	4.03	4.00
	.01	13.7	10.9	9.78	9.15	8.75	8.47	8.26	8.10	7.98	7.87	7.79	7.72
7	.10	3.59	3.26	3.07	2.96	2.88	2.83	2.78	2.75	2.72	2.70	2.68	2.67
	.05	5.59	4.74	4.35	4.12	3.97	3.87	3.79	3.73	3.68	3.64	3.60	3.57
	.01	12.2	9.55	8.45	7.85	7.46	7.19	6.99	6.84	6.72	6.62	6.54	6.47
8	.10	3.46	3.11	2.92	2.81	2.73	2.67	2.62	2.59	2.56	2.54	2.52	2.50
	.05	5.32	4.46	4.07	3.84	3.69	3.58	3.50	3.44	3.39	3.35	3.31	3.28
	.01	11.3	8.65	7.59	7.01	6.63	6.37	6.18	6.03	5.91	5.81	5.73	5.67
9	.10	3.36	3.01	2.81	2.69	2.61	2.55	2.51	2.47	2.44	2.42	2.40	2.38
	.05	5.12	4.26	3.86	3.63	3.48	3.37	3.29	3.23	3.18	3.14	3.10	3.07
	.01	10.6	8.02	6.99	6.42	6.06	5.80	5.61	5.47	5.35	5.26	5.18	5.11
10	.10	3.29	2.92	2.73	2.61	2.52	2.46	2.41	2.38	2.35	2.32	2.30	2.28
	.05	4.96	4.10	3.71	3.48	3.33	3.22	3.14	3.07	3.02	2.98	2.94	2.91
	.01	10.0	7.56	6.55	5.99	5.64	5.39	5.20	5.06	4.94	4.85	4.77	4.71

TABLE C.3   (continued)

df for de-nomi-nator (error)	α	\multicolumn{12}{c}{df for numerator (systematic)}
		1	2	3	4	5	6	7	8	9	10	11	12
11	.10	3.23	2.86	2.66	2.54	2.45	2.39	2.34	2.30	2.27	2.25	2.23	2.21
	.05	4.84	3.98	3.59	3.36	3.20	3.09	3.01	2.95	2.90	2.85	2.82	2.79
	.01	9.65	7.21	6.22	5.67	5.32	5.07	4.89	4.74	4.63	4.54	4.46	4.40
12	.10	3.18	2.81	2.61	2.48	2.39	2.33	2.28	2.24	2.21	2.19	2.17	2.15
	.05	4.75	3.89	3.49	3.26	3.11	3.00	2.91	2.85	2.80	2.75	2.72	2.69
	.01	9.33	6.93	5.95	5.41	5.06	4.82	4.64	4.50	4.39	4.30	4.22	4.16
13	.10	3.14	2.76	2.56	2.43	2.35	2.28	2.23	2.20	2.16	2.14	2.12	2.10
	.05	4.67	3.81	3.41	3.18	3.03	2.92	2.83	2.77	2.71	2.67	2.63	2.60
	.01	9.07	6.70	5.74	5.21	4.86	4.62	4.44	4.30	4.19	4.10	4.02	3.96
14	.10	3.10	2.73	2.52	2.39	2.31	2.24	2.19	2.15	2.12	2.10	2.08	2.05
	.05	4.60	3.74	3.34	3.11	2.96	2.85	2.76	2.70	2.65	2.60	2.57	2.53
	.01	8.86	6.51	5.56	5.04	4.69	4.46	4.28	4.14	4.03	3.94	3.86	3.80
15	.10	3.07	2.70	2.49	2.36	2.27	2.21	2.16	2.12	2.09	2.06	2.04	2.02
	.05	4.54	3.68	3.29	3.06	2.90	2.79	2.71	2.64	2.59	2.54	2.51	2.48
	.01	8.68	6.36	5.42	4.89	4.56	4.32	4.14	4.00	3.89	3.80	3.73	3.67
16	.10	3.05	2.67	2.46	2.33	2.24	2.18	2.13	2.09	2.06	2.03	2.01	1.99
	.05	4.49	3.63	3.24	3.01	2.85	2.74	2.66	2.59	2.54	2.49	2.46	2.42
	.01	8.53	6.23	5.29	4.77	4.44	4.20	4.03	3.89	3.78	3.69	3.62	3.55
17	.10	3.03	2.64	2.44	2.31	2.22	2.15	2.10	2.06	2.03	2.00	1.98	1.96
	.05	4.45	3.59	3.20	2.96	2.81	2.70	2.61	2.55	2.49	2.45	2.41	2.38
	.01	8.40	6.11	5.18	4.67	4.34	4.10	3.93	3.79	3.68	3.59	3.52	3.46
18	.10	3.01	2.62	2.42	2.29	2.20	2.13	2.08	2.04	2.00	1.98	1.96	1.93
	.05	4.41	3.55	3.16	2.93	2.77	2.66	2.58	2.51	2.46	2.41	2.37	2.34
	.01	8.29	6.01	5.09	4.58	4.25	4.01	3.84	3.71	3.60	3.51	3.43	3.37
19	.10	2.99	2.61	2.40	2.27	2.18	2.11	2.06	2.02	1.98	1.96	1.94	1.91
	.05	4.38	3.52	3.13	2.90	2.74	2.63	2.54	2.48	2.42	2.38	2.34	2.31
	.01	8.18	5.93	5.01	4.50	4.17	3.94	3.77	3.63	3.52	3.43	3.36	3.30
20	.10	2.97	2.59	2.38	2.25	2.16	2.09	2.04	2.00	1.96	1.94	1.92	1.89
	.05	4.35	3.49	3.10	2.87	2.71	2.60	2.51	2.45	2.39	2.35	2.31	2.28
	.01	8.10	5.85	4.94	4.43	4.10	3.87	3.70	3.56	3.46	3.37	3.29	3.23

(continued)

TABLE C.3   (continued)

df for denominator (error)	α	1	2	3	4	5	6	7	8	9	10	11	12
						df for numerator (systematic)							
22	.10	2.95	2.56	2.35	2.22	2.13	2.06	2.01	1.97	1.93	1.90	1.88	1.86
	.05	4.30	3.44	3.05	2.82	2.66	2.55	2.46	2.40	2.34	2.30	2.26	2.23
	.01	7.95	5.72	4.82	4.31	3.99	3.76	3.59	3.45	3.35	3.26	3.18	3.12
24	.10	2.93	2.54	2.33	2.19	2.10	2.04	1.98	1.94	1.91	1.88	1.85	1.83
	.05	4.26	3.40	3.01	2.78	2.62	2.51	2.42	2.36	2.30	2.25	2.21	2.18
	.01	7.82	5.61	4.72	4.22	3.90	3.67	3.50	3.36	3.26	3.17	3.09	3.03
26	.10	2.91	2.52	2.31	2.17	2.08	2.01	1.96	1.92	1.88	1.86	1.84	1.81
	.05	4.23	3.37	2.98	2.74	2.59	2.47	2.39	2.32	2.27	2.22	2.18	2.15
	.01	7.72	5.53	4.64	4.14	3.82	3.59	3.42	3.29	3.18	3.09	3.02	2.96
28	.10	2.89	2.50	2.29	2.16	2.06	2.00	1.94	1.90	1.87	1.84	1.81	1.79
	.05	4.20	3.34	2.95	2.71	2.56	2.45	2.36	2.29	2.24	2.19	2.15	2.12
	.01	7.64	5.45	4.57	4.07	3.75	3.53	3.36	3.23	3.12	3.03	2.96	2.90
30	.10	2.88	2.49	2.28	2.14	2.05	1.98	1.93	1.88	1.85	1.82	1.79	1.77
	.05	4.17	3.32	2.92	2.69	2.53	2.42	2.33	2.27	2.21	2.16	2.13	2.09
	.01	7.56	5.39	4.51	4.02	3.70	3.47	3.30	3.17	3.07	2.98	2.91	2.84
40	.10	2.84	2.44	2.23	2.09	2.00	1.93	1.87	1.83	1.79	1.76	1.73	1.71
	.05	4.08	3.23	2.84	2.61	2.45	2.34	2.25	2.18	2.12	2.08	2.04	2.00
	.01	7.31	5.18	4.31	3.83	3.51	3.29	3.12	2.99	2.89	2.80	2.73	2.66
60	.10	2.79	2.39	2.18	2.04	1.95	1.87	1.82	1.77	1.74	1.71	1.68	1.66
	.05	4.00	3.15	2.76	2.53	2.37	2.25	2.17	2.10	2.04	1.99	1.95	1.92
	.01	7.08	4.98	4.13	3.65	3.34	3.12	2.95	2.82	2.72	2.63	2.56	2.50
120	.10	2.75	2.35	2.13	1.99	1.90	1.82	1.77	1.72	1.68	1.65	1.62	1.60
	.05	3.92	3.07	2.68	2.45	2.29	2.17	2.09	2.02	1.96	1.91	1.87	1.83
	.01	6.85	4.79	3.95	3.48	3.17	2.96	2.79	2.66	2.56	2.47	2.40	2.34
200	.10	2.73	2.33	2.11	1.97	1.88	1.80	1.75	1.70	1.66	1.63	1.60	1.57
	.05	3.89	3.04	2.65	2.42	2.26	2.14	2.06	1.98	1.93	1.88	1.84	1.80
	.01	6.76	4.71	3.88	3.41	3.11	2.89	2.73	2.60	2.50	2.41	2.34	2.27
∞	.10	2.71	2.30	2.08	1.94	1.85	1.77	1.72	1.67	1.63	1.60	1.57	1.55
	.05	3.84	3.00	2.60	2.37	2.21	2.10	2.01	1.94	1.88	1.83	1.79	1.75
	.01	6.63	4.61	3.78	3.32	3.02	2.80	2.64	2.51	2.41	2.32	2.25	2.18

TABLE C.4   Critical values of r (Pearson product–moment correlation coefficient)

df	Level of significance for two-tailed test*		
	.10	.05	.01
1	.988	.997	.9999
2	.900	.950	.990
3	.805	.878	.959
4	.729	.811	.917
5	.669	.754	.874
6	.622	.707	.834
7	.582	.666	.798
8	.549	.632	.765
9	.521	.602	.735
10	.497	.576	.708
11	.476	.553	.684
12	.458	.532	.661
13	.441	.514	.641
14	.426	.497	.623
15	.412	.482	.606
16	.400	.468	.590
17	.389	.456	.575
18	.378	.444	.561
19	.369	.433	.549
20	.360	.423	.537
25	.323	.381	.487
30	.296	.349	.449
35	.275	.325	.418
40	.257	.304	.393
45	.243	.288	.372
50	.231	.273	.354
60	.211	.250	.325
70	.195	.232	.303
80	.183	.217	.283
90	.173	.205	.267
100	.164	.195	.254

*The significance level is halved for a one-tailed test.

Glossary

alpha level The probability of incorrectly rejecting the null hypothesis that is used by a researcher to decide whether an outcome of a study is statistically significant (most commonly, researchers use a probability of .05).

alternative explanation Part of causal inference; a potential alternative cause of an observed relationship between variables.

analysis of variance *See F* test.

archival data Information that is obtained from stored records including written, video, audio, and digital sources.

archival research The use of existing sources of information for research. Sources include statistical records, survey archives, and written records.

attrition The loss of subjects who decide to leave an experiment. *See* mortality.

autonomy (Belmont Report) Principle that individuals in research investigations are capable of making a decision of whether to participate.

bar graph A visual presentation that uses bars to depict frequencies of responses, percentages, or means in two or more groups.

baseline In a single case design, the subject's behavior during a control period before introduction of the experimental manipulation.

beneficence (Belmont Report) Principle that research should have beneficial effects while minimizing any harmful effects.

between-subjects design An experiment in which different subjects are assigned to each group. Also called independent groups design.

carry-over effect A problem that may occur in repeated measures designs if the effects of one treatment are still present when the next treatment is given.

case study A descriptive account of the behavior, past history, and other relevant factors concerning a specific individual.

ceiling effect Failure of a measure to detect a difference because it was too easy (*also see* floor effect).

central tendency A single number or value that describes the typical or central score among a set of scores.

cluster sampling A probability sampling method in which existing groups or geographic areas, called clusters, are identified. Clusters are randomly sampled and then everyone in the selected clusters participates in the study.

coding system A set of rules used to categorize observations.

cohort A group of people born at about the same time and exposed to the same societal events; cohort effects are confounded with age in a cross-sectional study.

conceptual replication A type of replication of research using different procedures for manipulating or measuring the variables.

conclusion validity Extent to which the conclusions about the relationships among variables reached on the basis of the data are correct.

concurrent validity The construct validity of a measure is assessed by examining whether groups of people differ on the measure in expected ways.

confederate A person posing as a participant in an experiment who is actually part of the experiment.

confidence interval An interval of values within which there is a given level of confidence (e.g., 95%) where the population value lies.

confounding An uncontrolled variable varies systematically with an independent variable; it is impossible to separate the effect of the independent variable from the confounding variable.

confounding variable A variable that is not controlled in a research investigation. In an experiment, the experimental groups differ on both the independent variable and the confounding variable.

construct validity The degree to which a measurement device accurately measures the theoretical construct it is designed to measure.

content analysis Systematic analysis of recorded communications.

content validity An indicator of construct validity of a measure in which the content of the measure is compared to the universe of content that defines the construct.

control series design An extension of the interrupted time series quasi-experimental design in which there is a comparison or control group.

convergent validity The construct validity of a measure is assessed by examining the extent to which scores on the measure are related to scores on other measures of the same construct or similar constructs.

correlation coefficient An index of how strongly two variables are related to each other.

correlational method *See* nonexperimental method.

counterbalancing A method of controlling for order effects in a repeated measures design by either including all orders of treatment pre-

sentation or randomly determining the order for each subject.

covariation of cause and effect Part of causal inference; observing that a change in one variable is accompanied by a change in a second variable.

criterion variable The variable/score that is predicted based upon an individual's score on another variable (the predictor variable). Conceptually similar to a dependent variable.

Cronbach's alpha An indicator of internal consistency reliability assessed by examining the average correlation of each item (question) in a measure with every other question.

cross-sectional method A developmental research method in which persons of different ages are studied at only one point in time; conceptually similar to an independent groups design.

curvilinear relationship A relationship in which changes in the values of the first variable are accompanied by both increases and decreases in the values of another variable.

debriefing Explanation of the purposes of the research that is given to participants following their participation in the research.

deception Misinformation that a participant receives during a research investigation.

degrees of freedom (df) A concept used in tests of statistical significance; the number of observations that are free to vary to produce a known outcome.

demand characteristics Cues that inform the subject how he or she is expected to behave.

dependent variable The variable that is the subject's response to, and dependent on, the level of the manipulated independent variable.

descriptive statistics Statistical measures that describe the results of a study; descriptive statistics include measures of central tendency (e.g., mean), variability (e.g., standard deviation), and correlation (e.g., Pearson *r*).

discriminant validity The construct validity of a measure is assessed by examining the extent to which scores on the measure are not related to scores on conceptually unrelated measures.

double-blind A procedure wherein both the experimenter and the participant are unaware of whether the participant is in the experimental (treatment) or the control condition.

effect size The extent to which two variables are associated. In experimental research, the magnitude of the impact of the independent variable on the dependent variable.

electroencephalogram (EEG) A measure of the electrical activity of the brain.

electromyogram (EMG) A measure of the electrical activity of muscles, including muscle tension.

empiricism Use of objective observations to answer a question about the nature of behavior.

error variance Random variability in a set of scores that is not the result of the independent variable. Statistically, the variability of each score from its group mean.

exact replication A type of replication of research using the same procedures for manipulating and measuring the variables that were used in the original research.

experimental control Eliminating the influence of an extraneous variable on the outcome of an experiment by keeping the variable constant in the experimental and control groups.

experimental method A method of determining whether variables are related, in which the researcher manipulates the independent variable and controls all other variables either by randomization or by direct experimental control.

experimenter bias (expectancy effects) Any intentional or unintentional influence that the experimenter exerts on subjects to confirm the hypothesis under investigation.

external validity The degree to which the results of an experiment may be generalized.

extraneous variable *See* third variable.

F test (analysis of variance) A statistical significance test for determining whether two or more means are significantly different. *F* is the ratio of systematic variance to error variance.

face validity The degree to which a measurement device appears to accurately measure a variable.

factorial design A design in which all levels of each independent variable are combined with all levels of the other independent variables. A factorial design allows investigation of the separate main effects and interactions of two or more independent variables.

falsifiability The principle that a good scientific idea or theory should be capable of being shown to be false when tested using scientific methods.

field experiment An experiment that is conducted in a natural setting rather than in a laboratory setting.

filler items Items included in a questionnaire measure to help disguise the true purpose of the measure.

floor effect Failure of a measure to detect a difference because it was too difficult (*also see* ceiling effect).

frequency distribution An arrangement of a set of scores from lowest to highest that indicates the number of times each score was obtained.

frequency polygon A graphic display of a frequency distribution in which the frequency of each score is plotted on the vertical axis, with the plotted points connected by straight lines.

functional MRI Magnetic resonance imaging uses a magnet to obtain scans of structures of the brain. Functional magnetic resonance imaging (fMRI) provides information on the amount of activity in different brain structures.

galvanic skin response (GSR) The electrical conductance of the skin, which changes when sweating occurs.

haphazard (convenience) sampling Selecting subjects in a haphazard manner, usually on the basis of availability, and not with regard to having a representative sample of the population; a type of nonprobability sampling.

histogram Graphic representation of a frequency distribution using bars to represent each score or group of scores.

history effect As a threat to the internal validity of an experiment, refers to any outside event that is not part of the manipulation that could be responsible for the results.

hypothesis An assertion about what is true in a particular situation; often, a statement asserting that two or more variables are related to one another.

independent groups design An experiment in which different subjects are assigned to each group. Also called between-subjects design.

independent variable The variable that is manipulated to observe its effect on the dependent variable.

inferential statistics Statistics designed to determine whether results based on sample data are generalizable to a population.

informed consent In research ethics, the principle that participants in an experiment be informed in advance of all aspects of the research that might influence their decision to participate.

Institutional Review Board (IRB) An ethics review committee established to review research proposals. The IRB is composed of scientists, nonscientists, and legal experts.

instrument decay As a threat to internal validity, the possibility that a change in the characteristics of the measurement instrument, including human observers, is responsible for the results.

interaction Situation in which the effect of one independent variable on the dependent variable changes, depending on the level of another independent variable.

internal consistency reliability Reliability assessed with data collected at one point in time with multiple measures of a psychological construct. A measure is reliable when the multiple measures provide similar results.

internal validity The certainty with which results of an experiment can be attributed to the manipulation of the independent variable rather than to some other, confounding variable.

interrater reliability An indicator of reliability that examines the agreement of observations made by two or more raters (judges).

interrupted time series design A design in which the effectiveness of a treatment is determined by examining a series of measurements made over an extended time period both before and after the treatment is introduced. The treatment is not introduced at a random point in time.

interval scale A scale of measurement in which the intervals between numbers on the scale are all equal in size.

interviewer bias Intentional or unintentional influence exerted by an interviewer in such a way that the actual or interpreted behavior of respondents is consistent with the interviewer's expectations.

item-total correlation The correlation between scores on individual items with the total score on all items of a measure.

IV × PV design A factorial design that includes both an experimental independent variable (IV) and a nonexperimental participant variable (PV).

justice (Belmont Report) Principle that all individuals and groups should have fair and equal access to the benefits of research participation as well as potential risks of research participation.

Latin square A technique to control for order effects without having all possible orders.

longitudinal method   A developmental research method in which the same persons are observed repeatedly as they grow older; conceptually similar to a repeated measures design.

main effect The direct effect of an independent variable on a dependent variable.

manipulation check A measure used to determine whether the manipulation of the independent variable has had its intended effect on a subject.

matched pairs design A method of assigning subjects to groups in which pairs of subjects are first matched on some characteristic and then individually assigned randomly to groups.

maturation effect As a threat to internal validity, the possibility that any naturally occurring change within the individual is responsible for the results.

mean A measure of central tendency, obtained by summing scores and then dividing the sum by the number of scores.

measurement error   The degree to which a measurement deviates from the true score value.

median A measure of central tendency; the middle score in a distribution of scores that divides the distribution in half.

meta-analysis A set of statistical procedures for combining the results of a number of studies in order to provide a general assessment of the relationship between variables.

minimal risk research Research in which participants are exposed to risks that are no greater than those encountered in daily life or in routine physical or psychological tests.

mixed factorial design A design that includes both independent groups (between-subjects) and repeated measures (within-subjects) variables.

mode A measure of central tendency; the most frequent score in a distribution of scores.

moderator variable A variable that influences the nature of the relationship between two other variables (an independent variable and a dependent variable). In a factorial design, the effect of the moderator variable is revealed as an interaction.

mortality The loss of subjects who decide to leave an experiment. Mortality is a threat to internal validity when the mortality rate is related to the nature of the experimental manipulation.

multiple baseline design Observing behavior before and after a manipulation under multiple circumstances (across different individuals, different behaviors, or different settings).

multiple correlation   A correlation between one variable and a combined set of predictor variables.

naturalistic observation Descriptive method in which observations are made in a natural social setting. Also called field observation.

negative case analysis   In field observation, an examination of observations that do not fit with the explanatory structure devised by the researcher.

negative linear relationship A relationship in which increases in the values of the first variable are accompanied by decreases in the values of the second variable.

no relationship Outcome of research in which two variables are not related; changes in the first variable are not associated with changes in the second variable.

nominal scale A scale of measurement with two or more categories that have no numerical (less than, greater than) properties.

nonequivalent control group design A quasi-experimental design in which nonequivalent groups of subjects participate in the different experimental groups, and there is no pretest.

nonequivalent control group pretest-posttest design A quasi-experimental design in which nonequivalent groups are used, but a pretest allows assessment of equivalency and pretest-posttest changes.

nonexperimental method Use of measurement of variables to determine whether variables are related to one another. Also called correlational method.

nonprobability sampling Type of sampling procedure in which one cannot specify the probability that any member of the population will be included in the sample.

null hypothesis The hypothesis, used for statistical purposes, that the variables under investigation are not related in the population, that any observed effect based on sample results is due to random error.

one-group posttest-only design A quasi-experimental design that has no control group and no pretest comparison; a very poor design in terms of internal validity.

one-group pretest-posttest design A quasi-experimental design in which the effect of an independent variable is inferred from the pretest-posttest difference in a single group.

operational definition Definition of a concept that specifies the method used to measure or manipulate the concept.

order effect In a repeated measures design, the effect that the order of introducing treatment has on the dependent variable.

ordinal scale A scale of measurement in which the measurement categories form a rank order along a continuum.

panel study Research in which the same sample of subjects is studied at two or more points in time, usually to assess changes that occur over time.

partial correlation The correlation between two variables with the influence of a third variable statistically controlled for.

participant observation A technique of observing a situation wherein the observer takes an active role in the situation.

participant (subject) variable A characteristic of the research participant such as gender, age, personality, or ability.

Pearson product-moment correlation coefficient A type of correlation coefficient used with interval and ratio scale data. In addition to providing information on the strength of relationship between two variables, it indicates the direction (positive or negative) of the relationship.

peer review The process of judging the scientific merit of research through review by other scientists with the expertise to evaluate the research.

pie chart Graphic display of data in which frequencies or percentages are represented as "slices" of a pie.

pilot study A small-scale study conducted prior to conducting an actual experiment; designed to test and refine procedures.

placebo group In drug research, a group given an inert substance to assess the psychological effect of receiving a treatment.

plagiarism Presentation of another person's work as your own instead of properly citing the actual source.

population The defined group of individuals from which a sample is drawn.

positive linear relationship A relationship in which increases in the values of the first variable are accompanied by increases in the values of the second variable.

posttest-only design A true experimental design in which the dependent variable (posttest) is measured only once, after manipulation of the independent variable.

power The probability of correctly rejecting the null hypothesis.

practice effect Improvement in participant performance with repeated testing.

prediction An assertion concerning what will occur in a particular research investigation.

predictive validity The construct validity of a measure is assessed by examining the ability of the measure to predict a future behavior.

predictor variable A variable that is used to make a prediction of an individual's score on another variable (the criterion variable). Conceptually similar to an independent variable.

pretest-posttest design A true experimental design in which the dependent variable is measured both before (pretest) and after (posttest) manipulation of the independent variable.

probability The likelihood that a given event (among a specific set of events) will occur.

probability sampling Type of sampling procedure in which one is able to specify the probability that any member of the population will be included in the sample.

program evaluation Research designed to assess procedures (e.g., social reforms, innovations) that are designed to produce certain changes or outcomes in a target population.

propensity score matching A method of pairing individuals for assignment to a treatment and control condition based upon a combination of scores on participant variables.

pseudoscience Claims that are made on the basis of evidence that, despite appearances, is not based on the principles of the scientific method.

psychobiography A type of case study in which the life of an individual is analyzed using psychological theory.

purposive sample A type of haphazard sample conducted to obtain predetermined types of individuals for the sample.

quasi-experimental design A type of design that approximates the control features of true experiments to infer that a given treatment did have its intended effect.

quota sampling A sampling procedure in which the sample is chosen to reflect the numerical composition of various subgroups in the population. A haphazard sampling technique is used to obtain the sample.

random assignment Use of a random "chance" procedure (such as a random number generator or coin toss) to determine the condition in which an individual will participate.

randomization Controlling for the effects of extraneous variables by ensuring that the variables operate in a manner determined entirely by chance.

ratio scale A scale of measurement in which there is an absolute zero point, indicating an absence of the variable being measured. An implication is that ratios of numbers on the scale can be formed (generally, these are physical measures such as weight or timed measures such as duration or reaction time).

reactivity A problem of measurement in which the measure changes the behavior being observed.

regression equation A mathematical equation that allows prediction of one behavior when the score on another variable is known.

regression toward the mean Also called statistical regression; principle that extreme scores on a variable tend to be closer to the mean when a second measurement is made.

reliability The degree to which a measure is consistent.

repeated measures design An experiment in which the same subjects are assigned to each group. Also called within-subjects design.

replication Repeating a research study to determine whether the results can be duplicated.

research hypothesis The hypothesis that the variables under investigation are related in the population—that the observed effect based on sample data is true in the population.

response rate The percentage of people selected for a sample who actually completed a survey.

response set A pattern of response to questions on a self-report measure that is not related to the content of the questions.

restriction of range A problem when scores on a variable are limited to a small subset of their possible values; this makes it more difficult to identify relationships of the variable to other variables of interest.

reversal design A single case design in which the treatment is introduced after a baseline period and then withdrawn during a second baseline period. It may be extended by adding a second introduction of the treatment. Sometimes called a "withdrawal" design.

risk-benefit analysis Evaluation of the ethical implications of a research procedure by considering the benefits of the research in relation to the potential risks to participants.

role-playing An alternative to deception in which individuals indicate how they or others would respond to an independent variable.

sampling The process of choosing members of a population to be included in a sample.

sampling distribution Theoretical distribution of the frequency of all possible outcomes of a study conducted with a given sample size.

sampling frame The individuals or clusters of individuals in a population who might actually be selected for inclusion in the sample.

scatterplot Graphic representation of each individual's scores on two variables. The score on the first variable is found on the horizontal axis and score on the second variable is found on the vertical axis.

selection differences Differences in the type of subjects who make up each group in an experimental design; this situation occurs when participants elect which group they are to be assigned to.

sensitivity The ability of a measure to detect differences between groups.

sequential method A combination of the cross-sectional and longitudinal design to study developmental research questions.

significance level *See* alpha level.

simple main effect In a factorial design, the effect of one independent variable at a particular level of another independent variable.

simple random sampling A sampling procedure in which each member of the population has an equal probability of being included in the sample.

single case experiment An experiment in which the effect of the independent variable is assessed using data from a single participant.

Solomon four-group design Experimental design in which the experimental and control groups are studied with and without a pretest.

split-half reliability A reliability coefficient determined by the correlation between scores on half of the items on a measure with scores on the other half of a measure.

standard deviation The average deviation of scores from the mean (the square root of the variance).

statistical significance Rejection of the null hypothesis when an outcome has a low probability of occurrence (usually .05 or less) if, in fact, the null hypothesis is correct.

stratified random sampling A probability sampling method in which a population is divided into subpopulation groups called strata; individuals are then randomly sampled from each of the strata.

structural equation modeling Statistical techniques that are used to evaluate a proposed set of relationships among variables.

systematic observation Observations of one or more specific variables, usually made in a precisely defined setting.

systematic variance Variability in a set of scores that is the result of the independent variable; statistically, the variability of each group mean from the grand mean of all subjects.

temporal precedence Part of causal inference; the cause occurs before the effect.

testing effect A threat to internal validity in which taking a pretest changes behavior without any effect on the independent variable.

test-retest reliability A reliability coefficient determined by the correlation between scores on a measure given at one time with scores on the same measure given at a later time.

theory A systematic, coherent, and logical set of ideas about a particular topic or phenomenon that serves to organize and explain data and generate new knowledge.

third variable In descriptions of the relationship between two variables, a third variable is any other variable that is extraneous to the two variables of interest. True experiments control for the possible influence of third variables.

true score An individual's actual score on a variable being measured, as opposed to the score the individual obtained on the measure itself.

t-**test** A statistical significance test used to compare differences between means.

Type I error An incorrect decision to reject the null hypothesis when it is true.

Type II error An incorrect decision to accept the null hypothesis when it is false.

validity *See* construct validity, external validity, internal validity.

variability The amount of dispersion of scores about some central value.

variable Any event, situation, behavior, or individual characteristic that varies—that is, has at least two values.

variance A measure of the variability of scores about a mean; the mean of the sum of squared deviations of scores from the group mean.

within-subjects design An experiment in which the same subjects are assigned to each group. Also called repeated measures design.

References

Abel, E. L., & Kruger, M. L. (2010). Smile intensity in photographs predicts longevity. *Psychological Science, 21,* 542–544. doi:10.1177/0956797610363775

American Psychological Association. (2010). *Concise rules of APA style* (6th ed.). Washington, DC: Author.

American Psychological Association. (2010). *Publication manual of the American Psychological Association* (6th ed.). Washington, DC: Author.

Anderson, C. A., Lindsay, J. J., & Bushman, B. J. (1999). Research in the psychological laboratory: Truth or triviality? *Current Directions in Psychological Science, 8,* 3–9.

Arnett, J. J. (2008). The neglected 95%: Why American psychology needs to become less American. *American Psychologist, 63,* 602–614.

Aronson, E., Brewer, M., & Carlsmith, M. (1985). Experimentation in social psychology. In G. Lindzey & E. Aronson (Eds.), *Handbook of social psychology* (3rd ed.). New York, NY: Random House.

Asch, S. (1956). Studies of independence and conformity: A minority of one against a unanimous majority. *Psychological Monographs,* 709 (Whole No. 416).

Aseltine, Jr., R. H., Schilling, E. A., James, A., Murray, M., & Jacobs, D. G. (2008). An evaluation of National Alcohol Screening Day. *Alcohol & Alcoholism, 43*(1), 97–103.

Bakeman, R. (2000). Behavioral observation and coding. In H. T. Reis & C. M. Judd (Eds.), *Handbook of research methods in social and personality psychology* (pp. 138–159). New York, NY: Cambridge University Press.

Bakeman, R., & Brownlee, J. R. (1980). The strategic use of parallel play: A sequential analysis. *Child Development, 51,* 873–878.

Bamberger, M., Rugh, J., Church, M., & Fort, L. (2004). Shoestring evaluation: Designing impact evaluations under budget, time and data constraints. *American Journal of Evaluation, 25,* 5–37.

Bangerter, A., & Heath, C. (2004). The Mozart effect: Tracking the evolution of a scientific legend. *British Journal of Social Psychology, 43,* 605–623.

Barlow, D. H., Nock, M. K., & Hersen, M. (2009). *Single case experimental designs: Strategies for studying behavior change* (3rd ed.). Boston, MA: Allyn & Bacon.

Baron, R. M., & Kenny, D. A. (1986). The moderator-mediator variable distinction in social psychological research: Conceptual, strategic, and statistical considerations. *Journal of Personality and Social Psychology, 51,* 1173–1182.

Barrett, L. F., & Barrett, D. J. (2001). Computerized experience-sampling: How technology facilitates the study of conscious experience. *Social Science Computer Review, 19,* 175–185.

Baum, A., Gachtel, R. J., & Schaeffer, M. A. (1983). Emotional, behavioral, and psychological effects of chronic stress at Three Mile Island. *Journal of Consulting and Clinical Psychology, 51,* 565–572.

Beach, F. A. (1950). The snack was a boojum. *American Psychologist, 5,* 115–124.

Bem, D. J. (1981). Writing the research report. In L. H. Kidder (Ed.), *Research methods in social relations.* New York: Holt, Rinehart & Winston.

Bem, D. J. (2003). Writing the empirical journal article. Retrieved July 16, 2008 from http://dbem.ws/WritingArticle.pdf

Blanchflower, D. G., & Oswald, A. J. (2008). Is well-being U-shaped over the life cycle? *Social Science & Medicine, 66*(8), 1733–1749.

Borenstein, M., Hedges, L. V., Higgins, J. P. T., & Rothstein, H. R. (2009). *Introduction to meta-analysis*. Hoboken, NJ: John Wiley & Sons.

Bornstein, B. H. (1998). From compassion to compensation: The effect of injury severity on mock jurors' liability judgments. *Journal of Applied Social Psychology, 28,* 1477–1502.

Bortnik, K., Henderson, L., & Zimbardo, P. (2002). The Shy Q, a measure of chronic shyness: Associations with interpersonal motives and interpersonal values. Retrieved November 10, 2002, from http://www.shyness.com/documents/2002/SITAR2002poster_handout.pdf

Bowman, L. L., Levine, L. E., Waite, B. M., & Gendron, M. (2010). Can students really multitask? An experimental study of instant messaging while reading. *Computers & Education, 54,* 927–931. doi:10.1016/j.compedu.2009.09.024

Bröder, A. (1998). Deception can be acceptable. *American Psychologist, 53,* 805–806.

Brogden, W. J. (1962). The experimenter as a factor in animal conditioning. *Psychological Reports, 11,* 239–242.

Brooks, C. I., & Rebata, J. L. (1991). College classroom ecology: The relation of sex of student to classroom performance and seating preference. *Environment and Behavior, 23,* 305–313.

Brown, A. S., & Rahhal, T. A. (1994). Hiding valuables: A questionnaire study of mnemonically risky behavior. *Applied Cognitive Psychology, 8,* 141–154.

Buchanan, T., & Williams, J. E. (2010). Ethical issues in psychological research on the Internet. In S. D. Gosling & J. A. Johnson (Eds.), *Advanced methods for conducting online behavioral research* (pp. 255–271). Washington, DC: American Psychological Association.

Bushman, B., Wang, M., & Anderson, C. (2005). Is the curve relating temperature to aggression linear or curvilinear? Assaults and temperature in Minneapolis reexamined. *Journal of Personality and Social Psychology, 89*(1), 62–66.

Bushman, B. J., & Wells, G. L. (2001). Narrative impressions of the literature: The availability bias and the corrective properties of meta-analytic approaches. *Personality and Social Psychology Bulletin, 27,* 1123–1130.

Buss, D. M. (2011). *Evolutionary psychology: The new science of the mind* (4th ed.). Needham Heights, MA: Allyn & Bacon.

Byrne, G. (1988, October 7). Breuning pleads guilty. *Science, 242,* 27–28.

Cacioppo, J. T., & Tassinary, L. G. (1990). Inferring psychological significance from physiological signals. *American Psychologist, 45,* 16–28.

Campbell, D. T. (1968). Quasi-experimental design. In D. L. Gillis (Ed.), *International encyclopedia of the social sciences* (Vol. 5). New York, NY: Macmillan and Free Press.

Campbell, D. T. (1969). Reforms as experiments. *American Psychologist, 24,* 409–429.

Campbell, D. T., & Stanley, J. C. (1966). Experimental and quasi-experimental designs for research. Chicago, IL: Rand McNally.

Carroll, M. E., & Overmier, J. B. (Eds.). (2001). *Animal research and human health: Advancing human welfare through behavioral science.* Washington, DC: American Psychological Association.

Chaiken, S., & Pliner, P. (1987). Women, but not men, are what they eat: The effect of meal size and gender on perceived femininity and masculinity. *Personality and Social Psychology Bulletin, 13,* 166–176.

Chambless, D. L., Sanderson, W. C., Shoham, V., Bennett, S. B., Pope, K. S., Crits-Christoph, P., Baker, M., . . . McCurry, S. (1996). An update on empirically validated therapies. *The Clinical Psychologist, 49,* 5–18.

Chandra, A., Martino, S. C., Collins, R. L., Elliott, M. N., Berry, S. H., Kanouse, D. E., & Miu, A. (2008). Does watching sex on television predict teen pregnancy? Findings from a national longitudinal survey of youth. *Pediatrics, 122,* 1047–1054.

Chastain, G. D., & Landrum, R. E. (Eds.). (1999). *Protecting human subjects: Department subject pools and institutional review boards.* Washington, DC: American Psychological Association.

Christensen, L. (1988). Deception in psychological research: When is its use justified? *Personality and Social Psychology Bulletin, 14,* 664–675.

Clark, K. B., & Clark, M. P. (1947). Racial identification and preference in Negro children. In T. M. Newcomb & E. L. Hartley (Eds.), *Readings in social psychology.* New York, NY: Holt, Rinehart & Winston.

Clay, R. A. (2010). Psychology's voice is heard. *APA Monitor, 41*(7), 22.

Codd, R. T., III, & Cohen, B. N. (2003). Predicting college student intention to seek help for alcohol abuse. *Journal of Social and Clinical Psychology, 22,* 168–191.

Cohen, D., Nisbett, R. E., Bowdle, B. F., & Schwarz, N. (1996). Insult, aggression, and the southern culture of honor: An "experimental ethnography." *Journal of Personality and Social Psychology, 70*, 945–960.

Cohen, J. (1988). *Statistical power analysis for the behavioral sciences.* Hillsdale, NJ: Erlbaum.

Cohen, J. (1994). The earth is round ($p <$ OS). *American Psychologist, 49*, 997–1003.

Coile, D. C., & Miller, N. E. (1984). How radical animal activists try to mislead humane people. *American Psychologist, 39*, 700–701.

Collins, B. E. (2002). Coping with IRBs: A guide for the bureaucratically challenged. *APS Observer, 15*(10). Retrieved January 15, 2005 from http://www.psychologicalscience.org/observer/2002/1202/irb.cfm

Coltheart, V., & Langdon, R. (1998). Recall of short word lists presented visually at fast rates: Effects of phonological similarity and word length. *Memory & Cognition, 26*, 330–342.

Cook, T. D., & Campbell, D. T. (1979). *Quasi-experimentation: Design and analysis issues for field settings.* Boston: Houghton-Mifflin.

Costa, P. T., Jr., & McCrae, R. R. (1985). *The NEO Personality Inventory manual.* Odessa, FL: Psychological Assessment Resources.

Cramer, S., Mayer, J., & Ryan, S. (2007). College students use cell phones while driving more frequently than found in government study. *Journal of American College Health, 56*, 181–184. doi:10.3200/JACH.56.2.181-184

Crawford, F. (2000). Researcher in consumer behavior looks at attitudes of gratitude that affect gratuities. *Cornell Chronicle.* Retrieved February 28, 2005 from http://www.news.cornell.edu/Chronicle/00/8.17.00/Lynn-tipping.html

Cunningham, M. R., Druen, P. B., & Barbee, A. P. (1997). Angels, mentors, and friends: Tradeoffs among evolutionary, social, and individual variables in physical appearance. In J. A. Simpson & D. T. Kenrick (Eds.), *Evolutionary social psychology* (pp. 109–140). Mahwah, NJ: Erlbaum.

Curtiss, S. R. (1977). *Genie: A psycholinguistic study of a modern-day "wild child."* New York, NY: Academic Press.

Danner, D. D., Snowden, D. A., & Friesen, W. V. (2001). Positive emotions in early life and longevity: Findings from the Nun Study. *Journal of Personality and Social Psychology, 80*, 804–813.

Denmark, F., Russo, N. P., Frieze, I. H., & Sechzer, J. A. (1988). Guidelines for avoiding sexism in psychological research: A report of the Ad Hoc Committee on Nonsexist Research. *American Psychologist, 43*, 582–585.

Devlin, B., Daniels, M., & Roeder, K. (1997). The heritability of IQ. *Nature, 388*(6641), 468–471.

Dill, C. A., Gilden, E. R., Hill, P. C., & Hanslka, L. L. (1982). Federal human subjects regulations: A methodological artifact? *Personality and Social Psychology Bulletin, 8*, 417–425.

Dillman, D. A. (2000). *Mail and Internet surveys: The tailored design method* (2nd ed.). New York, NY: Wiley.

Duncan, S., Rosenberg, M. J., & Finklestein, J. (1969). The paralanguage of experimenter bias. *Sociometry, 32*, 207–219.

Dunn, A. L., Trivedi, M. H., Kampert, J. B., Clark, C. G., & Chambliss, H. O. (2005). Exercise treatment for depression. *American Journal of Preventive Medicine, 28*(1), 1–8.

Elliot, A. J., & Niesta, D. (2008). Romantic red: Red enhances men's attraction to women. *Journal of Personality and Social Psychology, 95*, 1150–1164.

Ennett, S. T., Tobler, N. S., Ringwalt, C. L., & Flewelling, R. L. (1994). How effective is drug abuse resistance education? A meta-analysis of Project D.A.R.E. outcome evaluations. *American Journal of Public Health, 84*, 1394–1401.

Epstein, Y. M., Suedfeld, P., & Silverstein, S. J. (1973). The experimental contract: Subjects' expectations of and reactions to some behaviors of experimenters. *American Psychologist, 28*, 212–221.

Finkel, E. J., Eastwick, P. W., & Matthews, J. (2007). Speed-dating as an invaluable tool for studying romantic attraction: A methodological primer. *Personal Relationships, 14*, 149–166.

Fiske, S. T., & Taylor, S. E. (1984). *Social cognition.* New York, NY: Random House.

Fisman, R., Iyengar, S. S., Kamenica, E., & Simonson, I. (2006). Gender differences in mate selection: Evidence from a speed dating experiment. *The Quarterly Journal of Economics, 121*, 673–697.

Flavell, J. H. (1996). Piaget's legacy. *Psychological Science, 7*, 200–203.

Fowler, F. J., Jr. (2009). *Survey research methods.* (4th ed.). Thousand Oaks, CA: Sage.

Fraley, R. C., & Shaver, P. R. (1998). Airport separations: A naturalistic study of adult attachment dynamics in separating couples. *Journal of Personality and Social Psychology, 75,* 1198–1212.

Frank, M. G., & Gilovich, T. (1988). The dark side of self- and social perception: Black uniforms and aggression in professional sports. *Journal of Personality and Social Psychology, 54,* 74–85.

Freedman, J. L., Klevansky, S., & Ehrlich, P. R. (1971). The effect of crowding on human task performance. *Journal of Applied Social Psychology, 1,* 7–25.

Freedman, J. L., Levy, A. S., Buchanan, R. W., & Price, J. (1972). Crowding and human aggressiveness. *Journal of Experimental Social Psychology, 8,* 528–548.

Frick, R. W. (1995). Accepting the null hypothesis. *Memory and Cognition, 25,* 132–138.

Friedman, H. S., & Martin, L. R. (2011). *The longevity project.* New York, NY: Hudson Street Press.

Furnham, A., Gunter, B., & Peterson, E. (1994). Television distraction and the performance of introverts and extroverts. *Applied Cognitive Psychology, 8,* 705–711.

Gallup, G. G., & Suarez, S. D. (1985). Alternatives to the use of animals in psychological research. *American Psychologist, 40,* 1104–1111.

Gardner, G. T. (1978). Effects of federal human subjects' regulations on data obtained in environmental stressor research. *Journal of Personality and Social Psychology, 34,* 774–781.

Gardner, L. E. (1988). A relatively painless method of introduction to the psychological literature search. In M. E. Ware & C. L. Brewer (Eds.), *Handbook for teaching statistics and research methods.* Hillsdale, NJ: Erlbaum.

Garvin, A. W., & Damson, C. (2008). The effects of idealized fitness images on anxiety, depression and global mood states in college age males and females. *Journal of Health Psychology, 13,* 433–437.

Gilovich, T. (1991). *How we know what isn't so: The fallibility of human reason in everyday life.* New York, NY: Free Press.

Goldstein, N. J., Cialdini, R. B., & Griskevicius, V. (2008). A room with a viewpoint: Using social norms to motivate environmental conservation in hotels. *Journal of Consumer Research, 35,* 472–482. doi:10.1086/586910

Goodstein, D. (2000). How science works. Retrieved from http://www.its.caltech.edu/~dg/HowScien.pdf

Graesser, A. C., Kennedy, T., Wiemer-Hastings, P., & Ottati, V. (1999). The use of computational cognitive methods to improve questions on surveys and questionnaires. In M. G. Sirkin, D. J. Hermann, S. Schechter, N. Schwarz, J. M. Tanur, & R. Tourangeau (Eds.), *Cognition and survey methods research* (pp. 199–216). New York, NY: Wiley.

Graham, K., Tremblay, P. F., Wells, S., Pernanen, K., Purcell, J., & Jelley, J. (2006). Harm, intent, and the nature of aggressive behavior: Measuring naturally occurring aggression in barroom settings. *Assessment, 13,* 280–296. doi:10.1177/1073191106288180

Greenfield, D. N. (1999). *Nature of Internet addiction: Psychological factors in compulsive Internet use.* Paper presented at the meeting of the American Psychological Association, Boston, MA.

Greenwald, A. G. (1976). Within-subjects designs: To use or not to use? *Psychological Bulletin, 83,* 314–320.

Gross, A. E., & Fleming, I. (1982). Twenty years of deception in social psychology. *Personality and Social Psychology Bulletin, 8,* 402–408.

Groves, R. M., Fowler, J. J., Couper, M. P., Lepkowski, J. M., Singer, E., & Tourangeau, R. (2009). *Survey methodology* (2nd ed.). Hoboken, NJ: John Wiley & Sons.

Guo, S., & Fraser, M. W. (2010). *Propensity score analysis: Statistical methods and applications.* Thousand Oaks, CA: Sage Publications.

Haney, C., & Zimbardo, P. G. (1998). The past and future of U.S. prison policy: Twenty-five years after the Stanford Prison Experiment. *American Psychologist, 53,* 709–727.

Harris, R. (2002). Anti-plagiarism strategies for research papers. Retrieved September 10, 2002, from http://www.virtualsalt.com/antiplag.htm

Hawking, S. W. (1988). *A brief history of time: From the big bang to black holes.* New York, NY: Bantam Books.

Hearnshaw, L. S. (1979). *Cyril Burt, psychologist.* Ithaca, NY: Cornell University Press.

Henle, M., & Hubbell, M. B. (1938). "Egocentricity" in adult conversation. *Journal of Social Psychology, 9,* 227–234.

Henrich, J., Heine, S., & Norenzayan, A. (2010). The weirdest people in the world? *Behavioral and Brain Sciences, 33*(2–3), 61–83. doi:10.1017/S0140525X0999152X

Henry, P. J. (2008). College sophomores in the laboratory redux: Influences of a narrow data base on social psychology's view of the nature of prejudice. *Psychological Inquiry, 19,* 49–71.

Herman, D. B., Struening, E. L., & Barrow, S. M. (1994). Self-reported needs for help among homeless men and women. *Evaluation and Program Planning, 17,* 249–256.

Hermans, R., Herman, C., Larsen, J., & Engels, R. (2010). Social modeling effects on snack intake among young men. The role of hunger. *Appetite, 54,* 378–383.

Hill, L. (1990). Effort and reward in college: A replication of some puzzling findings. In J. W. Neuliep (Ed.), *Handbook of replication in the behavioral and social sciences* [Special issue]. *Journal of Social Behavior and Personality, 5*(4), 151–161.

Holden, C. (1987). Animal regulations: So far, so good. *Science, 238*(4829), 880–882. doi:10.1126/science.3672130

Hölzel, B. K., Carmody, J., Vangel, M., Congleton, C., Yerramsetti, S. M., Gard, T., & Lazar, S. W. (2011). Mindfulness practice leads to increases in regional brain gray matter density. *Psychiatry Research: Neuroimaging Section, 191,* 36–43.

Hood, T. C., & Back, K. W. (1971). Self-disclosure and the volunteer: A source of bias in laboratory experiments. *Journal of Personality and Social Psychology, 17,* 130–136.

Hostetler, A. J. (1987, May). Fraud inquiry revives doubt: Can science police itself? *APA Monitor, 1,* 12.

Huchting, K., Lac, A., & LaBrie, J. W. (2008). An application of the Theory of Planned Behavior to sorority alcohol consumption. *Addictive Behaviors, 33,* 538–551.

Humphreys, L. (1970). *Tearoom trade.* Chicago: Aldine.

Jones, R., & Cooper, J. (1971). Mediation of experimenter effects. *Journal of Personality and Social Psychology, 20,* 70–74.

Judd, C. M., Smith, E. R., & Kidder, L. H. (1991). *Research methods in social relations* (6th ed.). Ft. Worth, TX: Holt, Rinehart & Winston.

Kamin, L. G. (1974). *The science and politics of IQ.* New York, NY: Wiley.

Kazbour, R. R., & Bailey, J. S. (2010). An analysis of a contingency program on designated drivers at a college bar. *Journal of Applied Behavior Analysis, 43*(2), 273–277.

Kazdin, A. E. (1995). Preparing and evaluating research reports. *Psychological Assessment, 7,* 228–237.

Kazdin, A. E. (2001). *Behavior modification in applied settings* (6th ed.). Belmont, CA: Wadsworth.

Kazdin, A. E. (2011). *Single-case research designs: Methods for clinical and applied settings* (2nd ed.). New York, NY: Oxford University Press.

Kelman, H. C. (1967). Human use of human subjects: The problem of deception in social psychological experiments. *Psychological Bulletin, 67,* 1–11.

Kenny, D. A. (1979). *Correlation and causality.* New York, NY: Wiley.

Kim, H., Sherman, D., & Taylor, S. (2008). Culture and social support. *American Psychologist, 63*(6), 518–526. doi:10.1037/0003-066X

Kimmel, A. (1998). In defense of deception. *American Psychologist, 53,* 803–805.

Kintz, N. L., Delprato, D. J., Mettee, D. R., Persons, C. E., & Schappe, R. H. (1965). The experimenter effect. *Psychological Bulletin, 63,* 223–232.

Kirsch, I. (2010). *The emperor's new drugs: Exploding the antidepressant myth.* New York, NY: Basic Books.

Kitayama, S., Markus, H. R., Matsumoto, H., & Norasakkunkit, V. (1997). Individual and collective processes in the construction of the self: Self-enhancement in the United States and self-criticism in Japan. *Journal of Personality and Social Psychology, 72,* 1245–1267.

Korn, J. H. (1997). *Illusions of reality: A history of deception in social psychology.* Albany: State University of New York Press.

Korn, J. H. (1998). The reality of deception. *American Psychologist, 53,* 805.

Koss, M. P. (1992). The underdetection of rape: Methodological choices influence incident estimates. *Journal of Social Issues, 48*(1), 61–75.

Kraut, R., Olson, J., Banaji, M., Bruckman, A., Cohen, J., & Couper, M. (2004). Psychological research online: Report of board of scientific affairs advisory group on the conduct of research on the Internet. *American Psychologist, 59,* 105–117.

Kremer, P., Spittle, M., McNeil, D., & Shinners, C. (2009). Amount of mental practice and performance of a simple motor task. *Perceptual and Motor Skills, 109*, 347–356.

Labranche, E. R., Helweg-Larsen, M., Byrd, C. E., & Choquette, R. A., Jr. (1997). To picture or not to picture: Levels of erotophobia and breast self-examination brochure techniques. *Journal of Applied Social Psychology, 27*, 2200–2212.

Lana, R. E. (1969). Pretest sensitization. In R. Rosenthal & R. L. Rosnow (Eds.), *Artifacts in behavioral research*. New York, NY: Academic Press.

Langer, E. J., & Abelson, R. P. (1974). A patient by any other name . . : Clinical group difference in labeling bias. *Journal of Consulting and Clinical Psychology, 42*, 4–9.

Larson, J., Newell, K., Topham, G., & Nichols, S. (2002). A review of three comprehensive premarital assessment questionnaires. *Journal of Marital and Family Therapy, 28*, 233–239.

Latané, B., Williams, K., & Harkins, S. (1979). Many hands make light the work: The causes and consequences of social loafing. *Journal of Personality and Social Psychology, 37*, 822–832.

Lee, S. S., Schwarz, N., Taubman, D., & Hou, M. (2010). Sneezing in times of a flu pandemic: Public sneezing increases perception of unrelated risks and shifts preferences for federal spending. *Psychological Science, 21*, 375–377. doi:10.1177/0956797609359876

Levin, J. R. (1983). Pictorial strategies for school learning: Practical illustrations. In M. Pressley & J. R. Levin (Eds.), *Cognitive strategy research: Educational applications* (pp. 213–238). New York, NY: Springer-Verlag.

Levine, R. V. (1990). The pace of life. *American Scientist, 78*, 450–459.

Levy, K. N., & Kelly, K. M. (2010). Sex differences in jealousy: A contribution from attachment theory. *Psychological Science, 21*, 168–173.

Lilienfeld, S., Lynn, S., & Lohr, J. (Eds.). (2003). *Science and pseudoscience in clinical psychology*. New York, NY: Guilford Press.

Lofland, J., Snow, D. A., Anderson, L., & Lofland, L. H. (2006). *Analyzing social settings: A guide to qualitative observation and analysis* (4th ed.). Belmont, CA: Wadsworth.

Loftus, E. (1979). *Eyewitness testimony*. Cambridge, MA: Harvard University Press.

Luria, A. R. (1968). *The mind of a mnemonist*. New York, NY: Basic Books.

Macintosh, N. J. (Ed.). (1995). *Cyril Burt: Fraud or framed?* New York, NY: Oxford University Press.

Marlatt, G. A., & Rohsenow, D. R. (1980). Cognitive processes in alcohol use: Expectancy and the balanced placebo design. In N. K. Mello (Ed.), *Advances in substance abuse* (Vol. 1). Greenwich, CT: JAI Press.

Martino, S. C., Collins, R. L., Elliott, M. N., Strachman, A., Kanouse, D. E., & Berry, S. H. (2006). Exposure to degrading versus non-degrading music lyrics and sexual behavior among youth. *Pediatrics, 118*, 430–441. doi:10.1542/peds.2006-0131

Matsumoto, D. (1994). *Cultural influences on research methods and statistics*. Belmont, CA: Brooks/ Cole.

Matteson, M. T., & Ivancevich, J. M. (1983). Note on tension discharge rate as an employee health status predictor. *Academy of Management Journal, 26*, 540–545.

Mazer, J. P., Murphy, R. E., & Simonds, C. J. (2009). The effects of teacher self-disclosure via Facebook on teacher credibility. *Learning, Media and Technology, 34*, 175–183. doi:10.1080/17439880902923655

McCutcheon, L. E. (2000). Another failure to generalize the Mozart effect. *Psychological Reports, 87*, 325–330.

McGuigan, F. J. (1963). The experimenter: A neglected stimulus. *Psychological Bulletin, 60*, 421–428.

Melzack, R. (2005). The McGill Pain Questionnaire: From description to measurement. *Anesthesiology, 103*, 199–202.

Meston, C. M., & Buss, D. M. (2007). Why humans have sex. *Archives of Sexual Behavior, 36*, 477–507. doi:10.1007/s10508-007-9175-2

Middlemist, R. D., Knowles, E. S., & Matter, C. F. (1976). Personal space invasion in the lavatory: Suggestive evidence for arousal. *Journal of Personality and Social Psychology, 33*, 541–546.

Middlemist, R. D., Knowles, E. S., & Matter, C. F. (1977). What to do and what to report: A reply to Koocher. *Journal of Personality and Social Psychology, 35*, 122–124.

Milgram, S. (1963). Behavioral study of obedience. *Journal of Abnormal and Social Psychology, 67*, 371–378.

Milgram, S. (1964). Group pressure and action against a person. *Journal of Abnormal and Social Psychology, 69,* 137–143.

Milgram, S. (1965). Some conditions of obedience and disobedience to authority. *Human Relations, 18,* 57–76.

Miller, A. G. (1986). *The obedience experiments: A case study of controversy in social science.* New York, NY: Praeger.

Miller, C. T., & Downey, K. T. (1999). A meta-analysis of heavyweight and self-esteem. *Personality and Social Psychology Review, 3,* 68–84.

Miller, G. A. (1969). Psychology as a means of promoting human welfare. *American Psychologist, 24,* 1063–1075.

Miller, J. G. (1999). Cultural psychology: Implications for basic psychological theory. *Psychological Science, 10,* 85–91.

Miller, N. E. (1985). The value of behavioral research on animals. *American Psychologist, 40,* 423–440.

Montee, B. B., Miltenberger, R. G., & Wittrock, D. (1995). An experimental analysis of facilitated communication. *Journal of Applied Behavior Analysis, 28,* 189–200.

Mook, D. G. (1983). In defense of external invalidity. *American Psychologist, 38,* 379–387.

Murray, B. (2002). Research fraud needn't happen at all. *APA Monitor, 33*(2). Retrieved July 31, 2002, from http://www.apa.org/monitor/feb02/ fraud.html

National Commission for the Protection of Human Subjects of Biomedical and Behavioral Research. (April 18, 1979). *The Belmont Report: Ethical principles and guidelines for the protection of human subjects of research.* Retrieved March 19, 2003, from http://ohsr.od.nih.gov/mpa/belmont.php3

Nelson, D., & Knight, A. (2010). The power of positive recollections: Reducing test anxiety and enhancing college student efficacy and performance. *Journal of Applied Social Psychology, 40*(3), 732–745. doi:10.1111/j.1559-1816.2010.00595.x

NICHD Early Child Care Research Network (Eds.). (2005). *Child care and child development.* New York, NY: Guilford Press.

Nicol, A. A. M., & Pexman, P. M. (2003). *Displaying your findings: A practical guide for creating figures, posters, and presentations.* Washington, DC: American Psychological Association.

Nisbett, R. E., & Ross, L. (1980). *Human inference: Strategies and shortcomings of social judgment.* Englewood Cliffs, NJ: Prentice-Hall.

Nisbett, R. E., & Wilson, T. D. (1977). Telling more than we can know: Verbal reports on mental processes. *Psychological Review, 84,* 231–259.

Oczak, M. (2007). Debriefing in deceptive research: A proposed new procedure. *Journal of Empirical Research on Human Research Ethics, 2,* 49–59.

Ono, H., Phillips, K. A., & Leneman, M. (1996). Content of an abstract: De jure and de facto. *American Psychologist, 51,* 1338–1340.

Orne, M. T. (1962). On the social psychology of the psychological experiment: With particular reference to demand characteristics and their implications. *American Psychologist, 17,* 776–783.

Orth, U., Trzesniewski, K. H., & Robins, R. W. (2010). Self-esteem development from young adulthood to old age: A cohort-sequential longitudinal study. *Journal of Personality and Social Psychology, 98,* 645–658. doi:10.1037/a0018769

Osgood, C. E., Suci, G. J., & Tannenbaum, P. H. (1957). *The measurement of meaning.* Urbana: University of Illinois Press.

Paulus, P. B., Annis, A. B., Seta, J. J., Schkade, J. K., & Matthews, R. W. (1976). Crowding does affect task performance. *Journal of Personality and Social Psychology, 34,* 248–253.

Peterson, R. A., (2001). On the use of college students in social science research: Insights from a second-order meta-analysis. *Journal of Consumer Research, 28*(3), 450–461.

Petty, R. E., & Cacioppo, J. T. (1986). *Communication and persuasion: Central and peripheral routes to attitude change.* New York, NY: Springer-Verlag.

Pew Internet. (2010). *Demographics of internet users.* http://www.pewinternet.org/Static-Pages/Trend-Data/Whos-Online.aspx

Pfungst, O. (1911). *Clever Hans (the horse of Mr. von Osten): A contribution to experimental, animal, and human psychology* (C. L. Rahn, Trans.). New York, NY: Holt, Rinehart & Winston. (Republished 1965.)

Piaget, J. (1952). *The origins of intelligence in children.* New York, NY: International Universities Press.

Plous, S. (1996a). Attitudes toward the use of animals in psychological research and education: Results from a national survey of psychologists. *American Psychologist, 51,* 1167–1180.

Plous, S. (1996b). Attitudes toward the use of animals in psychological research and education: Results from a national survey of psychology majors. *Psychological Science, 7,* 352–363.

Popper, K. (2002). *The logic of scientific discovery.* New York, NY: Routledge.

Pryor, J. H, Hurtado, S., DeAngelo, L. Palucki Blake, L., & Tran, S. (2011). *The American freshman: National norms for Fall 2010.* Los Angeles, CA: UCLA Higher Education Research Institute.

Psi Chi (2005). Tips for paper/poster presentations. Retrieved March 1, 2005, from http://www.psichi.org/conventions/tips.asp

Ramirez, G., & Beilock, S. L. (2011). Writing about testing worries boosts exam performance in the classroom. *Science, 331*(6014), 211–213.

Rauscher, F. H., & Shaw, G. L. (1998). Key components of the Mozart effect. *Perceptual and Motor Skills, 86,* 835–841.

Rauscher, F. H., Shaw, G. L., & Ky, K. N. (1993). Music and spatial task performance. *Nature, 365,* 611.

Raykov, T., & Marcoulides, G. A. (2000). *A first course in structural equation modeling.* Mahwah, NJ: Lawrence Erlbaum Associates.

Reed, J. G., & Baxter, P. M. (2003). *Library use: A handbook for psychology* (3rd ed.). Washington, DC: American Psychological Association.

Reeve, D. K., & Aggleton, J. P. (1998). On the specificity of expert knowledge about a soap opera: An everyday story of farming folk. *Applied Cognitive Psychology, 12,* 35–42.

Rentfrow, P., Gosling, S., & Potter, J. (2008). A theory of the emergence, persistence, and expression of geographic variation in psychological characteristics. *Perspectives on Psychological Science, 3,* 339–369. doi:10.1111/j.1745-6924.2008.00084.x

Reverby, S. M. (Ed.). (2000). *Tuskegee's truths: Rethinking the Tuskegee syphilis study.* Chapel Hill, NC: University of North Carolina Press.

Reverby, S. M. (2011). "Normal exposure" and inoculation syphilis: A PHS "Tuskegee" doctor in Guatemala, 1946–1948. *Journal of Policy History, 23,* 6–28. doi:10.1017/S0898030610000291

Rhoades, G., & Stocker, C. M. (2006). Can spouses provide knowledge of each other's communication patterns? A study of self-reports, spouses' reports, and observational coding. *Family Process, 45,* 499–511. doi:10.1111/j.1545-5300.2006.00185.x

Rhodes, N., Roskos-Ewoldsen, D., Eno, C. A., & Monahan, J. L. (2009). The content of cigarette counter-advertising: Are perceived functions of smoking addressed? *Journal of Health Communication, 14*(7), 658–673. doi:10.1080/10810730903204262

Ring, K., Wallston, K., & Corey, M. (1970). Mode of debriefing as a factor affecting subjective reaction to a Milgram-type obedience experiment: An ethical inquiry. *Representative Research in Social Psychology, 1,* 67–68.

Riordan, C. A., & Marlin, N. A. (1987). Some good news about some bad practices. *American Psychologist, 42,* 104–106.

Roberson, M. T., & Sundstrom, E. (1990). Questionnaire design, return rates, and response favorableness in an employee attitude questionnaire. *Journal of Applied Psychology, 75,* 354–357.

Robinson, J. P., Athanasiou, R., & Head, K. B. (1969). *Measures of occupational attitudes and occupational characteristics.* Ann Arbor, MI: Institute for Social Research.

Robinson, J. P., & Martin, S. P. (2009). Social attitude differences between internet users and non-users: Evidence from the General Social Survey. *Information, Communication & Society, 12*(4), 508–524. doi:10.1080/13691180902857645

Robinson, J. P., Rusk, J. G., & Head, K. B. (1968). *Measures of political attitudes.* Ann Arbor, MI: Institute for Social Research.

Robinson, J. P., Shaver, P. R., & Wrightsman, L. S. (1991). *Measures of personality and social psychological attitudes* (Vol. 1). San Diego, CA: Academic Press.

Rosenbaum, D. P., & Hanson, G. S. (1998). Assessing the effects of school-based drug education: A six-year multilevel analysis of Project D.A.R.E. *Journal of Research in Crime and Delinquency, 35,* 381–412.

Rosenthal, R. (1966). *Experimenter effects in behavior research.* New York, NY: Appleton-Century-Crofts.

Rosenthal, R. (1967). Covert communication in the psychological experiment. *Psychological Bulletin, 67,* 356–367.

Rosenthal, R. (1969). Interpersonal expectations: Effects of the experimenter's hypothesis. In R. Rosenthal & R. L. Rosnow (Eds.), *Artifacts in behavioral research.* New York, NY: Academic Press.

Rosenthal, R. (1991). *Meta-analytic procedures for social research* (Rev. ed.). Newbury Park, CA: Sage.

Rosenthal, R., & Jacobson, L. (1968). *Pygmalion in the classroom: Teacher expectation and pupils' intellectual development.* New York, NY: Holt, Rinehart & Winston.

Rosenthal, R., & Rosnow, R. L. (1975). *The volunteer subject.* New York, NY: Wiley.

Rosnow, R. L., & Rosnow, M. (2009). *Writing papers in psychology* (8th ed.). Belmont, CA: Cengage Learning.

Rossi, P. H., Freeman, H. E., & Lipsey, M. W. (2004). *Evaluation: A systematic approach* (7th ed.). Thousand Oaks, CA: Sage.

Ruback, R. B., & Juieng, D. (1997). Territorial defense in parking lots: Retaliation against waiting drivers. *Journal of Applied Social Psychology, 27,* 821–834.

Rubin, Z. (1973). Designing honest experiments. *American Psychologist, 28,* 445–448.

Rubin, Z. (1975). Disclosing oneself to a stranger: Reciprocity and its limits. *Journal of Experimental Social Psychology, 11,* 233–260.

Ryan, C. S., & Hemmes, N. S. (2005). Effects of the contingency for homework submission on homework submission and quiz performance in a college course. *Journal of Applied Behavior Analysis, 38,* 79–88. doi:10.1901/jaba.2005.123-03

Schachter, S. (1959). *The psychology of affiliation.* Stanford, CA: Stanford University Press.

Schaie, K. W. (1986). Beyond calendar definitions of age, time, and cohort: The general developmental model revisited. *Developmental Review, 6,* 252–277.

Schlenger, W. E., Caddell, J. M., Ebert, L., Jordan, B. K., Rourke, K. M., Wilson, D., et al. (2002). Psychological reactions to terrorist attacks: Findings from the National Study of Americans' Reactions to September 11. *Journal of the American Medical Association, 288,* 581–588.

Schultz, W. (Ed.). (2005). *Handbook of psychobiography.* Oxford: Oxford University Press.

Schumann, K., & Ross, M. (2010). Why women apologize more than men: Gender differences in thresholds for perceiving offensive behavior. *Psychological Science, 21,* 1649–1655. doi:10.1177/0956797610384150

Schwarz, N. (1999). Self-reports: How the questions shape the answers. *American Psychologist, 54,* 93–105.

Scribner, S. (1997). Studying literacy at work: Bringing the laboratory to the field. In E. Torbach, R. J. Falmagne, M. B. Parlee, L. M. W. Martin, & A. S. Kapelman (Eds.), *Mind and social practice: Selected writings of Sylvia Scribner.* Cambridge: Cambridge University Press.

Sears, D. O. (1986). College sophomores in the laboratory: Influences of a narrow data base on social psychology's view of human nature. *Journal of Personality and Social Psychology, 51,* 515–530.

Shadish, W. R., Cook, T. D., & Campbell, D. T. (2002). *Experimental and quasi-experimental designs for generalized causal inference.* Boston: Houghton Mifflin.

Shepard, R. N., & Metzler, J. (1971). Mental rotation of three-dimensional objects. *Science, 171,* 701–703.

Sidman, M. (1960). *Tactics of scientific research.* New York, NY: Basic Books.

Sieber, J. E. (1992). *Planning ethically responsible research: A guide for students and internal review boards.* Newbury Park, CA: Sage.

Sieber, J. E., Iannuzzo, R., & Rodriguez, B. (1995). Deception methods in psychology: Have they changed in 23 years? *Ethics and Behavior, 5,* 67–85.

Siegel, S., & Castellan, N. J. (1988). *Nonparametric statistics for the behavioral sciences.* New York, NY: McGraw-Hill.

Silverman, L., & Margulis, S. (1973). Experiment title as a source of sampling bias in commonly used "subject-pool" procedures. *Canadian Psychologist, 14,* 197–201.

Singh, D., Dixson, B., Jessop, T., Morgan, B., & Dixson, A. (2010). Cross-cultural consensus for waist–hip ratio and women's attractiveness. *Evolution and Human Behavior, 31*(3), 176–181. doi:10.1016/j.evolhumbehav.2009.09.001

Skinner, B. F. (1947). 'Superstition' in the pigeon. *Journal of Experimental Psychology, 38,* 168–172.

Skinner, B. F. (1953). *Science and human behavior.* New York, NY: Macmillan.

Smart, R. (1966). Subject selection bias in psychological research. *Canadian Psychologist, 7,* 115–121.

Smith, C. P. (1983). Ethical issues: Research on deception, informed consent, and debriefing. In L. Wheeler & P. Shaver (Eds.), *Review of personality and social psychology* (Vol. 4). Newbury Park, CA: Sage.

Smith, R. J., Lingle, J. H., & Brock, T. C. (1978). Reactions to death as a function of perceived similarity to the deceased. *Omega, 9,* 125–138.

Smith, S. M., & Shaffer, D. R. (1991). Celerity and cajolery: Rapid speech may promote or inhibit persuasion through its impact on message elaboration. *Personality and Social Psychology Bulletin, 17,* 663–669.

Smith, S. S., & Richardson, D. (1983). Amelioration of harm in psychological research: The important role of debriefing. *Journal of Personality and Social Psychology, 44,* 1075–1082.

Smith, S. S., & Richardson, D. (1985). On deceiving ourselves about deception: A reply to Rubin. *Journal of Personality and Social Psychology, 48,* 254–255.

Smith, V. L., & Ellsworth, P. C. (1987). The social psychology of eyewitness accuracy: Misleading questions and communicator expertise. *Journal of Applied Psychology, 72,* 294–300.

Snowden, D. A. (1997). Aging and Alzheimer's disease: Lessons from the Nun Study. *Gerontologist, 37,* 150–156.

Solomon, R. L. (1949). An extension of control group design. *Psychological Bulletin, 46,* 137–150.

Springer, M. V., McIntosh, A. R., Winocur, G., & Grady, C. L. (2005). The relation between brain activity during memory tasks and years of education in young and older adults. *Neuropsychology, 19,* 181–192.

Stabell, A., Eide, H., Solheim, G. A., Solberg, K. N., & Rustoen, T. (2004). Nursing home residents' dependence and independence. *Journal of Clinical Nursing, 13,* 677–686.

Steele, K. M., Bass, K. E., & Crook, M. D. (1999). The mystery of the Mozart effect: Failure to replicate. *Psychological Science, 10,* 366–369.

Steinberg, L., & Dornbusch, S. M. (1991). Negative correlates of part-time employment during adolescence: Replication and elaboration. *Developmental Psychology, 27,* 304–313.

Stephan, W. G. (1983). Intergroup relations. In D. Perlman & P. C. Cozby (Eds.), *Social psychology.* New York, NY: Holt, Rinehart & Winston.

Sternberg, R. J. (2003). *The psychologist's companion: A guide to scientific writing for students and researchers* (4th ed.). Cambridge: Cambridge University Press.

Stevenson, H. W., & Allen, S. (1964). Adult performance as a function of sex of experimenter and sex of subject. *Journal of Abnormal and Social Psychology, 68,* 214–216.

Stewart, R. E., & Chambless, D. L. (2009). Cognitive-behavioral therapy for adult anxiety disorders in clinical practice: A meta-analysis of effectiveness studies. *Journal of Consulting and Clinical Psychology, 77,* 595–606.

Stone, V. E., Cosmides, L., Tooby, J., Kroll, N., & Knight, R. T. (2002). Selective impairment of reasoning about social exchange in a patient with bilateral limbic system damage. *Proceedings of the National Academy of Sciences, 99*(17), 11531–11536. Retrieved November 1, 2002, from http://www.pnas.org/cgi/content/full/99/17/11531

Strassberg, D. S., & Holty, S. (2003). An experimental study of women's Internet personal ads. *Archives of Sexual Behavior, 32*(3), 253–260. doi:10.1023/A:1023465601718

Sullivan, D. S., & Deiker, T. E. (1973). Subject-experimenter perceptions of ethical issues in human research. *American Psychologist, 28,* 587–591.

Szabo, A., & Underwood, J. (2004). Cybercheats: Is information and communication technology fuelling academic dishonesty? *Active Learning in Higher Education, 5,* 180–199.

Tabachnick, B. G., & Fidell, L. S. (2007). *Using multivariate statistics* (5th ed.). New York, NY: Allyn & Bacon.

Terman, L. M. (1925). *Genetic studies of genius: Vol. 1. Mental and physical traits of a thousand gifted children.* Stanford, CA: Stanford University Press.

Terman, L. M., & Oden, M. H. (1947). *Genetic studies of genius: Vol. 4. The gifted child grows up: Twenty-five years' follow-up of a superior group.* Stanford, CA: Stanford University Press.

Terman, L. M., & Oden, M. H. (1959). *Genetic studies of genius: Vol. 5. The gifted group in mid-life: Thirty five years' follow-up of the superior child.* Stanford, CA: Stanford University Press.

Thomas, G. V., & Blackman, D. (1992). The future of animal studies in psychology. *American Psychologist, 47,* 1678.

Thombs, D. L. (2000). A retrospective study of DARE: Substantive effects not detected in undergraduates. *Journal of Alcohol and Drug Education, 46,* 27–40.

Thompson, W. F., Schellenberg, E. G., & Husain, G. (2001). Arousal, mood, and the Mozart effect. *Psychological Science, 12,* 248–251.

Trochim, W. M. (2006). *The research methods knowledge base* (2nd ed.). Retrieved May 1, 2008 from http://www.socialresearchmethods.net/kb/

Tucker, W. H. (1997). Re-considering Burt: Beyond a reasonable doubt. *Journal of the History of the Behavioral Sciences, 33,* 145–162.

Tufte, E. R. (1983). *The visual display of quantitative information.* Cheshire, CT: Graphics Press.

Tufte, E. R. (1990). *Envisioning information.* Cheshire, CT: Graphics Press.

Tufte, E. R. (1997). *Visual explanations: Images and quantities, evidence and narrative.* Cheshire, CT: Graphics Press.

Tufte, E. R. (2006). *Beautiful evidence.* Cheshire, CT: Graphics Press.

Ullman, J. B. (2007). Structural equation modeling. In B. G. Tabachnick & L. S. Fidell, *Using multivariate statistics* (5th ed.). Boston, MA: Allyn & Bacon.

U.S. Department of Health and Human Services. (2001). *Protection of human subjects.* Retrieved from http://www.hhs.gov/humansubjects/guidance/45cfr46.htm

U.S. Department of Justice. (1999). *Eyewitness evidence: A guide for law enforcement.* Retrieved from http://www.nij.gov/pubs-sum/178240.htm

Vitz, P. C. (1966). Preference for different amounts of visual complexity. *Behavioral Science, 11,* 105–114.

Wampold, B. E., Minami, T., Tierney, S., Baskin, T. W., & Bhati, K. S. (2005). The placebo is powerful: Estimating placebo effects in medicine and psychotherapy from randomized clinical trials. *Journal of Clinical Psychology, 61,* 835–854. doi:10.1002/jclp.20129

Webb, E. J., Campbell, D. T., Schwartz, R. D., Sechrest, R., & Grove, J. B. (1981). *Nonreactive measures in the social sciences* (2nd ed.). Boston: Houghton Mifflin.

Wells, G. L. (2001). Eyewitness lineups: Data, theory, and policy. *Psychology, Public Policy, and Law, 7,* 791–801.

Wells, G. L., Small, M., Penrod, S. J., Malpass, R. S., Fulero, S. M., & Brimacombe, C. A. E. (1998). Eyewitness identification procedures: Recommendations for lineups and photospreads. *Law and Human Behavior, 22,* 603–647.

West, S. L., & O'Neal, K. K. (2004). Project D.A.R.E. outcome effectiveness revisited. *American Journal of Public Health, 94,* 1027–1029.

Wilkinson, L., & the Task Force on Statistical Inference. (1999). Statistical methods in psychology journals: Guidelines and explanations. *American Psychologist, 54,* 594–604.

Wilson, D. W., & Donnerstein, E. (1976). Legal and ethical aspects of nonreactive social psychological research. *American Psychologist, 31,* 765–773.

Wilson, W. H., Ellinwood, E. H., Mathew, R. J., & Johnson, K. (1994). Effects of marijuana on performance of a computerized cognitive neuromotor test battery. *Psychiatry Research, 51,* 115–125.

Winograd, E., & Soloway, R. M. (1986). On forgetting the location of things stored in special places. *Journal of Experimental Psychology: General, 115,* 366–372.

Wolpe, J. (1982). *The practice of behavior therapy* (3rd ed.). New York, NY: Pergamon.

Yin, R. K. (2009). *Case study research: Design and methods* (4th ed.). Thousand Oaks, CA: Sage.

Zimbardo, P. G. (1973). The psychological power and pathology of imprisonment. In E. Aronson & R. Helmreich (Eds.), *Social psychology.* New York, NY: Van Nostrand.

Zimbardo, P. G. (2004). Does psychology make a significant difference in our lives? *American Psychologist, 59,* 339–351.

Zitek, E. M., Jordan, A. H., Monin, B., & Leach, F. R. (2010). Victim entitlement to behave selfishly. *Journal of Personality and Social Psychology, 98,* 245–255.

Credits

Chapter 2 p. 29 The partial PsycINFO record is reprinted with the permission of the American Psychological Association, publisher of the PsycINFO database. All rights reserved. **Chapter 4** p. 71 Copyright 1983, Wong-Baker FACES™ Foundation, www.WongBakerFACES .org. Used with permission. **Chapter 7** Fig. 7.1 Adapted from *Monitoring the Future,* http:// monitoringthefuture.org/data/10data/fig10_3 .pdf. Fig. 7.2 Adapted from "Does watching sex on television predict teen pregnancy? Findings from a national longitudinal survey of youth" by A. Chandra, S. C. Martino, R. L. Collins, M. N. Elliott, S. H. Berry, D. E. Kanouse, and A. Miu, 2008, *Pediatrics,* 122, pp. 1047–1054. **Chapter 8** Fig. 8.2 Adapted from "Mental Rotation of Three-Dimensional Objects" by Shepard & Metzler, *Science* 171: 701–703 (1971). Copyright © 1971 American Association for the Advancement of Science. **Chapter 9** p. 187 From R. Rosenthal (1967), "Covert Communication in the Psychological Experiment," *Psychological Bulletin,* 67, pp. 356–367. Copyright 1967 by the American Psychological Association. Reprinted by permission of the author. **Chapter 11** Figs. 11.4 and 11.5 From D. T. Campbell (1969), "Reforms as Experiments," *American Psychologist,* 24, pp. 409–429. Copyright © 1969 by the American Psychological Association. Reprinted with permission of the American Psychological Association. **Appendix C** Table C.1 Adapted from Fisher and Yates, *Statistical Tables for Biological, Agricultural, and Medical Research,* 1963, 6th ed. London: Longman; New York: Hafner.

Index